Evaluation of Health Promotion, Health Education, and Disease Prevention Programs

THIRD EDITION

RICHARD WINDSOR

School of Public Health and Health Services
George Washington University Medical Center

NOREEN CLARK

School of Public Health
University of Michigan

NEAL RICHARD BOYD

School of Public Health and Health Services
George Washington University Medical Center

ROBERT M. GOODMAN

School of Public Health
University of Pittsburgh

Boston   Burr Ridge, IL   Dubuque, IA   Madison, WI   New York
San Francisco   St. Louis   Bangkok   Bogotá   Caracas   Kuala Lumpur
Lisbon   London   Madrid   Mexico City   Milan   Montreal   New Delhi
Santiago   Seoul   Singapore   Sydney   Taipei   Toronto

Higher Education

EVALUATION OF HEALTH PROMOTION, HEALTH EDUCATION, AND DISEASE PREVENTION PROGRAMS, THIRD EDITION
Published by McGraw-Hill, a business unit of The McGraw-Hill Companies, Inc., 1221 Avenue of the Americas, New York, NY 10020. Copyright © 2004 by The McGraw-Hill Companies, Inc. All rights reserved. Previous editions © 1994, 1984 by Mayfield Publishing Company. No part of this publication may be reproduced or distributed in any form or by any means, or stored in a database or retrieval system, without the prior written consent of The McGraw-Hill Companies, Inc., including, but not limited to, any network or other electronic storage or transmission, or broadcast for distance learning.

Some ancillaries, including electronic and print components, may not be available to customers outside the United States.

3 4 5 6 7 8 9 0 FGR/FGR 0 9 8 7

Vice president and editor-in-chief: *Thalia Dorwick*
Publisher: *Jane Karpacz*
Sponsoring editor: *Vicki Malinee*
Development editor: *Kirstan Price*
Marketing manager: *Pamela Cooper*
Production services manager: *Jennifer Mills*
Production service: *Penmarin Books*
Manuscript editor: *Sheryl Rose*
Art director: *Jeanne M. Schreiber*
Design coordinator: *Mary Kazak*
Cover designer: *Asylum Studios*
Interior designer: *Ellen Pettengell*
Art manager: *Robin Mouat*
Illustrator: *John and Judy Waller, Lotus Art*
Production supervisor: *Rich DeVitto*

The text was set in 10/13 Janson Text by G & S Typesetters, Inc. and printed on 45# New Era Matte by Quebecor World, Fairfield.

Library of Congress Cataloging-in-Publication Data

Evaluation of health promotion, health education, and disease prevention programs / Richard Windsor ... [et al.]. — 3rd ed.
    p. cm.
  Previously published: Mountain View, Calif. : Mayfield Pub. Co., c1994.
  Includes bibliographical references and index.
  ISBN   978-0-07-253034-6
  MHID 0-07-253034-0
  1. Health education—Evaluation.   2. Preventive health services—Evaluation.
3. Educational accountability.   I. Windsor, Richard A.
RA440.5.E93   2003
613—dc21
                                                                    2003051257
www.mhhe.com

Brief Contents

Contents

CHAPTER 7   Cost Evaluation 264

Preface

The third edition of *Evaluation of Health Promotion, Health Education, and Disease Prevention Programs* represents a substantially restructured and updated volume. The primary audiences are (1) masters and advanced undergraduate students who are specializing in health promotion/health education/health behavior and (2) experienced public health practitioners who are responsible for the planning and evaluation of health promotion/disease prevention programs. The text should also serve as a primary reference for medical, nursing, and related health professionals who direct and supervise health promotion/health education/disease prevention program managers and coordinators.

CONTENT AND ORGANIZATION OF THE THIRD EDITION

The third edition has been revised to reflect advances in the field and recommendations of multiple external peer reviewers. Chapter 8 of the second edition, "Simple Methods to Analyze Program Data," was dropped because the majority of users indicated they were required to complete a statistics course prior to enrolling in their health promotion evaluation course.

Chapter 1 has been considerably updated and expanded to reflect national and professional activities in the field of health promotion. The utility of the *Healthy People 2010* objectives and consensus documents that contribute to stronger science/policy/practice linkages are discussed. A new section on defining "evaluation phases" has been added as an important process to ascertain the scientific foundation of a health promotion program for specific populations and problems. Program evaluation as a core competency of public health practice is discussed and a current description of competencies for health promotion specialists is presented.

Chapter 2 has been completely revised and reflects our decision to provide specific guidance about the model and methods to "plan an evaluation." The PRECEDE/PROCEED model is reviewed, and a detailed case study that applies the model to a population of elderly citizens at risk is presented. Many concepts discussed in Chapters 2 and 3 of the second edition have been integrated into the third edition, including an introduction to the basic principles of budgeting. A new author, Dr. Neal Richard Boyd, who represents 20 years of program evaluation experience in health education, prepared this chapter.

Chapter 3, "Measurement in Evaluation," is a synthesis and updated discussion, including new and old case studies from Chapters 6 and 7 of the second edition. It is presented earlier in this edition because measurement and data quality are the foundations of all evaluations. What and how to measure are the most important procedures of an evaluation plan.

Having drafted an evaluation plan (Chapter 2), including what to measure (Chapter 3), a program must define its intervention. Chapter 4, "Process Evaluation," provides a detailed model for all health promotion programs and core assessment and intervention procedures. Without successful implementation of the program and the application of a variety of quality assessment methods, an impact is unlikely to occur.

New to this edition is Chapter 5, "Qualitative Evaluation." Contemporary health promotion practice and research demands an understanding of qualitative and quantitative methods and analyses. Multiple cases are presented to represent examples of how to conduct and use data from qualitative studies. A new author, Dr. Robert M. Goodman, a nationally recognized qualitative researcher, prepared this chapter.

Chapter 6, "Formative and Impact Evaluations," is an expansion of Chapter 5 from the second edition. A newly published case study on formative evaluation is presented. Several of the original case studies on impact evaluation are retained for continuity; and two new case studies on a hospital-based breastfeeding program evaluation and on a school-based nutrition education program evaluation are introduced.

Chapter 7, "Cost Evaluation," is an edited version of the previous edition's Chapter 9. The cases are retained for continuity. They represent good examples of the systematic application of the basic principles and methods of cost-effectiveness, cost benefit, and sensitivity analyses of health promotion programs.

The appendixes from the second edition have been retained. Appendix A, "The Evaluation Report," presents the basic purpose and elements of an evaluation report. Appendix B, "Specification of the Role of the Entry-Level Health Educator," describes the minimum functions, skills, and knowledge (credentials) necessary to evaluate health education and promotion programs.

SUPPLEMENTS

New for the third edition is the **Instructor's Resource CD-ROM** (ISBN 0-07-293328-3). This CD-ROM includes a detailed sample syllabus with lecture outlines and a student course project assignment; it also includes two sample exams. The syllabus can also be downloaded from the book's Web site (www.mhhe .com/windsor3e); contact your McGraw-Hill sales representative to obtain a password.

Also new for the third edition is **PageOut** (www.pageout.net), a free, easy-to-use program that enables instructors to quickly develop Web sites for their courses. PageOut can be used to create a course home page, an instructor home page, an interactive syllabus, Web links, online discussion areas, an online gradebook, and much more. Contact your McGraw-Hill sales representative to obtain a password for PageOut and for additional information on other course management systems.

Students who buy a new copy of the text receive a free registration code for **PowerWeb: Health and Human Performance.** This Web site provides current articles in the field of health and human performance, weekly updates, and a daily news feed specifically on issues related to health and human performance. Students who buy a used book can purchase access to PowerWeb separately (www.dushkin.com/powerweb).

ACKNOWLEDGMENTS

A special note of appreciation for their helpful suggestions and insights is extended to our colleagues who served as reviewers for this edition:

Randy Black, Purdue University

Robert E. Fullilove, Columbia University

Kimberly M. Harper, Florida A & M University

John Sciacca, Northern Arizona University

Robert F. Valois, University of South Carolina

The authors of the third edition thank Dr. Tom Baranowski for his contributions to the first and second editions of this text.

About the Authors

RICHARD WINDSOR, BS, MS, MPH, PhD, received his BS with honors (1969) in health education from Morgan State College and MS (1970) and PhD (1972) in health education from the University of Illinois. Currently, he is a professor at the George Washington University School of Public Health, appointed in 2000. He was an assistant professor in the College of Education at Ohio State University (1972 to 1975). He received a postdoctoral fellowship and an MPH in maternal and child health, and he was an assistant professor in the School of Hygiene and Public Health at Johns Hopkins University (1976–1977).

He was professor of public health and chair of the Department of Health Behavior, School of Public Health, at the University of Alabama at Birmingham (UAB) (1977–1991) and professor (1994–2000). He was a senior scientist (1978–1991) and associate director for the Cancer Prevention and Control Program of the Comprehensive Cancer Center of Alabama at the UAB School of Medicine (1987–1991). He was associate director for Prevention, Education, and Control of the National Heart, Lung, and Blood Institute (NIH)—U.S. Public Health Service, and member of the Senior Executive Services of the U.S. government (1991–1993).

He has been the principal investigator or co-PI of 10 randomized clinical trials and 20 other research studies funded by the NIH, CDC, and NCHSR to test the efficacy and cost-effectiveness of public health education methods. He has been an advisor to the NICHD, NCI, NHLBI, IOM, CDC, Robert Wood Johnson Foundation, and the WHO, Ministries of Health of Canada, Ireland, Scotland, Singapore, and the CDC of the People's Republic of China.

He has been vice-president and president (1979–1981) of the Society for Public Health Education (SOPHE) and is a distinguished SOPHE fellow (1999). He is a recipient of the C. Everett Koop Award (1997) for his scientific and programmatic leadership of the Smoking Cessation or Reduction in Pregnancy Treatment (SCRIPT) Model. SCRIPT has been cited by the AHCPR (1996) and AHRQ Clinical Practice Guidelines (2000) as the most effective and cost-effective treatment methods for patients in Medicaid maternity care.

NOREEN M. CLARK, PhD, is dean of the University of Michigan School of Public Health and Marshall H. Becker Professor of Public Health. She serves as national program director for the Robert Wood Johnson Foundation Allies Against Asthma Program. She was a member of the Advisory Council of the National Institute of Environmental Health Sciences from 1999 to 2002. She has served as chair of the Behavioral Science Section of the American Thoracic Society, as a member of the Pulmonary Diseases Advisory Committee for the NHLBI, and is a member of the Institute's Advisory Committee on Prevention, Education, and Control. Dr. Clark is a member of the Coordinating Council of the National Asthma Education and Prevention Program and has chaired the American Lung Association (ALA) Technical Advisory Group on Asthma, and the Lung Diseases Care and Education Committee. She has served on both the Board and Council of the ALA. She is the former editor of *Health Education and Behavior.* She has been president of the Society for Public Health Education and chair of the Public Health Education Section of the American Public Health Association (APHA).

She is the recipient of the Distinguished Fellow Award from the Society for Public Health Education; the Derryberry Award for outstanding contribution to health education in behavioral science, given by the APHA; the Health Education Research Award, conferred by the National Asthma Education Program for leadership and research contributions; the Distinguished Career Award in Health Education and Promotion, given by the APHA; and the Healthtrac Education Prize.

Dr. Clark's primary research specialty is self-regulation and management of disease, and she has conducted many large-scale program evaluations. Her studies have demonstrated that educational interventions can decrease asthma hospitalizations and medical emergencies. Her work has resulted in an archetype educational program for health care facilities distributed by the National Institutes of Health and used in hundreds of clinics nationally and internationally. It is also being disseminated by the ALA and has reached 400,000 American schoolchildren.

Dr. Clark has extensive international experience in Kenya and in the Philippines. She has been a consultant for a wide range of organizations, including the Ethiopian Women's Welfare Association, the Ministry of Education in Nepal, the Asia Foundation in Pakistan, the Directorate of Health in Portugal, the World Bank, the United Nations Development Program, the Synergos Institute, the Community Health Authority of Madrid, and the Beijing Heart, Lung, and Vessel Institute. She serves on the board of directors of World Education, Inc. and Family Care International. Dr. Clark is a member of the Council on Foreign Relations and served on the board of the Aaron Diamond Foundation. She is a member of the Institute of Medicine of the National Academy of Sciences.

NEAL RICHARD BOYD, EdD, MSPH, MS, is professor and director of the Health Promotion Program in the Department of Prevention and Community Health in the School of Public Health and Health Services at George Washington University. He received a BA in history from Carson-Newman College (1971), an MS in safety (1978) and an EdD in health education (1981) from the University of Tennessee at Knoxville, and a postdoctoral MSPH in public health with a concentration in behavioral science (1991) from the School of Public Health at the University of Alabama at Birmingham. He was a postdoctoral fellow in cancer prevention and control at the Comprehensive Cancer Center of Alabama (1989–1991) and was a Cancer Prevention Fellow at the National Cancer Institute (1991–1993). He was an assistant professor/associate professor in the Department of Health and Safety Education at the University of Southern Mississippi (1981–1989) and a member of the faculty of the Fox Chase Cancer Center (1993–1999). His research interests include evaluation of the efficacy/effectiveness of minimal contact/self-help interventions in tobacco control and chronic disease risk reduction with a variety of modalities, including self-help guides, live proactive telephone counseling, computer-based interactive voice response telephone systems, and computer-generated tailored print communications. He has been a smoking-cessation consultant with numerous state, regional, and national public health organizations.

ROBERT M. GOODMAN, PhD, MPH, MA, is the Chair of the Department of Behavioral and Community Health at the Graduate School of Public Health, University of Pittsburgh. Formerly he was the Usdin Family Professor in Community Health Sciences at Tulane University School of Public Health and Tropical Medicine. He directed the Center for Community Research at Wake Forest University School of Medicine and was a faculty member at the University of North Carolina and University of South Carolina Schools of Public Health. Dr. Goodman has written extensively on issues concerning community health development, community capacity, community coalitions, evaluation methods, organizational development, and the institutionalization of health programs. He has been the principal investigator and evaluator on projects for the Centers for Disease Control and Prevention, the National Cancer Institute, the Centers for Substance Abuse Prevention, the Children's Defense Fund, and several state health departments.

In 1992, the Health Education and Health Promotion Section of the American Public Health Association awarded Dr. Goodman its Early Career Award, and in 1994, the Association of State and Territorial Directors of Health Education and Centers for Disease Control and Prevention jointly honored him with the Health Promotion and Education Advocacy Award for advocacy at the state and national levels.

Recently, Dr. Goodman served as the PI of a 3-year study funded through the CDC Prevention Research Centers that utilized qualitative case studies as a first phase in developing valid measurements for community capacity and related social protective factors. Additionally, he was the PI of a multisite qualitative evaluation of the Centers for Excellence in Women's Health of the National Institutes of Health.

1 | Introduction to Evaluation

Program evaluation is a core competency of public health practice. Its theories, principles, and methods are derived from multiple academic disciplines including anthropology, economics, communications, education, political science, psychology, sociology, and statistics. *Evaluation of Health Promotion, Health Education, and Disease Prevention Programs* incorporates theories and methods from an additional set of core public health specialties including biostatistics, epidemiology, health education–behavioral science, and health services research, policy, and administration.

The measurement science that produces health promotion (HP) program evaluation biomarkers is defined by multiple biomedical and basic science disciplines. Thus, state-of-the-art evaluations of HP programs reflect a maturing continuum of basic science to public health science methods. The primary objective of all disciplines that contribute to the intellectual and practice foundations of program evaluation is the search for valid, empirical evidence to confirm that an HP program was delivered, and to attribute a significant impact on the behavior and health status of a population at risk to the intervention.

OVERVIEW

This chapter presents an introduction to multiple salient dimensions of evaluation, reflecting a synthesis of general and specific principles and methods from the disciplines noted. It introduces the evaluation student or evaluation team member to the range of enduring, complex issues encountered by a health program evaluation. The chapter presents a synopsis of Evaluation Progress Reviews from the 1960s and 1970s, representing the early development period of HP evaluations, and from the 1980s and 1990s, representing a significant maturation period in the field of health promotion program evaluation. A discussion of the development process and the utility of the national Healthy People Objectives for program evaluation follows the Evaluation Progress Reviews. These reports are primary references for planning evaluations of HP programs and are important, independent contributions to an Evaluation Progress Review.

Contemporary evaluations demand that scientists, program managers, and practitioners, all critical stakeholders, develop successful collaborative relationships. We strongly promote a basic principle in evaluation planning and implementation: public health science and practice partnerships. In this chapter we define the different types and purposes of evaluation, and we examine the role of evaluation in an organization and the need for an evaluability assessment. We discuss the importance of documenting, by meta-evaluation and meta-analysis methods, the strength of evidence and the degree of maturation in the evaluation phase. We define and discuss the salience of science, policy, and practice domains in planning health promotion intervention for a defined population at risk and defined setting. Because members of an evaluation team need to know and be able to use an accurate technical language, we identify and define a set of common evaluation terms.

We explore the issues of professional competence in evaluation and its importance as a core responsibility of graduate level–trained public health professionals. Specific skills for master's level–trained health education–promotion specialists are presented. Most of the issues introduced in Chapter 1 are discussed in detail in following chapters of the text. Throughout the text, we frequently use the term *health promotion (HP)* to refer to health promotion, health education (HE), and disease prevention (DP).

EVALUATION PROGRESS REVIEW: THE 1960S AND 1970S

Evaluation of health education–health promotion programs in the 1960s and 1970s paralleled a national interest in evaluation of public health, education, medical care, and social services programs. In the 1960s, Rosenstock (1960), Hochbaum (1962, 1965), Campbell and Stanley (1966), Suchman (1967), Deniston and Rosenstock (1968a, 1968b), and Campbell (1969) stressed the need to improve the quality and the quantity of evaluation research and program evaluation. The inseparable relationship between planning and evaluation received consistent emphasis. The health promotion literature, however, reported very few examples of rigorous evaluation research.

A concern typically expressed in the literature was that evaluation reports only measured and reported resource expenditures and staff effort: They were structure and process evaluations. Evaluations of behavioral impact were rarely reported. Significant behavioral changes reported to be attributable to program inputs, if documented, were typically of questionable internal validity. During this period a considerable number of epidemiological studies documented significant levels of attributable and relative risk for multiple diseases for specific behavioral risk factors. The science-evidence base, however, documenting the efficacy of HP interventions to reduce these risks and to improve health through significant behavior change among populations at high risk was very limited.

The large gap between scientific theory and professional practice was frequently discussed in the social and behavioral science research and health program evaluation literature. The problems of adapting and applying the range of social and behavioral science methods to evaluations of HP programs were well documented. Seminal evaluation texts and reports were published in the 1970s by Rossi and Williams (1972), Weiss (1972, 1973a, 1973b), Deniston and Rosenstock (1973), Green (1974), Green and Figa-Talamanca (1974), Green et al. (1975), Rosenstock (1975), Bernstein et al. (1976), Shortell and Richardson (1978), Green et al. (1978), Cook and Campbell (1979), and Rossi et al. (1979). Rigorous designs and quantitative methods, presented in Campbell and Stanley (1966), Campbell (1969), and Cook and Campbell (1979), were rarely employed in the evaluation of health education–health promotion programs. During this period Green and colleagues (1974, 1977) began to promote a philosophy and to define core principles and methods for systematic planning and evaluation of health education programs.

The *Report of the President's Committee on Health Education* (Larry 1973) noted the paucity of evaluation literature. It confirmed the need to document program efficacy and efficiency in a variety of settings: schools, hospitals, public health clinics, and workplaces. Program evaluation was identified as a required part of health systems plans by the National Health Planning and Resources Act of 1975 (Public Law 93-641) and the National Consumer Health Information and Health Promotion Act of 1976 (Public Law 94-317). The report from the Task Force on Consumer Health Education, *Promoting Health: Consumer Education and National Policy* (Somers 1976), also stimulated national interest in evaluation. The need for greater precision in program evaluation was the basis for Task Force recommendation #6: "Provide federal support for research and development in consumer health education techniques, methodologies, and programs, and their evaluation" (Somers 1976). In a survey of 23 consumer health programs, Little (1976) indicated that the field began to show a modest increase in evaluation studies.

Qualitative evaluation methods, beginning with the foundation work on grounded theory by Glaser and Strauss (1967), began to receive increased attention in the 1970s (Scriven 1972; Patton 1980). Glass published the first article on "meta-analysis" in 1976 and one of the first books (Glass et al.) in 1981. Cook and Reichardt, editors of *Qualitative and Quantitative Methods in Evaluation Research* (1979), affirmed, with multiple contributors, the philosophy that the methods should be complementary.

The decade of the 1970s was an early gestational period for HP evaluation research documenting intervention efficacy. Several large-scale efficacy studies were initiated, representing first-generation evaluation models of community- and clinic-based health promotion programs: the North Karelia Cardiovascular Risk Reduction Projects of 1972–1978 in Finland (Puska et al. 1979), the Stanford Heart Disease Prevention Study of 1973–1976 in California (Farquahar et al. 1977), and the National Multiple Risk Factor Intervention Trial (MRFIT) of 1974–1982 (Neaton et al. 1981). Initial progress and impact reports from each of these studies documented the methodological complexity of designing and implementing an evaluation of health promotion programs for defined communities.

EVALUATION PROGRESS REVIEW: THE 1980s AND 1990s

At the onset of the decade, the World Health Organization (WHO) published *Health Program Evaluation: Guiding Principles for Application of the Managerial Process for National Health Development* (1980) and a companion book, *Development of Indicators for Monitoring Progress Toward Health for All by the Year 2000* (1981). These and other WHO documents provided an international and country-level focus on evaluation. They confirmed the importance of using evaluations to improve HP programs and to guide planning and resource allocation. The need to develop a knowledge base through the standardization of planning procedures, the strengthening of evaluation designs, and the replication of evaluation studies in diverse settings was a strong, consistent theme in health education at the onset of the 1980s (Green et al. 1980; Windsor et al. 1984).

A significant expansion of more rigorous evaluation research literature began in this decade. Zapka (1982) suggested the following strategies to expand the health education and promotion knowledge base:

- Commitment to rigorous experimental or quasi-experimental evaluation research
- Application of qualitative research strategies
- Integration of formative and summative approaches to evaluation design
- Diversification of the settings and focus of evaluative research
- Increased case studies by field practitioners to demonstrate modest evaluation methods applied to well-planned programs
- Evaluation studies placed in larger, health education–quality assurance frameworks
- Critical analysis of broader issues of research and evaluation

Green, Kreuter, Deeds, and Partridge (1980), in the first edition of their text, *Health Education Planning: A Diagnostic Approach*, introduced the first comprehensive health education planning model: PRECEDE. Chapter 8, "Evaluation and the Accountable Practitioner," presented one of the first detailed discussions in health education on this topic. It confirmed to the field that evaluation was an integral part of planning and application of the PRECEDE framework. The first edition of this evaluation text by Windsor, Baranowski, Clark, and Cutter was published in 1984 and the second edition in 1994.

Multiple federal agencies, especially the National Institutes of Health (NIH), and nongovernmental organizations (NGOs), such as the American Cancer Society, the American Heart Association, and the Robert Wood Johnson Foundation, funded prevention, behavioral, demonstration, and health education–promotion research programs in the 1980s and 1990s. The National Heart, Lung, and Blood Institute (NHLBI), the National Cancer Institute (NCI), the National Institute for Drug Abuse (NIDA), and the Centers for Disease Control (CDC) served as major sources of support for evaluation studies in multiple-risk-factor areas.

Second-generation reports became available from three NIH-funded evaluations of large-scale community health promotion programs designed to document the efficacy of community health education programs. The Minnesota Heart Health Project (MHHP) (Leupker et al. 1994) was designed to evaluate the reduction of cardiovascular disease using a comprehensive, community-wide risk-factor-reduction approach. The Pawtucket Heart Health Project (Carlton and Lasater 1995) used a variety of community-based interventions including citizen participation at work sites, religious organizations, schools, grocery stores, and restaurants; screening education; and referrals to mobilize community involvement in heart health planning. The Stanford Five City Projects (Farquahar et al. 1990) principally used mass media (broadcast and print), interventions, and a wide variety of community health education methods and materials in their community-based programs.

Each of these three NHLBI-funded programs represented models for community health education planning and evaluation. Multiple reports from each project demonstrated the complexity of measuring and evaluating population behavior change and risk reduction over a 10- to 15-year period. Shea et al. (1996) presented excellent reviews and discussions of the salient issues faced by community-based HP-DP evaluation studies.

Multiple examples of health promotion evaluation reports reflecting a broader variation in setting and populations became available in the 1980s. Iverson and Kolbe (1983) and Kreuter (1985) discussed evaluation of health education and promotion strategies in schools. Stone et al. (1989) synthesized behavioral research in cardiovascular youth health promotion programs and identified a variety of evaluation issues for future studies with this population. Rimer et al. (1986) made an important contribution in their report, "Research and Evaluation Programs Related to Health Education for Older Persons." This report, a synthesis of the methodological and evaluation design issues and findings, covering approximately a 15-year period, presented a comprehensive review of the literature for this population.

Three special issues of *Health Education Quarterly* are noteworthy in a synthesis of evaluation progress in the 1990s: "Toward Integrating Qualitative and Quantitative Methods" (Steckler et al. 1992), "Arthritis Health Education" (Daltroy and Goeppinger 1993), and "Worksite Health Programs" (Heaney and Goldenhar 1996). The first special issue, which focused on qualitative-quantitative methods, was one of the first comprehensive presentations of the complementary nature of both methodological paradigms for the health promotion and education profession. One of its objectives was to put to rest the either/or debate over qualitative vs. quantitative methods. It provided a foundation reference for future evaluation discussions in this area.

The second special issue highlighted the evaluation research studies of Lorig and Holman (1993). Their contributions to the science base of the profession, reflecting a synthesis of 12 years of research on patient education for adults with arthritis, deserve special attention. Their evaluation research team demonstrated how to use health education principles and planning and evaluation methods as building blocks to systematically produce knowledge about chronic disease management. They documented feasibility, quality, efficacy, effectiveness, and cost-effectiveness.

The third special issue, by Heaney and Goldenhar and a 14-member editorial board, described the variety of methods that health education specialists can apply in HP and occupational health and safety programs. They identified three core themes for future planners and evaluators: (1) the need for broader, more integrative conceptual frameworks, (2) the application of theory in program development, and (3) the use of multiple assessment and evaluation methodologies.

Excellent examples of process evaluation models and methods applied to programs with a national scope were presented by Stone et al. (National Heart, Lung, and Blood Institute, 1994), "Process Evaluation in the Multi-Center Child and Adolescent Trial for Cardiovascular Disease: CATCH"; Baranowski and Stables (National Cancer Institute, 5-a-Day, 2000), "Learning What Works and How: Process Evaluation of the 5-Day Projects"; and Windsor et al. (Robert Wood Johnson Foundation—Smoke Free Families—National Program Office, 2000), "A Process Evaluation Model for Patient Education Programs for Pregnant Smokers." Steckler and Linman (2002), in their reference text, *Process*

Evaluation for Public Health Interventions and Research, provided the first thorough methodological review, with numerous case studies, of this type of evaluation.

Patton provided comprehensive discussions of *Creative Evaluation* (1987) and *Qualitative Research and Evaluation Methods* (1980, 1990, 2000). Green and Lewis made an important contribution to the evaluation literature in *Evaluation and Measurement in Health Education* (1986). *Fourth Generation Evaluation* (Guba and Lincoln 1989) and *Foundations of Program Evaluations* (Shadish, Cook, and Leviton 1991) represented comprehensive, insightful discussions about the evolution of evaluation theory, methods, and practice. Rossi and Freeman published their fifth edition (1993) and sixth edition (1999) of *Evaluation: A Systematic Approach*. These books provided detailed discussions about how to conceptualize, design, and implement comprehensive evaluations. Collectively, they provided a complete range of complementary insights about the technical complexity and political and programmatic issues related to evaluation. All are excellent references for the advanced student of evaluation.

Two notable contemporary contributions specific to health education and health promotion program planning and evaluation were made: *Health Promotion Planning: An Educational and Ecological Approach* (3rd ed.) by Green and Kreuter (1999) and *Intervention Mapping: Designing Theory- and Evidence-Based Health Promotion Programs* by Bartholomew, Parcel, Kok, and Gottlieb (1999). Chapter 7 of the former book and Chapter 9 of the latter described the steps to systematically plan and evaluate HP interventions in the context of setting and population.

The prominence of HIV/AIDS as an enduring, major public health problem and the role of evaluation in dealing with it deserve attention in this synopsis. *How Effective Is AIDS Education?* (U.S. Congress 1988), from the Office of Technology Assessment, and *Preventing AIDS: A Guide to Effective Education for the Prevention of HIV Infection* by Freudenberg (1989), were the first documents to describe the evolving state of the art and science of interventions and evaluation. As Freudenberg (1989) noted, "Evaluation is the single most valuable way to learn what works and what does not work. It is the only way AIDS educators can develop a body of knowledge that can guide their practice." Two major conclusions about evaluation were made: No single intervention appears to have maximal effectiveness even within a single geographic area, and effectiveness of interventions has been handicapped by program designs that do not lend themselves to rigorous evaluation.

Coyle et al. (1991), in *Evaluating AIDS Prevention Programs*, provided a report of the Panel on the Evaluation of AIDS Interventions convened by the National Research Council Committee. Six chapters in Coyle covered the following topics: (1) designing and implementing evaluation research; (2) measuring outcomes; (3) evaluating media campaigns; (4) evaluating health education and risk-reduction projects; (5) evaluating HIV-testing and counseling projects; and (6) evaluating the effectiveness of AIDS prevention programs. In February 1997, a nonfederal, 12-member multidisciplinary panel prepared an NIH Consensus Development Statement on HIV/AIDS. It provided health care providers, patients, and the general public with a current assessment of the efficacy of behavioral intervention methods to reduce the risk of HIV infection. This panel described how to plan, implement, and evaluate programs. "The Compendium of HIV Prevention Interventions with Evidence of Effectiveness" by the CDC (1999) provided an update on the state of the science at the end of the decade.

Progress Review Summary

This eclectic synopsis highlighted the rich resource base available to both new and experienced professionals for planning and evaluating health promotion programs. Comprehensive descriptions of the theoretical and methodological issues and practical problems in planning and conducting evaluations are readily available. Multiple, rigorous evaluations were conducted in the 1980s and 1990s that documented the quality, feasibility, efficacy, and cost-effectiveness of programs for specific health problems among well-defined populations at risk. Because of the strong science-evidence base created during the years 1980 to 2000, we know how to plan interventions, what to measure, and how to conduct all major types of rigorous HP evaluations.

HEALTHY PEOPLE OBJECTIVES FOR THE NATION

The next sections introduce the Objectives for the Nation Reports for 1990, 2000, and 2010, dealing with health promotion–disease prevention. The development of the objectives was one of the most important national- (and state-) level activities for program evaluation in HP-DP. The methods used to synthesize the available HP databases and the intervention literature have produced a sound framework for evaluation planners. The evaluation targets (goals) in *Healthy People: The Surgeon General's Report of Health Promotion and Disease Prevention* (1979b) were based on expert assessments of historical trends, combined with an estimate of the extent to which interventions would accelerate potential gains among defined populations at risk. Each report and the 1985 and 1995 Mid-Course Reviews are salient, independent contributions to the Evaluation Progress Review literature.

Healthy People Objectives for the Nation: 1990

The U.S. Department of Health and Human Services (DHHS), in *Promoting Health/Preventing Disease: Objectives for the Nation* (1980c), identified 227 measurable objectives in 15 health priority areas in three program areas: (1) Health Promotion Services, (2) Preventive Health Services, and (3) Health Protection Services.

The report confirmed the importance of establishing valid baseline data and monitoring data and trends for each objective over a 10-year period. The Office of Disease Prevention and Health Promotion (ODP-HP) was established in DHHS to coordinate HP-DP progress reviews. As part of its National Health Interview Survey (NHIS), the National Center for Health Statistics (NCHS) initiated the 1985 Health Promotion–Disease Prevention Study to monitor progress. The DHHS published a Mid-Course Review in 1985 to document the status of the 1990 objectives and projections for their accomplishment, finding that 108 (48%) of the objectives were likely to be met by 1990. It is worth noting that of the 226 objectives specified, 58 (26%) were written without baseline data. Thus, the true number of measurable, achievable objectives was 168.

DHHS, lead, and collaborating federal agencies are responsible for documenting the status of measurable objectives specific to each disease and to improving the health of high-risk populations, e.g., the NHLBI's National High Blood Pressure Program and National Cholesterol Education Program objectives. Every two or three years, the office of the director of each lead federal agency, in partnership with multiple federal and nonfederal agencies and organizations, conducts and presents a Progress Review to the secretary of DHHS and to Congress. The types of data used by the lead agencies to document achievement of HP-DP objectives for each priority area include health status; risk factors; public and professional awareness; use of appropriate clinical, prevention, and/or screening services; and knowledge, belief, or skills.

Healthy People Objectives for the Nation: 2000

Because of the success in achieving more than 50% of the 1990 objectives and their utility in measuring national progress, a new set of 336 *Healthy People 2000* HP-DP objectives was prepared in the 22 priority areas. In September 1990, the secretary of DHHS, Dr. Louis Sullivan, presented to the nation *Healthy People 2000: National Health Promotion and Disease Prevention Objectives* (1990b). A Mid-Course Review was conducted and disseminated in 1996. As noted in Table 1.1, a new category of special importance to program evaluation was created: Priority Area 22, Surveillance and Data Systems.

Healthy People Objectives for the Nation: 2010

In January 2000 the DHHS secretary, Dr. Donna Shalala, released *Healthy People 2010* as the United States' contribution to the World Health Organization's

TABLE 1.1   *Healthy People 2000:* Twenty-two Priority Areas

Health Promotion	Health Protection	Preventive Services
1. Physical activity	9. Unintentional injuries	14. Maternal and infant health
2. Nutrition	10. Occupational safety	
3. Tobacco	11. Environmental safety	15. Heart disease and stroke
4. Alcohol and other drugs	12. Food and drug safety	16. Cancer
	13. Oral health	17. Diabetes and chronic disabling conditions
5. Family planning		18. HIV infection
6. Mental health and mental disorders		19. Sexually transmitted diseases
7. Violent and abusive behavior		20. Immunization and infectious diseases
8. Educational and community-based programs		21. Clinical preventive services
		22. Surveillance and data systems

Source: U.S. Department of Health and Human Services (1990b).

"Health for All" strategy. Through *Healthy People 2010,* the United States provided a model for population health improvement and program evaluation. The *Healthy People 2010* objectives were distinguished from the 2000 objectives by a richer prevention science base; a heightened demand for preventive health services and quality health care; and improved surveillance and data systems. The 2010 objectives represent, in combination with the 50 states' HP-DP objectives, the most current and comprehensive statement about the status and trends of public health problems in the United States. Collectively, they define the foci of future public health intervention programs and their evaluation. Academic courses and training programs on planning and evaluation of health promotion programs need to use the development process and content of the 28 focus areas and 467 objectives as basic planning and evaluation references. Examples of *Healthy People 2010* objectives are presented in Table 1.2.

Data are the foundation of *Healthy People 2010* objectives and the evaluation of HP-DP progress. Information on current health status, behavioral rates and risks to health, and use of health services served as the baseline (1980, 1985, 1990, 1995, 2000) for the proposed year 2010 measurable objectives. The experiences from 1980 to 2000 demonstrated that this framework was useful in identifying missing data and information and where improvements were/were not occurring. *Healthy People 2010* objectives identified what was important to measure and influenced the development of new data-evaluation systems.

TABLE 1.2   *Healthy People 2010:* Examples of Objectives

Type	Objective
Health Status	To reduce coronary heart disease mortality to no more than 51 per 100,000. (Baseline: age-adjusted 108/100,000 in 1995)
Risk Reduction	To increase to 90% the number of infants who are put to sleep on their back. (Baseline: 76% in 1996)
Service and Protection	To increase to at least 75% the proportion of people aged 50+ who have received a colorectal exam–fecal occult test within last 2 years (Baseline: 30% in 1992)

Source: USDHHS, *Healthy People 2010* (Nov. 2000).

TABLE 1.3   Criteria for Health Indicators

Criteria	Description
Interpretability	Understandable by the public, opinion leaders, and the health and medical communities
Population Applicability	Broad applicability to diverse national population
Problem Impact	Addresses a problem of substantial impact on mortality, morbidity, and costs
Link to Objectives	Linked to one or more of the 2010 objectives
Representative	Clear reflection of overall level and direction of issues and problems
Measurable Data	Data from an established source on a regular (biennial) basis
Multilevel Trackability	Data anticipated at multiple levels and for multiple groups and available at the national, state, and county levels, by age, gender, and ethnicity
Sensitivity to Change	Accurate reflection of change over a short period of time
Profile Balance	A balance among targets that does not overemphasize any one group or condition
Relevance to Policy and Individual Action	Useful in directing policy and operational initiatives

Source: USDHHS, *Healthy People 2010* (Nov. 2000).

Using the 2000 objectives as a reference base, DHHS agencies convened working groups, including the National Academy of Science–Institute of Medicine (IOM), to develop leading 2010 Health Indicators. The 10 criteria used to select the indicators and a brief description are listed in Table 1.3. These criteria should be considered in the preparation of evaluations of HP-DP programs.

Elimination of 2010 Health Disparities: Implications for Evaluation

Progress toward the *Healthy People 2000* objectives reflected achievement primarily among higher socioeconomic groups. *Healthy People 2010* established special population targets for racial and ethnic minority groups and specific age groups. The commitment was made to eliminate health disparities in six public health areas:

1. Infant mortality
2. Cancer screening and management
3. Cardiovascular disease
4. Diabetes
5. HIV/AIDS
6. Childhood and adult immunizations

Elimination or significant reduction of the disparities by the year 2010 will require new knowledge about disease determinants and about the feasibility, efficacy, cost, and effectiveness of HP programs. Well-designed qualitative, process, impact, and cost evaluations of HP-DP programs for diverse populations and settings will be needed to provide new evidence about how to reduce disparities.

Clinical Practice Guidelines

Program evaluations designed to change patients' health-related behaviors and to improve the incidence or prevalence of health status or outcome rates of populations at high risk need to reflect an understanding of the science base for patient assessment diagnosis and treatment: Clinical Practice Guidelines and/or NIH Consensus Conference Reports. A large number of practice guidelines and empirically based discussions about their dissemination have been presented in the last decade, e.g., for HIV/AIDS, smoking cessation, high blood pressure, asthma, cholesterol, and diabetes. Evaluators need to look to these sources and to their methods to improve evaluations of behavior change among providers and patients in health care settings. They are essential referents for an HP-DP evaluation plan for disease management, control, and prevention programs.

Congress established the Agency for Health Care Policy and Research (AHCPR) in 1989 and the Agency for Healthcare Research and Quality (AHRQ) in 2000. AHRQ has two major responsibilities:

1. To develop and review clinically relevant guidelines to be used by physicians/educators and health care practitioners to assist in determining how diseases can be most effectively prevented, diagnosed, and clinically managed

2. To establish standards of quality, performance measures, and medical review criteria

Clinical Practice Guideline Development: Methodology Perspective (McCormick and Moore, USDHHS, 1994) describes the development process. Practice guidelines for public health have also been developed by the Council on Linkages between Academia and Public Health Practice (October 1995). Evidence-based medicine (EBM) and evidence-based practice centers have been funded to promote the systematic synthesis and application of methods to improve health outcomes and cost (Matchar and Samsa 1999).

Emphasis on evaluation of dissemination and adoption of health promotion–disease prevention methods based on Clinical Practice Guidelines needs to increase substantially in the coming decade. HP evaluation research specialists, in collaboration with clinical specialists, need to be knowledgeable about the current philosophy, policies, and operational characteristics of managed health care systems and disease management programs, e.g., National Committee on Quality Assurance (NCQA) and Health Plan Employer Data and Information Set (HEDIS). To be successful, future evaluations of the process, impact, and cost-effectiveness of the guidelines should focus on provider behavior practices, systems of care, and promotion of changes in program policies.

PRACTICE–SCIENCE PARTNERSHIPS

The importance of enduring, productive relationships between academic and nonacademic health promotion specialists and their colleagues in clinical, work site, school, or community–public health practice settings is self-evident. In reflecting on the 1988 Institute of Medicine (IOM) *Report on the Future of Public Health,* Clark (1999) noted, "neither academia nor practice can work at the desired level of excellence without the perspective and insights garnered from the other." Specialists in each setting have much to contribute to problem definition, to the creation of solutions, and to the selection of evaluation methods, designs, and procedures. A contemporary philosophy of evaluation demands that the gap be bridged through improved communications and real partnerships. It is critical to increase the perception of the value of individual and collective contributions by both parties.

Two conference reports are notable in this discussion: the 1994 Disease Prevention and Health Promotion Conference at CDC and the 1996 Consensus Conferences on Bridging the Gap Between Research and Practice. The first CDC consensus conference was designed to establish a research agenda for public health education, primarily focusing on intervention and evaluation research. The second CDC conference was designed to develop strategies for research and practice partnerships. Six specific strategies were reported at the 1996 conference to bridge the gap:

1. Establish profession-wide standards of practice or protocols for research and evaluation.
2. Promote the incorporation of research and evaluation protocols into professional preparation programs in health education.
3. Synthesize health education research through the commission of a meta-analysis.
4. Disseminate results of a meta-analysis through professional organizations, leadership training, professional journals, and conferences.
5. Establish a research agenda for the health education profession.
6. Expand researcher and practitioner collaboration in participatory research.

Neiger et al. (2000) provided an excellent synopsis of the 1994 and 1996 conferences in their report, "Unifying Research and Practice in Health Education. . . ."

Additional insights about the problems and about ways to enhance science–practice partnerships have also been described in McLeroy et al. (1995), "Creating Capacity: A Health Education Research Agenda," and Sanstad and Stall (1999), "Collaborative Community Research Partnerships Between Research and Practice." Excellent partnerships will improve the quality and success of evaluations and will accelerate the dissemination and impact of public health evaluation research and program evaluation.

PURPOSES OF PROGRAM EVALUATION

Although criteria will vary from organization to organization, most evaluations will continue to focus on the effectiveness and cost-efficiency of services provided, usually measured in behavioral, health, and/or economic terms. One of the most important decisions by an evaluation team is to determine why, how, and what types of evaluation will be conducted. Comprehension and application of the science base and creating a good science–practice partnership, two essential public health leadership competencies, will substantially facilitate the definition of realistic purposes. When either or both competencies are absent, a program will not succeed.

Evaluators, program managers, and colleagues in practice need to recognize that the principal reasons for conducting a program evaluation differ from situation to situation, and from program to program. The expectations and demands of multiple stakeholders and audiences for the evaluation significantly influence its purposes.

The following are 10 common purposes of evaluation:

1. To determine the degree of achievement of program objectives
2. To document program strengths and weaknesses in making planning decisions
3. To establish quality assurance and control methods and to monitor performance
4. To determine the generalizability of a program to other populations/settings
5. To identify hypotheses about human behavior for future evaluations
6. To contribute to the science base of health education programs
7. To improve staff skills required for planning, implementation, and evaluation
8. To fulfill grant or contract requirements
9. To promote positive public relations and community awareness
10. To meet public and fiscal accountability requirements

Although it is not realistic to expect each evaluation to achieve all purposes, a competent, reality-based team of practitioners and scientists will consider the relevance of each purpose for its program plan. A skilled and creative practice–science team will accomplish most of these purposes.

ROLE OF EVALUATION IN AN ORGANIZATION

The ability of a program to document implementation and behavioral impact is directly related to the competency of the evaluation team and the support it has from management, the evaluation purposes and the characteristics of the health problem, the setting, and the population at risk. The organizational mission and program purposes always play a dominant role in defining the following evaluation issues:

- Program objectives
- Type(s) of evaluation
- Evaluation design
- Measures of program input, quality, process, impact, and outcome
- Types of data collected
- Impact analysis methods
- Resources, time, staff, and budget

Agencies typically fund an evaluation, in theory, to provide evidence about the quality and impact of a program in order to make current and future decisions about resource allocation. In practice, fiscal, philosophical, and political orientations may play a substantial (perhaps greater) role than science issues in policy making and resource allocation to a program and/or its evaluation. It is important to realize that the interest in, expectations of, and funding for evaluations tend to have a tidal quality in an organization: they will ebb and flow. Evaluators need to recognize the politics of decision making and resource allocation and develop leadership competencies to influence the decision-making process and outcome.

Regardless of the perspective of individual stakeholders, an evaluation team must conduct an evaluation that meets an agency's purposes and expectations. Program managers and the evaluators must agree on the criteria for success before conducting an evaluation: Compromise and consensus are typically the products of this process. Each staff member may see program evaluation in a different way. It may be viewed as a method to ascertain the extent to which a program has succeeded or failed. The "worth," "merit," or "value" of a program evaluation plan and report will be debated and defined by each stakeholder. Some may see evaluation as a management tool, a method to improve the planning and implementation process or to improve public health programs or policies. Others may believe evaluation is a way to gain insight into what happened and why, collecting data from participants and staff to determine their degree of satisfaction with or acceptance of the program's process, content, and quality. Some staff or managers may believe an evaluation is a waste of staff, time, and money: a necessary evil or meaningless exercise. Unless there is strong philosophical support by each organization level and sufficient program resources (staff, money, and time), an evaluation will be a poor investment by an agency.

EVALUATION DOMAINS

Figure 1.1 presents three distinct but interrelated domains that evaluation planners need to consider: the science domain, the policy domain, and the practice domain. The contribution of each perspective needs to be well understood by all members of an evaluation team. The science domain refers to the evidence base for health promotion interventions derived from a meta-evaluation or meta-analysis. The basic questions for this domain are: How valid, reliable, representative, and conclusive is the evidence confirming the feasibility, efficacy, and cost of a proposed program for a well-defined population, health problem, and setting? The peer-reviewed scientific literature defines what a "best practice" intervention is, what to measure, and what behavioral impact levels (effect size) are realistic. The science domain documents the validity of the theoretical behavior change model for an HP program and its evaluation.

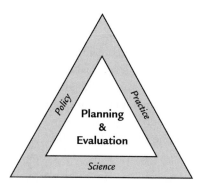

FIGURE 1.1   Primary Domains for
Planning an Evaluation of an HP-DP
Program

The policy domain refers to the philosophical, political, financial, and organizational base of support for an HP program and its evaluation. Who really supports or opposes the program and its evaluation? Who will define the questions to be answered and the type(s) of evaluation to be conducted or not to be conducted? Is the program and its evaluation politically sensitive? What is the level and duration of commitment, especially budgetary, made by the agency and/or management? What does current health policy mandate or prohibit, e.g., services, counseling, or referral, for a specific program and population at risk?

The practice domain refers to the current "state of the art" in an HP specialty area and for program providers and agencies. What is the infrastructure and capacity for the new HP program, or is a significant revision of an existing program planned? What are the characteristics, structure, process, and content of the "old" vs. the "new" program, e.g., time, staffing, complexity, cost, frequency? What are the competencies and attitudes of HP program staff about the existing or new program, its target population, and its evaluation? How much time and what resources are available for staff training, ongoing technical assistance, pilot testing, and formative evaluation? Are the input and perspectives of the staff and the target population reflected in planning the intervention and evaluation? What are the salient characteristics of the population at risk and the setting that need to be considered?

How compatible or contentious are each of these domains? Is there a specific plan describing how to reduce the barriers that typically exist between them?

Advocates within each domain will have a significant impact on what types of evaluations will be conducted and whether an evaluation can be implemented successfully. The involvement of managers, practitioners, and representatives of the target audience is critical in defining an evaluation's philosophy, purposes, and type and in preparing a realistic time line. The evaluation planning process and consensus will be enhanced significantly if program managers and staff are active participants. Do all stakeholders perceive the evaluation as an opportunity for professional growth and program improvement? A director of program evaluation or evaluation research needs to be able to apply his/her leadership skills to optimize successful reconciliation of the perspective of each domain.

The science domain, however, is and should be the foundation of reference for an evaluation team and its leaders. It defines what core qualitative and quantitative methods and research design must be applied to produce valid, defensible evaluation results. Evidence-based insight to a parent agency, to a funding source, to the peer-reviewed science base, and to practice peers is most likely to be produced by referring to the science domain.

EVALUABILITY ASSESSMENT

One of the many initial planning tasks an evaluation team must perform is to conduct a candid assessment of the science, policy, and practice domains. How ready is the agency to conduct an evaluation? A comprehensive process-impact-cost program evaluation may not be possible, given the time, resources, type of problems, and setting of an ongoing or new program. An evaluability assessment asks:

- Does the evaluation plan have well-defined program objectives and measures of impact and outcome?
- Does the plan specify tasks, methods, and procedures and specify by whom, for whom, and over what period of time they will be employed?
- Does the plan clarify what resources will be allocated to achieve the core objectives?

Program and evaluation staff must determine what a program can achieve and what it cannot achieve. A consensus on reasonable expectations is an essential product of negotiations among team members. Drafting objectives, discussing them, and reaching agreement on a small number of core objectives will help an evaluation team set realistic targets. In general, teams should set more realistic and more modest expectations for their programs.

Trying to evaluate what cannot be evaluated, given limited resources, time, and expertise; evaluating a program before it has had a chance to become established in a setting; and poorly measuring impact rates, all represent common, serious evaluation deficiencies. An evaluation team also needs to take a common-sense approach in their deliberations. Every component of a program usually cannot and, in most cases, should not be evaluated. The evaluation team should focus on core objectives and allocate maximal resources to produce excellent results.

Evaluation Planning

An evaluation needs a well-defined planning framework, such as the PRECEDE/ PROCEED model discussed in detail in Chapter 2. Program evaluation teams need to approach the creation and revision of an evaluation plan with specific insight into how different parts, methods, and designs relate to one another conceptually and operationally. Adjustments in one component or method almost always affect another care component. A well-defined, written evaluation plan assists program staff and the evaluator in resetting objectives (if needed) during the evaluation. Program and evaluation staff must also recognize that there may not be a "perfect" evaluation design or definitive measurement method to apply to their setting and population. Designs and methods are better or worse, or more or less appropriate, for specific settings, problems, and behaviors. Data are of better or poorer quality or can be collected more or less easily or expensively in different settings for different risk factors. The best evaluation information will be produced, however, when valid program methods and evaluation designs are matched to the program questions being asked.

When the evaluation plan is prepared, a number of decisions and assumptions are also made. Not all dimensions of a program evaluation, however, are evident during the planning and early implementation stages. Opportunities to examine and change selected components of a program may exist prior to or in the early stages of program pilot testing and implementation but typically will not exist at a later time. One primary purpose of this book is to improve an evaluator's ability to confidently participate in preparing or revising a program plan, comprehending as fully as possible the alternatives and consequences of each alteration.

A rigorous evaluation, e.g., a randomized, clinical trial with experimental and control groups and with extensive resources, may not always produce a definitive answer to a specific research or program evaluation question. Unequivocal proof of intervention impact is difficult to document. All programs and evaluation studies experience implementation problems. The best an ongoing program evaluation may be able to do is rule out several less plausible reasons for an observed change and support one or two reasons why the program worked. The serendipity of both positive and negative program impact in an evaluation also needs to be acknowledged.

EVALUATION PHASES FOR HP-DP PROGRAMS

Planning an evaluation requires a comprehensive synthesis of the quality of the HP-DP intervention literature: a meta-evaluation (ME) or meta-analysis (MA). As noted in the definition of terms later in this chapter, an ME is an evaluation of completed evaluation studies, a qualitative assessment of the internal validity

TABLE 1.4   Evaluation Phases for Health Promotion–Disease Prevention Programs: Defining the Policy–Science–Practice Base

Phase 1	Phase 2	Phase 3	Phase 4
Evaluation Research		Program Evaluation	
Formative Evaluation	Efficacy Evaluation	Effectiveness Evaluation	Impact Dissemination Evaluation
Internal Validity of Health Policy, Program, and/or Practice		Internal and External Validity of a Health Policy, Program, and/or Practice	
Meta → Qualitative → Process → Cost Evaluations and Meta-Analyses			

of HP methods. An evaluation team needs to know what is known about how to intervene with specific groups, problems, and settings, and what to measure. The meta-evaluation tells us what the successful and unsuccessful interventions for a population at risk are. If a sufficient number of evaluation studies of high quality exist to confirm internal validity, a meta-analysis is performed to document external validity.

MA and ME define the quality, strengths, and weaknesses of the science base for specific HP intervention methods. They define the evaluation phase for an intervention program for a specific population at risk, problem, and setting. Table 1.4 identifies four evaluation phases to consider in reviewing the science, practice, and policy bases for a specific HP program. As noted in Table 1.4, qualitative, process, and cost evaluations are foundation (core) methods to be applied in all four evaluation phases. The arrows reflect the continuous refinement, by empirical study, of the HP science-policy-practice base.

Phases 1 and 2 are developmental evaluation phases that can be described as evaluation research. They are designed to determine intervention feasibility, acceptability, efficacy, and cost for a defined population at risk. In Phase 1 and 2 evaluations, specialized HP intervention and assessment staff, typically under the supervision of faculty/senior scientists at academic research centers, implement studies to answer specific questions about the value of a new "best practice" program. An experimental (E) group vs. usual care control ($\underline{C}$) group comparison is made.

Phases 1 and 2 should be theory-based evaluations (TBE). A specific model, such as social cognitive theory or the theory of reasoned action and related literature, is used to create multiple HP program intervention procedures and measurement methods. An excellent first reference for a description of the major behavioral science theories commonly used to develop health promotion interventions is Glanz and Rimer, "Theory at a Glance: A Guide for Health Promotion Practice" (1997).

The primary objective of Phase 1 and 2 evaluations is to document the internal validity of an HP intervention. If very few or no rigorous evaluations have been conducted, a Phase 1 formative evaluation should be planned to document efficacy. If several rigorous formative evaluations have been conducted and internal validity is confirmed for a specific population at risk, a larger, Phase 2 efficacy evaluation, with more sites and participants, is planned. The behavioral impact (effect size) and the feasibility of a new program is documented under "ideal" practice conditions in Phase 1 and 2 evaluations.

In Phase 1 and 2 evaluations, critical questions to be answered are: Can the new, untested program be delivered by staff (process evaluation) under optimal circumstances to the target population? Was the intervention used by the target group (qualitative evaluation)? Did the intervention produce a significant change in behavior (impact evaluation)? What resources were expended and saved (cost evaluation)? How valid was the model used by the TBE? Approximately 90% of all HP published intervention studies are Phase 1 and 2 evaluation research.

Phases 3 and 4, program evaluations, in theory should not be conducted unless the evidence from Phases 1 and 2 is positive, consistent, and conclusive. Was the efficacy—internal validity—of an HP intervention based on a sufficiently large number of studies among multiple samples and sites of the population at risk? Phase 3 and 4 evaluations should include large samples of participants, e.g., 500 to 1,000 or more per study, and involve multiple sites, e.g., 4 to 50. Phase 3 and 4 program evaluations ideally should use representative cohorts of participants from a defined population for specific health problems for which behavioral and population-attributable risk factors (PAR) are established. A significant, direct association exists between improvements in the behavior of the target population and improvements in a health outcome rate. The epidemiological evidence (PAR) should be confirmed for all phases. Phase 3 and 4 program evaluations, because they are evaluations of effectiveness, should be designed to answer questions about both internal and external validity.

In its ideal application, a Phase 4 study is an evaluation of an ongoing HP program for a defined population. Quality, efficacy, and cost have been documented. Almost without exception, Phase 1, 2, and 3 evaluations should apply randomized experimental designs. Typically, the objective of a Phase 4 impact-dissemination evaluation is to confirm the behavioral impact of routine delivery of evidence-based methods for an existing program for a defined delivery system and staff. It is an evaluation of the dissemination and routine application of "best practice" methods by regular staff. An experimental or quasi-experimental design is typically selected. Although a randomized experimental design is preferred, a nonequivalent comparison group design or a single or multiple time series design may be strong alternative evaluation designs for a Phase 4 impact-dissemination evaluation.

Phase 3 and 4 program evaluations should answer four questions:

1. Are the HP intervention methods feasible and effective when delivered with fidelity by regular staff to the target population under normal practice conditions?

2. Are the numbers of evaluation participants and sites of sufficient size to meet statistical power and impact analysis assumptions?

3. Is the evaluation sample and number of study sites sufficiently large and representative to provide new, additional evidence to support the external validity (generalizability) of these methods and results to a defined population at risk?

4. Were the costs, cost-effectiveness, and, if appropriate, cost-benefits associated with the existing vs. new program documented?

Rigorous reviews of evaluation studies will provide insights to help a program define and plan the next phase of HP intervention development for a specific public health problem and setting. Only from a comprehensive review of valid evidence can an HP program define the scientific horizon and decide what to evaluate next and how. Once the phase has been defined from a rigorous review and synthesis of the literature (ME or MA), the next evaluation phase should be designed to answer specific new questions about quality, process, impact, and cost. The evidence base will define the evaluation phase and define the measurement and intervention methods of each new evaluation.

An insightful discussion of how to improve the evidence base for health education and health promotion interventions is presented by Rimer, Glanz, and Rasband in *Health Education and Behavior* (2001). They and their colleagues noted in their review of methodological issues that the science base could be derived only from well-designed evaluation studies. The maturation of the science-evidence base for all health promotion programs is a continuous process. It needs to be grounded in evaluation methods that produce strong qualitative and quantitative empirical results. The major challenge for the next decade in health promotion is to significantly expand the quality and quantity of evaluation research and program evaluation for all phases. In future evaluations, we need to complement the strong science base in changing the individual behavior of populations at high risk with a broader focus on changes in environment settings—clinics, schools, school systems, families, and communities—and changes in public health policy for large at-risk populations.

Evaluation Terms

Good communication by an evaluation team using accurate technical language is essential. Although there may be some variation in these definitions, we present a set of common terms frequently used in this text. These definitions will help you to synthesisze, comprehend, and discuss the evaluation literature, and to actively contribute to planning an evaluation.

- **HP Intervention (Program):** A planned and systematically implemented combination of standardized, replicable methods designed to produce changes in cognitive, affective, skill, behavior, or health status objectives for a defined population at risk at specified sites and during a defined period of time.

- **Efficacy:** An evaluation of the extent to which a new (untested) intervention produced significant changes in a behavioral impact or a health outcome rate: Did the intervention produce significant changes among a sample of the population at risk under *optimal* program-practice conditions?

- **Internal Validity:** The degree to which an observed significant change in a behavioral impact or health status outcome rate (A) among a sample of a population at risk (B) can be attributed to an intervention (C): "Did C cause A to change among B?"

- **Effectiveness:** An evaluation of the extent to which an existing (tested) intervention with documented internal validity produced a significant change in a behavioral impact or health outcome rate: Did the intervention produce a significant change among a large, representative sample of a well-defined population at risk under *normal* program-practice conditions?

- **External Validity:** The degree to which an observed significant change in an impact (behavior) or outcome (health status) rate attributable to an HP intervention can be generalized from a representative sample to a large, well-defined population at risk.

- **Process Evaluation (Feasibility Study):** An evaluation designed to document the degree to which replicable program procedures were implemented with fidelity by trained staff according to a written plan: How well and how much of the assessment and intervention procedures were provided, to whom, when, and by whom?

- **Qualitative Evaluation:** An evaluation designed to explain why a program succeeded or failed, using a systematic process of in-depth, open-ended interviews, indirect and direct observations, and written reports to inductively assess and to describe the perceived value of HP intervention procedures by program staff, participants, and the community.

- **Formative Evaluation:** An evaluation designed to produce qualitative and quantitative data and insight during the early developmental phase of an intervention, including an assessment of (1) the feasibility of program implementation; (2) the appropriateness of content, methods, materials, media, and instruments; and (3) the immediate (e.g., 1 hour to 1 week) or short-term (e.g., 1 week to 6 months) cognitive, psychosocial, psycho-motor (skill), and/or behavioral impact of an intervention for a well-defined population at risk.

- **Evaluation Research (ER):** An evaluation using an experimental or quasi-experimental design designed to establish the feasibility, efficacy, and cost-effectiveness or cost-benefit of a *new* intervention for a specific behavioral impact or health outcome rate during a defined period of time among a well-defined population at risk.

- **Program Evaluation (Summative Evaluation):** An evaluation using an experimental or quasi-experimental design to assess the feasibility, effectiveness, and cost-effectiveness or cost-benefit of a *tested* intervention in producing long-term (e.g., 1 to 5 years) cognitive, psychosocial, skill, and/or behavioral impact during a defined period of time among a well-defined population at risk.

- **Health Outcome Evaluation:** An evaluation using an experimental or quasi-experimental design to document intervention feasibility, efficacy or effectiveness, and cost-effectiveness or cost-benefit in producing long-term changes (e.g., 1 to 10 years) in the incidence or prevalence of a morbidity or mortality rate or other health status indicator for a clinically diagnosed medical condition among a well-defined population at high risk.

- **Cost-Effectiveness Analysis (CEA):** An evaluation designed to document the relationship between intervention program costs (input) and an impact rate (output); a ratio of cost per unit to percent impact.

- **Cost-Benefit Analysis (CBA):** An evaluation designed to document the relationship between intervention program costs (inputs) and a health outcome rate, expressed as a monetary benefit-consequence (outputs) or a ratio of costs per unit of economic benefit and net economic benefit (savings).

- **Meta-Evaluation:** An evaluation of the methodological quality of impact or outcome evaluation studies, using standardized rating criteria in six areas, to document internal validity: (1) evaluation design; (2) sample size and sample representativeness; (3) population characteristics; (4) measurement validity and reliability; (5) appropriateness and replicability of intervention methods; and (6) process evaluation.

- **Meta-Analysis:** An evaluation using quantitative analysis and standardized procedures to review completed experimental evaluation research with high internal validity for a well-defined population at risk to estimate the degrees of external validity of a health promotion intervention.

TYPES OF EVALUATIONS

This section provides a synopsis of five common types of evaluation: process evaluation, qualitative evaluation, formative evaluation, evaluation research, and program evaluation. Each type requires time, training, skill, and resources. A detailed discussion of the methods and technical issues related to each type of evaluation is provided in Chapter 4 (process), Chapter 5 (qualitative), and Chapter 6 (formative and impact).

Process Evaluation

Program implementation success is an enduring methodological concern in all evaluations. Basch and colleagues (1985) have described the failure to implement a health education intervention as a "Type III error." Process evaluation data provide essential insight about what types of assessment and intervention methods can (and cannot) be routinely delivered for specific settings, behaviors, types of providers, and clients. This method should be used by a program as a primary quality control mechanism to assess staff delivery of core HP program procedures. It should be conducted in all evaluation phases.

It also has a very practical function, providing empirical information about salient structure and operational procedures within and across programs for specific settings. Process evaluation activities should include periodic review of department activity, staff performance, and performance of a new system for monitoring participants. In a process evaluation, criteria and standards for determining acceptable performance are derived from independent professional judgment or available guidelines from accrediting agencies, procedure manuals, consultants, and professional practice associations.

A process evaluation documents program feasibility and fidelity. It assesses the existence of a structure and the implementation by staff of process components and content delivered. Part of a process evaluation consists of observing and assessing the quality and quantity of procedures performed by program staff. This involves staff examination of the situation, events, problems, people, and interactions during program development, implementation, and field-testing. Evaluators assess components of the program for congruence between staff adherence to a written plan and participants' responses. This assessment of quantitative and qualitative data suggests ways to improve the program design and operational plan.

Qualitative Evaluation

Qualitative assessment methods typically include participant observations or stakeholder interviews to probe for and to identify insights about the evaluation team and participants' interactions. Qualitative evaluation methods should be applied in all four evaluation phases. Qualitative assessments assist in identifying strategies for "mid-course" corrections if the desired plan is not being followed. Scheirer et al. (1995) describe this process as a "breaking down" of cause and effect into "micro steps." Establishing internal validity may depend largely on examination of the "micro-connections" for many community-based evaluation studies. The evaluation team begins with the original program model and, through observations, interviews, and document reviews, detects how and why the model is altered when implemented from one setting to the next. During formative testing, assessment teams may develop visual maps of program components (logic models) to identify progress markers and roadblock indicators. Qualitative assessments may be used to discover unintended positive and negative results. In the case study approach, several assessment methods are used in combination (triangulated) to produce a rich, nuanced portrait of a program. When used in concert with quantitative methods, qualitative assessments enhance internal and external validity.

A qualitative case study can be conducted as part of Phases 1 to 4 evaluations, but also independently. Yin (1994) suggests that a qualitative evaluation best answers the "how" or "why" questions: How was the program a success? Why didn't the program produce a specific change? How might the program be revised to produce better results? This clarifies the dynamic interaction of program personnel, clients, organizations, and other environmental factors that influence program delivery and results.

Green and Kreuter (1999) have suggested that many health issues, e.g., teen pregnancy or substance abuse, are embedded in the social fabric of a community: its environmental or ecologic dimensions. The embedded nature of these health concerns suggests that HP interventions may be more effective when they operate at multiple social levels—individual, social, network, organizational, community, and macro-policy—and are integrated across levels. Because multiple interventions are mutually reinforcing, boundaries typically become blurred. Yin emphasized that the qualitative case study is most suited for blurred levels of analysis but may be hard to achieve. The evaluation team develops themes that emerge from the systematic analysis of notes and document reviews. Emergent themes are translated into a narrative story about the program, why it worked, and what larger lessons emerged.

Formative Evaluation

A formative evaluation answers an immediate question: Can the program be implemented, and is it efficacious? All HP intervention and measurement methods are applied in a formative evaluation at a small number of program sites. Program impacts most likely to be observed would be improvements in knowledge, skill, and immediate or short-term behavior change, e.g., within 1 week or 1 to 6 months after program exposure. Data and information derived from this type of evaluation are used to revise intervention components, instruments, and data-collection procedures to estimate effective size, as well as time and task plans. Failure to conduct a Phase 1 formative evaluation and process evaluation is a major reason why Phase 2, 3, and 4 evaluations and interventions fail.

Conducting a formative evaluation assumes that the methods and procedures to conduct a process evaluation have been well defined and all intervention and data-collection methods have been developed. This type of evaluation should be as rigorous as all others that attempt to assess the internal validity of an HP program. A detailed formative evaluation is presented as the first case study in Chapter 6.

Evaluation Research

The primary purpose of evaluation research (ER) is to document the level of impact of a new intervention among a defined population at risk: Phase 1 and 2 evaluations. ER represents the best method for empirically assessing "age-old truths" and "new fads." ER is the primary method for testing the validity of a theoretical model or a behavior change and for establishing the feasibility, efficacy, and costs of a health promotion intervention. ER attempts to produce evidence to support or reject research hypotheses and to demonstrate a cause-effect relationship between the intervention and the impact or outcome rate. Alternative explanations for an observed, significant behavioral impact should be ruled out by ER. The HP intervention typically consists of multiple components and may apply individual, group, or mass communication methods. Because the ER should be concerned with the policy implications of results, it should be designed to yield convincing, generalizable conclusions.

The purposes and complexity of evaluation research, especially Phase 2 evaluations, demand extensive resources: typically $1–3 million for total costs (direct and indirect) for 3 to 5 years. It requires infrastructure and staff capacity well beyond what a school, community, work site, business, or hospital-based program typically has available. ER requires the collaborative effort of investigator-scientists with doctoral training in the psychosocial, quantitative, and health sciences. Specialists in public health education–health promotion, social and behavioral science, epidemiology, biostatistics, health services research, and nursing typically collaborate on the research team. Extensive training and experience in measurement, evaluation design, statistical analysis, research methods, and especially creation of HP interventions are essential for the principal investigator and team.

A critical step in proposing and conducting ER is a meta-evaluation or meta-analysis. This provides an understanding of the newest evidence-based developments in a specialized area of health behavior change. Thus, an ER team develops interventions based on accumulated knowledge derived from a sound theoretical grounding. ER uses the following standard procedures:

- Specification of research questions and hypotheses
- Definition and selection of an appropriate population at risk to test the hypotheses
- Selection of data sources and measurement of high validity and reliability
- Specification of sample size–effect size estimates
- Selection of an evaluation design to maximize internal validity
- Application of a data-monitoring system to produce ongoing estimates of immediate and short-term program effects and estimates of long-range effects
- Application of a standardized, replicable HP intervention

Program Evaluation

The objective of a Phase 3 and 4 program evaluation is to determine if the efficacious intervention from Phase 1 and 2 studies, when applied under normal practice conditions at specific locations to a defined population, produced significant behavior change. Synonyms for *program evaluation* are *impact evaluation, dissemination evaluation,* and *summative evaluation.* As noted, there are two phases of program evaluation. Because of time and resource limitations and because programs are (and should be) concerned about what works in their setting for their clients, emphasis should be placed on both internal validity and external validity. An assumption apparent in a program (impact) evaluation is that the *efficacy* of the intervention has been confirmed by evaluation research. Conducting a meta-evaluation or meta-analysis (discussed in Chapter 2) is essential for creating and evaluating "best practice" methods. A common problem that may contribute to program failure is not looking at comparable, previously conducted evaluations of programs to learn what can be implemented and what level of impact can be achieved. When multiple Phase 3 evaluations confirm the effectiveness of a "best practice" intervention, it is likely to be widely disseminated to be routinely used and evaluated in Phase 4 studies.

A principal difference between evaluation research and program evaluation is that public health programs usually deal with a fluid situation and have to adapt to organizational, policy, fiscal, and situational changes. Evaluation research tends to be more rigid in its inputs and methods, attempting not to deviate from a protocol and research design and methods. Experience and resources are also typically more limited among an ongoing program evaluation staff vs. evaluation research staff.

A Phase 3 or 4 program evaluation is concerned with both internal and external validity. Would the program produce a comparable impact at other sites with a comparable defined population? Program impact-dissemination evaluation attempts to determine the congruence between performance (i.e., what occurred) and objectives (i.e., what was supposed to occur). It attempts to isolate the most plausible reasons for an effect. Program evaluation and evaluation research objectives and the rigor of methods used should be very similar. Both should be designed to supplement real-world decision making and to add valid new knowledge to the health promotion literature.

EVALUATION PRACTICE STANDARDS

Regardless of the type of evaluation, an HP evaluation plan needs to reflect the application of nationally disseminated professional performance-practice standards. The Evaluation Research Society published its evaluation practice standards in *New Directions for Program Evaluation* (P. Rossi, ed., 1982). The 1982 practice standards were updated by a joint committee of sixteen professional associations in *Program Evaluation Standards* (J. Sanders, chair, 2nd ed., 1994). As noted in Table 1.5, the joint committee identified four attributes of a standard that when addressed should result in improved program evaluations. A total of 30 standards were defined as basic elements of the four attributes by the committee. Evaluations of health promotion programs should demonstrate an application of the four attributes:

- **Utility:** An evaluation serves the information needs of intended users.
- **Feasibility:** An evaluation is realistic, prudent, and efficient.
- **Propriety:** An evaluation is conducted ethically and with due regard for the welfare of the evaluation participants and people affected by its results.
- **Accuracy:** An evaluation produces technically adequate and valid information about the measures that define program worth or merit.

Contemporary evaluation plans and reports need to reflect an application of these four attributes and 30 standards.

TABLE 1.5   Basic Attributes and Standards of Program Evaluation

Utility	Propriety	Feasibility	Accuracy
U1: Stakeholder Identification	P1: Service Orientation	F1: Practical Procedures	A1: Program Documentation
U2: Evaluator Credibility	P2: Formal Agreements	F2: Political Viability	A2: Context Analysis
U3: Information Scope and Selection	P3: Rights of Human Subjects	F3: Cost-Effectiveness	A3: Described Purposes and Procedures
U4: Values Identification	P4: Human Interactions		A4: Defensible Information Sources
U5: Report Clarity	P5: Complete and Fair Assessment		A5: Valid Information
U6: Report Time-liness and Dissemination	P6: Disclosure of Findings		A6: Reliable Information
U7: Evaluation Impact	P7: Conflict of Interest		A7: Systematic Information
	P8: Fiscal Responsibility		A8: Analysis of Quantitative Information
			A9: Analysis of Qualitative Information
			A10: Justified Conclusions
			A11: Impartial Reporting
			A12: Meta-Evaluation

Source: J. R. Sanders, chair, Joint Committee on Standards for Educational Evaluation, Evaluation Center, Western Michigan University, Kalamazoo, MI (1994).

PROFESSIONAL COMPETENCE IN EVALUATION IN PUBLIC HEALTH

In 1988 the Committee for the Study of the Future of Public Health of the Institute of Medicine defined the core functions of public health. As noted in Table 1.6, a Public Health Functions Steering Committee (1988), representing government, public health agencies, and nonprofit public health groups, defined three core functions of public health. Each has important implication for evaluations of HP-DP programs.

These functions require specific competencies related to planning and evaluation in 10 categorical areas:

1. Monitor health status to identify community health problems
2. Diagnose and investigate health problems and health hazards in the community

TABLE 1.6   Functions of Public Health

Core Function	Definition
Assessment	Regularly and systematically collect, assemble, analyze, and make available information on the community, including statistics on health status, community health needs, and epidemiologic and other studies of health problems.
Policy Development	Exercise responsibility to serve the public interest in the development of comprehensive public health policies by promoting the use of the scientific knowledge base in decision making about public health and by leading in developing public health policy. Agencies must take a strategic approach developed on the basis of a positive appreciation for the democratic political process.
Assurance	Assure constituents that services necessary to achieve agreed-upon goals are provided, either by encouraging actions by other entities (public or private sector), by requiring such action through regulation, or by providing services directly.

Source: Committee for the Study of the Future of Public Health, Institute of Medicine (1988).

3. Inform, educate, and empower people about health issues

4. Mobilize community partnerships to identify and solve health problems

5. Develop policies and plans that support individual and community health efforts

6. Enforce laws and regulations that protect health and ensure safety

7. Link people to health care and services when otherwise unavailable

8. Assure a competent public health and personal health care workforce

9. Evaluate effectiveness, accessibility, and quality of personal and public health services

10. Conduct research for new insights and innovative solutions to health problems

Graduate-trained health promotion and education specialists should be knowledgeable about all functions and have specific skills to contribute to all 10 areas.

Credentialing and Professional Preparation in Health Promotion and Education

The quality of an evaluation plan depends heavily on the competency, experience, and confidence of the evaluation staff. Evaluation has also been identified as an integral component of school, public, patient, work site, and community

Table 1.7   Guidelines for the Preparation and Practice of Professional
Health Educators: Area Four—Research and Evaluation

Skill Area	Master's Level Function
1. Statistical Methods	Collect and use quantitative data and perform standard statistical tests to understand and analyze the relationships between variables and draw inferences for interventions.
2. Research Design and Research Methods	Design and conduct studies on health-related behavior, health education methods, and behavior-change problems.
3. Design Methods of Evaluative Research	Design health education programs so that evaluative measures are incorporated with provision for continuing process evaluation.
4. Methods of Data Collection and Analysis	Determine which data are needed to analyze a health problem and where they can be obtained. Use standardized measurement instruments. Analyze research findings relevant to health-related behavior change. Draw implications for application. Design action research and demonstration projects.
5. Computer Science: Technologies	Understand appropriate applications of computer technology to plan, conduct, and evaluate research.
6. Knowledge and Skills Possessed by Other Disciplines in Research and Evaluation	Use expert help as needed for design and conduct of research.

Source: Society for Public Health Education (1977b, 75–89).

health education programs by standard-setting organizations such as the World Health Organization (1954, 1969, 1980, 1981), American Public Health Association (1957), Association of Schools of Public Health (Boatman et al. 1966), and the Society for Public Health Education (1968, 1977a).

The health education specialist is expected to perform a number of evaluation functions and be skilled in selected technical areas. Training programs and professional leaders in public health education have consistently defined evaluation as a core competency of graduate-trained health professionals. The Society for Public Health Education (SOPHE; 1977a) has described the research and evaluation skills needed by a health education specialist with a master's degree (Table 1.7). The importance of having a baccalaureate-trained health education specialist (see Appendix B) to assist in program evaluation has also been defined (SOPHE 1977b; USDHHS 1980a).

The President's Committee on Health Education, the U.S. Coalition of Health Education Organizations, and the leadership in the field of health education and health promotion throughout the 1970s called for improvements in

TABLE 1.8   A Competency-Based Framework for Graduate-Level
Health Educators

Area of Responsibility I	Assessing Individual and Community Needs for Health Education
Area of Responsibility II	Planning Effective Health Education Programs
Area of Responsibility III	Implementing Health Education Programs
Area of Responsibility IV	Evaluating Effectiveness of Health Education Programs
Area of Responsibility V	Coordinating Provision of Health Education Services
Area of Responsibility VI	Acting as a Resource Person in Health Education
Area of Responsibility VII	Communicating Health and Health Education Needs
Area of Responsibility VIII	Applying Appropriate Research Principles and Techniques in Health Education
Area of Responsibility IX	Administering Health Education Programs
Area of Responsibility X	Advancing the Profession of Health Education

Source: American Association for Health Education, National Commission for Health Education Credentialing, Inc., Society for Public Health Education (1999).

training programs and competency of health educators. The academic and practice leadership in school health education, public health education, patient health care education, and work site health education agreed that major commonalities existed in the functions and skills of health education specialists. These deliberations produced a landmark meeting in April 1978, convened by the Bureau of Health Manpower, Department of Health Resources Administration: "Preparation and Practice of Community, Patients and School Health Educators." A National Task Force on Professional Preparation was established at this time. These activities led to the creation of a credentialing commission.

Two major initiatives of the National Commission for Health Education Credentialing Inc. (NCHEC) are ongoing: (1) promotion of improved competency through professional certification of health education specialists, and (2) continued promotion and application of "A Guide for the Development of Competency-Based Curricula for Entry-Level Health Educators" by baccalaureate and graduate programs in the United States. The NCHEC has two publications describing these two initiatives: *A Competency-Based Framework for Professional Development of Certified Health Education Specialists* (1996) and *The Certified Health Education Specialist: A Self-Study Guide for Professional Competency* (1998). The competency in area of responsibility V—Evaluation is included in the appendix to this chapter. Table 1.8 defines the ten areas of responsibility for certified health education specialists (CHES). Specialist staff with these skills and credentials are essential for planning, implementing, and evaluating HP programs.

SUMMARY

Contemporary thinking dictates that the professional preparation and practice of health education–health promotion specialists be approached from both an experimental and a qualitative perspective. Evaluation should serve as a mechanism not only to assess and to improve existing programs but also to test new interventions and innovations. It represents one of the most important channels for improvement of health education, health promotion, and disease prevention professional practice.

Program evaluation and health education practice need to be perceived as a fertile ground for collaboration between scientists, trainers, trainees, managers, and practitioners, regardless of setting. Program evaluation should become a major source of personal and professional growth. All evaluation phases provide opportunities to bridge the gap between academically oriented and practice-oriented professionals. The work of both types of professionals can improve or diminish the opportunity for new methods, technology, and advancement of the field. Both groups may experience frustration at the energy, patience, and sophistication needed to plan, implement, and evaluate a program, often with limited resources. Individuals in practice and academic settings need to discover how they can do better with what they have so they can get more of what they need. Future HP evaluations need to reflect a full appreciation for the contribution of the science, policy, and practice domains.

The development, implementation, and adaptation of an evaluation plan to unanticipated situations, although at times frustrating, can be one of the most creative exercises for members of an evaluation team. If health education and promotion are to continue to prosper as an integrated part of the public health, health care, work site, and educational systems of the United States, greater technical skill and improved sophistication are needed. Responsibility for the extra effort it takes to master the technical, interpersonal, and organizational development skills needed to conduct health program evaluations rests with the graduate-trained professional. With improved skill and experience, and good mentoring, a program evaluator should be able to better perceive what is possible, probable, or impossible given the science base, available resources, time, and the existing political environment. This book provides guidance and structure to optimize the process of staff and program resource development.

APPENDIX

Specification of the Role of the Entry-Level Health Educator

Area of Responsibility V: Evaluating Health Education

Function:	A.	Participate in developing an evaluation design.
Skill:		1. Specify indicators of program success.
		2. Establish the scope for program evaluation.
		3. Develop methods for evaluating programs.
		4. Specify instruments for data collection.
		5. Determine samples needed for evaluation.
		6. Select data useful for accountability analysis.
Function:	B.	Assemble resources required to carry out evaluation.
Skill:		1. Acquire facilities, materials, personnel, and equipment.
		2. Train personnel for evaluation as needed.
		3. Secure the cooperation of those affecting and affected by the program.
Function:	C.	Help implement the evaluation design.
Skill:		1. Collect data through appropriate techniques.
		2. Analyze collected data.
		3. Interpret results of program evaluation.
Function:	D.	Communicate results of evaluation.
Skill:		1. Report the processes and results of evaluation to those interested.
		2. Recommend strategies for implementing results.
		3. Incorporate results into planning and implementation processes.

Source: U.S. Department of Health and Human Services, Public Health Service, *Initial Role Delineation for Health Education. Final Report,* prepared for the National Center for Health Education, DHHS Publication no. (HRA) 80-44 (Washington, D.C.: Government Printing Office, 1980), pp. 78–82.

2 | Planning an Evaluation

In Chapter 1, we focused on the role of the evaluator and the potential for evaluation to produce change within an organization, a community, or a population at high risk. In this chapter, we discuss development of the health education program to be evaluated. In many, if not most, instances the health education specialist oversees the planning, implementation, and evaluation of an educational program. The program plan is a road map—the blueprint to ensure that the program is logical, addresses learning needs, and can be evaluated. The plan consolidates staff thinking. Among the collaborators in the planning process are, of course, the program participants.

Besides ensuring that the program is well conceived, good planning helps to mobilize essential information, people, and resources critical to program success. A plan provides guidelines for program instructors and enables programs to be replicated. The plan, then, is the comprehensive document to ensure that a program is sound and that it will engender the support needed for implementing it.

In this chapter, we focus on the steps in developing a program plan and emphasize program evaluation as part of the planning process. Initially, we discuss several important, basic concepts for program developers: the organizational context for planning, the planning network, and the step-by-step process of developing the program and its evaluation plan.

THE ORGANIZATIONAL CONTEXT FOR HEALTH PROMOTION AND EDUCATION

When scientists plan health education and promotion interventions, they try to manipulate the environment by applying theories and testing hypotheses. In the day-to-day implementation of health education, however, practitioners must accept realities and try to build into their plan ways to manage existing situations. Often, staff have limited control over the conditions in which programs are developed and delivered. Nonetheless, a standard of practice and a program should be based on valid principles and theories. Successfully planning and evaluating a theory-based program can be difficult, however. For example, existing theory suggests that developing ongoing peer support groups in which the same members meet over a period of time may enable chronically ill people to acquire the social support needed to manage their illness (Israel and Rounds 1987). But, given patients' work schedules, the available meeting places, a limited budget, or other factors, it may be very difficult to fully apply this principle.

In practice, staff should try to translate theoretical principles that enable positive behavior change to occur. They continually try to encourage needed changes in parent organizations and communities to enable them to come closer to creating optimum conditions for behavior changes (Clark 1978). Phases 1 and 2 evaluation research, discussed in Chapter 1, is designed to manipulate the environment to test hypotheses. Phases 3 and 4 effectiveness evaluations contribute to the knowledge base of health promotion and education by assessing and describing the application of knowledge in similar settings and situations. Ultimately, the program evaluations you will conduct as part of your daily health promotion and education work form the basis on which a theory becomes accepted as generally valid. The challenge for those in the field of health promotion and education is to develop programs and to conduct evaluations to bridge the gap between theory and practice.

Philosophy of the Organization

Health promotion and education specialists are employed by agencies and organizations to develop programs. Working with an organization means that you must represent not only your own views, objectives, and philosophy but also those of your employing organization. Sometimes there is conflict between what an individual believes and the goals of the organization. If you find yourself in such a quandary and no reconciliation of ideas can be achieved, you need to make a personal and professional decision about whether to work with organizational goals unlike your own. Deciding to proceed is likely to create a difficult situation and would probably preclude effective work. You may, instead, find another organization whose philosophy and views are more in line with yours. Some educators volunteer their assistance to individuals and groups to develop programs that espouse particular political and philosophical views. Educators can then emphasize views they believe are particularly important, unencumbered by the need to represent an employer. In presenting the steps of program development, we assume that staff must pay attention to the mission and interests of an employing organization.

Impetus for the Program

In the field of practice, there are three basic ways in which health promotion and education programs are created. The educator sees the need to design a program: "We really need to develop a hypertension education program for the elderly. We've got to improve the quality and the cost-effectiveness of our service. Shall I develop something for you and the budget people?" Or you are asked to design a program that, according to someone else, the agency's clients need: "Larry, given the data on hypertension in the elderly, the board of directors feels we should get a hypertension education program off the ground. Develop something that we might get the budget to support." Or you are asked to design a program on the basis of what clients want: "Joan, what kind of health education do our elderly clients need and want? Find out and put something together. Then let's see what kind of budget we'd need."

Orientation and Goals of the Organization

Regardless of who initiates the program, it is likely to be organized in one of two ways: (1) as part of ongoing activities providing related health services directly to clients, or (2) as a project by groups that provide no direct medical or nursing services. For example, hypertension education may be part of the senior citizens program of a local health department. The health department may have contracts with physicians or nurses who are on staff and available to screen and to treat program participants diagnosed as hypertensive. Similarly, the program may be part of the services of a general primary care clinic that has a large elderly population, where physicians routinely see hypertensive clients. The health promotion and education program may be developed to be integrated into the ongoing services of an organization with a wider set of health service activities.

On the other hand, the hypertension education program might be developed as an activity of a community-based senior citizens center where the aim is to assist the elderly with many concerns, including health. In this case, participants will be referred elsewhere if they need medical or nursing services. Similarly, a community health education program may be developed by a private voluntary agency, say, Citizens for a Better Community, and directed to all the elderly in an area. Such a program might recruit physicians and nurses to participate, if they are needed, or might refer people to available Medicare-supported services when necessary. The important aspect to note about these latter two examples is that the health promotion program is part of a broader community effort and not part of medical or nursing services.

It is also likely that, in organizations where health promotion and education are part of a larger set of medical and nursing activities, *health* may be narrowly defined to mean primarily those conditions that document the absence or reduction of the diseases of organizational interest. Health related to hypertension, for example, may mean having normal blood pressure (120/80). In organizations where health promotion and education are not tied to medical and nursing services, health may have a much broader definition. Health for the senior citizens, for example, may include such things as practicing a range of good personal health habits (Simmons et al. 1989) or having social contact with other people (Shinn et al. 1984).

The purposes of evaluations conducted by an organization will depend on how it defines health. Both the goals of health promotion and education and the goals of evaluations are greatly influenced by the mission of the sponsoring organization. Organizations give priority to programs that further their primary goals. Health care organizations tend to be oriented primarily toward communities or individuals and toward disease treatment, management, or prevention.

If an organization serves individuals, it will tend to focus on what people can do to improve their health. Such an organization (e.g., a community hospital) might develop patient education programs to teach diabetic patients to self-administer medications. The focus is on the individual and an individual solution to the health problem. If an organization has a community orientation, it tends to focus more on a broader kind of change; it looks for community-wide solutions.

As an example, assume a health problem exists in an area because health services are inadequate or because people cannot afford to eat nutritious food or buy necessary medications. A community-based organization (CBO) might organize and educate people to work collectively to bring about changes in health care delivery or might develop cooperatives to cut the costs of buying food or medications. In other words, health education favored by a CBO might focus on assisting groups of people to change conditions in the physical, social, or political environment that have a negative impact on their health.

For the program planner, a cardinal rule is to know the organizational context well before starting a program. You must understand organizational goals and mission as they relate to the problem in question. As you consider your program in light of the variety of organizations that sponsor it, you may ask a question frequently posed: Is the objective of education always behavior change? We would answer yes, in the sense that behavior change is sought within the context of social change. Rarely is an individual's behavior under that person's total control. Public health education almost always tries to stimulate organizational and community changes to enable people to acquire the resources and services necessary for healthful living. This is particularly apparent when education has a community-action orientation, but it is also the case when the program is oriented toward individual change.

All programs operate on the assumption that people will change as a result of their participation. This assumption is easy to understand when a program focuses on individuals and disease management. Hypertension education for an elderly woman, for example, should enable her to take her medication and to reduce her sodium intake—to behave regularly in a new way. It is more difficult to see behavior change as the goal if the program focuses on communities and prevention. Assume that a program wants to help people improve inadequate housing in their community. A goal may be to organize groups to demand service from the city housing authority or to bring suit against recalcitrant landlords. Although housing may improve because the housing department or landlords sent workers to make repairs, participant behavior presumably led to this outcome. Even when the goal is to change the conditions that obstruct good health, it is people who bring about the change by behaving in a different way. These new behaviors may include such things as being more assertive, being more vocal, exercising more community leadership, and participating more in cooperative activities (Clark and Gakuru 1982; Clark and Pinkett-Heller 1977). An important part of planning a program evaluation is to anticipate what changes in behavior may occur, what other related changes might occur, and how such changes might be measured. We will discuss this further in a later section.

THE HEALTH PROMOTION PLANNING NETWORK

Regardless of the type of sponsoring organization, planning is rarely a unilateral activity. The design, implementation, and evaluation of a program always involve a network of people: representatives of the target group, the program planner/evaluator, other staff in an organization, and representatives of outside organizations who provide needed services and resources. Another cardinal rule of program development is that, to be effective, programs should always be planned with the participation of major interest groups. Good health seems to be everyone's goal, but views on what it is and how to get it differ enormously. Therefore, part of program planning is to collaborate with those who can provide insight to a program.

If a program fails to account for the learner's perspective, it cannot possibly appeal to their motives or enable them to see the relevance of the learning to their situation. Without the participation of potential learners, you might plan a program leaving out the vital ingredient that will enable participants to behave in a new way or that will change conditions that inhibit healthful behavior (Bruner 1973). Without the views of those who provide needed related services, it is very difficult to mobilize the resources and cooperation to carry out a comprehensive program.

PRECEDE/PROCEED Planning Model

Many frameworks exist for planning and evaluating health education, health promotion, and disease prevention programs. One of the most rigorous is the PRECEDE/PROCEED model (Figure 2.1). This framework is a data-driven model that recognizes that health problems and health behaviors are caused by multiple factors; thus, these causes must be systematically evaluated to identify the specific intervention components. PRECEDE/PROCEED is so comprehensive that planners can use it in virtually all settings, e.g., community, school, medical/clinic, and work site.

The PRECEDE planning and evaluation framework, originally developed by Green (Green, Kreuter, Deeds, and Partridge 1980), first appeared in the 1970s. PRECEDE (an acronym for Predisposing, Reinforcing, and Enabling Constructs in Educational Diagnosis and Evaluation) was developed to enable health education practitioners to design interventions utilizing a planning process based upon a thorough, systematic assessment of each component's antecedents or underlying causes. The PROCEED part of the framework (Policy, Regulatory, and Organizational Constructs in Educational and Environmental Development) was added in the late 1980s in recognition of the need for health promotion interventions that go beyond traditional education approaches in changing unhealthy behaviors. PRECEDE and PROCEED work in tandem by allowing the planner to execute a continuous series of steps to plan, implement, and evaluate programs. In PRECEDE, planners identify priorities that form the basis of quantifiable objectives, which become goals in the implementation of the project in PROCEED.

The application of the PRECEDE/PROCEED planning model (Green and Kreuter 1999) involves a nine-step process. It utilizes guidelines for prioritizing aims and objectives so that the resources the planners need to develop a project can be accurately identified and used. For example, some public health planners think that all they need to do to change health behavior is to inform the public about the consequences of a health threat. However, planners who do not carefully consider the extent to which the target population lacks knowledge, beliefs, values, skills, and program resources may be misdirected in their efforts. Thus, they may develop and implement a program in which no behavioral impact is observed. Planners may avoid such misguided efforts through a thorough assessment and prioritization of all phases in the PRECEDE/PROCEED model.

PRECEDE/PROCEED is based upon the principle of participation. This principle assumes that success in achieving behavior change in any population is enhanced when individuals in the target population have the opportunity to assist in the prioritization of problems and in developing and implementing the

PRECEDE

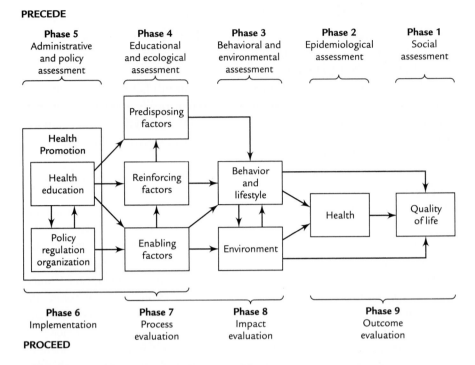

FIGURE 2.1   PRECEDE/PROCEED Model   *Source:* Green and Kreuter (1999). Reproduced with permission of The McGraw-Hill Companies, Inc.

solutions. The idea of participation is rooted in the community organization and empowerment ideas described in the writings of Friere (1970) and more recently in the work of Wallerstein (1992). Planners must make considerable efforts to include the target population in all aspects of program planning, implementation, and evaluation.

PROCEED highlights the importance of the social environment in healthy and unhealthy behavior. Although many individual behaviors lead to serious health consequences, many behaviors are influenced by powerful factors in the physical and social environment. The acknowledgment of the impact of the environment on behavior is a central component of the ecological approach to health promotion. Thus, PRECEDE/PROCEED considers not only the individual but also the environmental factors that influence health behaviors. In the next sections we discuss the stages of the PRECEDE/PROCEED model. Case Study 2.1 presents an application of this model.

Phase 1: Social Assessment

One of the first tasks in planning is to determine the target population's perceptions of their quality of life. There are many reasons why the social assessment is important. Green and Kreuter (1999) indicate that health and quality of life are reciprocal, i.e., each affects the other. For example, individuals living in poverty are more likely to have poor health. When impoverished people are unhealthy, it is more difficult for them to escape poor living conditions. Green and Kreuter (1999) acknowledge that the notion of health is not an end in itself but rather a means to an end. Individuals will value their health because of what good health brings.

Planners need to understand a target group's quality-of-life concerns. This understanding enables a program to be designed that is relevant to the needs of the target population. When a program is developed that meets their needs, it increases the chances that the group will embrace the program and it will be effective. There are numerous ways for planners to collect social data. Methods used for social assessment may include discussion groups, the nominal group process, the Delphi technique, focus groups, and surveys.

Discussion groups   If the aim is to discover how social problems are perceived or which social problem is most important to a group, a *discussion group* may be convened. Representatives of the community should comprise the group: volunteers who agree to discuss issues they consider most pressing or of most concern to them. Members might be people who hold positions with community groups or other organizations, or they may simply be interested individuals who experience the problems and are likely to know the viewpoint of their peers. Such a discussion group has the advantage of allowing people to discuss and even vote on topics of immediate significance.

When conducting group discussions, make clear what actions a sponsoring organization is prepared to take in light of the perceptions and concerns of the group. The domain of community organization and action within the field of health education is based on this principle. McKnight (1978) used a very effective approach of combining discussion groups, analysis of secondary data, and action. He assisted members of community organizations in translating statistics from their local hospital, health department, or some other source into a picture of the actual problems experienced in their neighborhood. By examining available data, community representatives can explore how the problem occurs in their area and select aspects of the problem to address.

Health promotion staff may convene meetings specifically to discuss the priorities of individuals or community groups. In such a meeting, group members, led by staff, determine which problem or aspects of the problem are most important. In situations where varying points of view must be reconciled, staff frequently use the nominal group process or Delphi technique (Delbecq 1974). These techniques enable group members to select problems and to reach consensus on aspects of problems without letting individuals' views dominate. The nominal group process is an interactive method for determining needs by listing opinions without critique from the group and then rating them by secret ballot. The secret ballot minimizes the influence of interpersonal dynamics on the ratings. The Delphi technique (Delbecq 1974) is a method of sampling opinions of a small group of individuals, usually experts, community leaders, or key informants. This technique uses a succession of mailed questionnaires that request the recipient to rank a series of issues. The results are mailed to the same individuals in subsequent rounds for further refinement of the initial issues.

A disadvantage of discussions by volunteers is that you never know exactly whose views the group represents. Some representatives of organizations may have clear-cut constituencies, and their statements may accurately present the case for their constituencies; but this is not always the case. Similarly, concerns expressed by unaffiliated individuals may be uniquely felt. The views and attitudes of one suburban mother of young children do not necessarily reflect those of similar women. In other words, it is difficult to know how far to generalize the opinions and experiences of these volunteers. If a disparity eventually emerges between the views of the representatives and the target population you aim to reach, fundamental problems can plague your program. Nonetheless, discussion groups can generally shed light on the problems and can provide rich insights on dimensions of the problems.

Focus groups   A *focus group* is a discussion about specific aspects of a problem or program among people similar to the target population. The term is borrowed from marketing, where groups of consumers are convened and paid to tell manufacturers or advertisers the characteristics of products they prefer or the elements of advertisements that capture their attention. Focus group techniques have been widely adopted in program planning (Basch 1987). The primary difference between a focus group and a discussion group is the specificity of issues or questions concerning the program. The intention is to discover useful information about issues of most concern to the group. No consensus is required. As in discussion groups, focus group members may not represent the opinion of all members of a community.

Surveys   The purpose of a *survey*, whether a mailed questionnaire, telephone questionnaire, or face-to-face interview, is to elicit specific information from a defined population at risk. Like information collected from discussion and focus groups, survey data are used to delineate the problem and to describe population perspectives. If the survey is of a sample of people who will eventually be in the program, the answers may also be used as baseline data for measuring change.

In conducting a survey, the first step is to select a sample population. Sampling has been defined as the selection of as few observations as is necessary to serve as the basis for general conclusions (Kish 1987). Sampling and techniques for conducting different types of surveys are described in Chapter 3. Sampling overcomes the problem of representativeness. By selecting people at random (e.g., women who come to the clinic) or using a systematic procedure (e.g., every third woman who visits the clinic), you can collect representative data. The sample collected views are likely to be similar to those of people not surveyed, whereas volunteers might be different in some respect from the larger population you hope to reach.

After gathering data, staff can use the findings to establish a link between the problems they identified in their social assessment and specific health problems in the community, which may become the focus of health promotion interventions.

Phase 2: Epidemiological Assessment

An *epidemiological assessment* identifies health problems that are most prevalent in the target population's community. At this stage one of two approaches is utilized: reductionist or expansionist. In the reductionist approach, staff use data on the most important quality-of-life concerns that were found in the social assessment and identify the contributing health problems that appear to be causally linked with these social concerns. In the expansionist approach, staff begin the initial planning by selecting an important health problem and then attempt to link it to quality-of-life concerns among members of the target population. Those planning HP-HE-DP interventions and evaluations will utilize the expansionist approach far more often than the reductionist approach because funding opportunities are more often associated with health problems or health risk behaviors among specific populations at risk. When beginning with the expansionist approach, it is important to identify relationships with a health concern and a quality-of-life concern.

Two questions need to be answered: (1) What is the problem? (2) Who has the problem? In conducting an epidemiological assessment, consider conducting secondary data analyses with existing data sets such as vital statistics from the state and local data sets; results of local, state, and national health surveys; and medical and administrative records. Data from these sources will yield information on morbidity and mortality in the target population. Analyses of these data will show which subgroups are most affected and who is at greatest risk. Disaggregate the data into the following categories: gender, age group, educational status, income level, family structure, occupation, and geographic location. Analyze each level of data to determine its contribution to the health problem. Be aware that although national and state surveys give a larger perspective, you may need to collect original data on smaller groups to ensure that the information obtained from the larger data banks is appropriate for your setting.

Writing health objectives   Once the health problems have been defined in terms of risk factors, staff should be ready to develop objectives. This step is crucial to the program planning, implementation, and evaluation process. Objectives should be written with specificity and should answer four questions:

1. Who is the target of the program?
2. What is the health benefit the target population will receive?
3. How much benefit should be achieved?
4. When should the benefit be achieved, or for how long should the program run?

The information collected and analyzed in the epidemiological assessment should be valid and reliable data for writing measurable program objectives. Although these decisions will be guided by the needs of the target population, the program objectives will be a statement of the program's ultimate benefit in changing health. For example, an objective in a health program on highway safety could be to reduce alcohol-related driving mortality. The program objective would be to answer the questions: "What health improvements will be achieved in whom? By how much? By when?" These questions might be answered in the objective "Alcohol-related traffic deaths will be reduced by 25% among drivers aged 16–24 in County X by the year 2007." Measurable program objectives are essential, not only to guide appropriate allocations of resources, but also to evaluate the program's success. Staff planning programs and evaluations should utilize national and regional public health consensus documents as a guide for setting reasonable targets for change. For example, the U.S. Public Health Service document *Healthy People 2010*, which identifies health promotion–disease prevention objectives for the nation, is a good reference for beginning this process. State-level companion documents to *Healthy People 2010* are other examples of excellent references for establishing measurable objectives.

Phase 3: Behavioral and Environmental Assessment

The third phase of PRECEDE/PROCEED is the *behavioral and environmental assessment*. This step identifies behavioral and environmental risk factors for the health problems that were identified in the epidemiological assessment: population-attributable risk. In this phase we seek an answer to the question: "Why do those individuals with the health problem have it?"

Simply stated, behavioral factors are aspects of the lifestyle of the target population that contribute to the prevalence and the severity of the health problems. Typically, environmental factors are external to the individual and are frequently beyond personal control. However, in most instances, these factors can

	More Important	Less Important
More Changeable	High priority (Quadrant 1)	Low priority except for political purposes (Quadrant 3)
Less Changeable	Priority for innovative program; assessment is critical (Quadrant 2)	No program (Quadrant 4)

FIGURE 2.2   Dimensions of Importance and Changeability
Source: Green and Kreuter (1999). Reproduced with permission of The
McGraw-Hill Companies, Inc.

be altered by changes in the social environment through policies, laws, and regulations to support behavior change that may influence the health outcome.

As the planner, consider an inventory of influential behaviors that contribute to the social and health problems identified in Phases 1 and 2. Documentation of the top behavioral causes of disease and death is easily accessible. There are also many nonbehavioral causes of health problems. Note both behavioral and nonbehavioral causes in an assessment. Even if nonbehavioral causes cannot be changed through a health promotion intervention, they should be considered in program planning.

Once an inventory of influential behavior factors has been developed, your next task is to rate each one in terms of its importance to the social concerns/health problems. Two considerations are important in this evaluation. The importance of the behavior is evident when data show that (1) it occurs frequently, and (2) it is positively/strongly associated with the health problem.

The next step is to rate the behaviors in terms of changeability. Be aware that even if a behavior is strongly associated with a health problem, it may not be appropriate to target it unless you can reasonably expect it to change through an HP intervention. Green and Kreuter (1999) identify several rules to assist in assessing changeability. A behavior is considered highly changeable if it (1) is still in its developmental stage, (2) has only recently been established, (3) is not deeply rooted in culture and lifestyle, and (4) has been found to change in previous intervention attempts. The selection of which behaviors to target in an intervention is based on importance and changeability.

Utilizing the matrix shown in Figure 2.2 is a good way to select which behaviors should be targeted in the intervention and to identify where the most effective intervention methods can be applied. Choose intervention targets by combining importance and changeability ratings. Select only those behaviors that are important, i.e., contribute significantly to a health problem, and are considered highly changeable.

Writing behavioral objectives   The next task is to write measurable objectives for change for each of the target behaviors. To estimate behavior change when writing objectives, search the literature regarding the behavioral impact researchers have observed in other settings. As described in the section on writing health objectives for an epidemiological assessment, write objectives to answer the following questions:

1. Who in the target population is expected to change?
2. What behavior in the target population is expected to change?
3. How much of the behavior is expected to change?
4. By when is the behavior expected to change?

Like the assessment of behaviors, the environmental assessment requires an evaluation of several criteria. The first step is to identify which environmental factors that are causing health problems may be changed. When the behavioral assessment was conducted, nonbehavioral organizational, economic, and environmental factors were identified that have an impact on health and/or quality of life. The second step is to rate these factors in terms of their relative importance. This involves analyzing them on the basis of the strength of their impact on health and quality of life, their incidence and prevalence, and the number in your population that are affected by them. The third step is to rate the environmental factors in terms of changeability. This differs from the task completed in step 1. In this step the environmental factors that would be least likely to change through policy, regulation, or organizational change are deleted. This task will be easier if only the factors that emerged in step 2 are utilized. The last step is to choose the environmental factors that will become targets for change. Application of the matrix that was utilized in the behavioral assessment to prioritize behaviors should be used to complete the evaluation of environmental factors. Factors that are rated more important and more changeable should become priorities for environmental change (see Figure 2.2).

Writing environmental objectives   After you have determined the environmental factors that need to be changed, the last task is to write environmental objectives. To do this, slightly alter the criteria that you used for writing health and behavioral objectives. Environmental objectives will address these questions:

1. What environmental factor will change?
2. By how much should this factor change?
3. By when in the time line of the project should the change occur?

For example, a priority of a comprehensive tobacco control project may be to reduce environmental tobacco smoke exposure in restaurants by reducing the number of restaurants that allow smoking. A possible environmental objective could be: "The proportion of restaurants that allow smoking will be reduced by 50% within three years of the initiation of the project."

Reviewing literature   How much behavioral impact can an intervention produce? The answer to this question is essential to planning an evaluation. One of the first steps all evaluators should take in the development of an intervention and evaluation plan is a thorough review of the literature. This review will help estimate effect size and sample size for different types of interventions.

There are two methods to use in reviewing the literature: meta-evaluation (ME) and meta-analysis (MA). The distinction between the two methods rests primarily on the maturity of the literature base. In the early stages of an intervention's use, documentation of its efficacy is usually limited. Often, only a few published evaluation studies exist to provide insight about the estimated impact of intervention methods or programs for a defined population and risk factor. In this case, only an ME is performed.

Meta-evaluation   *Meta-evaluation* is a method of assessing the quality of published intervention studies. It applies standard rating criteria in six methodological areas to assess the internal validity of the impact of health promotion–disease prevention programs:

1. Type of evaluation design
2. Sample representativeness and sample size
3. Specification of population characteristics
4. Measurement quality
5. Appropriateness and replicability of experimental and control procedures
6. Feasibility of routine delivery of program procedures

For a detailed example of the application of the ME method, see Windsor and Orleans (1986), who studied eight smoking-cessation programs for pregnant women, all that were available at the time of their review in 1985. They included only studies with a quasi-experimental or experimental design in their ME. Table 2.1 presents their overall methodological ratings for each criterion area and a total rating score for the eight studies critiqued. They recommended the following minimal standards for future program evaluations of health education methods for pregnant smokers:

- Only use an experimental design with an inception cohort of at least 80% of the smoking patients at all sites.

TABLE 2.1 Methodological Ratings of Completed Smoking-Cessation Intervention Research Studies for Pregnant Women[a]

Investigators (years)	Criteria					
	1: Design	2: Sample	3: Charac- teristics	4: Measure- ment	5: Inter- vention	Rating Score
1. Baric et al. (1975)	4.0	3.0	2.0	1.0	0.0	10.0
2. Donovan et al. (1972–1973)	4.0	3.0	1.0	0.0	1.0	9.0
3. Loeb et al. (1979–1981)	4.0	3.0	2.0	0.0	1.0	10.0
4. Ershoff et al. (1980–1981)	2.0	2.0	3.0	1.0	4.0	12.0
5. Bauman et al. (1981)	4.0	3.0	4.0	1.0	3.0	15.0
6. Burling et al. (1983)	4.0	2.0	1.0	2.0	2.0	11.0
7. Sexton and Hebel (1979–1983)	5.0	3.0	3.0	3.0	3.0	17.0
8. Windsor et al. (1982–1984)	5.0	5.0	4.0	3.0	5.0	22.0
Range	1–5	1–5	1–5	1–5	1–5	5–25

Source: Windsor, R. A., and Orleans, C. T. 1986. Guidelines and methodological standards for smoking cessation intervention research among pregnant women: Improving the science and art. *Health Education Quarterly* 13(2): 131–161. Copyright © 1986 by the Society for Public Health Education. Reprinted by permission of Sage Publications, Inc.

[a] Includes only studies that have used quasi-experimental or experimental designs.

- Confirm representatives of study participants at all sites.
- Estimate sample size and documented effect size needs based on power = 0.80, including at least 100 subjects in each experimental and control group.
- Provide complete baseline demographic, behavioral, and clinical assessments with standardized definitions using minimal exclusionary criteria.
- Use self-reports based on patient knowledge of the test combined with independent biochemical tests—cotinine (COT)/thiocynate (SCN) measures using specified cutoffs at baseline, midpoint, and end of pregnancy and ideally at the first postpartum visit.
- Document a 90% or more follow-up rate for all patients at each observation point.

- Provide a complete intervention description with specification of cessation methods to permit replication and documentation of pilot testing of procedures and training to staff to deliver the program.

- Conduct a process evaluation to document intervention exposure and costs, including exposure by type, frequency, and duration for each program procedure.

It is essential to systematically apply well-established meta-evaluation standards to determine the extent to which the health promotion and health education literature provides insight about the intervention science and practice base. Boyd and Windsor (1993) and Windsor, Boyd, and Orleans (1998) provide additional examples of a meta-evaluation.

Meta-analysis   *Meta-analysis* is a statistical analysis of the results of completed empirical research. The objective of the MA is to provide an accurate and impartial quantitative description from completed experimental studies of the impact of an intervention for samples of populations for a specific risk factor and setting. MA differs from ME in that it presumes the publication of a large number of completed experimental evaluation studies with sufficient rigor to define the evidence–science base for a specific HP-DP program. The first step is a comprehensive review of the literature to identify published studies through a meta-evaluation. At this stage, a serious bias may occur from an incomplete review of the literature. An explicit set of ME rules should be established to exclude studies with serious methodological flaws. For example, (1) review only experimental studies with experimental and control groups, (2) use only studies that have sample sizes for both the experimental and control groups in excess of 100 subjects, and (3) use only studies that provide confirmed evidence of measurement validity and reliability of the impact or outcome rate used to document change. In addition, the intervention for a specific population at risk and the effect size (ES) need to be specified and replicable for each evaluation study. ES, as previously noted, refers to the difference in impact rate between the experimental and control groups.

The MA aggregates prior studies into a quantitative estimate of the impact of an intervention. It is a weighted average of the individual results, providing more weight for larger studies and less weight for smaller ones. The methodology for combining findings from studies is not new, and the techniques are straightforward. The primary difficulty of the MA is, typically, the selection of the studies to be used. One study is rarely a replicate of another: populations, research procedures, and settings differ. The use of published literature can also lead to biased results, because journals choose not to publish negative or statistically insignificant results. Thus, performing the MA on the basis of published literature alone may produce results with a biased effect.

Performing an MA is an essential step for all evaluations. If researchers and evaluators fail to adequately use available information, they may find themselves "reinventing the wheel." For a thorough discussion of meta-analysis, two excellent references are Glass et al. (1981) and Hunter and Schmidt (1990).

Snyder and Hamilton (2002) provide an excellent discussion of the application of MA methods to estimate the effect of media campaigns on behavior change. They identified 48 media studies from the published literature and calculated an effect size for each campaign. Their method was to identify the campaign's effect size from the statistics reported in the publication. If the effect was not reported as a correlation (r), the published statistic (e.g., chi-square, F-ratio, p-value, means, standard deviations) was calculated to a correlation using standard formulas. Taking effects from posttest-only control group studies and pretest–posttest studies with no control group where percentages were reported, they calculated a difference statistic (d) from software and then converted to a correlation (r). For studies that reported pretest and posttest percentages in the treatment and control/comparison communities ($k = 24$), effect size was calculated by the formula below, where c represents the control community, i represents the intervention community, and the subscript specifies the pretest (1) or posttest (2). In this formula the effect size d is equal to the change over time in the treatment community minus the change over time in the control/comparison community divided by the standard deviation of the average pretest score. The result of this calculation was d, which was then converted to r.

$$d = \frac{(i_2 - i_1) - (c_2 - c_1)}{\sqrt{\frac{(i_1 + c_1)}{2} \cdot \left(1 - \frac{(i_1 - c_1)}{2}\right)}}$$

In Snyder and Hamilton's review of 48 studies, they found the average short-term campaign effect of behavior change was 0.09. In persuasive campaigns that did not use a legal enforcement message, the average campaign behavioral effect size was 0.05. For campaigns with an enforcement message, the average campaign effect size was 0.17. Results from the 10 largest studies and 10 smallest studies in Snyder and Hamilton's MA are shown in Table 2.2. This MA review provided a detailed discussion of the study selection criteria, sampling methods, measures, message content, campaign reach, control group trends, campaign length, outcomes, and effect size. Mullen et al. (1997) present additional discussions and examples of MA.

Some MA techniques merely combine the results of studies based on whether they were successful (statistically significant). The implicit assumption

TABLE 2.2 The 10 Largest and 10 Smallest Media Campaigns Used in the Meta-Analysis Performed by Snyder and Hamilton

Campaign	Citation	Behavior[a]	Campaign Effect Size	Sample Size	Reach	Message Variables[b]	Length (years)	Control Trend
A Su Salud	McAlister et al. (1992); Ramirez & McAlister (1998)	Smoking cessation	.20	175	.50	R	4	
AIDS Community Demonstration Project	Fishbein, Guenther-Grey, Johnson, et al. (1996)	Condom use, vaginal sex, bleach use	.03	6,184	.43	R	2	
America Responds to AIDS	Snyder (1991)	Risky sex	.01	163	.17		.17	
CA Tobacco Education Media Campaign	Popham, Potter, Hetrick Muthen, Duerr, & Johnson (1994)	Smoking	.03	10,339	.47		1	
Cancer Control in a TX Barrio	McAlister et al. (1995); McAlister, Ramirez, Amezcua, Pulley, Stern, & Mercado (1992)	Mammography screen, Pap smear	.05	309	.42	N, R, S	1	
COMMIT	COMMIT Research Group (1995a; 1995b; 1996); Corbett, Thompson, White, & Taylor (1990–1991); Wallack & Sciandra (1990–1991)	Quit smoking	.02	20,347	.17		4	
Decreasing Binge Drinking at College	Haines and Spear (1996)	Binge drinking	.07	4,258	.50		4	
Headstrong	Rouzier & Alto (1995)	Bike helmets	.41	121		N	2	.02

(continues)

TABLE 2.2 (*continued*)

Campaign	Citation	Behavior[a]	Campaign Effect Size	Sample Size	Reach	Message Variables[b]	Length (years)	Control Trend
Know When to Say No	Werch & Kersten (1992); Werch, Kersten, & Young (1992)	Drinking	.12	314	.99	N	.17	
Minority Smoking Cessation in Chicago	Jason, Tate, Goodman, Buckenberger, & Gruder (1988)	Smoking cessation	.16	137	.31		.05	
MMHP, MN Adult Smoking Prevention	Jacobs, Leupker, Mittlemark et al. (1986); Lando, Pechacek, Pirie, et al. (1995); Leupker, Murray, Jacobs, et al. (1994)	Smoking, physical activity	.05	7,400	.17		7	.05
MN/WI Adolescent Tobacco Use	Murray, Perry, Griffin, et al. (1992); Murray, Pirie, Leupker, & Pallonen (1989); Murray, Prokhorov, & Harty (1994)	Smoking	.07	15,396	.17		5	.00
Mpowerment Project	Kegeles, Hays, & Coates (1996)	Unprotected anal sex	.12	188	.87		.75	−.01

Parents Magazine Intervention	Kischchuck, Laurendeau, Desjardin, & Perreault (1995)	Positive, negative interactions with kids	.02	307	.95	N	3	
Programma Latino Para Dejar de Fumar	Marin (1990); Marin, Perez-Stable, Marin, & Hauck (1994)	Smoking	.06	5,701	.45	R	1.5	
Seat Belt Contest	Foss (1989)	Child seat belt use	.09	6,072	.59	N	.5	
Seat Belt Use	Robertson, Kelley, O'Neill, Wixom, Eiswirth, & Haddon (1974)	Seat belt use	.01	2,720	.17		.75	−.09
Seat Belts in VA	Roberts and Geller (1994)	Seat belt use	.16	40,493		E	.6	−.01
Smoking: VA Hospital Clinic	Mogielnicki, Neslin, Dulac, Balstra, Gillie, & Corson (1986)	Smoking abstinence	.19	127	.61		.42	−.15
Weight-a-Thon	Wing & Epstein (1982)	Weight loss (PH)	.08	189	.50		.12	

Source: Excerpted from Snyder, L. B., and Hamilton, M. A. 2002. A meta-analysis of the U.S. health campaign effects on behaviors. In R. C. Hornik, ed., *Public Health Communication: Evidence for Behavior Change.* Mahway, N.J.: Erlbaum. Used with permission of Lawrence Erlbaum Associates, Inc.

[a] Physiological measures are marked by (PH).

[b] Message variables: N = new information, E = enforcement, R = role model messages, S = services.

when performing this type of summarization is that lack of significance is equal to a zero effect; this assumption may not be valid. In addition, just counting statistical significance can also cause problems. Fleiss and Gross (1991) provide four primary uses of properly performed meta-analyses: (1) to increase statistical power for important endpoints and subgroups; (2) to resolve controversy when studies disagree; (3) to improve estimates of effect size; and (4) to answer new questions that were not posed in the studies.

The planning staff must have a clear idea of the potential impact of the intervention and must establish realistic objectives. This is accomplished in two ways: (1) performing an ME and/or MA, depending on the maturity of the literature, and (2) conducting a formative evaluation that represents an application of the best intervention and evaluation methods synthesized from the ME and from program experience of staff. The application of these two procedures, ME and/or MA, and a formative evaluation will provide the best evidence with which to initiate a program evaluation.

Phase 4: Educational Assessment

At this point the planning staff should have a thorough understanding of the social, health, and behavioral and environmental problems that affect the target population. In the educational phase an assessment of the possible antecedents of the behaviors and environmental conditions that were identified in the behavioral and environmental assessment takes place. The outcome of this evaluation will become the focus for planning health promotion–intervention components.

Green and Kreuter (1999) identified three general areas of factors that influence behavior:

1. Predisposing factors occur prior to the behavior, and they provide the motivation to perform the behavior.

2. Enabling factors occur prior to the behavior, and they allow the motivation to be realized.

3. Reinforcing factors take place after the behavior, and they provide the reward that encourages the behavior to be repeated.

Predisposing, enabling, and reinforcing factors work collectively to explain health behavior. Application of PRECEDE/PROCEED is based on the premise that health behavior is multifactorial. Therefore, planning for and evaluating changes in health behavior and the environment must consider the part each of these "causal" factors plays in increasing or decreasing the likelihood of action taking place and its potential for an effect on the other factors.

Consider the nature of each factor. Predisposing factors are primarily psychosocial. They include cognitive and affective aspects of knowledge, feelings, beliefs, values, and self-confidence or self-efficacy. There are a host of other factors that could predispose behavior. These include personality factors, socioeconomic status, age, gender, and ethnicity. In most instances these other factors do not lend themselves to health promotion interventions, because they are either unchangeable (e.g., age, gender, ethnicity) or less changeable (e.g., personality factors) within the resources and limitations of health promotion programs. Some of the factors could be useful in planning an intervention. For example, the age range within certain ethnic groups would be useful in targeting an intervention.

Predisposing factors that are commonly addressed in interventions include knowledge, health beliefs, values, attitudes, self-efficacy, behavioral intentions, and existing skills. Some or all of these factors may be relevant to the target population. Some may play a more important role in influencing behavior than the others. A careful review of the influence of each factor is essential in helping you understand what to target in your intervention.

Enabling factors facilitate the action of an individual or organization. They include the availability, accessibility, and affordability of health care and the location of community resources. They may include living conditions that act to prohibit or inhibit actions and skills that are needed to enact a behavior. Enabling factors may become the immediate focus of community organization or organizational development and training components of a new HP program. They include new resources and skills necessary to perform health actions and organizational actions that are needed to modify the environment. Resources include the organization and accessibility of the health facilities, personnel, schools, outreach centers/clinics, and any similar resource. Personal health skills can be used to enable specific health actions. Skills in influencing the community, such as those necessary to promote social action and organizational change, influence the physical and health care environment.

Reinforcing factors are what take place after behavior occurs: the reaction, either positive or negative, that individuals receive from others after taking specific action. Such feedback influences whether the behavior will be repeated. These influences may come from social support, peers, significant others, and health care providers. Two or more of these may combine to influence whether a positive behavior is repeated or a negative behavior is ceased. Physical consequences of behavior are also acknowledged as reinforcing factors. This may be the relief that asthmatics feel from the correct use of medication or the positive feelings of physical conditioning that result from participating in an exercise program. Reinforcing factors may also include adverse consequences of behavior. For example, people who get too much sun exposure experience sunburn. The sunburn then serves to reinforce the affected individuals' need to use sunscreen on future outings.

Three tasks help select which predisposing, enabling, and reinforcing factors should be targeted for modification in the intervention to promote health behavior or environment change:

1. Identifying and sorting factors into three categories
2. Setting priorities in the categories
3. Establishing priorities within categories

The first task is to identify and sort the factors into three categories. This list should be as comprehensive as possible. The data in this list may be obtained through either informal or formal methods. Informal methods may begin with planners using their own intuition as to why behaviors exist. For example, planners may suspect that knowledge, health beliefs, and lack of confidence are important predisposing factors related to the behavior in question. Such estimates are most often confirmed through interaction with members of the target population. Additional insight may be obtained from use of focus groups, interviews, discussion groups, and questionnaires. These same methods should be used to gather data from those who are involved in the delivery of intervention components and those delivering services in organizations collaborating with the planning group. Based on these informal data the planning staff may want to conduct a more formal assessment. Standard measures of many constructs are available in the literature to adapt for this purpose, including measures of health beliefs, self-efficacy, attitudes, behavioral intentions, and social support. Results from a formal survey may be used to confirm the findings from the informal approaches.

The second step is to set priorities among the categories. Even if a complete inventory of target behaviors exists, they cannot be analyzed and prioritized at the same time. A sequencing of factors in the intervention must be determined. For example, consider a health promotion program that seeks to reduce prostate cancer mortality among inner-city African American men. Enabling factors such as providing a prostate screening service must be in place before an educational campaign to address predisposing factors calling for the use of the service can begin. Once the enabling and predisposing factors are in place, attention can then be directed to reinforcing factors. This situation demands the following order of development: enabling, predisposing, and reinforcing factors.

The last is step is to establish priorities within the categories. In this step, planners will again use the criteria of importance and changeability (see Figure 2.2). Just as in the behavioral and environmental assessment, emphasize those variables that are highly important and highly changeable. When evaluating importance, consider prevalence, immediacy, and necessity. Prevalence refers to how widespread the factor is; immediacy refers to the urgency of the factor; and necessity refers to factors that are low in prevalence yet necessary for change.

When assessing changeability, planners need to know how much change they can expect. A review of the literature can provide considerable insight. Application of the meta-evaluation and meta-analysis methods described in this chapter should be applied to the selected literature. The outcomes will enable the planning staff to make sound inferences when projecting the level of change in the prioritized factors.

Writing educational objectives   Health promotion programs should write objectives for each predisposing, enabling, and reinforcing factor in the intervention. These objectives are crucial; thus, it is critical to have a complete understanding and knowledge of each particular factor before specifying it as an objective. Write the objectives using four criteria that were used in writing behavioral and health objectives: who, what, how much, and by when.

Phase 5: Administrative and Policy Assessment

In Phase 5 the intervention strategies and final planning for implementation are completed. The primary purpose at this development point is to identify the policies, resources, and circumstances in the organization that could hinder or facilitate program implementation. At this stage the intervention strategies are enumerated based on the previous steps in the PRECEDE/PROCEED assessment. An assessment of the availability of necessary time, staff, and resources is conducted. Barriers to implementation, such as lack of staff commitment or space, should be identified and resolved. In addition, any organizational policies or regulations that could affect implementation should be considered and addressed accordingly. Administrative and policy assessment is specific to the context of the program and its sponsoring organization and thus requires political savvy as much as knowledge.

Developing interventions   Successful health education and promotion programs are based on an understanding of why people behave as they do relative to their health and what causes or enables them to change. Base the HP intervention on the prevailing theories of learning and behavior change. Select the theoretical principles most relevant to the people, problem, and program goals in question. The available theories considered in light of the data that have been collected in the educational and ecological assessment, the behaviors that have been selected as important and changeable, and the nature of the target population will dictate the type of learning techniques and materials that are most likely to be effective in the program being developed. Two levels of concern must be satisfied when designing interventions: (1) the content of the materials, and (2) the processes by which people learn to behave differently. Process and content are interrelated.

When evaluating programs, researchers think that it is "cleaner" to assess different interventions separately (Green and Kreuter 1991) to discern whether rehearsal of skills is a more effective intervention than problem-solving groups or individual counseling. In the daily practice of health education, this separation of approaches makes sense only if previous studies and direct experience say it is the most effective way to proceed. Answering the effectiveness question is currently an important area in evaluation research. Theoretically, combined approaches should be better. With the design of learning events, however, the behavior to be learned dictates the approach and determines the resources and materials needed to support the approach.

Intervention methods and materials   Materials in health education (e.g., videotapes, audiotapes, PowerPoint slide presentations, self-help guides, computer-generated tailored print communications, and interactive voice response systems) in and of themselves are not learning methods. Learning is a process supported by materials. Materials can provide information, stimulate discussion, and reinforce the information provided in a learning session. However, you can choose the kinds of materials you need only after you have decided on the learning objectives and theoretical underpinnings.

For each learning event, planners must determine how members of the target population will demonstrate that they learned the behavior. For example, participants in a nutrition intervention program might simply complete a checklist of low-fat foods at the end of the session on menu selection. For each learning event for which there is a specific objective, however, planners must identify how to determine whether the objective has been satisfactorily achieved. Monitoring provides important benchmarks of mastery for both the learners and program personnel (Bandura 1986). There must be signs that the program has momentum and is moving the participants along.

Intervention structure   The duration and frequency of learning sessions and of the program itself are of great concern to program developers in terms of both learning and cost. Some studies have shown that important behavior change has occurred in a single learning session (Green 1977; Weingarten et al. 1976). At least one study has found that attending more sessions was associated with change in one setting (Clark et al. 1981). Attending fewer sessions was associated with similar change in another setting (Evans et al. 1987). Green (1974) postulates that extended health education reaches a point of diminishing returns. Highly focused, standardized 10- to 15-minute counseling sessions and the provision of self-help materials may also be very effective (Windsor et al. 1985, 1993, 2000). Unless specific data are available from evaluation research to suggest a particular time frame for the type of education you are planning, the determination should be based on the following criteria:

- What is best for the participants, in their view?
- What have previous studies and programs of a similar type shown to be effective?
- What is manageable, given the context in which the program must operate?
- What has been effective in your previous experience?
- How much material must be covered?
- What is the location of the program in relation to the participants?

The location of interventions is an important consideration. If the intervention site is not the place where participants spend the bulk of their time (i.e., school, home, and work), then you must consider a practical question: How often and how far can people be expected to travel to and from the site? If education is part of other health services, then location and frequency of sessions may be geared to them, e.g., the sessions will coincide with monthly clinic visits. If school, work, or home will coincide with the site monthly, more frequent educational sessions for shorter durations may be best. Base decisions on available data and what makes the most sense for participants.

Similarly, the number of participants to include in a program is based on three criteria: (1) the number best suited to the educational approaches selected, (2) the number of populations to be reached, and (3) the practicalities of cost and manageability.

Assume that group discussion will be the format for a work site program on diet and exercise. From the review of literature, 6 to 8 members in a group is optimum to ensure full participation in discussion. However, there are almost 1,000 men to be reached. Therefore, holding information sessions for medium or large groups (30 to 50) with numerous visual aids, self-tests, and a lecturer may be the most feasible approach. These will alternate with discussion and support groups of small numbers (5 to 20). In this way, you can meet the objective of reaching a big audience with information and meet the necessary conditions of the more intensive learning approaches at a reasonable cost.

Developing organizational arrangements, logistics, and personnel training If members of the program-planning network have been involved in the planning process, the resources and support needed to mount the program should be evident and available. For example, if the employee health service has agreed to give medical checkups to employees enrolling in a weight-loss program, now is the time to work out the details of referral, record keeping, and so forth. If a program has been developed without internal or external input, expect problems in trying to secure assistance now.

At this point administrative and logistical details are determined from participants. What departments, people, and resources are needed and available? Who must give their approval before the program proceeds? Which facilities are needed for events? Have all the parties that are needed to implement the program committed themselves and, where necessary, put their participation in writing? Have all organizational and legal constraints been considered?

Consider the example of asthma management education. Assume a decision has been made to evaluate fewer school absences as a related outcome of better management. Will the local school let you use its records? Will parents sign releases? Or perhaps tenant organizers have been invited to the clinic to talk with parents about improvements in housing. Will the organizers need passes to visit the clinic? Must these visits be noted as referrals in clinic records? Each step of the program must be reviewed while asking: Have the planning staff accounted for the administrative, legal, and logistical aspects of this element?

Next, personnel training needs to be determined. Each member of the staff who will have an influence on the participants must be oriented. Many may need special training to implement education, to collect data, to keep records, and so on. Those who will facilitate discussion groups must be trained. Every program and group of participants is different. The staff must be prepared to work with a particular group of people in a specific context.

The design of staff training, like the education program, operates on two levels: (1) those who must be briefed regarding the content or health condition, and (2) those who must be trained to deliver the intervention. Physicians, who play a role as counselors in an asthma education program, may be very well versed in clinical aspects of asthma but need training in counseling techniques. Health educators may be highly skilled in facilitating discussion groups but need a background in the clinical dimensions of asthma. The extent of training is determined by the tasks to be performed, the information to be provided, and the existing skill levels of the personnel.

Developing a budget and administrative plan   When a program is developed, costs and administrative needs result because the program is new. Costs of planning and development of methods, materials, and evaluation tools are, in large part, one-time expenses. The configuration of staff/personnel needed to carry out initial planning and development may be different from the pattern needed when the program becomes institutionalized or part of an organization's routine.

The elaborateness of a program is likely to be proportional to the resources made available. Failure to allocate sufficient money has been cited as a major reason for the limited success of some health education programs (Green and Kreuter 1991). A budget should justify all personnel and all tasks to be undertaken during program development and delivery. The budget justification should convince the sponsoring organization or funder that initial allocations are warranted and that the program will be affordable over time. Job descriptions must be written and personnel costs estimated. The following kinds of personnel may be needed: a program director to assume overall responsibility, program coordinators to manage logistics, consultants in particular areas (content specialists, educational methods specialists, etc.), educators to carry out the learning program, and secretarial and clerical staff.

Many of the staff may be available in the organization or are members of the planning network. Individuals from other organizations may participate, and their services will show on the budget as contributions. To determine the cost of personnel, the simplest method is to estimate the number of hours per week, month, or year a person will need (percentage of effort) to devote to program activities and to calculate the amount that person will be paid per week, month, or year. One person may have several program responsibilities. A health educator might serve as both program coordinator and instructor, for example.

A budget must show the direct costs, which are defined as the anticipated costs of implementing an HP intervention project. Direct costs include salaries of personnel and fringe benefits. All organizations have established rates for these costs. There are other unseen costs in a program. What is the cost of housing the program? What about services provided by other divisions or departments of the organization, such as the financial office and the personnel office, to support program personnel? The indirect costs are the costs associated with the project's overhead. These costs include but are not limited to rent for office space, utilities, and the like. These costs must be calculated; the organization is likely to have an established rate for this.

Items other than personnel services will be needed to develop the program. Some will be ongoing expenses, but others will be required only during program development. Expenses likely to be incurred initially include space, if program housing is not available; office equipment and supplies; telephone, fax, and e-mail services; postage and photocopying charges; acquisition of studies, articles, and books (i.e., secondary data); printing costs for primary data (collection and evaluation materials); printing costs for educational materials; computer costs for data analysis; travel costs to and from learning sites; and training costs.

Once it has been determined who and what are needed to carry out the HP program, the budget must be developed. Table 2.3 illustrates an example of how to present program costs for the first development year and the following 2 years. Table 2.4 presents the rationale that might accompany this budget to justify why the amounts are requested.

TABLE 2.3 Budget for Program Development and Implementation: Year 1 (2003)

	Hours/Week	Percent of Effort	Salary/Annum	Fringe Benefits[a]	Total	Amount
Personnel						
Program director: Susan Greenbaum	40	100	$50,000	$10,000	$60,000	—
Program coordinator-educator: (To be named)	40	100	36,000	7,200	43,200	—
Program evaluator: James Sinclair	4	10	6,000	1,200	7,200	—
Secretary: Robert Murphy	40	100	20,000	4,000	24,000	—
Consultants:						
Carlos Velez (educational materials)	2	5	(Contributed by Heart Association)			—
Rachel Polanowski (data analysis)	2	5	(Contributed by university)			
Total personnel costs						$134,400
Costs other than personnel services						
Books, materials, and acquisition of background data						1,000
Printing of questionnaires						2,000
Printing of evaluation materials						2,400
						$139,800
Indirect costs[b]						$41,940
Total Year 1 request						$181,740
Total Year 2 request (.04)						$189,010
Total Year 3 request (.04)						$196,570

[a] Computed as 20% of salary.
[b] Computed as 30% of total direct costs.

TABLE 2.4   Budget for Program Development and Implementation: Year 1 (2003)

PERSONNEL SERVICES

Program Director Susan Greenbaum will devote 100% time during Year 1 of program development. She will assume overall responsibility for the program, maintain links with all cooperating agencies, and oversee day-to-day program activities. The yearly department budget provides for the cost of the program director. In Years 2 and 3, it is estimated that Greenbaum will spend approximately 10% time supervising ongoing program implementation.

Program Coordinator-Educator A person will be hired at 100% time to coordinate all day-to-day aspects of program development and to carry out the actual teaching in the program. The cost of the coordinator-educator is requested at 100% for all years of the program. After the first year of program development and evaluation, the program coordinator-educator will devote 100% time to the ongoing program and to its expansion to four sites by Year 3 of program implementation.

Program Evaluator James Sinclair will spend 10% time in all years of the program and will coordinate all evaluation tasks.

Secretary Robert Murphy will spend 100% time handling correspondence and record-keeping tasks. The department budget provides for the cost of this position.

Consultants Each cosponsor of the program, the local Heart Association and the local university, will contribute the equivalent of 5% consultation time by Carlos Velez and Rachel Polanowski for development of educational materials and for analysis of initial survey data, respectively. In Years 2 and 3, consultation will be provided regarding program expansion and evaluation.

OTHER THAN PERSONNEL SERVICES

Books, Materials, and Background Data Although many resources are available in our own resource center and in the library of the nearby university, we will need to acquire some specialized materials from outside sources. This collection of materials should be updated yearly.

Printing of Questionnaires and Evaluation Materials Most of the materials that will be needed for the program are available through existing sources, such as the Heart Association and other cooperating agencies. However, some costs will be incurred in the printing of specialized questionnaires to be used for needs assessment and for evaluation; these costs are likely to be incurred yearly.

YEARS 2 AND 3

To compute costs for Years 2 and 3, the Year 1 budget has been increased each year by 4% to cover inflation and salary increases.

Table 2.3 shows that the formula the sponsoring organization uses to calculate fringe benefits is 20% of a person's salary. Indirect costs are determined to be 30% of total direct costs in this example. Outside contributions are included in the budget with an indication that no funds are requested from the department for the services listed. Showing contributed time in the budget more accurately

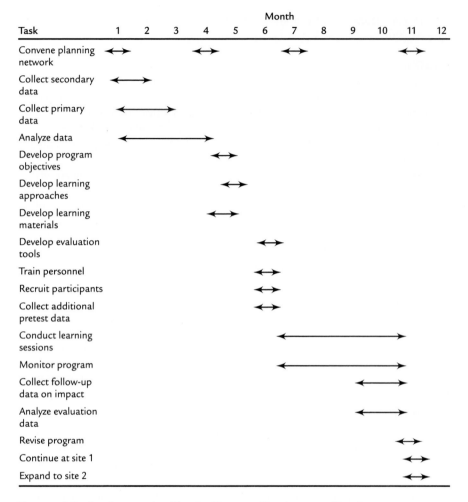

FIGURE 2.3 Implementation Plan for Program Development, Year 1

reflects the percentage of effort that will be expended. The bottom of the budget notes that requests will be made in Years 2 and 3.

The budget rationale explains that, during the first year, the program director will spend 100% of her time administering program activities. This is likely to be considered a reasonable ongoing program expense. The rationale also states that, in the next 2 years, the program will be expanded to four sites with no addition of staff. Each additional year the budget has been increased by 4% to cover changes in salaries and prices of materials.

Once the budget and budget justification have been developed, an outline of the time frame for carrying out major tasks is needed. Figure 2.3 gives an example of how the first year of tasks might be presented. Note that representatives of organizations and groups from the planning network will meet regularly over the first year of development. The program will also be monitored continuously during the 4 months it is operating and will only be expanded to the second site after evaluation and revision.

With a program description, including the evaluation plan, an outline of personnel and their responsibilities, a time frame, a budget, and a budget rationale, you are ready to seek funding, or, if money is in hand, to implement the work plan. In addition, on completion of the evaluation, you should be able to conduct cost analyses (see Chapter 7) of your program.

Phase 6: Implementation

In Phase 6 the health promotion intervention project is implemented according to the plans that are specified in the administrative and policy assessment (Phase 5).

Phases 7–9: Evaluation

The final steps in PRECEDE/PROCEED are to conduct a process evaluation (Phase 7), impact evaluation (Phase 8), and outcome evaluation (Phase 9). Process evaluation determines the extent to which the intervention was delivered as planned. Impact evaluation determines whether changes occurred in the predisposing, reinforcing, and enabling factors. In addition, impact evaluation assesses whether changes took place in the targeted behaviors and in the environment. The outcome evaluation determines whether the program had an effect on health status and quality of life. In each of the evaluation phases the evaluator uses the objectives that were written in the planning process (Phases 2–4) as standards against which to compare the observed results and decide whether the project succeeded. For a complete discussion of the methods of conducting a process evaluation, impact evaluation, and outcome evaluation see Chapters 4, 6, and 7.

CASE STUDY 2.1

Clear Horizons—An Application of PRECEDE/PROCEED

This case study describes how program planners/researchers at the Fox Chase Cancer Center in Philadelphia, Pennsylvania, applied the PRECEDE/PROCEED model to plan, implement, and evaluate a smoking-cessation program for midlife and older smokers (Rimer et al. 1994). At the time this project began there was new epidemiological evidence showing that smokers of all ages benefited from quitting smoking. However,

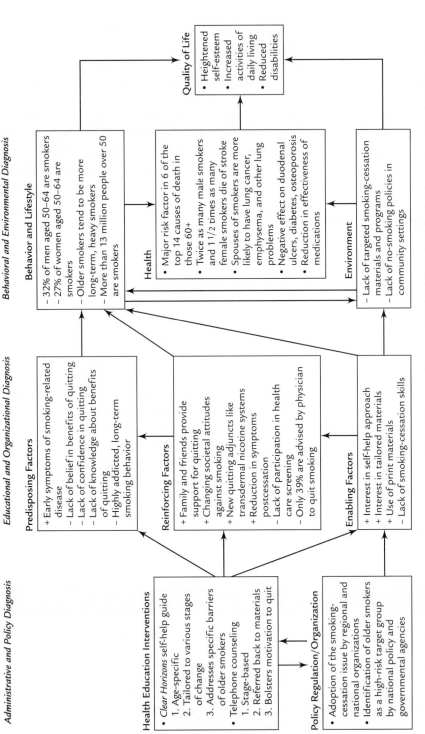

FIGURE 2.4 Clear Horizons, a Minimal-Contact Smoking-Cessation Program for Midlife and Older Adults *Source:* Rimer et al. (1994, 69–84).

there were no programs or smoking cessation materials specifically designed for older smokers. This was perhaps due to a common misconception among lay and professional groups that "it was too late for older smokers."

The objective of the project, known as Clear Horizons, was to develop a program that would dispel the misconceptions about whether it is beneficial to quit smoking at midlife or later and to address the "unique" barriers and facilitators to quitting in this vulnerable, underserved population. The information shown in Figure 2.4 provides a diagrammatic depiction of PRECEDE/PROCEED used to plan, implement, and evaluate the smoking cessation program for midlife and older smokers.

EPIDEMIOLOGICAL ASSESSMENT

The project planners applied the expansionist approach of PRECEDE/PROCEED in developing Clear Horizons (see Figure 2.4). The first step was a literature search to gather epidemiological data to document the health consequences of smoking for older people and the health benefits that result when older smokers quit smoking.

Approximately 94% of smoking-related deaths occur after age 50, making smoking a problem that affects older people. At that time, smoking was a risk factor in 7 of the top 14 causes of death for those aged 65 years and older (Special Committee on Aging 1986). Twice as many older smokers and one and one-half as many older female smokers died from stroke than older nonsmokers of both genders. In addition, spouses of older smokers are more likely to have lung cancer, emphysema, and other lung conditions. Smoking also complicates many illnesses and conditions common among older people, including heart disease, high blood pressure, circulatory and vascular conditions, duodenal ulcers, osteoporosis, periodontal disease, age-related macular degeneration, cataracts, lens opacities, and diabetes (Boyd and Orleans 1999). In addition, smoking interacts with and restricts the effectiveness of many medications that are used to treat many of these conditions (Moore 1986). For example, an older diabetic who smokes typically needs twice as much insulin as an older diabetic nonsmoker.

The literature review also documented that quitting smoking even in the later years is beneficial. In 1990 the *Surgeon General's Report* (USDHHS 1990c) reviewed the existing medical and epidemiological data and concluded: "It is never too late to stop smoking." This document provided evidence that smoking cessation leads to significant health benefits regardless of how long a person has smoked. Although the improvement in health that results from quitting smoking is well documented, many older smokers were unaware of these benefits. Stopping smoking can reduce or prevent the likelihood of heart disease, cancer, and respiratory diseases (USDHHS 1989a; Paganini-Hill and Hsu 1994). The literature also showed that quitting can also stabilize chronic obstructive pulmonary disease (COPD). The conclusion of a review of large clinical trials was that smoking cessation even during one's 60s increased both longevity and independent functioning (Abramson 1985).

Although smoking leads to considerable physical damage, the body responds immediately to quitting smoking. Within 1 month of a person's having stopped smoking, the body begins to repair itself. Data from the Coronary Artery Surgery Study (Hermanson et al. 1988) demonstrated that subjects who quit smoking at age 55 or older immediately began to reduce their chances of a heart attack. In comparison with nonsmokers, smokers had a 70% higher risk of death. Other findings revealed that survival benefits were more pronounced in the moderately ill patients.

SOCIAL ASSESSMENT

Given the unequivocal epidemiological evidence that documented the health consequences of smoking and the considerable health benefits that result from quitting, program planners began to gather literature to connect the health data with issues of quality of life to complete the social assessment (see Figure 2.4). The literature revealed that an overlooked benefit of quitting smoking is the improvement in the quality of life that takes place when older smokers quit. Fries, Green, and Levine (1989) advocated that the most important outcome from smoking cessation might be not a longer life span but a longer *active* life span. This result would become most apparent in the delay or compression of chronic diseases and illnesses to the very later years of life. Another important outcome of smoking cessation is that quitters are more likely to remain living independently for a longer period of time (Haug and Ory 1987). Planners confirmed these findings and their importance in the lives of older smokers through numerous focus groups completed with the target population.

BEHAVIORAL ASSESSMENT

At the time this project began, more than 13 million Americans over age 50 smoked cigarettes (see Figure 2.4). Approximately 32% of men between the ages of 50 and 64 were smokers and about 27% of the women in the same age range smoked. This group of smokers, for the most part, had smoked for many decades, some for more than 50 years. Most smoked heavily and were highly addicted to nicotine as a result. Many began their smoking behavior when smoking was considered a glamorous part of American social culture and long before its health consequences were well known.

ENVIRONMENTAL ASSESSMENT

An evaluation of the environment revealed two significant issues (see Figure 2.4). One was a lack of targeted smoking-cessation programs and related materials for midlife and older smokers. A second issue was the lack of no-smoking policies in community dwellings for older citizens. These factors contributed to the continuation of the smoking behavior among older citizens.

EDUCATIONAL ASSESSMENT

Focus groups with 61 older smokers recruited from communities and work sites in the Philadelphia area specifically included questions on predisposing, reinforcing, and enabling factors (see Figure 2.4). The sociodemographic composition of the groups was diverse. The participants were equally divided by gender and between midlife (50–64 years of age) and older (65 years and older) adults. Only 22% had a high school education. One-fourth were minorities, predominately African American.

To ensure consistency among the groups, a facilitator's guide was written with targeted questions designed to test older participants' positions on these variables and how they affected their smoking behavior: positive and negative aspects of smoking; attitudes toward quitting; personal experiences with quitting; and reactions to specific smoking cessation programs and methods. Also, focus group participants responded to a structured questionnaire prior to group discussions. The content of this survey included items on smoking behavior, motivation to quit, sources of health information, program preferences, and sociodemographics. Results from this questionnaire rendered key background information on the group participants and served as a pretest for a large survey mailed to older smokers identified by the American Association of Retired Persons.

Predisposing Factors

Information presented in Figure 2.4 shows factors that were considered important in the development of the special health education program for midlife and older smokers. These predisposing factors were suggested by focus group participants: lack of perceived susceptibility to smoking-related illnesses, lack of belief in the benefits of quitting, lack of self-efficacy, and addiction to tobacco. Data from the target population acknowledged and confirmed a lack of belief in the benefits of quitting. More than one-half (51%) did not believe the health consequences of smoking. In fact, 52% believed that smoking did not pose as much of a health threat as being 20 pounds overweight. Almost one-half (47%) reported that they were skeptical about the health benefits of smoking cessation. Also, 59% indicated a lack of confidence in their ability to quit smoking. Almost all said that they were highly addicted to cigarettes. Members of the target population informed the project planners in focus groups that they wanted methods they could use on their own.

Reinforcing Factors

An essential dimension assessed by the project planners was reinforcing factors (see Figure 2.4). A number of reinforcing factors were addressed, including social support, cessation messages from physicians, and an improved sense of well-being from reduction of smoking-related symptoms. Data revealed that 62% had significant support systems from family and friends to help in smoking-cessation efforts. Focus group information also confirmed that 61% of midlife and older smokers had never been advised by their physicians to quit smoking. However, 58% of older smokers did say that a physician's advice to quit would be a compelling reason to try to quit.

Enabling Factors

Several major factors were apparent in the assessment of enabling factors (see Figure 2.4). The most important was that there was no smoking cessation program designed specifically for midlife and older smokers. Another important factor was data that revealed most (77%) of the target population lacked sufficient smoking-cessation skills. Most (82%) indicated that they were interested in self-help smoking-cessation approaches, especially methods that were tailored to their specific needs. Only 7% reported that they would be interested in a group smoking-cessation program. Reasons for not using a group program included lack of transportation, lack of privacy, the group being too structured, and the burden of record keeping. Also, the majority of the participants reported that they rarely listened to audiotapes (68%) or used a videotape player (67%). However, the majority reported that they "sometimes" or "often" read the newspaper (87%) or magazines (75%). These data provided additional support for developing a tailored self-help publication as a viable health communication medium with this population.

Regulations were designed to advocate adoption of smoking cessation as an issue by regional and national organizations for midlife and older smokers. Another closely related component was the identification of older smokers as a high-risk group by national policy and governmental agencies.

ADMINISTRATIVE AND POLICY ASSESSMENT

Program planners utilized information obtained from focus groups and the national survey of older smokers on predisposing, reinforcing, and enabling factors to create a new smoking-cessation program for midlife and older smokers (see Figure 2.4). This program included a new self-help guide and telephone-based counseling to support smoking-cessation efforts.

HEALTH EDUCATION METHODS

Program planners decided to develop Clear Horizons to fill the void of the lack of smoking-cessation programs for midlife and older smokers. This program also met the older population's preference for a program that they could use on their own. A 4-color, 48-page guide, *Clear Horizons,* was specifically targeted to the smoking habits, quitting concerns, and lifestyle of older smokers (Orleans et al. 1989). Its magazine-style format was similar to the American Association of Retired Persons (AARP) publication *Modern Maturity.* The guide's content blended entertainment and information, used large, clear type, and was written at an eighth-grade reading level. Multiracial smokers who ranged in age from the 50s to the 70s were depicted in photographs to provide inspiration to a wide audience of older smokers. Much of the content was based on the data retrieved from focus groups and survey participants. Information in the guide highlighted the specific health harms of smoking for older adults and the health benefits of quitting. The guide also described how smoking interacts with many common medications to restrict their efficacy. Prochaska and DiClemente's transtheoretical model (1983) was used to present relevant self-change methods appropriate for smokers in various stages of quitting. Tips on the use of pharmaceutical adjuncts (e.g., nicotine gum) were also featured.

A final important step in the development of the *Clear Horizons* guide was a pretest with potential users in the target population. In-depth interviews were conducted with 29 smokers who were at least 50 years old. These smokers were recruited from Philadelphia-area community groups and organizations. Interviews assessed smokers' perceptions of the guide's appeal; the acceptability and relevance of its content, including cover art; the realistic nature of the characters depicted in the photovignettes; new information; and the overall usefulness of *Clear Horizons.* Eighty-six percent of the interviewees overwhelmingly endorsed the guide and confirmed its format, style, and print size as appropriate for midlife and older smokers. Three-fourths of those interviewed agreed that the guide was written for persons like themselves.

Telephone counseling calls were added to the program because of their influence in facilitating behavior change in other smoking-cessation projects. The telephone counseling in this project consisted of two 10- to 15-minute calls that were placed 4–6 weeks and 16–30 weeks after the smoker received the guide. The content of these calls was based on the social learning theory of Bandura (1982) and the theory of short-term counseling developed by Janis (1983). The calls were designed to bolster quitting motivation and confidence and to promote adherence to the quitting strategies presented in the guide by (1) providing positive, nonjudgmental feedback and reinforcement geared to the stage of change; (2) addressing the individual's unique quitting motives and barriers; and (3) following the individual's preferences regarding methods and committing to a personalized quitting plan using the strategies described in *Clear Horizons.* Each call was tailored to the particular needs of the older smoker being called.

Counselors assisted participants to identify their strong quitting motives and overcome unique quitting barriers. Counselors also aimed to boost self-efficacy and provide timely reinforcement and social support. These calls combined tailoring and support elements in addition to serving as cues to action. The counselor mediated the guide by encouraging the smoker to try the recommended strategies and by providing personalized quitting advice.

IMPLEMENTATION

Clear Horizons was a research project, and the program was implemented as a randomized community trial (see Figure 2.4). Smokers aged 50–64 from across the United States were recruited to the study through an advertisement placed in *Modern Maturity* magazine. Those who were interested were directed to return a postage-paid postcard with their name, address, and telephone number. One thousand eight hundred sixty-seven responded and were mailed a brief recruitment survey that contained questions about smoking history, barriers to quitting, and sociodemographics. All respondents were randomly assigned to one of three groups: (1) a control group, which received the National Cancer Institute's *Clearing the Air* (USDHHS 1991), a 24-page nontailored smoking-cessation guide; (2) a group that received only the *Clear Horizons* guide; or (3) a group that received the *Clear Horizons* guide plus two telephone counseling calls 4–6 weeks and 16–30 weeks after the guide was mailed. The third group was also offered the Clear Horizons Quitline, a telephone helpline for further quitting assistance should smokers need more help.

EVALUATION

Process, impact, and outcome evaluation methods were applied in the Clear Horizons project. Baseline sociodemographic characteristics and baseline smoking characteristics of the study population are shown in Table 2.5 and Table 2.6, respectively. There were no statistically significant differences among the groups on these characteristics.

Process Evaluation

In the 3-month follow-up telephone interviews, the three groups were asked to rate the program's quality, their overall satisfaction, and their use of their respective guides (Table 2.7). Respondents rated the guides on several dimensions, including whether the information contained in the guide was new; whether the guide depicted people like the ones they knew; whether the content in the guide was useful; whether the guide was written for someone like themselves; and whether the guide was easy to use. Overall, the groups who used *Clear Horizons* rated that guide higher than control group members rated *Clearing the Air* on four of the five dimensions. The only variable that did not favor *Clear Horizons* was "depicting people like ones they knew." There were significant differences on the other four ratings. Compared with control subjects, higher proportions of subjects in both the tailored guide groups rated their guide highly.

There was a significant difference in the distribution of guide rating scale scores: Higher proportions of controls had low or medium guide rating scores; higher proportions of tailored guide alone and tailored guide and calls subjects had high scores ($P < 0.001$). For example, 28% of the control group gave their guide a high overall score

TABLE 2.5   Demographic Baseline Characteristics of Program Participants

	Control (n = 537) (% or mean)	Clear Horizons Guide Only (n = 511) (% or mean)	Clear Horizons Guide Plus Calls (n = 505) (% or mean)
Mean age (in years)	62	61	61
Aged less than 65	63	66	69
Education			
Less than high school graduate	8	5	8
High school graduate	33	34	36
More than high school graduate	59	62	56
Sex: female	62	63	64
Race			
White	98	96	96
African American	2	2	2
Other	1	2	1
Household size: live alone	35	35	32
Marital status: married	55	56	57
Employed for salary/wages			
Not employed	62	59	57
Part-time	12	12	12
Full-time	27	29	31
Region of residence			
Northeast	32	31	31
Midwest	23	23	23
South	26	28	30
West	19	18	15

Source: Rimer et al. (1994, 69–84).

Chi-square or Kruskal-Wallis test; all variables not significant; $P > 0.05$.

compared with 36% of the tailored guide alone subjects and 41% of the tailored guide and calls subjects.

Study groups also differed significantly in the amount of the guide they read ($P < 0.001$). The amount read may reflect the intensity of treatment. The control group had the highest proportion of subjects who read none of their guide (14%, compared with 12% of the tailored-guide-alone group and 5% of the tailored guide and calls group). The tailored-guide-alone group had the highest proportion who read some of the guide. The tailored-guide-plus-calls group had the highest proportion who read the entire guide. There was also a significant difference among the study groups in whether a subject re-read the guide ($P < 0.001$). Compared with the control subjects, larger proportions of subjects in both tailored-guide groups re-read *Clear Horizons*. Whether a subject re-read the guide was significantly associated with the guide rating scale ($P < 0.001$). A higher proportion who re-read their guides rated them highly.

TABLE 2.6   Smoking-Related Baseline Characteristics of Program Participants

	Control (n = 537) (% or mean)	*Clear Horizons* Guide Only (n = 511) (% or mean)	*Clear Horizons* Guide Plus Calls (n = 505) (% or mean)
Mean number of cigarettes/day	26	27	27
Heavy smoker	51	54	55
Smoke within 30 min. of arising	90	91	90
Doctor advised quitting within past year (at baseline)	65	64	67
One or more past quit attempts	93	92	91
Tried quit-smoking clinic	39	39	36
Tried Nicorette	44	44	41

Source: Rimer et al. (1994, 69–84).

Chi-square or Kruskal-Wallis test; all variables not significant; $P > 0.05$.

TABLE 2.7   Ratings of Guides

	Control (%)	*Clear Horizons* Guide Only (%)	*Clear Horizons* Guide Plus Call (%)	P-value
Ideas are new				0.001
Not at all/A little	46	36	30	
Somewhat	29	29	33	
Quite a bit/Completely	26	35	37	
People you know				0.861
Not at all/A little	14	14	16	
Somewhat	26	23	24	
Quite a bit/Completely	61	62	60	
Helpful				0.001
Not at all/A little	11	7	4	
Somewhat	22	16	14	
Quite a bit/Completely	67	77	82	
Written for you				0.005
Not at all/A little	8	8	7	
Somewhat	23	18	14	
Quite a bit/Completely	69	74	80	
Easy				<0.001
Not at all/A little	8	6	4	
Somewhat	19	12	9	
Quite a bit/Completely	74	81	86	

Source: Rimer et al. (1994, 69–84).

Scale: 0, not at all; 1, a little; 2, somewhat; 3, quite a bit; 4, completely. Test: chi-square test.

A process evaluation of telephone counseling received by those in the group using *Clear Horizons* and follow-up phone calls also revealed high ratings (not shown). About three-fourths of those who were interviewed about the calls rated them helpful (70%), felt that the counselor understood how they felt (77%), and felt that the counselor was encouraging (88%). To explore the characteristics of subjects responding favorably to the calls, a summary call rating scale form consisting of the four items was calculated (Cronbach's alpha = 0.73). Significantly more subjects under age 65 rated the counselor calls highly (41%) compared with those over age 65 ($P < 0.05$). Subjects who rated the calls highly had significantly higher scores on the variable "How much do you want to quit?" ($P < 0.05$) and a composite "How much will quitting help your health?" and "How much will continuing to smoke hurt your health?" ($P < 0.01$).

In sum, the process evaluation showed high levels of program delivery and high program acceptance of the tailored intervention materials.

Impact Evaluation

The impact of the intervention on smoking cessation was assessed at 3 months and 12 months postbaseline (see Table 2.8). Quit rates at the 3-month follow-up were significantly higher for the *Clear Horizons*-plus-telephone-counseling group (13%) than for the groups receiving *Clear Horizons* alone (9%) or *Clearing the Air* (7%) (see Table 2.8). By the 12-month follow-up, however, the quit rate of the group receiving the *Clear Horizons* guide alone (21%) had edged ahead of the quit rate of those who had received *Clear Horizons* plus telephone counseling (19%) and was significantly higher than the quit rate of the participants receiving the nontargeted *Clearing the Air* guide (14%) (see Table 2.8). These findings indicated that a targeted self-help guide alone may benefit older smokers more than generic quitting guides.

The cessation rates in this community trial increased over time. This is not unusual in self-help smoking-cessation programs and is, in fact, one of the highly attractive features of self-help quitting. A possible reason for this increase in quitting success over time is that those who do not succeed with their initial quitting attempt often put aside their self-help materials and then use them again in another quit attempt. Research in quitting success confirms that the more times those who fail try to quit, the more likely they are to succeed eventually.

A second randomized controlled trial evaluated the *Clear Horizons* guide in conjunction with tailored physician interventions with older smokers in primary care practices in Pennsylvania and New Jersey. Statistically significant outcomes were observed for the group using *Clear Horizons*. See Morgan et al. (1996) for a complete presentation of the methods and results of this project.

Outcome Evaluation

In this phase of PRECEDE/PROCEED the program is evaluated on changes in health status indicators and quality of life. Improvements in morbidity and mortality from smoking-related diseases due to quitting smoking in the older age group could not be studied because of time limitations and budgetary constraints. However, the latest medical evidence on health benefits from quitting smoking among older age groups suggests that these benefits may be greater for older quitters than for their counterparts in younger age groups (Boyd and Orleans 2002).

TABLE 2.8   Quitting Outcomes at 3 Months and 12 Months

	Control (%)	Clear Horizons Guide Only (%)	Clear Horizons Guide Plus Call (%)	P-value
3-month quit rate	7	9	13	NS
12-month quit rate	14	21	19	<0.05

Source: Rimer et al. (1994, 69–84).

Test: chi-square test.

LESSONS LEARNED

The PRECEDE/PROCEED model proved to be effective in planning the design and evaluation of *Clear Horizons,* a self-help smoking-cessation guide for midlife and older smokers. This project, however, has some limitations that warrant discussion.

The project was limited by its choice of a marketing strategy to recruit older smokers for evaluating the new intervention. The placement of a recruiting advertisement in *Modern Maturity,* a magazine published by the American Association of Retired Persons, did not attract a large number of older minority smokers, including older African American smokers. Those who did respond to the advertisement were well educated. In fact, more than 50% completed high school. In retrospect, perhaps other methods of recruitment should have been employed to ensure that more older minority smokers and older smokers with less education were recruited. It is possible that *Clear Horizons* may not have been appropriate for those with lower literacy levels.

The goal of the process evaluation was to determine older smokers' reactions to various aspects of the *Clear Horizons* guide. It was not possible to relate the quit rates to a single aspect of the ratings. The ratings of the guide showed that midlife and older smokers responded more favorably to a tailored educational smoking-cessation guide than to the more general guide. That is, users rated *Clear Horizons* more highly and were significantly more likely to have quit smoking by 12 months but not at 3 months. From an educational perspective, tailored guides, or any tailored health education materials, may encourage more learning because they facilitate more exposure. In this project, this advantage may have been to increase repeated use and reference over time. Repeated use of the materials most likely affected the increase in quit rates at the 12-month follow-up.

SUMMARY

This chapter described the influence of the sponsoring organization on the health promotion program, emphasizing the need to establish and use a network to plan health promotion programs and evaluate them. The chapter presented an overview of the PRECEDE/PROCEED framework for planning and evaluating health promotion programs. This discussion underscored the need to write measurable objectives at each step of program development to serve as guides to designing effective process, impact, and outcome evaluations. The chapter also covered considerations of program implementation with regard to project timelines and cost of personnel and materials.

3 | Measurement in Evaluation

Chapters 1 and 2 established the importance of systematically defining intervention and assessment methods in planning and evaluation. As we will see in Chapter 6, "Formative and Impact Evaluations," measurement is identified as the most important bias to internal validity. Documentation of the validity, reliability, and representativeness of program data is the most critical of all the methodological issues an evaluation must address. An additional critical issue to be addressed in evaluation research studies is informed consent. A variety of complex issues must be considered in defining the scope, frequency, and type of measures for a program evaluation. In this chapter, we review multiple dimensions of validity and reliability, and we present specific, common data collection procedures. We introduce selected analysis methods, using a variety of case studies, to demonstrate application of measurement concepts.

MEASUREMENT AND DATA COLLECTION ISSUES

Concepts and Variables

Planning an evaluation of the behavioral impact of an intervention for a defined population should be approached using a conceptual framework, defining how the intervention and its specific components and procedures are supposed to work. A *conceptual framework* is a theory or, at a less formal level, a planning model, selected to hypothetically explain how the program's core intervention components are designed to affect predictor variables, e.g., the PROCEED model discussed in Chapter 2. A *model* is based on one or more theories that describe expected relationships between two or more variables. A theory or model defines a set of core concepts or independent variables to be measured and explains how the variables are correlated (positively or negatively) in specific ways with the impact (dependent) variable or impact rate. It is hypothesized that significant changes in intermediary variables attributable to an intervention will be strongly (positively or negatively) associated with significant changes in behavior.

A model and variables exist in the conceptual world. Constructs are made up of *variables* that typically exist in the mind of the behavioral scientist: positive to negative verbal or written abstractions about human experience, e.g., beliefs, attitudes, and emotions. No one has observed "self-efficacy" or "beliefs" to reduce salt in a diet or the perceived risk of smoking during pregnancy. They may be useful concepts, however, to organize an understanding of what may explain why some people are able to reduce salt in their diet or change their smoking behavior during pregnancy.

In many cases a public health program may not be based on theory but on professional judgment or intuition. The health promotion program in one state often represents what is being done in other states. The competent evaluator can serve an important leadership role to program staff by selecting and translating an evidence-based model that defines the explicit underlying theoretical concepts and relationships. If the program is based on a theory or model, it should be evaluated against the underlying variables of that theory or model. This is essential, because the evaluation may reveal that changes did not occur in one or more primary mediating variables, thereby decreasing the probability of behavior change. The impact results should guide program staff to change client interventions and staff training to increase the odds of significantly changing mediating variables and increasing the likelihood of significant behavioral changes. The term used in the evaluation literature to describe the application of behavior change models to planning an HP program is *theory-based evaluation* (TBE).

Theory-based evaluation Why is a theory or model necessary? There are multiple reasons. First, a program and its evaluations should be based on what is empirically known about the validity of theories of human behavior for a specific health problem or disease for a target population. A primary purpose of behavioral and social science is to conduct basic and applied survey and Phase 1 and 2 evaluation research to improve our understanding of the behavior of a human population at risk and how the behavior might be changed among the target group.

Behavioral theory provides a medium from which results across studies can be integrated to improve our comprehension of human behavior. If a theory-based model is validated by multiple applied empirical behavioral research studies, then program staff can have some degree of confidence that the theory may provide valid insights about behavior change among a new, comparable target population. In theory, a program will have a higher likelihood of being effective if it is based on the most valid theories and models of health behavior change. Planning an evaluation and designing interventions that effectively translate the underlying theoretical constructs of a model is a creative process: translation, synthesis application, and analysis of behavioral science theory into public health practice.

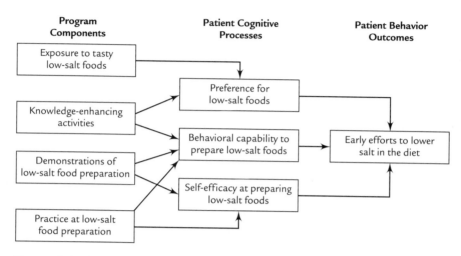

FIGURE 3.1   A Simple Application of SLT to Reduce Salt in the Diet

It is important to note that a theory-based evaluation will always encounter a number of major challenges and issues. As Weiss (1998) has noted, "problems beset its use, including inadequate theories about pathways to desired outcomes in many program areas, confusion between theories of implementation and theories of programmatic action, difficulties in eliciting or constructing usable theories, measurement error, complexities in analysis, and others." Additionally, most applications of TBE models do not meet rigorous, empirical standards of measurement of validity or reliability. We recommend that the scientist and practitioner team involved in planning an evaluation be cautious about assuming the applicability of a theory-based model, unless there is sufficient valid evidence from multiple studies to support its use for a specific behavior, disease, risk factor, or population at risk.

Nevertheless, with these caveats in mind, good TBEs need to be applied to enhance our knowledge base about how to help target populations at risk and to collaborate with professionals and systems that serve them. TBEs are a primary responsibility of Phase 1 and 2 evaluation research. As the science-evidence base confirms the validity of a model from multiple applications, Phase 3 and 4 program evaluations translate this insight into broader applications in routine professional practices.

Behavior change model   Consider, for example, a behavior change model that describes how adults can learn to lower their amount of dietary salt. Such a model is diagrammed in Figure 3.1, based on social learning theory (SLT) by

Bandura (1977) and Baranowski (1989–1990). It proposes that the probability of a person reducing salt in the diet is directly related to three mediating variables: preference for low-salt foods; behavioral capability, knowledge, and skills to perform the task; and self-efficacy or perceived self-confidence in being able to act. According to SLT, a program designed to reduce salt in a target group's diet would attempt to increase client preference, behavioral capability, and self-efficacy for salt reduction among members of the high-risk group.

The four components of a patient education program should affect the three mediating variables and, in theory, have a significant impact on behavior. The initial behavioral objective is to lower salt in the diet. As noted, the model specifies four positive relationships among these variables. The positive sign indicates that the higher the level of one variable, the more likely a higher level will be observed in another variable. This model of behavior is useful for three reasons:

1. It identifies the basic conceptual building blocks for an intervention program.
2. It describes specific directions for action.
3. It identifies variables to measure.

The direct method to evaluate the efficacy of a program based on this model would be to measure dietary salt consumption in the target group using a 24-hour food consumption questionnaire. The initial participant behaviors to lower salt intake may be to remove the salt shaker from the table and to buy low-salt or no-salt products. If the study's objective is to know whether the behavior change was "predictive" of the hypothesized model, the group's preferences, behavioral capability, and self-efficacy for lower-salt foods must be measured. Valid measurement of these variables requires instruments and observations to collect data.

Measurement and Instruments

The word *instrument* is used to identify a method to produce a measure of an impact or outcome rate of variables. In the physical sciences, an instrument refers to a machine or method designed to produce and reproduce very accurate, meaningful numbers. Although at times health promotion program evaluation may use machines as instruments to measure behavior change, more commonly they employ a sequence of questions, usually with precoded response alternatives, to measure a concept (construct). These sets of questions are also instruments. The numbers that are produced from applying the instrument to a person are called *measures*. Two or more instruments or questions may produce or attempt to produce the same measure. The instrument includes not only the specific questions but also instructions to the interviewer who will ask the questions or probe initial responses, and procedures for taking the responses and creating numbers to produce a measure. The terms *instrument* and *measure* can be used interchangeably in discussions of measurement categories. In this chapter, *instrument* will be used primarily to refer to the questions and procedures used to measure characteristics of human beings.

Types of Variables

Numerous types of variables exist to measure the characteristics of samples of a population. For each variable type, there are unique measurement and analysis procedures. The following variable categories are the most frequently measured in an evaluation of a health promotion program:

- Demographic
- Cognitive
- Skill
- Psychosocial
- Behavioral
- Environmental
- Health
- Cost (discussed in Chapter 7)

Demographic variables   Demographic variables and data describe the social characteristics of populations, such as age, sex, race or ethnicity, occupation, and education. These data are needed to define a target group—who participated (or refused) in a program—and to compare it to groups in other programs or to other samples of the population at risk. Demographic variables separate people into common groups that are useful to assess for differences in program impact (efficacy), or to define the population to which an evaluation's results can be generalized (effectiveness). Demographic data document the *representativeness* of an evaluation study sample.

Cognitive variables   Cognitive variables are often labeled *knowledge* variables. Measures of knowledge assume a correct or incorrect answer or score. The higher the percentage of correct answers, the more knowledgeable the person. Informational data are typically used to confirm levels of a target audience's awareness of a problem, program, or activity. Whether a percentage of people know that a service exists (availability) and when /where to find it (accessibility) are essential types of data needed to design or to refine a public health education campaign. Cognitive variables also measure the product of a mental process, e.g., synthesis, analysis, and/or application of knowledge, by which a person arrives at a conclusion or makes a decision about a behavior.

Skill variables   Skill or capacity variables represent a person's ability to perform a task: How well can a prevention, management, or self-care behavior be performed? A correct or incorrect score or answer confirms one component of a skill level. For example, persons with Type 2 diabetes need to know how to monitor sugar in their urine and how to inject insulin. Skill measures are essential, because people cannot effectively perform the behavior or task routinely in other settings unless they can demonstrate the skill in an assessment setting. Just because a person knows how to do it, however, does not necessarily mean he or she performs the task routinely.

Psychosocial variables   Attitude and belief variables, usually a multi-item psychosocial scale, measure people's feelings or opinions (constructs). Attitudes are typically considered to have three components: (1) a belief about a specific content-subject area; (2) a strongly positive to strongly negative value about the belief (5-point or 10-point scale); and (3) a predisposition to act or to behave. Value or motivational variables represent the factors that predispose or inhibit a person and thereby influence the person to act (Baranowski 1992–1993). Incentives, outcome expectancies, and preferences are different levels of value and motivational data.

- *Incentives*—extrinsic or intrinsic rewards or punishments that people expect to happen soon after they act, e.g., wanting a reward for having lost 10 pounds or wanting to avoid a penalty imposed by a program for not having lost 10 pounds.
- *Outcome expectancies*—events that people expect to occur from having performed a behavior, e.g., better health for their baby from breast-feeding (Baranowski, Bee, et al. 1989–1990).
- *Preferences*—a person's desires or wishes to engage in certain behaviors, e.g., preferences for eating fruits and vegetables to be healthy (Domel et al. 1992), e.g., increasing the concern for health in a person's life.

Behavioral variables   Routine performance of a behavior reflects whether or how frequently one or more behaviors or tasks are performed in daily life. All HP programs are concerned with specific health-enhancing behaviors. For example, is the hypertensive patient regularly consuming fewer high-salt foods or taking prescribed medications? Is the family doing more exercise? Was the child's urine tested for high blood sugar? Health screening or treatment service utilization variables are used to describe behavioral patterns among clients in their use of health, medical, social, or educational services. A subcategory of behavioral measures is whether and what kinds of people use specific types of services.

Environmental variables   The environment in which health-related behaviors occur is important in health promotion (Baranowski 1989–1990; McLeroy et al. 1990). For example, the physical proximity to fitness facilities or safe areas for exercise encourages physical activity (Sallis et al. 1990). Social and family support may either encourage or inhibit health behaviors (Baranowski, Bee, et al. 1989–1990). Parents influence whether their children engage in physical activity. Program evaluators may decide to measure environmental changes in a community to estimate changes in a process or impact rate.

Health variables   Health (clinical or biological) variables may be used for several purposes: as a measure of health status outcome or a change in one dimension of health risk. Blood pressure control and reduction is a primary measure of the impact of a patient hypertension education program. Urine sodium tests are approximate measures of the amount of salt consumed by an individual and may be used as a check on patient self-reports of salt consumption. High levels of high-density lipoprotein (HDL) cholesterol in a person's blood protect against heart attacks and are one estimate of the diet and amount of exercise the person habitually experiences. An evaluator may want to assess serum HDL cholesterol as a screen for whether a person should get an exercise intervention.

Measurement Bias

Measurement error is a basic issue that all evaluations must address. *Measurement bias* will almost always occur when not enough planning went into instrument development, the instrument was not pilot tested, or it was not used with care and attention to detail. Systematic errors produce differences between an obtained score and the true score for all variables. Bias reduces or destroys validity and reliability: It always attenuates effect size (behavioral impact) differences. A biased measure will lead an evaluation to conclude something different from a set of data than if it had the true measure. For example, assume that a person took the same tests on two occasions and the scores vary. Bias is the distance between the true response and the mean of the obtained responses. Of course, evaluators do not usually know what the true response is, although they may sometimes learn it from other information. With systematic errors, the mean of the obtained scores is systematically different from the true score by one or more units: a *systematic bias*.

Validity

Each evaluation study has to deal with the accuracy (validity) and reproducibility (reliability) of data collected in measuring all seven categories of data. *Valid-*

TABLE 3.1   Types and Definitions of Validity Measures

Type	Definition
Face	Extent to which the instrument appears to be measuring what it is supposed to measure.
Content	Extent to which an instrument samples items from the universe of content desired.
Criterion	Extent to which an instrument correlates with another more accurate (and usually more expensive) instrument (the criterion).
Concurrent	An instrument is administered at the same time as the instrument being tested for validity.
Predictive	An instrument is administered after administration of the instrument being tested for validity.
Construct	Extent to which the measure correlates with other measures in predicted ways, but for which no true criterion exists.
Convergent	Measure that strongly correlates with the variables with which it is predicted to correlate.
Discriminant	Measure that weakly correlates with the variables with which it is expected to be weakly correlated.

ity is the degree to which an instrument measures what the evaluator wants it to measure: predictor, impact, or outcome variables. In a more formal sense, validity is also the extent of concordance between a measure and its underlying theoretical variables. Psychometric analysis is a special methodology to evaluate instruments. Validity and reliability are inseparable dimensions of measurement. Table 3.1 presents four general types and definitions of validity: face, content, criterion, and construct validity.

Face validity   Face validity describes the extent to which an instrument appears to measure what it is supposed to measure. Thus, the question "How many minutes of running-jogging did you do today?" appears to measure one important component of a person's aerobic activity for a particular day. This question might produce good data for most adults, but probably not for children. There is little reason to believe that an accurate estimate of their exercise time could be made by children.

The question may lack validity even for adults. To gain cardiovascular benefit, a person must engage in aerobic activity for a minimum of 20 minutes at a time (without stopping), at least three times every week (American College of Sports Medicine 1980). Furthermore, the activity must reach a certain intensity to promote cardiovascular fitness. Sufficient intensity would produce a heartbeat of 60% or more of the person's maximum heart rate (calculated from commonly available tables for age and gender groups). Therefore, it may be difficult to interpret a response to the above question. Suppose the answer given is "20 minutes." Was the activity sufficiently intense to merit the label "aerobic"? Did the person cover 4 miles (high cardiovascular benefit) or 1½ miles (low cardiovascular benefit) in those 20 minutes? Were the 20 minutes continuous or two 10-minute segments?

Each variation raises issues about whether the question elicits accurate data. A measurement question, therefore, must be carefully written to assess an impact variable. A self-report measure for adults must assess distance traveled, intensity (e.g., heart rate), and continuous duration of activity (segments in minutes). A more complex questionnaire may work for marathon runners in training (who are highly motivated to keep necessary records to assess their progress) but may not work for casual early-morning joggers. Thus, the validity of the instrument may be high for one group (the marathon runners), but not valid for another group (the casual joggers).

A variety of complexities in assessing face validity have been introduced in the literature. The key issue in this literature is perspective. For example, a question posed by a highly trained clinician may have high validity in assessing a specific patient characteristic, but that validity may not be apparent to the person being assessed. Lack of perceived relevance of an item could affect how the respondent answers the item and thereby affect its validity.

Content validity   Another desirable characteristic of a measure is content validity. Most instruments cover multiple content areas. An instrument must sample items from each of these content areas to have content validity. For example, diabetes is a complex disease requiring knowledge and skills in multiple self-care areas. Windsor, Roseman, Gartseff, and Kirk (1981) developed an instrument to measure the knowledge and skill of 100 Type 2 diabetic patients to care for themselves, their level of instruction, and their degree of self-care behaviors. This measurement project used a consulting panel of clinical diabetologists, a common method to define the completeness of content. They identified seven diabetes self-care content areas, including foot/skin care, urine testing, diet, self-administration of insulin, safety measures, complications, and general information.

Multiple cognitive-knowledge ($n = 35$) and performance-skill ($n = 23$) items were developed by local medical and nursing specialists for each self-care area. Because of its comprehensiveness and rigorous development process, this instrument had high content validity. As the years pass, however, and more is learned about diabetes, patients may be expected to do more or to do different things to care for themselves. The content validity of this instrument may decrease, and the instrument may need further development and refinement. Thus, the content validity of an instrument may be time-limited: As the measurement science base matures, a disease- or risk factor–specific instrument must be updated.

Criterion validity   Criterion validity may be assessed by using two instruments at the same time (concurrent criterion validity) or by using a measure at one time to predict the measure of another instrument at the second time (predictive criterion validity). If the validity coefficient between the two methods is high ($r \geq 0.80$), the criterion validity of the instrument is considered high. Because multiple factors affect predictive validity, most baseline and follow-up measurement comparisons should occur within a short period of time, say, 3–6 months. There are instruments that produce highly valid measures of a characteristic but may be costly or difficult to apply. An evaluator faced with this situation may select a less costly measure. The less costly instrument can be assessed concurrently with the more costly instrument, e.g., self-reported cigarette use vs. a saliva cotinine test.

The assessment of salt in the diet provides a common example. Because salt intake is positively associated with high blood pressure, many patient education programs are interested in an instrument to measure salt intake. A relatively accurate measure (not subject to self-report errors and biases) is an assessment of the sodium excreted in the urine. Given the high day-to-day variability in an individual's consumption of salt, the lag time between episodes of unusually high salt ingestion, and the body's achievement of sodium balance, Liu et al. (1979) estimated that an evaluator needs 7 consecutive days of 24-hour urine samples to estimate daily salt consumption. Difficulties arise in obtaining these samples. People do not want to carry urine sample bottles to work, play, or other activities, because it is embarrassing and inconvenient. People forget to provide every sample. It is costly to furnish the multiple containers necessary to collect so much urine, not allow it to become contaminated, and pick it up at regular intervals.

Studies have been conducted to assess whether an overnight urine sample, testing for both sodium and creatinine, can obtain similar information and replace the tedious and expensive hourly urine samples. Other investigators have used self-report measures of dietary consumption. In both cases, however, the 7 consecutive days of 24-hour urine samples provided the criterion against which all other measures are assessed because it is the most accurate —valid—measure of the variable desired.

Measures of the validity of biological tests   There are four measures of validity to be considered in evaluating a biological test: (1) sensitivity, (2) specificity, (3) predictive value (+), and (4) predictive value (−). Figure 3.2 presents a ma-

	Gold Standard			
	Present	Absent	Total	Predictive Validity
Positive	a = True positives	b = False positives	$a + b$	Predictive value (+) $\dfrac{a}{a + b}$
Negative	c = False negatives	d = True negatives	$c + d$	Predictive value (−) $\dfrac{d}{c + d}$
Total	$a + c$	$b + d$	Grand total $a + b + c + d$	
	Sensitivity $\dfrac{a}{a + c}$	Specificity $\dfrac{d}{b + d}$		

(Row label: **Test Result**)

FIGURE 3.2   Measurement of the Validity of Biological Tests

trix to examine a screening test for a disease (rows) and a definitive diagnostic test (columns). An HP-DP program can determine how well the screening test performed in identifying individuals with or without a disease or behavior.

Sensitivity   The term to describe the accuracy of a test to correctly identify all screened patients who have the disease or risk factor is *sensitivity*. Sensitivity is defined as the number of true positives divided by the sum of the true positives and false negatives. In Figure 3.2, a total of $a + c$ individuals were determined to have the disease, according to an established definitive diagnosis "gold standard." For example, assume that in a sample of 100 adults, 12 actually have the disease. If the screening test correctly identified all 12 cases, sensitivity = 100%. If the screening test was unable to identify all individuals who should be referred for definitive diagnoses, then sensitivity $\leq$ 100%.

Specificity   The ability of the test to identify only nondiseased individuals who actually do not have the disease or risk factor is *specificity*. It is defined as the number of true negatives divided by the sum of false positives and true negatives. If a test is not specific, individuals who do not actually have the disease would be referred for additional diagnostic testing.

Predictive value (+)   This is the proportion of patients screened positive by the test that actually have the disease or condition. In Figure 3.2, a total of $a + b$ patients were screened positive by the test. Predictive value (+) is the proportion $a/(a + b)$ who actually have the condition as confirmed by the gold standard measure.

Predictive value (−) An analogous measure for those screened negative by the test; it is designated by the formula $d/(c + d)$. It describes the proportion who do not have a condition, as confirmed by the gold standard measure.

The only time these measures can be estimated is when the same group of individuals has been examined using the program measure test and the gold standard measure. The accuracy of a screening test is computed by the following formula: $(a + d)/(a + b + c + d)$. Accuracy measures the degree of agreement between the program measure test and the gold standard measure. The sensitivity, specificity, and positive predictive value need to be determined for each test used. Changing the cutoff for the positive or negative classification will change the % SP positive or negative.

CASE STUDY 3.1

Validity of Self-Reports

Data presented in Tables 3.2a, b, and c document the degree of accuracy of self-reports of smoking behavior at the first prenatal visit by a sample of 310 pregnant Medicaid women. A saliva thiocyanate (SCN) test was used as the independent criterion. Thiocyanate is a metabolite of nicotine. Data in Table 3.2a indicated that the self-report and the SCN test were needed to determine, with a high degree of accuracy, the women's smoking status: PPV = 94%. The deception rate (14/310) was 4.5%. Data in Table 3.2b also confirmed a very weak association between the number of cigarettes smoked and the biochemical value: $r = 0.12/0.03/0.11$. Analysis in Table 3.2c of multiple comparisons of self-reports of the number of cigarettes smoked indicated that the data are ordinal data and not interval.

Source: R. A. Windsor, J. Morris, G. Cutter, et al., "Sensitivity, Specificity and Positive Predictive Value of Saliva Thiocyanate among Pregnant Women," *Addictive Behaviors* 14 (1989): 447–452.

CONSTRUCT VALIDITY

As knowledge of a variety of concepts (e.g., anxiety, depression, or self-efficacy) increases, basic and behavioral scientists learn more about how specific biological and psychosocial measures correlate to other measures. For most psychosocial measures, however, a "gold standard" does not exist. The type and strength of these relationships—correlational validity evidence—define the underlying construct. For example, patients who are experiencing a high degree of anxiety would be expected to experience multiple physiological responses, e.g., more rapid heartbeat and breathing, higher blood pressure, and changed galvanic skin response. They are expected to be less efficient at cognitive tasks, e.g., memory, judgment. If an investigator believes that the existing measures of anxiety are

TABLE 3.2a   Sensitivity, Specificity, and Positive Predictive Value
for Pregnant Women

Thiocyanate Test	Behavior Present (+)	Behavior Absent (−)	Total
>101 μg/ml (+)	218	14	232
<100μg/ml (−)	54	24	78

Sensitivity = (218/218 + 54) = 80%
Specificity = (24/14 + 24) = 63%
PPV = (218/232) = 94%

TABLE 3.2b   Self-Reported Cigarette and SCN Levels

Number of Cigarettes/Day	n	Mean SCN	Std. Dev.	r	F	P
A. 1–10	48	141	63.9	.12	4.49	0.013
B. 11–20	50	171	68.5	.03		
C. 21–30	27	180	69.3	.11		
D. Total	125	163	67.3	.21		

TABLE 3.2c   Multiple Comparisons of SCN Levels by Group*

Comparisons	Ψ	Ψ	$\sqrt{(J1)}_{99}F_{2,122}$
A–B	−29.9 (−67.3, 7.5)$_{99}$	2.205	2.757
A–C	−44.8 (−89.2, −0.4)$_{99}$	2.778†	
B–C	−14.9 (−59.4, 29.2)$_{99}$	0.932	

*Scheffe method
†Significant at $\alpha = 0.01$

inadequate because they are highly related to another variable not related to anxiety, she or he might decide to develop and test the construct validity of a new instrument.

The evaluator hopes to document two results. First, the new measure will correlate more highly ($r \geq 0.80$) with the new physiological and cognitive performance changes (convergent validity) than the old measure. Second, the new measure of anxiety should correlate less well with variables not related to anxiety (discriminant validity) than the old measure. If the new instrument demonstrates such convergent and discriminant validity, it is considered to have higher construct validity than the old measure. Such a demonstration indicates a greatly increased capacity to define and to measure an important construct. Many studies of construct validity provide no or insufficient correlational evidence. If the correlational evidence indicates $r \geq 0.80$, it indicates approximately a 65% reduction in error of measurement compared to chance.

CASE STUDY 3.2

Validity of the Instrument

BACKGROUND

A measurement study was conducted to assess the quality of patient education assessment methods and instruments for 100 Type 2 adult diabetic in-patients. An examination of the degree of convergent and discriminant validity of the instrument was performed (Campell and Fiske 1959). A matrix comparing two different traits, e.g., urine knowledge (UK) vs. urine testing skill (UP), measured by different methods, e.g., interview vs. observation, was used. Statistical associations between a characteristic, e.g., urine testing knowledge, and a criterion variable, urine testing skill or routine testing behavior for the same individual at one point in time, were documented. In addition to assessing the evidence for convergent validity, the multitrait/multimethod approach can be used to confirm that a method of measurement is not highly correlated with another method of measurement from which it should differ (discriminant validity). Of the two types of validity, convergent and discriminant, discriminant is the stronger test of instrument-data validity.

RESULTS

A complete presentation of the data in Table 3.3 is presented in Table 9 of the article cited. The following is an excerpt from the original data: Data in the triangle for the concept area (trait) in urine testing measurement provided strong support for convergent validity. Data in Table 3.3 confirmed strong, direct relationships between urine instruction (UI), urine knowledge (UK), performance of urine testing (UP), and self-reported urine routine testing behavior (UB). Within the concept area (trait) of urine assessment, all convergent validity coefficients were much more strongly intercorrelated within (0.42, 0.39, 0.47, 0.65, 0.52, 0.59) urine measurement areas (UI-UK-UP-UB) than for all other content areas, e.g., insulin instructions (II) and diet instructions (DI), diet knowledge (DK), diet performance (DP), and diet behavior (DB).

Multiple, significant validity coefficients were also found between the total diabetes knowledge and performance index scores: $r = 0.60/>0.01$. With the exception of DB (0.13 and 0.17), multiple positive associations were documented ($r \geq 0.20$) between overall self-care knowledge and performance and three core traits: UI-UK-UP-UB, II-IK-IP-IB, and DI-DK-DP. Significantly higher scores on the cognitive, self-reported behavior and the performance indexes were noted for patients with higher levels of education, patients with more extensive exposure to diabetes education programs, and patients who perceived little need for additional instruction. Thus, general support for the construct validity of the total instrument was found. This analysis also provided

---

Source: R. A. Windsor, J. Roseman, G. Gartseff, and K. A. Kirk (1981).

TABLE 3.3   Validity Coefficients for Clinical Test Data of Diabetes Patients

Trait	Cognitive Index	Performance Index (P.I.)	Urine Instruction	Urine Knowledge	Urine Performance	Urine Behavior
P.I.	0.60					
UI	0.34	0.41				
UK	0.80	0.64	(0.42)			
UP	0.56	0.82	(0.39)	0.65		
UB	0.36	0.53	(0.47)	0.52	0.59	
II	0.34	0.32	0.66	0.37	0.29	0.31
IK	0.71	0.34	(0.15)	0.43	0.44	0.15*
IP	0.31	0.67	(0.32)	0.26	0.45	0.23
IB	0.24	0.32	(0.14)	0.21	0.30	0.19*
DI	0.42	0.20	(0.45)	0.38	0.14*	0.24
DK	0.57	0.40	(0.10)	0.24	0.31	0.07*
DP	0.46	0.50	(0.09)	0.27	0.27	0.13*
DB	0.13*	0.17*	(0.11)	0.19	0.14	0.12*

Source: Windsor, R. A., Roseman, J., Gartseff, G., and Kirk, K. A. 1981. Qualitative issues in developing educational diagnostic instruments and assessment procedures for diabetic patients. *Diabetes Care* 4(4): 468–475. Reprinted by permission of the American Diabetes Association.

Level of significance $\geq$ at 0.05 ($r \geq 0.20$/98 df).

Level of significance at 0.01 ($r \geq 0.26$/98 df).

* Did not meet minimum item criteria: $r \geq 0.20$.

good evidence of convergent validity for selected traits. Limited evidence, however, was observed to support the discriminant validity of several of the variables assessed.

Reliability

Reliability (consistency) is an empirical estimate of the extent to which an instrument produces the same result (measure or score), applied once or two or more times. Taking two or three blood pressure (BP) readings may result in different measurements. Imagine an assessor taking a blood pressure reading twice on the same person. On the first administration, a BP reading is 140/95: borderline hypertensive. The assessor, worried that something is wrong, takes another BP reading: 125/85. If a BP reading produced measures with this much variability, it is not reliable. Either the patient is clinically unstable or the assessor is poorly trained. The source(s) of error needs to be assessed.

FIGURE 3.3   Distribution of Scores of Multiple Tests with Random Error

Reliability may be better understood by considering the dimension of error. Almost all measures (M) have a true score (T) component and an error (E) component: $M = T + E$. What we want with any measure is a person's true score (T), but all measures have some associated error. We assume these errors are random. Random error is like "noise" on a radio. The more error, the more noise; more noise makes it harder to hear the true message. Random errors include any effects other than a true measure.

For example, suppose a patient takes the same blood/urine test on five different days and the scores are distributed as shown in Figure 3.3. Assume that the true response (measure) is depicted in the figure by the capital letter A. The deviations of each of the test administrations (a) from the true response are indicators of random error. Thus, errors are randomly distributed (plus or minus) around the true score. The five measures may have varied around the true response for many reasons: perhaps the person got up late one day and was rushed, was too tired another day, and was anxious about an incident at home another day. Because of random error, the obtained scores vary around the true response. If a large number of tests, say, 10, were performed on the same person or group, the mean of the obtained measures should be equal or very close to the true response.

The same test is rarely administered 5 or 10 times to look at the distribution of scores around a true score. When a test is administered once, the test result may be close to or far from the person's true score. We assume, however, that these errors are randomly distributed across all people being tested. Because randomness in the errors is assumed, the mean of the multiple administrations is used as a best estimate of the true score. Random errors decrease reliability, because they make it more difficult to detect the true score. Accordingly, error bias reduces or eliminates the probability of observing an impact of a program.

There may not be a stable true score over time for a person. The person's true score will vary from day to day. For example, the amount of physical activity a child gets on any day will vary. A measure of that activity will vary around the true score. Figure 3.4 presents a child's true activity scores for each of three days (A, B, C) and the measures of those activity levels (a, b, c). These measures (a, b, c) might come from three different observers following the same child for a defined period of time. In this case, we have variability among the true scores

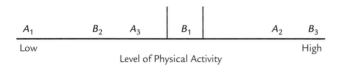

FIGURE 3.4   True Activity Scores (*A*, *B*, *C*) for Three Days with Three Measures (*a*, *b*, *c*) per Day

FIGURE 3.5   Interindividual (*A*, *M*) and Intraindividual (*A*, *A*, *A*) Variability for Two Measures

and variability among the measures. The variability among the true scores (σ_T) is called *intraindividual variability*. The variability among the measures (σ_E) is *error variability*. The smaller we can make those errors, the less statistical "noise" there is in detecting true activity levels. Some intraindividual variability will always exist.

Another level of complexity is produced by adding more people to this system. In Figure 3.5, we have three daily activity levels for persons *A* and *B*, with the true usual activity for *A* and *B* identified with vertical lines. Each of the day's estimates could come from multiple observers, but that is not expressed here. The variability between *A* and *M* is called *interindividual variability* (σ_I), and variability within an individual across days is called *intraindividual variability* (σ_T).

Methods of Assessing Reliability

Before an instrument is used to collect baseline and follow-up program data, its reliability should be documented. Reliability is an index of random measurement error. Reliability coefficients are highest if no error exists ($r = 1.0$) and lowest when there is only error or no association ($r = 0.0$) between two measures. Does the instrument make a distinction between two or more behaviors with a reasonable level of confidence? Reliability coefficients for psychosocial scales or tests should be $r = \geq 0.80$ for any type of behavioral change evaluation. Although $r = 0.80$ is very good, if it is less than this value, it confirms considerable error. Error always masks and attenuates effects.

For a few instruments, the reliability has been calculated with different groups; for most instruments, however, it has not. There are multiple approaches to assessing instrument reliability. Two factors are important to consider: the type of instrument (observer or external source vs. self-report) and the times at

		Time Instrument Applied: Same time	Time Instrument Applied: Different time
Type of Instrument	Observation	(A) Interobserver	(B) Intraobserver
	Self-reported	(C) Internal consistency	(D) Test-retest: stability

FIGURE 3.6 Four Types of Reliability

which the instrument is applied (same time vs. different times). Figure 3.6 presents the four possibilities with the different types of reliability.

Interobserver reliability If two observers collect data at the same time, reliability can be estimated by having the two observers rate the same performance of a task or skill: *interobserver* or *interrater reliability*. This documents whether two people are seeing and interpreting the same behaviors in the same way at the same time. Because both observers should measure the same actions, the perfect interobserver reliability and instrument would produce $r = 1.0$. The level of error variability decreases reliability downward from 1.0. If continuous variables are measured, the Pearson correlation is the common technique for measuring reliability. Because most observation scales use nominal or ordinal rating categories, Cohen's kappa is the accepted statistical technique (Cohen 1960). Kappa corrects the simple percentage agreement between two observers for chance agreement.

CASE STUDY 3.3

Rater Reliability

OVERVIEW

Utilizing a standardized instrument and assessment protocol, an observational trial of nine insulin-controlled adult diabetics was conducted using pairs of three trained patient assessors (MPH students): Raters A and B, B and C, and C and A. Information in Table 3.4 illustrates the methods used to document rater-observer reliability. Although

Source: R. A. Windsor (1981).

TABLE 3.4   Patient Education Assessment Methods to Document Agreement

Observer Pairs	Patients	Day
A & B	1, 2, 3	1
B & C	4, 5, 6	2
C & A	7, 8, 9	3

the overall mean percent agreement for the first assessment study was very good (90%), lack of agreement was noted for several important subcategories. A training program was conducted to improve accuracy, addressing the assessment problems found in the first assessment study.

METHODS

An observational study using nine insulin-controlled adult diabetic patients and three trained interviewers in pairs (A–B, A–C, B–C) was conducted during a two-week period to establish the objectivity of rater assessments. This method is a basic technique to determine the degree of interview/observer agreement. A standardized series of questions were asked of these patients to determine their demographic, educational, cognitive, instructional, and self-care behavioral characteristics. All nine patients also were given a standard set of materials and asked to demonstrate how they perform insulin injection and urine testing at home.

After the baseline level of agreement by category for the patient-education assessment staff was established (O_1), a formal in-service patient observation/interview skills training program was conducted (X). The objective of the training program was to reduce rater error in the patient educational assessment process identified in the first observational study. The rater improvement training program required approximately three hours and consisted of systematic question-by-question discussions of the instrument between the three assessment staff (MPH students), a group lecture-discussion of interview/observation techniques, and individual question-by-question discussions with the principal investigator. After the staff completed the training program, a second rater observation study (O_2) was performed one month after the first study.

RESULTS

Results of the first (O_1) and second (O_2) rater reliability studies are reported in Table 3.5 by category. The percent reported represents a mean agreement score of the assessments by the three pairs of interviewers for the nine patients in each of the five categories. Evidence from the first study confirmed a high level of agreement for the first four categories examined: demographic, lifestyle, instructional/behavior index, and cognitive index, but not for the performance index.

The second observation study confirmed a significant improvement in rater agreement using this instrument and method. The mean percentage rater agreement at O_1 was 90.9% and at O_2, 99%. A statistical analysis of interrater reliability of the performance indices produced a coefficient of $r = 0.93$. These data confirmed that the

TABLE 3.5 Percent of Rater Agreement and Change by Category

| | Observation Study | | | | |
| | 1st (%) | X | 2nd (%) | Change (%) | Gain (%) |
Category					
I. Demographic	97.3		99.0	+ 1.7	+ 1.8
II. Lifestyle	89.7		99.0	+ 9.3	+10.4
III. Instructional/Behavior Index					
A. Foot/skin care	93.3		100.0	+ 6.7	+ 7.2
B. Urine testing	86.3		98.7	+12.2	+14.1
C. Insulin	89.0		99.3	+10.3	+11.6
D. Reactions/ketoacidosis	94.7		98.7	+ 4.0	+ 4.2
IV. Cognitive Index					
A. Foot/skin care	91.3		100.0	+ 8.7	+ 9.5
B. Urine testing	96.0		96.7	+ 0.7	+ 0.0
C. Insulin injection	98.0		100.0	+ 2.0	+ 2.0
D. Reactions/ketoacidosis	96.0		100.0	+ 4.0	+ 4.2
V. Performance Index					
A. Urine testing	73.0		100.0	+27.0	+37.0
B. Insulin prep-injection	87.0		96.3	+ 9.3	+10.7
VI. Total	90.9		99.0	+ 8.1	+ 9.4*

Source: Reprinted from Windsor, R. A. 1981. Improving patient education assessment skills of hospital staff: A case study in diabetes. *Patient Counseling and Health Education* 3(1): 26–29. Copyright © 1981, with permission from Elsevier.

X = Staff assessment training intervention.

* 0.05, one-tailed paired t test.

extensive discussions with the principal hospital staff involved in educating the patients, including the patient assessors, prior to the first trial to standardize the instrument and procedures were fruitful (Case Study 3.2, Windsor, Roseman, Gartseff, and Kirk 1981). The target agreed upon before conducting the second study was to increase the percentage agreement beyond 95% for each category. As indicated, the average level of agreement at O_2 was 99%.

Analysis of the percent increase from O_1 to O_2, using a t test for independent samples, produced $t = 1.88$, which exceeded the 0.05 level of significance for a one-tailed t test of significance (1.72). A one-tailed test was used because a positive (directional) impact for the staff training program was hypothesized. It was implausible to expect that the same MPH students with more experience and training would exhibit lower patient assessment skills. This analysis confirmed a statistically significant, positive impact of the training program on the patient education assessment staff. Rater assessment error was almost eliminated. A superior level of interrater agreement was found for all categories of data: kappa $r = 0.99$. This study confirmed that routine assessment of patients should be periodically monitored, using the quality control methods described, to ensure valid program data.

Intraobserver reliability   If an observer assesses the same person at two different times, comparison of the consistency of the results is called intraobserver reliability. This type of reliability is not frequently performed, because it assumes no difference in the task being assessed between the two observation periods. Such a technique might be used if little change is expected, e.g., on mass assembly lines in factories or about perceptions of physical environments. Because the amount of change is usually the measurement issue, observer reliability is usually assessed at one time using two observers (interobserver reliability). The same statistical technique is used for intraobserver and interobserver reliability.

Reproducibility   Another dimension of reliability is the consistency of measurement over two or more assessments. If more than two assessments have been performed, the Pearson correlation analysis is not appropriate. In this case, the intraclass correlation coefficient is the method. In measurement theory, total variance (σ_x^2) can be divided into variability due to the true scores (σ_T^2) (interindividual variability; see Figure 3.6) and variability due to the error portion of the scores (σ_E^2) (see Figure 3.5): (σ_x^2) = (σ_T^2) + (σ_E^2). Theoretically, reliability is the proportion of total variance accounted for by variance in the true scores:

$$R_x = \frac{(\sigma_T^2)}{(\sigma_T^2) + (\sigma_E^2)} = \frac{(\sigma_T^2)}{(\sigma_x^2)}$$

where

$\quad\quad R_x$ = the index of reliability for test x

$\quad\quad (\sigma_T^2)$ = the variance for the true scores

$\quad\quad (\sigma_E^2)$ = the variance for the error portion of the scores

$\quad\quad (\sigma_x^2)$ = the variance for the whole test

When multiple assessments are obtained per person, the error term can be further divided into variability due to raters (σ_R^2) and due to error (σ_E^2):

$$(\sigma_x^2) = (\sigma_T^2) + (\sigma_R^2) + (\sigma_E^2)$$

This is important to show that rater variability is based on the error term rather than the subject's term. Using mean squares within an analysis of variance, the intraclass correlation coefficient (ICC) can be estimated by:

$$ICC = \frac{n(MS_B - MS_E)}{nMS_B + kMS_R + (nk - n - k)MS_E}$$

where

> n = the number of participants
>
> k = the number of assessments
>
> MS_B = the between-subject mean square (interindividual variability)
>
> MS_E = the mean square due to error
>
> MS_R = the mean square due to raters or times of assessment (intraindividual variability)

The ICC is sensitive to differences both in relative position and in mean values over times of assessment (k). High ICC values indicate high levels of consistency across all assessments in relative position, with little or no differences in mean values.

Multiple values or ratings may provide a more accurate estimate of quantity (Schlundt 1988). For example, there is much day-to-day (intraindividual) variability in what people eat (Schlundt 1988) and in how much physical activity they get (DuRant et al. 1992). One day's assessment is an unreliable estimate of what a person habitually or usually eats because of intraindividual variability and error variability. A more reliable estimate of what a person eats can be obtained by taking more than a 1-day assessment. More days (≥ 3 days) of assessment will increase the reliability for a given level of accuracy or will increase the accuracy for a given level of reliability. Several techniques are available to assess the reliability of self-report instruments applied at the same time.

Split-half reliability   If large numbers of items measure the same concept or construct, a split-half reliability assessment may be performed. Randomly assign items in the instrument to two sets of scores and conduct a Pearson correlation analysis for continuous variables or Cohen's Kappa for discrete variables. This correlation should be high, $r \geq 0.80$, because both halves are supposed to be measuring the same construct. This type of reliability is typically used with knowledge skill tests or psychosocial scales.

Test-retest reliability   Measuring reliability by using the same test at two different times with the same sample is defined as test-retest reliability. Reliability scores from this method may be lower than from the split-half method, because time has elapsed between the first and the second assessment. The longer this interval is, the more likely events will happen to some of the people to induce a real change in the measures the instrument provides. An $r \geq 0.80$ should be documented for a measure to have excellent test-retest reliability.

Internal Consistency

One of the most commonly used methods of assessing reliability is an index of internal consistency. Internal consistency measures the extent of interitem correlation among all items in an instrument. This is often called Cronbach's alpha, recognizing the contribution of its originator (Lee Cronbach). It is used for *continuous* measures, primary psychosocial scales. The Kuder-Richardson (KR) 20 is a form of internal consistency for *dichotomous* measures (Nunnally 1978), correct or incorrect knowledge or skill questions with multi-item test. Theoretically, multiple items in one test share true variation—i.e., the extent to which they commonly measure some underlying construct. The higher the interitem correlations, the more true variation is shared. The following is the equation to estimate coefficient alpha:

$$\alpha = \frac{k}{(k-1)}\left[1 - \left(\frac{\Sigma_i\sigma_{yf}^2}{\sigma_x^2}\right)\right] = \frac{k}{(k-1)}\left(1 - \frac{\Sigma_i\sigma_{yf}^2}{\Sigma_i\sigma_{yf}^2 + 2\Sigma_{i<j}\sigma_{yf}^2\Sigma_i\sigma_{yj}^2}\right)$$

where

α_x = the alpha value for the whole test

k = the number of items in a test

σ_{yf}^2 = the variance of individual item i

σ_{yj}^2 = the variance of the whole test

As seen in the description, if the covariance term $(2\Sigma_{i<j}\sigma_{yi}^2\sigma_{yj}^2)$ is large in comparison to the variance of the individual items, the value of the alpha will be close to 1. The larger the number of items, the larger will be the covariance terms in proportion to the variances. Although the minimum internal consistency for a total psychosocial scale, knowledge, or skill test is $r \geq 0.70$, the objective of all evaluations that examine any type of reliability should be to produce an $r \geq 0.80$ for the total scale or test. Individual instrument items/questions must have an item-to-total correlation of $r \geq 0.20$.

Psychometric Analysis

Data in Table 3.6 reflect a psychometric analysis of an 18-item social support scale from two assessments of a cohort of 310 pregnant patients who smoked at the onset of prenatal care, including internal consistency (Cronbach's alpha: $r = 0.90$), item-to-total correlation coefficients (range: $r = 0.24$ to 0.79), and test-retest/ scale stability ($r = 0.94$). All three analyses confirmed excellent psychometric statistics. Data in Table 3.7 present a psychometric analysis of a 16-item health

TABLE 3.6   Social Support Scale for Pregnant Smokers

Item	$\overline{X}$	s.d.	Var.	w/Item-to-Total r
1	6.2	3.5	12.3	0.74
2	7.4	3.0	9.0	0.69
3	5.6	3.5	12.3	0.49
4	5.7	3.8	14.4	0.57
5	5.0	3.6	13.0	0.59
6	4.1	3.6	13.0	0.59
7	7.6	2.8	7.8	0.62
8	6.9	3.0	9.0	0.58
9	6.8	3.2	10.2	0.55
10	6.6	3.2	10.2	0.72
11	4.6	3.5	12.3	0.79
12	6.5	5.2	27.0	0.46
13	4.4	3.6	13.0	0.24
14	3.7	3.5	12.3	0.67
15	4.4	3.5	12.3	0.79
16	8.7	2.1	4.4	0.59
17	7.9	2.6	6.8	0.61
18	6.9	3.2	10.2	0.75
Score	108.7	37.4	1,398.8	0.90

$n = 310$ patients

Cronbach's alpha (r) = 0.90

$\Sigma var_i = 209.5, k = 18$

$$r = \frac{k(1 - \Sigma VAR_i)}{k - 1(VAR_s)} = \frac{18(1 - 209.5)}{17(1,398.9)} = 1.06(1 - 0.15) = 1.06(0.85) = 0.90$$

Test-retest: $r = 0.94$

belief scale with the same sample of 310 patients. It included internal consistency data—Time 1: $r = 0.83$ and Time 2: $r = 0.89$, item-to-total correlation coefficients for both observations, and test-retest reliability: $r = 0.92$. When the poor belief questions ($r = <0.20$) were dropped at T_1 and T_2, the overall reliability increased: T_1: $r = 0.78$ to 0.83 vs. T_2: $r = 0.90$ to 0.92.

Factorial analysis reliability   An additional test of reliability is a factorial analysis. When multiple-item scales are used, some forms of component or factor

TABLE 3.7   Item-to-Total Correlation, Internal Consistency, and Stability Coefficients at Baseline, and Final Interviews for a Health Belief Scale for Pregnant Women

	Item-to-Total Correlation	
Item Description	T_1	T_2
Maternal Health Subscale		
1. Think about your health	.24	.28
2. Follow doctor's advice	−.01	.08
3. Effects known about smoking and pregnancy	.51	.63
4. Safe to smoke during pregnancy	.57	.62
5. Unhealthy to smoke during pregnancy	.55	.62
6. Smoking increases illness when pregnant	.35	.46
7. Smoking can harm health when pregnant	.54	.71
Fetal Health Subscale		
8. Other women worry about fetal health	.09	.21
9. You worry about fetal health	.17	.12
10. Improve your health through actions	.24	.24
11. Influence fetal health through actions	.33	.40
12. Stopping smoking improves fetal health	.57	.62
13. Fetus receives chemical from smoke	.46	.58
14. Effects known about smoking and fetus	.59	.71
15. Smoking increases illness for fetus	.47	.62
16. Smoking can harm fetal health	.65	.65
Internal Consistency	.78 → .83	.87 → .89
Stability		.90 → .92

T_1 = 1st visit; T_2 = 3rd trimester; ☐ = item dropped; n = 310

analysis can be applied (see, e.g., Baranowski, Tsong, and Brodwick 1990). If the items are supposed to measure a single underlying variable, applying factor analysis should produce the same number of factors with the same items loading on the same factors as in the original. Due to low reliability of assessment in individual items, items do not always load on the same dimensions as in the original study. When they do load in the same manner, greater confidence in the factors will exist. If multiple factors are found in a set of items that should be unidimensional, the measure may respond to an intervention in unpredicted ways. Even when loading on dimensions as desired, coefficient alpha should be calculated to obtain estimates of internal consistency. Component and factor analyses are sophisticated techniques (Nunnally 1978). Evaluators should seek the help of trained statistical consultants before using them.

Relationships Between Validity and Reliability

Although developers and users of instruments must be concerned about both validity and reliability, validity is a more important issue than reliability. If an instrument does not measure what it should be measuring, it is irrelevant that the measurement is reliable. Formulas exist to measure dimensions of reliability. Reliability sets an upper bound to validity. The procedures for using an instrument two times are straightforward. Thus, if r_R^2 is the reliability coefficient for a measure of a particular variable (e.g., dietary sodium) and r_V^2 is the reliability of a criterion variable (e.g., urinary sodium), the correlation (r_{RV}) between the measure and the criterion has the following limit (Schlundt 1988):

$$|r_{RV}| < \sqrt{r_V^2}\,\sqrt{r_V^2}$$

If a measure cannot be consistently reproduced from one occasion to the next, it cannot accurately measure the underlying construct. A method for estimating reliability should be employed every time an instrument is used. Tests of validity should be used prior to an evaluation to confirm that the instrument is measuring the desired variable(s) among the target population.

Sources of Validity and Reliability Error

There are multiple sources of random errors that produce invalid and unreliable data. Seven general sources of data error or bias have been identified:

1. Natural variation
2. Participant instructions
3. The instrument
4. The data collector
5. The respondent
6. The environment
7. Data management

Measurement error can be produced from any and all of these sources. Each source of error diminishes validity and reliability. Pay careful attention to anticipating possible sources of error and to developing plans to avoid or deal with them before or as they occur. Pilot tests are critical. Assessment of validity and reliability should be done each time an instrument is used, regardless of past experience or existing data on psychometric properties. The validity and reliability of an instrument/measure cannot be applied or assumed for a new population, problem, or setting.

Biases to Valid and Reliable Measurement

Any evaluation in which data are collected is subject to some form of bias. Although controlling all sources of bias is impossible, minimizing each major source in an evaluation is critical. Steps must be taken to select an instrument and methods of data collection to minimize the many probable sources of biases. Webb et al. (1966) identified 12 common biases in human measurements:

1. *Guinea pig effect:* People who are aware that they are being measured may respond in uncharacteristic ways.

2. *Role selection:* Awareness of being measured may influence people to feel that they have to play a special role.

3. *Measurement as a change agent:* The act of taking a measurement may affect the subsequent behavior of those being measured.

4. *Response sets:* People respond to questionnaires and interviews in "yea-saying" or socially desirable, predictable ways that have little or nothing to do with the questions posed.

5. *Interviewer effects:* Characteristics of the interviewer may affect respondents' receptivity and answers.

6. *Changes in the instrument:* If an instrument is used more than once, a learning effect is possible. Interviewers may become more proficient at or tired of implementing an interview schedule the longer they use it.

7. *Population restrictions:* The method of data collection may impose restrictions on the population to which the results can be generalized, e.g., telephone interviews require the respondent to have a telephone.

8. *Population stability over time:* An instrument administered at different times may not collect the same data on different populations.

9. *Population stability over areas:* The same way of collecting data in two different geographic areas may assess different types of people.

10. *Content restrictions:* A limited range of data can be reported by each method; e.g., self-report questionnaires cannot be used to study the cognitive mechanisms of moving information from short-term to long-term memory; observational data cannot be used to study relationships among a person's values.

11. *Stability of content over time:* If a program restricts a study to naturally occurring behavior, the content of the studied phenomenon may vary over time.

12. *Stability of content over an area:* A program may not be uniform in content throughout the area in which it is applied.

CRITERIA FOR SELECTING A DATA COLLECTION METHOD

Each instrument is based on a particular method of collecting data, e.g., interviewing, self-recording, observing, taking data from medical records. How do you select an instrument and, by inference, a method for data collection? Multiple issues are noted in Table 3.8 that should be considered when selecting a measurement instrument and method (Baranowski and Simons-Morton 1991). The primary concern in selecting an instrument and method is for high validity and reliability from previous experience, especially for the groups, situations, and purposes of your study. Each of these issues needs to be considered in an evaluation.

Instruments and methods may be appropriate or inappropriate for particular populations and settings. There are issues of developmental appropriateness to be considered, i.e., are the instruments and method appropriate to the cognitive and emotional abilities of respondents? What can be asked of normal adults may not be developmentally appropriate for children or the mentally impaired. Examples of ethnic and regional appropriateness could include whether a food-frequency technique includes foods common in a particular ethnic group or region of the country (e.g., greens in the South), and if the questions are phrased in a way understandable in that ethnic group or region (e.g., "turnips" in parts of Georgia means "turnip greens"). The instrument and method may also place undue burdens on the respondents or staff.

In summary, there are many issues to consider in the creation and use of an instrument and method. The procedures for a method should be explicitly detailed in a protocol that can be reviewed to assess their appropriateness for a particular population.

Measurement Cost

Another significant issue in data collection is cost. Cost has several characteristics: (1) dollar cost, (2) time spent by the evaluation staff, (3) time spent by respondents, (4) ease of setting up instruments, (5) difficulty of getting individuals to participate, (6) loss of accuracy due to increased work load, and (7) availability and quality of statistics. All instruments cost money, and some may be too costly. Some approaches may not be economically feasible (think of sending multiple observers to record clients' behaviors all day, every day, or supplying a personal computer for daily self-monitoring of some behavior to everyone in a health education program). Some approaches may produce other problems (think of

TABLE 3.8   Specification of Issues in Selecting a Measurement Method

Issue	Validity	Reliability
Prior Assessment	Do studies document that this method: • Appears to measure what it purports to measure (face validity)? • Taps all the areas of concern (content validity)? • Predicts some "gold standard" measure of the same variable (criterion or predictive validity)? • Is related to other variables as theoretically predicted (construct validity)?	Do studies document that this method • Has items that positively intercorrelate (internal consistency)? • Obtains similar values when administered twice in a short time period (test-retest reliability)? • Obtains similar values when administered twice over a long period of time (stability)? • Has two or more different forms that correlate highly when administered to the same people (identity)? • Obtains similar values when administered by two different interviewers or observers (intrarater or interobserver reliability)?
Precision		
Level of Detail	Does the method obtain data in sufficient detail to specify the variable desired?	Is the level of detail desired too refined given the capabilities of the collecting instrument?
Habitual Behavior	Does the method account for variation by season, weekends, sick days, and holidays?	Does the method allow for the collection of information across sufficient repeated time periods to produce a reliable estimate of usual behavior?
Reactivity	Does the method of collecting the data affect the variable of interest?	
Change	Does the method obtain data in sufficient detail to detect the level of change (pre to post)?	How many assessments must be conducted at pre- and posttest to detect the expected changes?
Appropriateness		
Developmental	Does the method require skills or other cognitive abilities the participant is not likely to have?	Are the questions and responses phrased and depicted in an appropriate manner?

(continues)

TABLE 3.8 *(continued)*		
Issue	Validity	Reliability
Ethnic	Does the method reflect dimensions common to an ethnic group?	Are the questions and responses phrased to respect ethnicity?
Regional	Does the method reflect regionality?	Are the questions and responses regionally sensitive?
Implementation		
Procedures	Is the method theoretically sound or otherwise reasonable to collect data of interest?	Is there a detailed protocol to collect the data, including procedures for training?
Conversions	Do the data need to be converted, e.g., converting foods to nutrient consumption?	Is there a detailed protocol for conversion of data, including training procedures?
Respondent Burden	Does the method take so much time, effort, or money that people are discouraged to participate or systematically distort responses?	Does the method take so much time, effort, or money that random error is increased?
Staff Burden	Does the method take so much time or effort that staff distorts the procedures (intentionally or unintentionally)?	

how hostile clients can become if they have to complete 1 hour of paperwork every day for a month). The key to selecting good measures is to choose a set sufficiently valid and reliable for your study's purposes, yet developed at minimal cost to the project and to the respondents.

An important aspect of economy is collecting no more data than are necessary to achieve the purposes of the particular study. Some investigators have developed a 300-question instrument requiring 2 hours to complete. Such a program bears a significant burden: costs in time, printing, collating, and data processing. Respondents must bear a considerable burden: time costs in completing the questionnaire. Investigators typically collect more data than they can reasonably analyze; the parties incur the costs of collection, but because of report deadlines nothing is ever done with the data. Ask: Why are we collecting this data?

The more valid and reliable instruments and methods usually incur more financial and staff costs to the investigator and time costs to the respondents. Sometimes an investigator must simply select the most valid and reliable instrument and method for the amount of money available and accept the resulting errors and problems. In some cases, an evaluation should not be done if resources are not available for instruments and methods that meet the minimum criteria for a particular project.

Purpose of the Study

A data collection method must clearly meet the purposes of a study, within resources and constraints. For a smoking cessation program, you might conduct an evaluation to assess impact (stopped smoking or not), the availability of resources in the environment (number of smokers willing to pay for a smoking cessation program), the quality of the resources, the appropriateness of the structure (well-designed program), whether the processes are occurring as planned (conducted according to program design), or whether the processes are being related to outputs (more sessions attended increases quit rates). Each topic can be the focus for an evaluation in a particular program. The type of question posed by the evaluator should determine the data collection method.

Hardness of Data

Another important criterion in selecting measures is the "hardness" of data. There is a belief among some investigators that certain types of data are "harder" and others "softer" and therefore more important to collect. According to Feinstein (1977), the following characteristics are typically associated with data hardness:

- The data are obtained objectively, e.g., physiological measures, rather than subjectively, e.g., urine sample vs. self-reports.
- The primary data can be preserved for repeated analyses, e.g., a videotape of an encounter, which can be reobserved and checked.
- The measurement is on a dimensional scale, e.g., a ratio or interval scale.

Although the reference may seem dated, the validity of the author's conclusions has contemporary application. Feinstein refuted each of these beliefs. For example, physiological measures can be highly unreliable. Rapid changes may occur in the values of the physiological measure, or there may be problems of mechanical determination of the physiological values by the laboratory. In some cases, a sufficient amount of a sample may not have been collected, or the sample was stored improperly or for too long to perform an accurate test. Some variables may be very difficult to quantify from videotape because they are not precisely specified or because they require too much observer interpretation. A ratio or an interval scale does not ensure reliability.

QUALITY CONTROL IN DATA COLLECTION

In this section, we examine multiple common methods of data collection, identify strengths and weaknesses (biases), consider issues in methods selection, and outline steps to develop an instrument and implementing method. There are many facets to collecting quality data. Quality control requires anticipating possible sources of problems, selecting the best methods for a particular evaluation, monitoring the data collection quality, and minimizing problems before or as they occur.

Sampling

We introduce methods in Chapter 6 to estimate the sample size needed for each group to make the desired analyses and inferences. We also discuss the salience of selection bias in accruing participants. Here, we briefly discuss how to obtain that sample. A major assumption in performing an analysis to test a hypothesis or relationship is that a study is conducted to generalize to a defined population.

A sample of evaluation participants needs to be assessed to determine how representative it is of the population at risk to which inferences of impact are to be made. There are multiple types of sampling techniques with random components, e.g., simple random, clustering, or stratified, presented in a large number of statistics texts (Sudman 1976). Randomness minimizes the likelihood that a systematic source of selection bias will occur among the sample, thereby influencing the degree of representativeness of the population. For example, selecting the next 50 participants in a program (a quota sampling) might not be representative. If you could be sure that the entry of any person into a service program was a random event, then quota sampling might be appropriate. Alternatively, the next 50 participants might all be obtained on Monday, but people who come on Wednesday might be different.

Evaluators are often faced with obtaining data from record systems, such as vital statistics or clinic records. A systematic sampling technique is often used to select cases from existing records. In systematic sampling, divide the population (e.g., 10,000 cases) by the sample size needed (e.g., 100 subjects, which results in a sampling interval of 100). Randomly select a number between 1 and 100. Start with that case. Thus, if 37 were randomly selected, the sample would consist of cases numbered 37, 137, 237, . . . , 9,937. The strength of systematic sampling is ease of implementation. If the sequence of cases is random, e.g., alphabetical order, then systematic sampling is very likely to produce an unbiased sampling method.

In developing the sampling procedures, specify inclusionary characteristics (e.g., participants in the program to be evaluated) and exclusionary characteristics (characteristics of people used to keep them out of the sample). Inclusionary and exclusionary characteristics define the population to which data and results can be generalized. Consult any of a variety of texts on sampling, and if necessary a biostatistician.

Obtrusive Measures

The term *obtrusive* indicates that the person is aware of being measured, assessed, or tested. Methods usually included in the obtrusive category are self-reporting questionnaires, interviews, and direct observations of behavior. *Unobtrusive* implies that an individual is not aware of being studied. The methods usually included in the unobtrusive category are record abstractions, physiological measures, and behavior trace methods. Unobtrusive measures are valued; because subjects are not aware of being measured, unobtrusive measures are supposed to produce less random error and bias. The differences between obtrusive and unobtrusive methods, however, are not always so clear-cut. If workers in a public health agency learn that they are continually being evaluated using the agency records they regularly complete, their record-completion behavior may change drastically.

Questionnaire development   A questionnaire obtains information on a respondent through self-reported answers to a series of questions, usually using paper and pencil, although computers can also be used. Good references on questionnaire development include Aday (1991) and Bradburn and Sudman (1979). Four general areas in questionnaire development are discussed next:

1. Instrument selection
2. Instrument development
3. Field testing
4. Quality control

Instrument selection   Many evaluations have developed and applied multiple types of instruments for a variety of purposes. Do not reinvent the wheel. When an instrument has been shown to be valid and reliable and that it directly measures the variables of interest for a specific problem and target population, starting with that instrument as a draft makes good sense. Using developed instruments is valuable for several reasons. First, capitalize on the conceptual work of other investigators in instrument design. Much time already will have been spent reviewing the literature and considering alternative questions. Second, other investigators would have spent time evaluating and revising the instrument to maximize validity and reliability. Most investigators go through multiple drafts of a questionnaire to increase its quality. Using their instrument should typically enhance some level of reliability and validity of measurement in a new application. Third, using an existing instrument and the same questions enables comparisons to be made across evaluation studies. Developed instruments, however, should not be used without a thorough review and pilot test.

Instrument development and field-testing In some cases, instruments have not been developed for a particular topic, or existing instruments are not appropriate. Even when instruments are available, you usually have to develop questions specific to your study. Refer to Bradburn and Sudman (1982) on questionnaire development.

In general, use close-ended questions. Respondents may not accurately understand an open-ended question; may not want to provide a full answer because it will take too much time; or may give what is a full and complete answer only in their view. Developing close-ended questions, however, requires more time and attention to detail than developing open-ended questions. Review the literature to ensure that the response categories are mutually exclusive. Pilot-test the questionnaire to ensure that the alternatives are understandable to the intended audience. When rating scales are used to obtain responses, the structure of the response scales can be important.

Open-ended questions can be useful when you want to learn something about which little is known. In this case, a close-ended question is posed (usually in a yes-no format), followed by an open-ended question asking for an explanation.

The questionnaire should be appealing to respondents. Keep the pages free of clutter and use empty space to make the form visually appealing. Asking several questions that are stimulating or pleasing early in the questionnaire increases the likelihood that respondents will maintain the motivation to complete the instrument. Developing and using clear and simple instructions increases the accuracy of responses to the questionnaire. Multi-item instruments should be constructed to avoid response sets that bias results. Overcome this problem by keeping the number of questions to which "yes" is the appropriate response equal to those to which "no" is appropriate and by including equal numbers of positive and negative items.

Windsor, Roseman, Gartseff, and Kirk (1981) proposed the following 10 steps in questionnaire instrument development:

1. Define program objectives in behavioral or performance terms.
2. Identify by internal review essential cognitive, affective, and psychomotor skills and descriptive information needs.
3. Review the literature—contact authors.
4. Review existing instruments and record-keeping systems.
5. Construct a draft instrument and agree on measurement procedures.

6. Identify measurement methods, coding, and staff training.

7. Pilot-test with 30 to 50 subjects from the target group at each study site to determine essential characteristics—instrument validity, reliability, adequacy of questions, ease of administration, degree of standardization, and efficiency (time).

8. Repeat the internal review and modification; perform an external review.

9. Conduct a formal instrument test with ≥50 to 100 target group members at each site; reexamine the characteristics in step 7.

10. Repeat the internal review; revise and finalize the measurement process and the instrument for routine application.

Quality control   Selecting, developing, and field-testing a questionnaire are necessary steps, but not sufficient to collect valid and reliable data. Questionnaire quality control checks should be made. Conduct other data-editing and -cleaning procedures after the data have been entered into the computer, for example, after reviewing 10% of the data-entry forms against printouts of the data set. The checks also detect data-entry errors. Check internal consistency, or multiple-form reliability. At a minimum, an investigator should calculate Cronbach's alpha (or the KR-20, as appropriate) and test-retest on all multi-item instruments to obtain an estimate of internal consistency and stability.

Self-completion questionnaires   A self-completion (or self-reporting) questionnaire is an instrument that the respondent completes by reading questions and providing answers. A questionnaire can be used with one person or a group.

Strengths   A self-completed questionnaire is a convenient and frequently used method of data collection for program evaluation. Data can be collected from a large sample in a short period of time at a low cost. Almost all types of measures can be assessed with a self-completed questionnaire. All participants are exposed to the same instrument.

Because no interviewer is involved in asking questions, a well-designed questionnaire controls for interviewer effects. The proportion of unusable data in a self-report questionnaire is typically low. All the questions are directed at the object of concern and replicability is high. The questionnaire is particularly useful when the variables studied are amenable to self-observation. Specific answers can be elicited to simple, straightforward questions. Self-report questionnaires, therefore, are most valid and reliable with short, simple, and straightforward questions. Good references on self-completion questionnaires include Aday (1991) and Bradburn and Sudman (1979).

Weaknesses   A self-completion questionnaire is susceptible to several biases. Although a self-completed questionnaire theoretically controls for possible interviewer effects, the person who distributes the questionnaire often answers questions about it and may give subtle or overt cues to how it should be answered. Respondents can easily fall into role selection when answering questionnaires, because no one is present to observe, clarify, or challenge their role taking. The phenomenon of response sets was originally identified using self-completed questionnaires. Other problems: The questionnaire may promote participant change; changes may occur in the respondents' understanding of the questionnaire; and limits may exist on the phenomena to which a questionnaire can be applied.

Self-completion mail surveys   When resources are scarce and the target population for the evaluation is dispersed across a broad geographic area, a mail survey may be the choice for collecting data. The mail survey uses a self-completion questionnaire with the postal system as the vehicle for delivering and retrieving the instrument. There are multiple references on mail survey research methods.

Strengths and weaknesses   Comments about the strengths and weaknesses of the self-completion questionnaire also apply to the mail survey. Given the relatively low cost of mail service, these surveys offer an inexpensive method of obtaining data from areas as large as a city, a state, or even a nation. The strengths of the mail survey method under some circumstances can be its weaknesses under others. A mail survey assumes a sampling frame exists with a particular respondent's accurate address and mail can be delivered to that address. Significant problems may exist with both assumptions. Many surveys reveal that 10% of the addresses may be in error, out of date, or for nonexistent locations. The greatest recommendation for the mail survey is its low cost as a method of obtaining data from a large geographic area. But because of the very low response rates, a major concern is the large selection bias of respondents.

Steps in conducting a mail survey   If a mail survey is contemplated, a sampling frame is necessary that contains names, addresses, and, if possible, phone numbers of the target group. Be concerned about the probable accuracy of existing information and whether some people who are of interest to the study may not be included or have not been accurately represented in the sampling frame. Follow these steps to implement a mail survey:

1. Develop a questionnaire.
2. Send a notification postcard or letter.
3. Send out the initial questionnaire.

4. Send a reminder postcard.

5. Send out a second questionnaire.

6. Call nonrespondents by phone.

Program staff members should expect some percentage of questionnaires to be returned marked "undeliverable." Attempt phone contact with these persons immediately to obtain new addresses for a mailing. Monitor the returned questionnaires, revise addresses and telephone numbers on the master list of names, addresses, and telephone numbers, and record attempts to reach respondents.

Self-completion diaries and logs   There are two problems in the usual methods of obtaining self-report measures: telescoping and memory loss. *Telescoping* means that respondents tend to remember certain events as having occurred more recently than they actually did. *Memory loss* refers to respondents failing to remember the occurrence of events. Studying children's dietary behaviors provides an illustrative example. Most dietary assessment methods require intensive recall for the past 24-hour period or for as long as 2 weeks. Children, however, demonstrate several limitations in reporting the frequency of consumption of specific foods:

- Unable to easily remember foods eaten for a full 24-hour period
- Difficulty reporting on frequencies of consumption of particular items across meals and snack times
- Unaware of the names and nutrient content of food products they consume
- Unaware of the methods of food preparation used in their family or by school cooks

Strengths and weaknesses   Verbrugge (1980) reviewed the available literature on health diaries and came to the following conclusions:

- Diaries produce higher frequencies for most phenomena than other methods.
- Diaries appear to be particularly better than other self-report methods for reporting low-salience phenomena, e.g., transient, low-impact health problems; symptoms; disability days.
- Telescoping is absent.
- Memory lapse is minimized.
- A high percentage of people contacted agree to complete diaries.

- Very few people who agreed to complete a diary failed to complete one during the full recording period.

This high completion rate happened without financial or other incentives to complete the forms. In addition, depending on how the diary data were collected, diaries may be a useful source of a wide variety of data.

Verbrugge (1980) also reported several problems with diaries. The quality of the data is roughly proportional to the effort expended to collect it. Frequent (e.g., weekly) attempts must be made to collect the diaries. These costs are higher per respondent than data collected by interviewers, because of the intensive efforts at data collection and extensive data coding. Two other methodological problems (biases) in diaries were noted: sensitization and conditioning. Respondents became more aware of the phenomena simply from monitoring their own behavior, at least initially. This increased sensitivity often results in behavior changes; e.g., the person is more likely to seek medical help when monitored. The frequency of events recorded typically decreases from 5% to 25% during the recording period. Respondents may increasingly lose interest in the task (i.e., become bored) over time, producing lower and or less accurate reported frequencies. All biases in the self-report questionnaire potentially apply to the diary, unless steps are taken to correct them. Diaries may be an attractive, though expensive, approach to data collection when the program staff have reason to believe that telescoping and memory loss may occur if other instruments are used.

CASE STUDY 3.4

Validity of a Paper Diary

BACKGROUND

Patient recall is often inaccurate and unreliable (biased) when collected over a period of time. Diaries have been developed to get more accurate information in an attempt to reduce this error. This study was designed to determine the validity of a paper diary. It asked the question: How objective is information from patients about chronic pain over a three-month period of time? The investigators compared use of an electronic diary designed to enhance validity and compliance versus use of a paper diary.

METHODS

Eighty adult patients with chronic pain, defined as at least 3 hours a day and rated as a 4 on a 10-point scale, were recruited. Forty were randomly assigned to keep a paper diary and 40 were randomly assigned to keep an electronic diary. A training session was

Source: E. Stone, S. Shiffman, R. Schwartz, et al., "Patient Non-Compliance with Paper Diaries," *British Medical Journal* 324 (May 18, 2002): 1193–1194.

TABLE 3.9   Compliance Rates for Paper and Electronic Diaries

Method	Paper (n = 40)	Electronic (n = 40)
30-Minute Window		
Total no. of episodes	2,445	2,435
Episodes excluded	126	7
Mean % compliance (95% CI):		
Actual	11 (8% to 14%)	94 (92% to 96%)
Reported	90 (86% to 94%)	

provided to each patient. All patients were paid $150, and all gave their informed consent. The paper diary was comprised of diary cards bound into an organizer binder. The cards contained a 20-question pain instrument. Patients were asked to record time and date as diary entries at 10 A.M., 4 P.M., and 8 P.M. within 15 minutes of the target times. The diary binders were unobtrusively fitted with photo sensors that detected light and recorded when the diary was opened and closed. This method had been previously tested and validated. The electronic diary was a palm-held computer with software for data collection in clinical trials. It presented the identical questions via a touch screen. It also recorded time and date of entry. The electronic diary entries could not be initiated outside a 30-minute window.

After 3 days to become familiar with the method and instrument, participants began a 21-day period of diary keeping. All patients completed the diaries over the 3-week period.

RESULTS

The reported compliance of patients keeping the paper diary was 90%; the actual compliance was 11%. The electronic diary compliance was 94%. Table 3.9 presents data for both groups.

DISCUSSION

This study reinforces the general discussions presented in the previous section of this chapter about problems with compliance and validity of diaries. As confirmed by the data, although patients reported high compliance, actual compliance was low and invalid. This case study documents the importance of establishing the validity and reliability of data collected by diary or any other method, because of the inherent possibilities of inaccurate data. For this method, as in all other data collection methods, the issue of social desirability by patients or evaluation program participants was evident.

Face-to-face interviewing   There may be no substitute for having an interviewer conduct a personal survey interview in some evaluations. The literature on survey interviewing methods seems infinite and is too complex to be conveniently summarized. Only an overview is presented here.

Strengths Conducted face-to-face, the interpersonal interview is usually preferable to the self-completion questionnaire when

- The content is not well defined.
- The questions are long or complex or require making subtle distinctions.
- The respondents have difficulty reading or writing.
- Personal effort may be needed to contact respondents.
- Data on other biological variables, e.g., blood pressure measurements, are needed.

The primary strength of the face-to-face interview is the use of a well-trained interviewer to ask the respondent intensive questions and to detect, clarify, and follow up on confusing answers or questions. A trained person can obtain answers to questions that are not well defined or for which in-depth answers are needed. Interviewers can be trained to probe interviewees with a variety of questions, attempting to get below-surface responses, that is, deeper than the flippant or simple answers a respondent may provide. For example, if you are interested in why mothers decide to breast-feed, you could ask a simple question—"Why did you decide to breast-feed or bottle-feed your baby?"—and leave several lines for the unstructured response.

Alternatively, you might have an interviewer ask the following series of questions:

- "What do you see as the benefits of breast-feeding (or bottle-feeding)?"
- "What do you see as the costs to you of bottle-feeding (or breast-feeding)?"
- "How important are the costs of breast-feeding to you?"
- "How important are the costs of bottle-feeding to you?"
- "Why did you select your method of infant feeding?"

A respondent finding these questions on a self-response questionnaire would probably answer them with the easiest responses. An interviewer can probe a little deeper, looking for things this mother might like about breast-or bottle-feeding.

Interview questions are best formed when the investigator is working from a theoretical framework of a model. For example, the breast-feeding interview was based on an expectancy model that assessed the benefits and costs of two behavioral alternatives (Baranowski 1992–1993). Questions can be designed to assess key variables in a model. The interviewer can be instructed about how far to probe respondents to collect the data of interest.

The interview is appropriate for long, complex questions and those requiring subtle distinctions for the same reasons it is valuable for poorly defined questions. The appropriateness of an interviewer for respondents who cannot read or write is obvious. The interview also provides the most flexible method for the use of descriptive cues. An interviewer can ask a variety of questions and make a variety of judgments about the state of the respondent. With careful attention to detail, an interview can almost always be replicated, which promotes reliability in data collection.

Weaknesses   The face-to-face interview is susceptible to several biases. In an interpersonal situation, respondents are likely to anticipate what the interviewer expects of them and act accordingly (role selection). The probing of particular content areas is likely to focus the respondent's attention on these issues (social desirability). This may change the way the respondent thinks about the issues and confound future attempts at measuring this content area—measurement as a change agent. All self-report measures are susceptible to a yea-saying or social desirability response set. Interviewers may also become more proficient and more subtle at asking questions, so that later interviews are different from earlier ones. The interview may not obtain accurate information on highly sensitive issues, for example, sexual or contraceptive behavior.

Realizing these biases, the evaluation staff must take steps to counter or minimize these effects. The interpersonal interview is an expensive method of data collection. Some combination of self-completed questionnaires and interviews may best achieve an investigator's objectives within the available budget.

Steps in conducting face-to-face interviews   A good face-to-face interview requires a well-designed interview schedule, a list of questions, and a well-trained interviewer. The guidelines presented in this chapter to develop questionnaires also apply to developing the interview. Training interviewers requires an equal attention to detail. The qualities of a good training program are:

- An understanding of the major ideas that underlie the questionnaire
- A guidebook or protocol on probing and on recording responses
- Materials for clarifying responses
- Procedures for collecting other data
- Clear instructions for obtaining and contacting a sample
- Experience in conducting the interview, especially probing
- Common experiences in recording or coding self-report information
- Sources of information to report or clarify problems
- Testing for reliability

Training should give interviewers enough knowledge of the subject area to enable them to ask intelligent questions. They should not, however, be informed of the study's specific hypotheses. This knowledge might bias the way in which they ask questions or interpret or record responses. An answer to any question may be ambiguous, unless clear guidelines or categories of response exist for recording a response. For example, to the question "Why do you smoke after eating?" a new smoker might answer, "Well, I'm not too sure. Er . . . well, it gives me a boost right after a meal. I try to puff enough to feel good, but not keep that terrible smoke in my mouth." This is a complex response to an apparently simple question. Some of the comments are positive; some are negative. The basic response to the question is equivocal. A set of rules is needed to guide the interviewer on the depth to probe for classification and which parts of a response to record. For some questions, an interviewer needs materials to show the respondent how to answer. Sometimes interviewers will collect data other than responses to questions. This might include blood pressure or saliva samples. Detailed guidelines, materials, and thorough training need to be provided. Criteria need to be formulated for screening and possibly rejecting potential interviewers who cannot collect data adequately.

Prepared with these materials and instructions, interviewers need experience in conducting interviews on a pilot basis. The pilot interviews test the questionnaire and enable the interviewers to develop confidence in implementing the interview. They clarify issues that did not arise in the initial review of materials and procedures. A valuable procedure is to have each interviewer tape-record a test interview and review the interview. During the review of the tape recordings, all interviewers individually record the taped responses to the questions; they then compare their recordings. While interviewers are recording the information from the interviewers, the program staff should collect the data and calculate the level of reliability. Such a review session should occur weekly thereafter, to ensure that interviewers are continuing to record in a reliable manner.

If an evaluation staff is conducting a community survey, interviewers must be given a phone number to call when they need clarification on interview techniques, sample locations, or other problems. If physiological measures are collected, the interviewers' basic data collection technique needs to be assessed at weekly intervals, and the machine used needs to be assessed to ensure calibration. Interview training time will vary and may take hours or days. Before they are sent into the field, interviewers must be furnished with identification. The program staff, in some cases, should announce the interview schedule and locations to the local authorities.

Telephone interviewing Telephone interviewing is an attractive alternative to face-to-face interviewing, because the information is cheaper to collect per interview and greater control can be exerted by evaluation staff over the methods of data collection in a central automated center. Telephone survey research centers currently use computerized random digit dialing centers for these interviews.

All comments made about face-to-face interviewing apply at some level to telephone interviewing, but telephone interviewing is susceptible to additional biases. A primary concern is population restrictions. Data reveal that more than 95% of all households have telephones; telephone unavailability is more common among people traditionally considered disadvantaged. Further population restriction problems arise when investigators try to reach people with unlisted phone numbers, those who have moved, and those who have changed phones for other reasons since the last public listing of phone numbers. Investigators typically propose the random digit dialing method to overcome the latter two problems. The shortcoming of this approach is that it cannot be used for contacting some known sampling of individuals, e.g., all the former participants in a particular project, or for contacting people in specific geographic areas, because the first three digits in the telephone number may not be specific to those areas. Differences may also exist in the populations that can be reached by telephone over a span of time or geographic area.

There are greater restrictions on content on the telephone than in the face-to-face interview. It is commonly reported that a telephone interview cannot last more than 30 minutes and is best conducted in 20 minutes or less. In contrast, face-to-face interviews commonly last 1 hour. Participant burden needs to be a concern of all evaluations.

Direct observation   The accuracy of self-reported behavior may be biased, reflecting a socially desirable response. In these cases, some investigators use direct observation. Observational methods are most useful for collecting behavioral and skill data. By definition, behavioral data are amenable to observation. Ability or skill data often require a person to perform a task in a controlled environment to see whether the person can do it. For example, a diabetic patient is often asked to perform self-injection to demonstrate that he or she can do it effectively (Windsor 1981; Windsor, Roseman, Gartseff, and Kirk 1981). As noted in Table 3.3, direct observation includes a variety of methods. Observational data can be obtained directly by the observers or by videotape or audiotape recorders, and other mechanical means. In some methods, the observer attempts to be an objective recorder of phenomena; in others, the observer frequently interacts with the subjects and may, in fact, participate with the subjects in various key social events. Observational studies may be concerned simply with identifying the frequency of certain phenomena or, at a more complex level, with the relationships between events.

There are multiple components necessary for direct observation:

- Observation instrument that reflects the theory, model, or other purposes of the study
- Definitions of observation-recording categories or symbols
- Protocol that outlines rules relating to observational data collection
- Observers trained to use the instrument and protocol
- Procedures to assess interobserver reliability
- Protocol for coding data
- Coders trained to use coding protocol
- Procedures to assess intercoder reliability

Direct observation, however, is one of the most expensive methods of obtaining behavioral data. One or more observers must be present for extended periods of time to document the behavior of concern; extensive observation records must be maintained; multiple coders must search the observation records and code the phenomena of concern; or expensive laptop computers must be used in the field to record the observations. A single investigator can use a self-report questionnaire with multiple respondents and in 1 hour obtain data from each respondent covering an hour, a day, a week, a year, or even a lifetime of experiences. In contrast, in 1 hour a single observer can obtain data on 1 hour in the life of one person or an interacting group of people. Observation, therefore, can be cost-effective when used with small samples to validate data obtained using other methods (Simons-Morton and Baranowski 1991). These other methods can then be used with larger samples.

The protocol must specify procedures for contacting, training, and/or interviewing the persons to be observed; times at which all activities are to be conducted; sequences of activities within observation sessions; and procedures for preventing or ameliorating anticipated problems. The protocol should include the definitions of items and examples of the cases that are difficult to distinguish. It should clarify whether single or multiple checks or entries are disallowed, allowed, encouraged, or required within time intervals of categories of observational items. Procedures for recording field notes should be stated. The protocol should also specify periodic times for joint observations to obtain interobserver reliability. A useful reference in discussing interobserver reliability is Windsor (1981). Observer training is a primary method of promoting the reliability of direct observational data.

Johnson and Bolstad (1973) identify five key problems in observation methods:

1. Reliability estimates may not be made in the same coding and time units.
2. The days on which reliability is assessed may not be representative of other days on which observations are conducted.
3. The instrument may decay due to the passage of time.
4. The observers may respond in some unknown way to having reliability assessed.
5. The people being observed may respond in some unknown way to being observed.

Methods for counteracting these problems have been developed. The following components of training are recommended for a reliability monitoring system to promote maximum reliability:

- Have all observers read and study the observation protocol.
- Have the observers complete programmed instruction materials on pre-coded interactions.
- Conduct daily intensive training programs in precoded scripts enacted on videotape or by actors.
- Provide field training with an experienced observer, followed by reliability testing.
- Randomly assess interobserver reliability in the field.

Observational techniques have been particularly useful in assessing the extent to which self-report methods have provided valid data (Simons-Morton and Baranowski 1991) and in assessing whether the usual counseling provided to patients in clinics resulted in their having the skills necessary to perform the desired self-care behaviors (Manzella et al. 1989; Windsor 1981; Windsor et al. 1981).

Unobtrusive Measures

There are a variety of methods of collecting unobtrusive data. Each method is subject to biases. For example, if people completing medical records become aware that someone has started using these records to evaluate their performance, they may complete the forms differently, thereby introducing a biased source of information. Similarly, hospital accounting records that contain total family income are probably biased downward, because a lower report of income will often mean a lower or no charge for care. The unbiased character of any unobtrusive method is maintained only as long as people are not aware they are being studied and there is no incentive to provide biased information. Here we review several unobtrusive methods used in health services research.

Abstraction of existing medical and clinical records   Some investigators consider the medical record a readily available and accessible source of rich data at little cost. Imagine the millions of medical records across the country describing millions of laboratory and physiological tests on a vast variety of health problems: It would appear to be a gold mine, but it may be fool's gold. There are occasions, however, when a medical record abstraction is appropriate and valuable. The Windsor, Roseman, Gartseff, and Kirk (1981) article in *Diabetes Care* is an example of this category.

Strengths and weaknesses   Entries are made in one or more medical records each time a patient receives care from a physician or other health care provider. This is an enormous quantity of data. If the health care provider or institution can be persuaded to share these records, the body of data becomes available for evaluation purposes. The primary cost is incurred by hiring staff to enter and abstract the desired data from all the data available. There are, however, many limitations. Not every person receives medical care for a specific problem. Although some of the major barriers to care have been overcome in the United States and Western Europe, multiple studies have indicated that the poor and ethnic minority groups may be less likely to receive care for a health problem than others. Because the evaluation team has little or no control over how much information is recorded or over the quality of that recorded information, an enormous set of problems can arise. Windsor, Roseman, Gartseff, and Kirk (1981), in conducting a retrospective medical record review of 996 diabetic in-patients, found that only 40% had a baseline admission assessment and only 6% a patient education–behavioral discharge assessment and documented an average level of completeness in data of 70%.

The quality, completeness, and stability of the content of medical records varies over time and across diseases and medical conditions. For example, the International Classification of Diseases (ICD) is a set of codes for major categories of causes of death and disability. Hospitals use several ICD codes in planning health services. Different hospitals may use different ICD codes, creating variations in data among locations. Moreover, the ICD codes are periodically updated to reflect the latest medical knowledge. Data collected before and after code changes are therefore not directly comparable because the diagnostic criteria for making a particular judgment may have changed.

Steps in abstracting medical records   A medical record abstraction can be useful when demographic data are simple, commonly recorded medical data are desired, and attempts to control for reliability are made. One study that attempted to abstract relevant information on hypertensive patients in a family medicine clinic illustrates the steps required in conducting abstractions of medical records. Six different drafts of this form were developed. The first three were revised to reflect the purposes of the study more clearly as these purposes became more clearly defined through staff decisions. Reliability analyses were conducted on the next two drafts by having sets of two out of three abstractors jointly abstract 20 records. Reliability indices were calculated on the 20 jointly abstracted records for each variable, for each pair of abstractors. All cases in which differing values were obtained were intensively reviewed against the medical record, and rules were generated to refine the search or the recording process.

On the second set of reliability abstractions, rules for abstraction were further refined, and variables for which a reliability of abstraction of 0.75 or higher was not achieved were dropped from the study. The sixth draft was used for the final abstractions. Search and coding rules were printed on the abstraction form to make their use convenient. A limited set of demographics, commonly recorded, and more serious variables were finally obtained from the medical records. Less than half the variables originally desired were included in the final form. Particular attention should be given to the development of rules for abstraction, because Boyd et al. (1979) show that explicit criteria for abstractions can more than double the interabstractor reliability value.

CASE STUDY 3.5

Record Review

Often too much or too little information is collected on participants in HP programs. The information collected often is not used. Despite the difficulty that may be encountered, a record-keeping system is an essential component of program implementation. All program-monitoring and data collection systems should be compatible with ongoing data systems. Program utilization and record review involves monitoring program participation or session exposure, improving record completeness, documenting program or session exposure, and monitoring the use of information services.

MONITORING PROGRAM PARTICIPATION OR EXPOSURE

Inherent in setting up a monitoring system is defining whom the program is attempting to serve and an estimated number of eligible participants for the target area or location. All target populations must be enumerated. This allows you to answer these questions: How many of those eligible were served? Were the people who participated those for whom the program was designed? For most programs, standard record forms are mandated. Programs almost always need minimum demographic and psychosocial characteristics and data concerning participants. Although this responsibility may

TABLE 3.10   Completed Items in Records of Diabetic Patients, in Rank Order

Item	Decile of Forms with Item Completed
Diabetes instructor	90–100%
Age	
Put on _____ calorie-ADA diet	80–89%
Diabetes mellitus diagnosed—year	
Demonstrated drawing up and injection of insulin	70–79%
Has been taught to use _____ urine test	
Personal hygiene and foot care items taught	
Educated in diabetic control	
After learning to use a urine test, knows how and when to test urine for sugar	60–69%
Knows how and when to test for acetone	
Knows how to use dextrostix	
Understands causes and symptoms of reactions, acidosis	
Understands need to call doctor if acidosis develops	
Attitude on admission	50–59%
Understands insulin adjustment for reactions, etc.	
Attitude on discharge	40–49%
Can test urine for sugar accurately	
Knows how to use booklet to follow diet	
Patient or member of family has been taught to use glucagon	
Pretest score	30–39%
Class attendance—insulin	
Class attendance—personal hygiene and foot care	
Class attendance—reactions and acidosis	
Class attendance—diabetes	20–29%
Class attendance—urine checks	
Diet restrictions	
Knows representative foods and amount of each exchange group	
Class attendance—diet	
Patient's physical or learning handicaps	10–19%
Posttest score	0–10%
Incapable of drawing up own insulin or testing urine	

Source: Windsor, Roseman, Gartseff, and Kirk (1981, 468–475). Reprinted by permission of the American Diabetes Association.

seem to present major difficulties, if staff members agree about the type of information needed for each participant and pay particular attention to efficiency in information collection, they should be able to gather complete documentation on service use.

Table 3.10 illustrates the amount of information that can be lost by a poor instrument and record-keeping system. A retrospective 12-month review of medical records of patients at a 40-bed diabetes care hospital was conducted to determine the quality of patient education assessment data of admitted diabetics (Windsor, Roseman, Gartseff, and Kirk 1981). Although it was hospital policy to assess each patient on admission, only 394 of 996 patients (39%) had a baseline assessment on file.

These 394 forms were reviewed to determine the quality of the assessments performed. A major problem identified, beyond nonperformance of the assessment, was ≥80% data incompleteness. From the standpoint of assessing educational needs, preparing an education prescription, or evaluating program effectiveness, data abstracted from the forms for this period were of no value. Serious questions about the quality, validity, and reliability of the data collected were apparent. Findings of this type are not uncommon in health care and public health settings.

Health promotion programs will improve their recording systems by developing a monitoring mechanism to meet staff and evaluation needs. It should be compatible with data processing or allow data to be aggregated by hand for quick periodic assessment, for example, monthly or per session. A record-keeping system is the only mechanism by which program evaluators can confirm how many of which demographic groups of clients were served. It is an essential process evaluation element.

Clinical or physiological measures   Clinical or physiological measures may be collected by a health promotion program. In some cases, the physiological measure is the primary outcome measure, e.g., a blood pressure reading to determine the effectiveness of a program. In other cases, physiological data may validate self-reported measures, e.g., urine or serum cotinine levels to validate smoking cessation during pregnancy. In some studies, physiological variables represent the subject's health status or disease risk, which may be affected by habitual behaviors. Examples include serum cholesterol, which may be affected by diet and exercise and is predictive of atherosclerosis, or a submaximal stress test, which measures physical fitness and should be affected by aerobic activity. The attraction of physiological measures is that they are not obtrusive in the many senses that behavioral measures are: It is not obvious to subjects that they are being observed, and the measures are reactive only to the extent that they encourage people to perform the desired behaviors when they are aware of the values. Despite the aura of complete objectivity of these "hard data" measures, they are subject to as many but different sources of error as the "soft data."

For example, physiological indicators are often subject to daily, weekly, and other cycles in values. Recent studies of blood pressure, using continuous- or frequent-monitoring instruments, show marked variations between waking and sleeping hours, between mornings and evenings, between conversation times and times alone. Blood pressure readings taken in an office or clinic are roughly 10 mm Hg higher than those taken in the home. Blood pressures rise and fall in response to the person's emotional or arousal state. Thus, systematic bias may occur in a study from simply taking a blood pressure measurement at different times in the day or in different settings. Because of minute-to-minute variability, resting blood pressure readings should be taken three or four times over successive minutes to obtain reliable estimates of resting blood pressure.

Although physiological measures seem simple and straightforward to make, detailed protocols have been developed for obtaining them, including:

- Extended training procedures even for well-credentialed individuals
- Specifications of the environmental conditions in which the measure is taken
- Specification of the state of the subject, e.g., an individual who has fasted for 12 hours before a blood sample for serum cholesterol analysis is taken
- Procedures for handling the specimen, if one was taken
- Identification of the specific machine and how it should be operated, periodically tested, and adjusted
- Procedures for ongoing quality control of all elements of the data-collection process

A primary difference between physiological measures and the behavioral and self-report measures is that the many sources of error in physiological measures are often known and more amenable to control if highly structured procedures are compulsively employed.

Human and other errors can occur at every stage in taking physiological measurements. Medication adherence provides an instructive example. Having enough medication flowing in a person's circulatory system to be effective to combat a disease (a therapeutic plasma concentrate) requires prescription of an adequate amount of medication for the size of the person, consumption of all the medication prescribed (patient adherence), and action by the body to make the medication available in the bloodstream as expected (bioavailability). Biron argued (1975) that most physicians do not know enough about pharmacotherapy to prescribe amounts that promote therapeutic bioavailability. There may also be adherence problems, for many reasons. There is high person-to-person variability in how the body absorbs, metabolizes, and stores the same medication (Alvares et al. 1979). With regard to bioavailability, a pharmaceutical company can make the same product within a relatively wide band of variation, some of which promote bioavailability of the product, while others retard it. These are all potential sources of error prior to taking a blood sample to test for bioavailability of the drug. Plasma concentrations at less than a therapeutic level may therefore be due to factors other than patient adherence.

An important source of error that has come to light from doing multicenter studies is interlaboratory variability (Laboratory Standardization Panel 1990; McShane et al. 1991). The most common procedure for handling this source of error variability is for a central quality control center to prepare several compounds with known, systematically controlled levels of the chemical of interest and to send samples of the compound to the participating laboratories. Based on the values obtained at each laboratory in comparison with the known values for each controlled compound, an adjustment value can be given to calibrate values obtained by the machine and procedures at each laboratory. This calibration must be done periodically to control laboratory drift (similar to observer drift).

A variety of other errors can occur. The needle for taking a blood sample from a child may be too narrow, destroying red blood cells and contaminating the serum sample. The blood sample may be collected in an inappropriate test tube, leading to coagulation and destroying the sample for a particular analysis. A fluid sample may evaporate. The centrifuge for separating red blood cells from serum may not be functioning properly. These and a host of other errors should disabuse program evaluation staff of blind faith in the value of physiological measures.

Steps in using physiological measures   The list of problems in implementing a physiological measure should not discourage program staff from selecting such a measure when it is appropriate. First, consult medical and other clinical specialists (such as a clinical pharmacist) on the appropriateness of a particular measure. The measure should clearly validate some behavioral measure, be the primary outcome of concern, or be a health or risk indicator of primary concern. Second, select (or develop) a protocol to monitor *all* phases of physiological data collection and processing. Almost all physiological measures that an evaluator may want to use have been used in other studies. The protocol that best meets the need of the evaluative study should be employed. Third, continually monitor data collection and processing for reliability to ensure that the same high-quality data are obtained throughout the project. Define a set of quality control procedures. It should be clear from this discussion that collecting physiological variables can be a very expensive process, not including the substantial costs for conducting the laboratory tests.

TOTAL QUALITY CONTROL OF DATA COLLECTION

Cummings (1992) identified four principles of quality control:

1. The quality of data collected is higher with more consistency in the development and implementation of procedures for collecting it.
2. Continuous monitoring of data collection provides an understanding of the process of data collection, points and times of failure, and opportunities to improve it.

TABLE 3.11   Steps in Quality Control of Data Collection

1. Select the instrument most appropriate to the particular need and targeted population; only in rare circumstances create your own instrument.

2. Pretest the instrument with a subsample of the target population; for self-report data, test for understanding of items, difficulty of recall-report, offensiveness of items, and other sources of difficulty (e.g., interviewer embarrassment).

3. Select data collectors with prerequisite skills.

4. Train data collectors in specific procedures to some preset level of reliability; use modeling, role playing, "fishbowl," double interviewing, and reliability testing with feedback throughout the training.

5. If a new instrument has been developed or an old instrument has been modified:
    a. identify a representative sample of the target population;
    b. collect data under circumstances as if in major study;
    c. re-collect same data within 1–4 weeks (to assess test-retest reliability);
    d. collect other variables with which the target variables should be related (to assess construct validity);
    e. estimate reliability and validity from collected data.
    If reliability and validity are unacceptable (e.g., less than $r = 0.80$ reliability), revise the instrument and reconduct the reliability and validity study; and
    If reliability and validity are acceptably high, find a way to abbreviate data collection to reduce participant burden yet collect acceptable quality data.

6. If using a validated instrument, devise an environment for optimal data collection and continuously monitor consistency (e.g., on a 10% subsample), including assessing interobserver or test-retest reliability, checking consistency daily, and retraining data collectors if reliability falls below a preset level.

7. Assess coding or transcription reliability.

8. Once data are fully collected, estimate reliability and validity of the data collected and include them in the report.

3. Reliable methods function well, even in difficult circumstances; use the most reliable methods appropriate to a study's purposes.

4. Provide evaluation data whose average quality is equal to that expected by those authorizing the evaluation and which meet scientific standards.

Consistent with these quality control guidelines, Table 3.11 gives the general procedures for total quality control of evaluation data collection.

SUMMARY

All methods are susceptible to various threats to reliability and validity. The issues in selecting and developing data collection methods are complex. Although many of these sources of error can be overcome, they are overcome at a cost. The responsibility of the evaluator is to select and develop the most reliable and valid methods and instruments appropriate to the issues at hand, within the funding and other resources available.

A common distinction is made between obtrusive and unobtrusive measurement techniques. Unobtrusive measures are often desired, because reactive bias is less likely to appear in these data. Under certain circumstances, however, even the measures that seem most unobtrusive can become obtrusive. Furthermore, unobtrusive measures are not always appropriate for collecting the type of information needed in a particular evaluation. The evaluator must be sensitive to bias issues in every evaluation conducted and must select and employ the most appropriate measurement methods.

Many skills are involved at each stage in selecting and developing methods and instruments. The novice evaluator should not become intimidated or discouraged. Despite the collective skills and intelligence of teams of evaluators, anticipated and unanticipated problems occur in the best of evaluative studies. No evaluative (or other) study has been perfect. Novice evaluators should, instead, have a realistic respect for the problems likely to be encountered, build their skills to the maximum level possible, and involve consultants knowledgeable in the particular type of evaluation contemplated. The best way to learn these skills is to participate in the selection and development of methods under the supervision of others already skilled in these tasks. Evaluators should seek professionals conducting program evaluations and volunteer or otherwise participate in these activities to build their skills.

4 | Process Evaluation

The primary objective of a process evaluation is to document what a health promotion program has provided to a client, patient, employee, student, or consumer and how well it was provided. The principle used to describe successful implementation is "fidelity." This type of evaluation assesses how changes are produced rather than assessing significant cognitive, skill, or behavioral impacts. A process evaluation (1) defines structure, process, and content to be delivered, (2) documents the delivery of each of the procedures, (3) conducts observational assessments and analyses of program sessions, and (4) monitors program-staff effort or activity. It provides routine (daily, weekly, monthly, quarterly, or annual), empirical feedback for individual staff and sites of what is being implemented.

Health promotion specialists have the responsibility of defining the salient structural and process components of a program. In the planning phases program staff should be able to describe:

- What process data and information to collect
- How they are going to be collected
- Who is going to collect them
- When they are going to be collected
- What instruments and observational methods will be used

Delineation of these steps will produce a richer insight about what happens as a program is implemented.

A process evaluation should answer questions about why a program succeeded or failed (efficacy or effectiveness) and document which components need to be revised. It defines components' strengths and weaknesses. It describes what actually happens as a new or existing program is started, implemented, and routinely provided. It applies existing performance standards for each procedure defined in the literature and/or derived by professional consensus through internal or external review. Although the health promotion literature has emphasized the need to conduct a comprehensive process evaluation, limited guidance has been presented about how to conduct one (McGraw et al. 1989; Norman et al. 1990; Windsor et al. 1994; Steckler and Linnan, 2002).

Information from a process evaluation provides important insights about the sequence of events and the interaction and linkage between client and program components. It provides empirical data reflecting the qualitative aspects of these program procedures and methods, including acceptance and participation rates by target groups for a specific setting. Data from these methods place the program manager in a more knowledgeable position to discuss how well the program and its parts are doing and how well the program works. A process evaluation allows a program manager, evaluator, or scientist to say with confidence that a 10% or 20% difference observed between an experimental group and a control group was attributable to the health promotion intervention.

This chapter presents a detailed description of a process evaluation model (PEM) and methods, including its application in several case studies. We also identify normative criteria and procedures—professional or practice performance standards—that a program should apply regularly during planning and implementation. At the end of several sections of the chapter, we define practice standards to guide an assessment of the quality of program and process evaluation components.

We also discuss complementary process evaluation–quality control methods, including:

- External program review
- Session or component observations
- Program component pretesting
- Readability testing
- Content analysis

PROCESS EVALUATION AND QUALITY

Several terms need to be reviewed in a discussion of an HP process evaluation: quality, quality control, and performance standards. *Quality* can be defined as a measure of the level of appropriateness of a set of well-defined (replicable) professional procedures—participant assessment and intervention methods—for a specific health problem. *Quality control* is the application of process evaluation methods to document the delivery and perceived value or worth of a program. A *performance standard* is the specification of a minimum acceptable level of competency set by experts in a specialty area. A standard can also be used to judge the quality of an individual's level of professional practice or to assess the degree of successful implementation of a program's procedures.

A *quality assurance review* (QAR) of a program is a multidimensional process, including documentation of the level of technical competence and professional preparation of the program-service provider, and the application of quality control methods to assess (and to improve, if they are inadequate) critical components of the health promotion practice. The review defines strengths and weaknesses and identifies practical solutions to problems or barriers to program implementation by staff and use of intervention methods by clients.

Two concepts are also frequently mentioned in discussions of program process and quality: efficacy and effectiveness rates. As noted in Chapter 1, *efficacy* is the impact of a program, applied under optimum conditions by specialist providers, to favorably alter the incidence rate of a behavioral risk factor for a defined population at risk. *Effectiveness* is the normal impact of a program, applied under typical practice conditions by regular providers, to favorably alter the incidence rate of a behavioral risk factor for a defined population at risk. *Neither type of impact rate will occur without full implementation of program procedures of high quality—fidelity.*

TYPE III ERROR

A major issue in all process evaluations is the level of implementation success—the degree of program feasibility and fidelity. Basch et al. (1985) have described the failure to implement a health education intervention as a "Type III error." Steckler and Goodman (1989), in an insightful discussion of a Type III error, used the qualitative case study approach to monitor data to complement an impact evaluation. They examined the implementation success of a cancer control program at industrial plants for United Rubber, Cork, Linoleum and Plastic Workers of America. Steckler and Goodman collected two types of process evaluation data, which provided insight about the degree to which a Type III error had occurred. The first were data from in-depth case studies from one intervention plan; the second was the monitoring of training activities and health educational events that occurred at all experimental (E) and comparison (C) industrial sites. Other process evaluation methods were used, including:

- Site visits
- Participant observations
- Interviews with key decision makers
- Record reviews of reports and documents related to program planning and implementation

Four additional types of process-monitoring data were also collected at all industrial study sites: (1) running records, (2) consultation logs, (3) phone logs, and (4) correspondence.

A general plan of how the project was intended to work was examined. This process evaluation example found that the cancer control programs were not used to any great extent by employees at the $\underline{C}$ group plant or by employees at most of the E group plants. Significant change did not occur among plant workers because of inadequate implementation of the planned health education program. The evaluation concluded that a Type III error had occurred.

The following conclusion, however, should not be made about the cancer control program: that its content and structure were inappropriate for this type of industrial site and for these types of workers. A more appropriate inference would be that for this setting and time, salient organizational barriers among and between management and workers prevented the introduction of this type of program. Without this kind of process-qualitative insight, evaluators cannot know why a health promotion program did or did not produce a behavioral impact. With such an empirically based insight, however, evaluators are in a stronger position to attribute observed significant change (if any) to an intervention. In cases where implementation is not successful, a process-qualitative evaluation should provide reasons why.

PROVIDERS' TECHNICAL COMPETENCE

The need to examine program procedures and skill and training levels of personnel who plan and deliver disease management programs has been confirmed by Donabedian (1966) on quality of medical care; Inui (1978) on quality assurance issues in patient education, physician training, and medical care; and Green and Brooks-Bertram (1978) on quality assurance and health education. The connections between structure–process–outcome continue to be an issue in examinations of the quality of health services (Salzer et al. 1997). In commenting on this issue from a legal perspective, Easton et al. (1977) referred to the lack of professional technical competence as "educational malpractice." They asserted that this could be as serious in consequences and in some cases as costly as medical malpractice.

A judgment by graduate-trained health promotion specialists based on existing performance standards is required to evaluate the structure, content, and quality of an HP program and its planning and delivery process. As noted in Chapter 1, there is long-standing historical concern about the need to improve the quality of professional preparation and practice in public health and in health promotion and health education. Provider competence can be assessed through external peer review methods. It requires examining the HP program providers' academic and professional training, program experience, professional performance and products, and current activities and plans in the development, implementation, administration, and evaluation of health promotion and education programs.

A brief synopsis of this topic and the credentialing process for a certified health education specialist (CHES) was noted in Chapter 1. Although codification of the competencies for health promotion and education practice continues to improve, widely disseminated documents confirm that HP professional competencies are well defined. Using the report on current competency from 1999 (see Chapter 1) on professional preparation in health education as a referent, we can examine two dimensions of provider competence here: (1) currency of knowledge and (2) adequacy of technical skill.

While the knowledge and evidence base continues to mature, the literature in health promotion and education and the underlying behavioral and social science–related disciplines offers a body of knowledge about human behavior in sickness or health for most major diseases and behavioral risk factors for most large populations at risk. A "competent" practitioner is knowledgeable about the most up-to-date literature and methods applicable to planning and evaluating HP programs. Accordingly, directors-coordinators of health promotion programs need to know what has been done, what can be done, and how it should be done for specific populations at risk. Knowledge, skill, and experience in conducting and translating meta-evaluations and meta-analyses into program plans are essential. Commonly cited reasons for program failure include:

- Lack of knowledge by program staff of what level of impact is possible or probable
- Lack of academic coursework or field experience in applying program skills
- Ignorance of published work
- Insufficient theoretical grounding about behavior change
- Weak or insufficient technical skill

Competent planners, directors, and program coordinators should be able to provide evidence that programs under their direction reflect high standards of practice and, within the context of available resources, reflect the latest HP evidence base. The level and type of academic training that should produce a professional with these competencies is a master's degree in health promotion, education, or behavior: MPH, MSPH, or MS. As noted in Table 4.1, staff responsible for planning, managing, and evaluating health education and promotion programs should provide documentation of a combination of appropriate baccalaureate and master's degree training and skills to meet these practice standards.

Deficiencies in competency exist in health promotion, in part, because of the very diverse backgrounds of mid- to senior-level staff who direct the planning and administration of health promotion programs; inadequate training in assessing the unique characteristics of a setting, target audience, and health problems; and lack of organizational clarity, direction, and/or resources in offering such

TABLE 4.1   Practice Standards for Health Promotion and Education Specialists

Practice-Performance Standard	Category
1. Interpret data on the distribution of the health problem/ risk factor for a defined population at risk.	Needs assessment
2. Describe, from available evidence and expert opinion, behavioral and nonbehavioral risk factors of a health problem.	Priority setting
3. Synthesize, from a meta-evaluation or meta-analysis, the evidence base for an intervention for a specified risk factor and population at risk to define the degree of potential behavior change.	Definition of objectives
4. Describe, from the scientific evidence and assessment methods, factors associated with the risk factor(s)/ behavior of a population at risk: • Target group: predisposing factors—attitudes, beliefs, skills, etc. • Setting: enabling factors—availability, accessibility, services, cost, etc. • Program-provider: reinforcing factors—staff attitudes, skills, etc.	Definition of contributing factors
5. Synthesize information and data from standards 1–4 into a plan as part of a science–practice partnership.	Definition of intervention and implementation plan
6. Design and evaluate appropriate communication, community organization, and organizational development-training methods to produce changes in the behaviors identified.	Definition of process and impact evaluation
7. Prepare process impact and cost analysis reports of publishable quality.	Preparation of valid evaluation reports
8. Conduct professional activities in an ethical manner, reflecting appreciation for human rights and peer review methods established by organizations that define professional-performance standards.	Application of ethical practices

programs. Employers also do not hold common views about appropriate academic and professional credentials in the recruitment and appointment of health promotion–education program personnel.

CULTURAL AND LINGUISTIC COMPETENCY

As discussed in Chapter 2, understanding the unique characteristics of communities, groups, and individuals at risk is an established principle of HP planning and evaluation. An application of the PRECEDE/PROCEED model requires

---

TABLE 4.2 Office of Minority Health CLAS Standards

1. Ensure clients receive effective, understandable, and respectful care, compatible with cultural dimensions.

2. Implement strategies to recruit, retain, and promote diversity in CLAS representative staff and leadership.

3. Ensure staff receive ongoing education/training.

4. Provide timely language assistance services at no cost to clients with limited English proficiency.

5. Provide to clients, in preferred language, verbal/written notices of the right to receive language services.

6. Ensure the competence of language assistance provided to limited-English-proficient clients by interpreters and bilingual staff. Family and friends should not be used to provide interpretation services (except on request).

7. Make available understandable patient-related materials and post signage in common languages.

8. Implement and promote a written strategic CLAS plan with clear goals, policies, methods, and management accountability mechanisms.

9. Conduct initial ongoing self-assessment of CLAS-related activities and integrate CLAS-related measures into audits, performance improvement programs, satisfaction assessments, and outcomes evaluations.

10. Ensure current data on the clients' race, ethnicity, and spoken/written language as part of information systems.

11. Maintain a community demographic, cultural, and epidemiological profile and a needs assessment.

12. Develop participatory, collaborative partnerships with communities and use formal and informal mechanisms to facilitate community and client involvement to design and implement CLAS-related activities.

13. Ensure CLAS conflict and grievance resolution processes are in place and able to identify, prevent, and resolve conflicts.

14. Encourage regularly informing the public about progress and innovations to implement CLAS standards.

---

that an evaluator's methodological and technical skills be complemented by an appreciation for the diversity of the ethnic groups served by the health promotion programs. Multiple excellent examples of how to systematically plan, implement, and evaluate a health promotion program for ethnically diverse populations is presented in a theme issue of *Health Promotion Practice:* "Eliminating Racial and Ethnic Health Disparities: Mapping a Course for Community Action and Research," K. Roe and S. Thomas, editors (Vol. 3 [2], April 2002).

Numerous resources are available on this topic, but the following represent accessible options: (1) "Cultural Competence for Evaluators" (USDHHS 1992a); (2) "Health Behavior Research in Minority Populations" (USDHHS 1992b). In addition, Policy Brief 3, "Cultural Competence in Primary Health Care: Partnerships for a Research Agenda" (summer 2000) and Policy Brief 2, "Linguistic Competence in Primary Health Care Delivery Systems: Implications for Policy Makers" (January 2001), are two cultural competence–specific publications available from the National Center for Cultural Competence at Georgetown University. Call the office of Minority Health Resource Center at 800-444-6472 for a list of journal articles on cultural competency, or go to http://gucdc.georgetown.edu/nccc/ncccpubs.html.

A set of core CLAS standards is presented in Table 4.2. The standards are organized into three themes: (1) culturally competent care (Standards 1–3), (2) language access services (Standards 4–7), and (3) organizational supports for cultural competence (Standards 8–14) (USDHHS 2001).

A PROCESS EVALUATION MODEL (PEM)

Process evaluation data provide essential empirical insight about what types of client assessment and intervention methods can (and cannot) be routinely delivered for specific settings, behaviors, types of providers, and program participants. Process evaluation methods should be used as standard quality control methods to assess staff provision of client intervention procedures. The PEM also has a very practical function: It provides empirical information about salient structure and operational procedures within and across health promotion programs in different sites and settings.

As noted in Chapter 2, in two meta-evaluations of 31 quasi-experimental and experimental evaluation studies of cessation methods for pregnant smokers, serious process evaluation deficiencies were reported (Windsor et al. 1985, and Windsor et al. 1998). Although space limitations in a publication may restrict a study from providing a complete description of intervention methods, many evaluation studies lacked an adequate description and/or documentation of the delivery of experimental and control group methods. Only 12 of the 31 evaluation studies reviewed adequately described the specific characteristics of core program methods, such as number, type, frequency, and duration of client contacts. Only three reported conducting a process evaluation.

Process evaluation data documenting the level of client exposure to each health education method are critical to coming to a conclusion about the following characteristics of an HP-DP intervention:

- Program fidelity—feasibility
- Efficacy or effectiveness
- Internal validity
- Costs and cost-effectiveness or cost-benefit
- External validity

In a structural assessment of a program, an evaluator examines the resources, personnel, facilities, and equipment for delivering services and asks: Are they adequate? Is the staff delivering the health promotion program qualified? In a process assessment, the ultimate questions are: What procedures were used to develop and implement the program? Are they consistent with normative criteria or performance standards, criteria developed by a consensus of experienced peers in health promotion and education with established professional credentials? A process assessment, using normative performance criteria, is indirectly an examination of provider competence. It provides an examination of the professional activities of the provider using peer group judgment. As in the practice of medicine and nursing, the key issue is: What constitutes good practice (care) for a specific health problem and population? How should a health promotion professional or program intervene to increase client knowledge, beliefs, skills, or behaviors?

The following section provides explicit practice guidelines to program staff about how to systematically evaluate program implementation using (1) a framework to describe client assessment and intervention procedures; (2) a description of the program (site) flow analysis method; (3) a description of the process evaluation model (PEM); and (4) case study examples of the application of the PEM, using data from several different health education projects. It describes a model that can be used to plan and to assess implementation of interventions of well-defined program structures and procedures.

PEM METHODS

Definition of HP Procedures

As discussed in Chapter 2, one of the first planning tasks all HP programs must perform is to describe what assessment and intervention methods clients with specific characteristics are supposed to receive. As noted in Table 4.3, the HP intervention procedures need to be described by specifying the following: (1) *what*, (2) *who*, (3) *when*, (4) *how much*, and (5) the *setting*. Descriptions of these process variables are essential to:

- Standardize methods
- Develop staff training programs
- Recommend specific modifications of methods during pilot testing and at the end of an evaluation study
- Replicate methods by future intervention programs and evaluation studies

Because "normal" health education methods and staff behavior often change because of the presence of an evaluation, documentation of salient program proce-

TABLE 4.3   Specification of HP Core Program Procedures

Process Variable	Program Task
What?	Describe the structure, procedures, and content of the health promotion program, including, e.g., audiovisuals, written materials, telephone or counseling methods.
Who?	Name each member of the staff that provides each health education procedure by degree/title.
When?	Specify the time (estimated or observed) to deliver each procedure at each contact.
How much?	Specify the frequency, duration, and periodicity of each participant contact by the type of method and type of provider.
Setting?	Specify where and how the procedures are delivered, e.g., group, one-to-one format, video, interactive computer.

dures at each client contact is essential *before* and *during* an evaluation study. These principles and methods apply to HP programs in school, community, or work site–based programs.

Table 4.4 presents an example of core patient education procedures for pregnant smokers in a maternity care program. It identifies staff that would provide the procedures, methods and materials, and time and cost involved for each procedure. This example should help HP project staff prepare descriptions of their client procedures, personnel methods, and materials and estimate time for each client contact. As noted in Table 4.4, this model defines what methods are supposed to be provided by whom at each visit. It is also an excellent method for documenting labor and nonlabor costs of an intervention. Each intervention program needs to provide descriptions of its core practice procedures.

Program (Site) Flow Analysis

After describing the core intervention procedures to be provided to clients at each site, programs must define how, when, and who would deliver the new methods. Program (site–staff–client) flow analysis (PFA) is an excellent method to be applied when a program is considering the introduction of new client assessment or counseling methods into program settings—services such as improving blood pressure control, smoking cessation, or increasing exercise. PFA documents exposure to specific services and staff at each client contact, from start to end of contact. It examines the average client time by type of contact, time to receive specific services, and proportion of time in contact and not in contact with each type of staff. It also helps site or program managers and staff document who can deliver what kinds of services and procedures to whom. It can be used

TABLE 4.4 Patient Education Procedures for Pregnant Smokers

Procedure	Staff	Methods and Materials	Time	Cost
First Visit: Obstetric, Pediatric				
I. Patient assessment procedure			5 min	?
A. Smoking status	RN or SW	Screening form (self-report)		
B. Collection of fluid	RN or SW	Vials, cotton rolls, saliva		
C. Psychosocial assessment	RN or SW	Baseline form		
II. Patient education procedure			10 min	?
A. Component 1	RN or SW	*A Pregnant Woman's Guide to Quit Smoking*		
B. Component 2	RN or SW	Patient counseling (patient education prescription form)		
Second Visit				
III. Patient assessment procedure 2	RN or SW	Self-report	1 min	?
IV. Patient education procedure 2	RN or SW	Chart reminder form	1 min	
Third Visit				
V. Patient assessment procedure 3	RN or SW	Self-report	1 min	?
VI. Patient education procedure 3	RN or SW	Staff reinforcement (chart reminder form)	1 min	
Fourth visit				
VII. Patient assessment procedure 4	RN	Self-report and vials, cotton rolls, saliva	1 min	?

RN = nurse; SW = social worker

to confirm the amount of time of services to estimate the cost for each program participant with each type of provider.

A sample of 5 to 10 HP program participants at each site where the new methods are being considered for adoption is needed to document the specific time (in minutes) a participant spends with each provider and the type of services received. A discussion of the program flow analysis methodology, developed by the CDC, is available (USDHHS, *Patient Flow Analysis: Data Collection Manual*, Rockville, Maryland: Centers for Disease Control and Prevention, National Center for Chronic Disease Prevention and Health Promotion, Clinical Management Unit, 1993).

PFA and Organizational Development

The introduction of any new set of procedures into a patient care, work site, or school system requires policy, management, and practice support. PFA should be a collaborative process between program staff and managers who deliver and plan services and staff who are responsible for evaluation. Without participation of all staff from each practice setting or site, it is very unlikely that a site flow analysis will be conducted and/or that its results will be useful or used by staff to plan how to integrate the new methods into that setting. A PFA study should start with a careful examination of the current program, policy, structure, process, and content to determine what will be delivered, where, and by whom. This method helps to identify normal patterns to gain insight about possible adjustments to those patterns to maximize the opportunity for routine delivery of new procedures.

Evaluation program staff should review their intervention program with managers and regular staff to determine how best to integrate new methods. Case Study 4.1 is an example of the application of the PEM to the Phase I and Phase II National Smoke Free Families Program (SFFP), supported by the Robert Wood Johnson Foundation (RWJF) and implemented from 1994 to 2004. It was applied to funded RWJF Phase I projects, eight in ob/gyn settings and three in pediatric care settings.

CASE STUDY 4.1

Process Evaluation

SFF PROCESS EVALUATION MODEL

Under the SFFP-PEM guidelines, each RWJF-SFF grantee had the responsibility of defining and implementing a set of new clinical procedures. As noted in Table 4.3, one

Source: R. Windsor, P. Whiteside, L. Solomon, et al., "A Process Evaluation Model for Patient Education Programs for Pregnant Smokers," *Tobacco Control* 9, suppl. III (2000): iii20–iii35.

of the first steps in the preparation of a process evaluation plan is to require each program to define its essential new patient assessment and intervention methods for each visit or patient-staff contact.

In a process assessment of a patient education program for pregnant smokers, the primary questions are as follows:

- What procedures should a trained professional provide to a pregnant smoker at her first visit and at follow-up visits?
- What is excellent clinical practice for this specific behavioral risk factor and defined patient population?
- Were the new procedures based on normative criteria (evidence) developed by a consensus of experts?
- Did staff participate in the development of the implementation plan?
- Did staff perform and/or provide the procedures to patients as planned at each OB visit?

Identification of the number of patients screened each week and recruitment of those who smoked—procedure 1—was the first task for all projects. Baseline data on patients screened, patients recruited, and patients who refused to participate documented the daily, weekly, monthly, and annual patient census for each project by site. Among each eligible cohort of 100 patients who smoke (A), a number of patients were recruited at each site (B). This method produces information to compute an exposure rate for each procedure ($B/A = C$). As noted in Table 4.5, at the first visit each SFF study typically planned a smoking status and psychosocial assessment of patients—procedures 2 and 3. Patients in this example were scheduled to receive each of the next seven procedures at future visits. Intervention patients would also receive procedures 7, 8, 9, and 10.

A performance practice standard (D) based on clinical practice guidelines defined the expected level of patient exposure to a procedure. The National Program Office (NPO) used 100% as an absolute performance standard (D) for each procedure. An implementation index (E) for each procedure was derived by dividing the exposure rate (C) by the practice performance standard (D). In this example, where the practice performance standard (D) is 100%, the implementation index (E) and exposure rate (C) are equal. A performance standard of 0.95 for an ongoing program would be an excellent level of implementation. A composite of all implementation indexes (ΣE) provides a summary indicator of the successful delivery of a patient assessment and education program: program implementation index (PII). A total PII ≥ 0.90 indicates an excellent level of implementation success.

APPLICATION OF THE PEM

Illustrative data for the 10 clinical practice procedures for the intervention group patients are presented in Table 4.5. These hypothetical data indicated that the project needs to increase patient exposure to procedures 6, 7, 8, 9, and 10.

Each SFF grantee had the responsibility of applying the PEM to patients at all sites to produce implementation data for its procedures. Implementation success, study progress, and problems using monthly, quarterly, and annual data reports for each procedure were to be reported to a project coordinator by the 10th of each month for all eligible patients and all procedures. A staff training plan can be prepared to improve a specific exposure rate (C) or implementation index (E) when problems are documented, for example, when a rate or index falls $\leq 90\%$.

TABLE 4.5   Process Evaluation Example

Patient Clinical Procedures (P)	Eligible Patients (A)	Exposed Patients (B)	Exposure Rate (B/A) (C)	Performance Standard (D)	Implementation Index (C/D) (E)
1. Smokers screened (S_1)	100	90	90%	100%	0.90
2. Baseline form (O_{1A})	100	100	100%	100%	1.00
3. Baseline cotinine (O_{1B})	100	100	100%	100%	1.00
4. Experimental group (X_1)	100	100	100%	100%	1.00
5. Experimental group (X_2)	100	95	95%	100%	0.95
6. Experimental group (X_3)	100	95	95%	100%	0.95
7. Follow-up O_{2A}	100	85	85%	95%	0.90
8. Follow-up O_{2B}	100	85	85%	95%	0.90
9. Follow up O_{3A}	100	80	80%	95%	0.84
10. Follow-up O_{3B}	100	80	80%	95%	0.84

Program implementation index:

$$\Sigma E/P_n = \frac{(0.90 + 1.00 + 1.00 + 1.00 + 0.95 + 0.95 + 0.90 + 0.90 + 0.84 + 0.84)}{10} = 0.928 - 1 = PII$$

P = procedure; X = intervention group–component; O = patient observation–smoking status

The following discussion is a synthesis of one study (#3) in the *Tobacco Control* article. Data and the PII in Table 4.6 are excerpted from the article. This pilot study involved 42 patients who smoked. After patients had undergone a telephone screening for inclusion in this study (Table 4.6), each was asked to set a quit date within the next two weeks and was mailed treatment materials (procedures 1, 2, 3). Women in the experimental group (usual care plus video) received the calendar, tip guide, and the six-video program: procedures 4 to 9. All follow-ups were conducted by telephone. Major patient assessments were conducted 2–3 days after the quit date, 4–5 weeks after the quit date, and 1 month postpartum (procedures 10, 11, 12). Measures of abstinence, negative affect, coping stress, and self-efficacy were obtained by phone interviews only. No counseling was provided during any of the phone follow-up visits.

RESULTS

The most significant difficulties encountered in this Pilot Study #3 were patient recruitment and patient retention. As noted, poor patient adherence was a major issue in this study. Although videos might appear useful as a minimal intervention, the lack of personal contact probably contributed to very poor compliance. It was hypothesized that it would be more convenient to keep a "video viewing" appointment in one's home, in contrast to keeping a clinic appointment with a cessation counselor. The freedom to watch a video at any time, however, also created an opportunity for significant distraction by the activities of daily living. Multiple factors, e.g., poor commitment and high nicotine dependence, may have contributed significantly to the overall poor adherence to the patient education procedures. The value of this pilot data in planning a

TABLE 4.6 Experimental Group Process Evaluation

Patient Clinical Procedures (P)	Eligible Patients (A)	Exposed Patients (B)	Exposure Rate (B/A) (C)	Performance Standard (D)	Implementation Index (C/D) (E)
1. Baseline assessment: psychosocial	42	42	100%	100%	1.00
2. Saliva collection*	42	26	62%	100%	0.62
3. Patient education	42	42	100%	100%	1.00
4. Video 1	42	31	74%	100%	0.74
5. Video 2	42	26	62%	100%	0.62
6. Video 3	42	22	52%	100%	0.52
7. Video 4	42	13	31%	100%	0.31
8. Video 5	42	6	14%	100%	0.14
9. Video 6	42	8	19%	100%	0.19
10. Follow-up 1: psychosocial	42	31	74%	100%	0.74
11. Follow-up 2: psychosocial	42	27	64%	100%	0.64
12. Postpartum follow-up: psychosocial	42	21	50%	100%	0.50

$$PII = \frac{(1.00 + 0.62 + 1.00 + 0.74 + 0.62 + 0.52 + 0.31 + 0.14 + 0.19 + 0.74 + 0.64 + 0.50)}{12} = 0.58$$

*Follow-up saliva samples requested only from women who reported abstinence during interviews.

future patient education program using six videos is self-evident: It confirmed the need for significantly revising the number and content of intervention procedures.

DISCUSSION

As documented in the examples, the primary value of the PEM is that it can and does provide data for regular site and procedure progress reviews. PEM data can be used to identify specific implementation problems by site and specific staff. Focus group methods with patients or staff training can also be performed to eliminate or significantly reduce barriers to routine delivery and/or use by patients. In the pilot study of 42 patients, for example, six videos for patients were created. The process data confirmed almost no use of the videos beyond video 3 or video 4. These data, combined with patient feedback, point to a reduction in the number of videos.

SUMMARY

The routine application of the PEM documents the degree to which the clinical staff had implemented all procedures as planned. The PEM provided empirical insight about the feasibility of routine delivery and the replicability of procedures at multiple comparable settings. It is also the primary method used to prepare a cost analysis of both new and existing health education programs. Future studies should apply the PEM in program planning and evaluation. Two additional process evaluation cases are presented to illustrate the utility of the PEM.

PRACTICE STANDARD

Health promotion programs should prepare a process evaluation model to provide documentation of the proportion of eligible participants served, the extent of participation of each client, and the program completion rate. A program implementation index (PII) should be reported for all health promotion programs.

CASE STUDY 4.2

Process Evaluation

This case study is based on the Eat Well, Live Well Nutrition Program. It represents a partnership between university faculty and a social service agency with extensive history in working with and providing services to African American communities in a large midwestern city. It is an excellent example of translating public health science into public health practice.

The primary objective of this nutrition program was to reduce cardiovascular-related risks, primarily through diet and weight control. The community-based, peer-delivered nutrition program was designed to promote dietary change among low-income African American women by "activation." As discussed in the source article, an activation approach emphasizes risk awareness, self-efficacy, and skill training through active learning exercises in the community.

The directors of the Eat Well, Live Well Nutrition Program recognized that a major weakness in community-based health promotion programs was the lack of attention to evaluating the delivery of the program with fidelity: process evaluation. They acknowledged that often much effort is placed on evaluating impact and not process. As they noted, "the critical product from process evaluation is a clear, descriptive picture of the quality of the program and what is going on as it is being implemented." Early detection of implementation problems provides opportunities for program staff to make adjustments. The impact evaluation results were presented in *Research in Social Work Practice, 2000*.

African American women who agreed to participate in the Eat Well, Live Well Nutrition Program were randomly assigned to either an experimental (E) condition ($n = 154$) or a control (C) group ($n = 148$). The program was delivered by peer educators in

---

Source: J. Williams, G. Belle, C. Houston, et al., "Process Evaluation Methods of a Peer-Delivered Health Promotion Program for African American Women," *Health Promotion Practice* 2, no. 2 (2001) 135–142.

3-month intervals to approximately 80 individuals in each condition. The program was administered in 12 sessions; peer educators led 6 group sessions that included 4–6 participants and 6 individual sessions. The following 6 group sessions were introduced over the course of the intervention:

1. Rate your plate
2. Label reading
3. Comparison shopping
4. Recipe modification
5. Eating out
6. Coping with high-risk situations

PEER TRAINING

African American women from the community were trained as peer educators to deliver the nutrition program that was designed to reduce high-fat dietary patterns among obese women at risk for developing non-insulin-dependent diabetes mellitus (NIDDM). They were recruited to serve as peer educators based on their leadership and communication skills and their ability to make their own dietary changes. The peer educators had four responsibilities: (1) to collaborate with the academic team; (2) to deliver components of the program to the target audience; (3) to work with the health promotion team to modify the program as needed to meet community needs; and (4) to participate in the process evaluation of the program.

The training program was designed to be delivered by the peer educators to improve their knowledge, dietary change strategies, basic nutrition, and teaching methods. It consisted of 4-hour sessions delivered 3 days a week for 16 weeks, for a total of 192 hours. This included 48 hours of nutrition-specific training, 48 hours of communication and group-facilitation training and problem-solving skills training, and 24 hours of administrative training. Peer educators were provided with weekly supervision during the program implementation phase of 1-hour meetings.

PROCESS EVALUATION

A detailed checklist and rating procedures were developed. The checklist was used as a guide by the peer educators in conducting each of the 12 sessions. A total of 144 sessions over four cohorts, 36 sessions per cohort, were delivered. For each cohort, 12 of the 36 sessions were randomly selected; 33% of the 144 sessions were audiotaped. Sessions typically lasted 45–90 minutes. Two outside raters independently performed a rating of the "comprehensiveness" of the content delivered; kappa (k) statistics were used to assess the percentage of content delivered. A registered dietitian conducted a third review to assess the accuracy of the nutrition content delivered.

RESULTS

This process evaluation had two primary objectives: (1) to document the comprehensiveness of the content delivered; and (2) to document the accuracy of the nutrition information delivered. Data in Tables 4.7a, 4.7b, and 4.7c are a synthesis and restructuring of the data presented in the tables in the original article.

TABLE 4.7a   Comprehensiveness of Program Items Delivered per Session

Session	Comprehensiveness (%)	Performance Standard (%)	Implementation Index
1	88.0	95	0.93
2	81.1	95	0.85
3	93.0	95	0.98
4	90.5	95	0.95
5	96.8	95	1.02
6	90.3	95	0.95
7	97.1	95	1.02
8	95.6	95	1.00
9	93.1	95	0.98
10	87.4	95	0.92
11	94.3	95	0.99
12	95.2	95	1.00
Total	91.4	95	0.96

$$PII = \frac{0.93 + 0.85 + 0.98 + 0.95 + 1.02 + 0.95 + 1.02 + 1.00 + 0.98 + 0.92 + 0.99 + 1.00}{12} = 0.97$$

TABLE 4.7b   Accuracy of Program Items Delivered per Session

Session	Accuracy (%)	Performance Standard (%)	Implementation Index
1	81.0	95	0.85
2	88.0	95	0.93
3	74.9	95	0.79
4	93.1	95	0.98
5	96.7	95	1.02
6	84.8	95	0.89
7	93.8	95	1.04
8	87.2	95	0.99
9	81.5	95	0.92
10	87.4	95	0.92
11	97.3	95	1.02
12	96.8	95	1.02
Total	88.5	95	0.93

$$PII = \frac{0.85 + 0.93 + 0.79 + 0.98 + 1.02 + 0.89 + 1.04 + 0.99 + 0.92 + 0.92 + 1.02 + 1.02}{12} = 0.95$$

TABLE 4.7c   Comprehensiveness and Accuracy of Program Items by Peer Educator

Peer Educator	Comprehensiveness (%)	Performance Standard (%)	Implementation Index	Accuracy (%)	Performance Standard (%)	Implementation Index
A	95.4	95	1.00	92.9	95	0.98
B	88.4	95	0.93	83.4	95	0.88
C	89.4	95	0.94	85.1	95	0.89

$$PIT = \frac{1.00 + 0.93 + 0.94 + 0.98 + 0.88 + 0.89}{6} = 0.95$$

Source: Tables 4.7a, 4.7b, 4.7c from Williams, J. H., Belle, G. A., Houston, C., Haire-Joshu, D., and Auslander, W. 2001. Process evaluation methods of a peer-delivered health promotion program for African American women. *Health Promotion Practice* 2(2): 135–142. Copyright © 2001 by the Society for Public Health Education. Reprinted by permission of Sage Publications, Inc.

DISCUSSION

This process evaluation case study provides an excellent example of how to gain explicit insight about the implementation of a community-based program. As discussed in the source article, the evaluators indicated that this process evaluation was an excellent method of monitoring the delivery of services and documenting accountability to agencies funding such projects. They noted:

> Studying the implementation of a program can also help planners learn how to modify programs and policies to improve their effectiveness. This article reaffirms from an evaluation perspective, that a process evaluation is necessary to insure that a Type III error does not occur: We did not make conclusions about the program's effectiveness, until we evaluated the extent to which the program was delivered.

The authors obviously perceived that this type of process evaluation was an integral part of an overall evaluation plan. Process, impact, and outcome are defined and implemented.

CASE STUDY 4.3

Process Evaluation

This case study was excerpted from a process evaluation of the Child and Adolescent Trial for Cardiovascular Health (CATCH). The objective of this paper was to demonstrate the importance of process evaluations to identify what actually occurred during program implementation. What program elements were implemented, to what extent, and how would these contribute to the outcome? This article presents an assessment of the curriculum component of the CATCH intervention based on the conceptual

Source: S. McGraw, D. Sellers, E. Stone, et al., "Using Process Data to Explain Outcomes: An Illustration from the Child and Adolescent Trial for Cardiovascular Health (CATCH)," *Evaluation Review* 20, no. 3 (1996): 291–312.

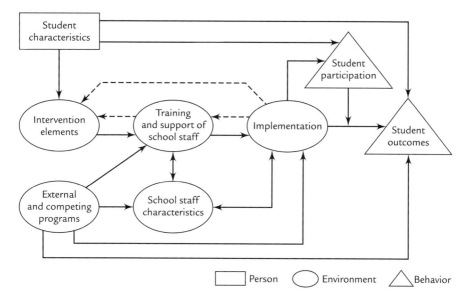

FIGURE 4.1   Conceptual Model for Process Evaluation of the Child and Adolescent Trial for Cardiovascular Health (CATCH) *Source:* McGraw et al. (1994).

framework in Figure 4.1. It is a good example of theory-based evaluation, discussed in Chapters 2 and 3.

This was a collaborative field trial funded by NIH, delivered at four study centers and at 96 schools. Its purposes were to determine the extent of the relationships between teacher characteristics, to measure the degree of curriculum implementation and competing influences, and to document student outcomes. There were 56 experimental (E) group schools and 40 control (C) group schools. A description of the process evaluation methods was presented in Edmundson et al. (1994).

As indicated in Figure 4.1, using a theory-based approach, the authors hypothesized that "process evaluation data can be useful for understanding how a program operated and might help explain outcomes." The CATCH trial was designed to assess the effectiveness of a food-service program, physical education, classroom curricula, and family activities to reduce cardiovascular disease risk factors. The classroom program components consisted of behavioral modeling, skills training, and goal setting. Each of these components focused on identifying and practicing lifestyle behaviors that would reduce cardiovascular disease risk factors.

PROCESS EVALUATION

The CATCH trial used two measures to determine the extent of implementation of the classroom components: (1) *dose,* the percentage of classroom activities (discussion topics, workbook pages, demonstrations) completed during a session; and (2) *fidelity,* the percentage of observed sessions modified. Three process measures were used: (1) *competing or confounding factors,* e.g., non-CATCH classroom education, special campaigns, clubs, school assemblies that were reported on the School Health Questionnaire; (2) CATCH *promotional activities* sponsored by the food-service staff; and (3) number of *support visits* made by CATCH staff during a 1-year period.

TABLE 4.8   Unadjusted Means of Implementation Measures

Activity	California	Louisiana	Minnesota	Texas	Total
Percentages of activities completed					
Grade 3	89%	75%	87%	79%	84%
Grade 4	78%	80%	88%	80%	80%
Grade 5	83%	81%	85%	83%	83%
Percentages of modified curriculum					
Grade 4	25%	11%	8%	5%	15%
Grade 5	9%	17%	0%	10%	9%
Number of competing events	17.2	14.6	16.5	20.0	17.2
Number of promotional activities	13.9	6.1	7.0	12.5	10.7
Number of visits					
Grade 4	19.70	14.89	2.50	11.03	13.21
Grade 5	6.46	13.07	3.79	4.78	7.19
	$n = 421$	$n = 195$	$n = 225$	$n = 230$	$n = 1,071$

Source: Excerpted from Table 2, McGraw et al. (1996). Copyright © 1996 by Sage Publications. Reprinted by permission of Sage Publications, Inc.

RESULTS

Program implementation had a direct effect on student outcomes and was not affected by teacher characteristics. The program implementation fidelity measure resulted in positive changes in self-efficacy and knowledge among students, indicating that CATCH sessions modified by teachers were more effective. This may indicate that teachers modified the curricula to better meet the needs and interests of the students, or that these teachers were more motivated, had stronger teaching skills, and so forth.

The E group showed a significant increase in dietary knowledge and motivation compared to the C group. The authors note that increases in self-efficacy were seen more from grades 3 to 4, when teachers modified the activities, but not from grades 4 to 5, which correlated with the decrease in curricula modifications from grades 4 to 5. The relationship of observed sessions increased the extent of each curriculum component implemented, which resulted in increased self-efficacy of the students.

As reported in Table 4.8, the number of activities completed was highest during grade 3 and lowest during grade 4. Competing events over the four sites during the 3-year trial period ranged from 14.6 to 20.0. Promotional activities conducted by food service averaged between 6.1 to 13.9. The number of support visits varied greatly during grade 4, 2.5 to 19.7, which may have contributed to the number and the extent of activities completed, and may be an indication of support from site staff.

The implementation measures dose and fidelity were reported as important in measuring the impact of the intervention. Intervention trials should not assume that program components will be implemented according to a standardized protocol; they may be modified during implementation to meet the specific needs and circumstances of the site/population. When planning and designing a program process evaluation, it is essential to take into account the modifications that may occur. These modifications will contribute to study results and outcomes.

SUMMARY

The CATCH study identified three implications for process evaluation as a part of intervention research:

1. It supported the importance of dose and fidelity as implementation measures.
2. It delineated and applied process model data and analysis in relation to study impact.
3. It promoted full implementation of all elements of an intervention.

Future process evaluation analyses need to link procedures explicitly to impact: How much of the impact is associated with exposure to the core HP program components? Through these empirical assessments, future HP programs and Phase 1 to Phase 2 evaluation research should be better able to tailor interventions to populations at risk.

QUALITY CONTROL METHODS

In addition to the process evaluation model presented, practitioners also need to be able to conduct assessments of specific health promotion program components in a systematic and technically acceptable fashion. Project staff can use a number of techniques to gain insight into how well each part of a program is being implemented, how well it is being accepted by a target client group, and what adjustments in methods and procedures might be made. One quality control technique is not necessarily superior to another. Each is useful in program planning and implementing. Each serves a specific purpose and provides unique information about the structure, content, and process of an ongoing program. All require allocations of resources: staff and time. Because of this, selecting the most appropriate and feasible methods for a specific program is important.

A combination of quality control methods is recommended to conduct a review of program components during implementation:

- Expert panel review
- Program utilization and record review
- Community and participant surveys
- Program/session observation
- Component pretesting
- Readability testing
- Content analysis

External Program Review

The importance of reviewing an evaluation plan during the early stages of preparation cannot be overstressed. An external program review (EPR) is an efficient way to assess the overall quality of a program. It assumes that a written program plan exists: structure, objectives, methods, activities, procedures, and tasks are described in detail. The plan defines the target group, staff, time, place, and resources. An EPR will help to determine if staff have followed a systematic process to plan and implement a program. The EPR examines major components, activities, materials, and procedures during program implementation, comparing documentation with a set of standards, using professional ratings. Common standards that can be used by program staff and expert panels are listed in Table 4.9. The panel reviews materials and discusses and rates each salient program component of a written implementation plan. Key questions are: Were each of these activities performed? Were they performed in a timely manner? Evidence from written documents and discussions can be gathered by panel members individually and as a group from the staff. In addition to ratings, the panel can provide comments on the degree of adequacy observed and suggest program revisions. This information gives the program staff an overall qualitative judgment of the structure and process of the ongoing program. The EPR should be a collaborative activity with staff and external reviewers. It should provide practical suggestions as part of a formative evaluation for immediate program improvement.

As noted in Table 4.9, the total program and individual components can be reviewed—for example, the implementation plan, evaluation design, data-collection procedures, mass-media components, instruments, or methods and content of the intervention. An EPR is particularly useful during planning and early stages of implementation. A review by experienced consultants, once in the first 6 months and again each year for a project, should provide sufficient independent insight into program progress. Practically speaking, it is important to have a small review panel. Two experts from the local area or state can be asked to visit the site and examine the HP program. Although EPR panel members must have experience with the health problem or risk factors the program is addressing, they need not be national leaders in health promotion. The EPR should not be a burden to participants and program staff, particularly if the staff is small.

PRACTICE STANDARD

Health promotion–education programs should document performance of an EPR during the first 6 months of operation and at least once a year thereafter.

TABLE 4.9 Program Standards for an EPR	
Standard	Rating
1. Documentation of the target population by number, characteristics, and proportion reached.	1 2 3 4 5 6 7 8 9 10
2. Consultation with state and local agencies and experts using data, literature, resources, and staff experience.	1 2 3 4 5 6 7 8 9 10
3. Documentation of a meta-evaluation or meta-analysis for the population at risk during intervention planning.	1 2 3 4 5 6 7 8 9 10
4. Program planning and revision reflects staff/client input.	1 2 3 4 5 6 7 8 9 10
5. Planning and written program objectives and behavioral-educational intervention content and methods, based on empirical needs assessment of knowledge, attitudes, and practices of target groups.	1 2 3 4 5 6 7 8 9 10
6. Staff tasks and time line clearly delineated and performed according to the program implementation plan.	1 2 3 4 5 6 7 8 9 10
7. Documentation of outreach plans to recruit target groups according to priorities dictated by the objectives.	1 2 3 4 5 6 7 8 9 10
8. Record-keeping system, forms, and instruments and observation methods pretested, and validity and reliability assessed.	1 2 3 4 5 6 7 8 9 10
9. Description of data collection and analysis plan and monitoring system in place prior to and during implementation.	1 2 3 4 5 6 7 8 9 10
10. Communication media and educational materials pretested and evaluated when implemented.	1 2 3 4 5 6 7 8 9 10
11. Allocation of resources according to implementation plan: identification of costs per client and cost-effectiveness.	1 2 3 4 5 6 7 8 9 10
12. Description and quality of evaluation design.	1 2 3 4 5 6 7 8 9 10

1 = poor, 10 = excellent. Scale = 1 to 10.

Monitoring Program Participant Exposure

Another program component to confirm is participant exposure to specific program sessions. A baseline and follow-up assessment of all participants or a sample should be conducted. Without exception, a health promotion program must document who received how much of what and when.

The observation form in Figure 4.2 was used to confirm patient exposure to a closed-circuit educational television (ETV) program for diabetic patients in a 40-bed hospital. For a 1-week period, patients' rooms were observed to determine whether the patients were viewing the ETV programs presented twice

Rm.	Patient						
___	_____						
	Monday	Tuesday	Wednesday	Thursday	Friday	Saturday	Sunday
A.M.							
P.M.							

Rm.	Patient						
___	_____						
	Monday	Tuesday	Wednesday	Thursday	Friday	Saturday	Sunday
A.M.							
P.M.							

Rm.	Patient						
___	_____						
	Monday	Tuesday	Wednesday	Thursday	Friday	Saturday	Sunday
A.M.							
P.M.							

Rm.	Patient						
___	_____						
	Monday	Tuesday	Wednesday	Thursday	Friday	Saturday	Sunday
A.M.							
P.M.							

FIGURE 4.2 Observation Form for Closed-Circuit Television Programming

daily. Using this method, whose results are noted in Table 4.10, the staff confirmed the proportion of patients exposed to each program and the proportion of programs to which each patient was exposed during the 1-week observation period.

As Table 4.10 indicates, on average, only 20% of approximately 30 eligible patients per day watched the closed-circuit programs, documenting a very low level of patient exposure to this channel of communication. These data confirmed a need to examine why so few patients used this program method.

Program or Session Observations

The purpose of observational data is to document the activities that took place at a specific time and place. These data also describe the people who participated and examine what happened between participants and staff during a session. The interpersonal skills of staff members are, in part, reflected in their actions with

TABLE 4.10 Patient Exposure to Closed-Circuit Television Program

Day	Program	Patients Exposed	Potential Patients	Percentage Exposed
Monday	1	19	29	34
	2	3	31	10
Tuesday	1	5	31	16
	4	3	29	10
	5	6	27	22
Wednesday	11	6	28	21
	7	6	30	20
Thursday	8	4	30	13
	9	7	31	23
Friday	10	4	30	13
	11	10	31	32
Saturday	4	6	31	19
Sunday	13	8	31	26
	14	7	30	23
Total	14	85	419	20

an audience. The audience may be consumers of a health education program, providers of a health care service, a group of administrators, or community leaders who play a principal role in setting organizational policy or providing community support. One quality control issue is the adequacy of verbal and nonverbal communication and group process skills demonstrated by staff members.

There are a number of ways to conduct observational assessments, but almost all include some type of overt or covert participant observation. Patton (1990) describes a number of variations of participant observations that a program may use singly or in combination. Chapter 5 of this book, "Qualitative Evaluation," describes multiple observation methods. The observer's activities may be concealed; a participant observer may be identified as an observer but not as a participant; the observer's activities may be publicly known; or the observer may act as a participant and not as an observer. Lofland notes four concerns in conducting observations:

1. The observer must get close enough to the people and situation being studied to be able to understand the depth and details of what goes on.

2. The observer must aim at capturing what people actually say: the perceived facts.

3. Observational data consist of a great deal of pure description of people, activities, and interactions.

4. Observational data consist of direct quotations from people, both what they say and what they write down. (1971, 136)

It is essential to identify beforehand what is to be observed, how and where it is to be observed, and the frequency and duration of the observations. The observation process may range from a casual period of personal observation of a session to video- or audiotaping full sessions. The evaluator should carefully examine the interaction between participants and staff. From this, the evaluator can assess what information was presented and how and the quality of interactions between presenter and audience. This method, commonly referred to as interactive analysis (Bales 1951; Flanders 1960), is often beyond the capability of the evaluator of an ongoing service project. Roter (1977) provides an excellent example of an interactive analysis study of patients and physicians.

Conducting program observations with limited resources is possible. Observations provide insights into what people do in a program, how they experience it, how activities are organized, and how participants behave and interact. A program may routinely apply a quality assurance system in which all instructors are evaluated by consumers. Miller and Lewis (1982) reported an excellent example of a 27-item instructor assessment form administered to 150 HMO clients of a program. The instrument was developed by the health education department to assess technical and interpersonal competence, providing feedback to its more than 70 facilitators per year from a sample of 3,000 program enrollees. Table 4.11 presents the items and the correlation for each question. An alpha $r = 0.94$ item-to-total (internal consistency) was found, and for individual items $r = \geq 0.40$. As discussed in Chapter 3, these are excellent psychometric data for this instrument.

Community and participant surveys   Program evaluators often need to survey target groups in a community or samples of participants in an organization. As discussed in Chapters 3 and 5, community assessment may involve the use of a range of methods, from a random sample of households to a convenience sample. The representativeness of your sample and the accuracy of your data are important issues to address in conducting a community survey. The program staff must carefully consider the limitations and disadvantages of using nonrandom sampling methods. Selecting a representative sample of respondents is always preferable, but you can use a number of practical, less rigorous approaches to obtain qualitative data on audience needs and perceptions of a program prior to or during the early stages of implementation. Although the purposes of a community survey will vary, it attempts to find out whether a program has:

- Reached a target audience.
- Increased the target audience's awareness of the program.
- Increased the level of community interest.

TABLE 4.11   Item-to-Total Correlations for Instructor Evaluation Form

Item	Item-to-Total Correlations
1. Instructor puts high priority on the needs of the class participants.	.51
2. Instructor makes a lot of mistakes in class.	.52
3. Instructor gives directions too quickly.	.52
4. Instructor helps me feel that I am an important contributor to the group.	.55
5. A person feels free to ask the instructor questions.	.61
6. Instructor should be more friendly than he/she is.	.58
7. I could hear what the instructor was saying.	.65
8. Instructor is a person who can understand how I feel.	.57
9. Instructor focuses on my physical condition but has no feeling for me as a person.	.65
10. Everyone who wanted to contribute had an opportunity to do so.	.57
11. There was too much information in some sessions and too little in others.	.52
12. Just talking to the instructor makes me feel better.	.60
13. Each session's purposes were made clear before, during, and after session.	.50
14. Covering the content is more important to the instructor than class needs.	.60
15. Instructor asks a lot of questions, but once he/she gets the answers he/she doesn't seem to do anything about them.	.62
16. Instructor held my interest.	.68
17. Instructor should pay more attention to the students.	.69
18. Instructor is often too disorganized.	.67
19. It is always easy to understand what the instructor is talking about.	.61
20. Instructor is able to help me work through my problems or questions.	.62
21. Instructor is not precise in doing his/her work.	.60
22. Instructor understands the content he/she presents in class.	.68
23. I'm tired of the instructor talking down to me.	.60
24. Instructor fosters sharing of ideas between class participants.	.58
25. Instructor is understanding when listening to a person's problems.	.72
26. Instructor could speak more clearly.	.60
27. Instructor takes a real interest in me.	.62

Source: Miller, J., and Lewis, F. 1982. Closing the gap in quality assurance: A tool for evaluating group leaders. *Health Education Quarterly* 9(1): 55–66. Copyright © 1982 by the Society for Public Health Education. Reprinted by permission of Sage Publications, Inc.

Alpha = 0.94

- Increased the number who use the program or service.
- Provided a satisfactory service.

Of the possible techniques by which an evaluator may systematically gather qualitative information about a program's progress, there are three common and feasible methods: (1) opinion leader survey, (2) community forum survey, and (3) central location survey. Each can be conducted in a short period of time at little cost; each has advantages and disadvantages. They do not provide a representative statement of the opinions of a defined population, however. More detailed discussions were presented on sampling procedures and other technical details of data collection in Chapter 3, but in the sections that follow, we briefly describe each community survey method and its limitation.

Stakeholder–opinion leader survey   Key lay or professional community informants, persons who should be familiar with the program, are selected as participants in an opinion leader survey. This type of survey is relatively easy and inexpensive to conduct. It is particularly useful in the discussion, planning, and early implementation stages of a program when support and interest from community leaders are crucial for program success. It may also generate familiarity with, awareness of, and interest in the program among these leaders. Generally, data from this survey are generated from person-to-person interviews. Using a nominal group process may also be effective (Delbecq et al. 1975).

Written questions should be prepared to elicit key information from the leaders about their impressions of a proposed or ongoing program. An opinion leader survey usually solicits a range of information. Results reflect the degree of consensus about the program from knowledgeable community people. This method plays an important role in assessing the political support for a program. It may be invaluable to an innovative program in identifying program barriers, acceptability, and initial participant satisfaction. Using this method, program planners should be able to document community and organizational input to and support for a program.

Community forum survey   In the community forum approach, several locations are selected for public meetings with a specific target audience. Community forums are inexpensive and usually easy to arrange and typically take 1–2 hours. The meetings may be open or by invitation. This method can be used to educate the current participants and to gather their impressions of the acceptance, diffusion, and levels of participation in the program. A list of key questions must be prepared to elicit audience input.

The forum method is most efficient when the meetings are small or when the audience is divided into smaller groups of 20–25. A staff member or trained layperson should facilitate the meeting and maintain records to ensure maximum participation. The forum encourages a wide range of community expressions about the problem. Its major disadvantages are (1) one group or individual may control the discussions or use the forum exclusively for expression of a grievance or opposition to the program; and (2) attendance may be limited and information covered very biased.

Central location survey   The central location survey is another technique commonly employed to gather information quickly and efficiently from a large number of people: 100 to 200 in a community. Two to 10 sites are typically selected, sites that are visited by a large number of people who possess the characteristics of the target audience for the health promotion program, e.g., a shopping center, movie theater, beach, or other pedestrian high-traffic areas in a metropolitan city or rural county. Interviewers identify a specific group, e.g., women of a certain racial, ethnic, or age group, and conduct short, 2- to 5-minute interviews of the people on the spot. Questions may concern the person's familiarity with a health problem, knowledge of the availability of the program and its purpose, or interest in a special program.

Focus group interview   A focus group interview is a group session method to explore the insights of target audiences about a specific topic. This method is discussed in greater detail in Chapter 5, "Qualitative Evaluation." Social marketing researchers and advertisers use this method to derive the perceptions, beliefs, language, and interests of an audience to whom a product or service would be marketed. The focus group interview usually involves eight to ten people. Following a detailed discussion outline, a moderator keeps the group session within the appropriate time limits but gives considerable latitude to participants to respond spontaneously to a set of general or specific questions. The moderator has the opportunity to probe and gain in-depth insights from the interviews. These sessions are often video- or audiotaped.

Particularly used in the concept development stage of the communications development process, focus group interviews help health communications/media planners identify key concepts that may trigger awareness and interest in participation. This method is often used to complement population-based, representative-sample surveys on specific topics. Qualitative information is issued in combination with the survey data to make judgments about the perceptions, beliefs, and behaviors of the target population and subgroups within it.

Component pretesting: *CD Cynergy*   Pretesting is a quality control method used to document the perceptions of target audiences. All programs should have core assessment and intervention elements pretested prior to routine application.

Good pretesting is a continuing issue in the field, because it requires technical skill from the staff and resources and time that often are not available. The three most common program elements that should be pretested are instruments, media, and materials, both written and visual. The following sections discuss the purposes and methods of pretesting these elements.

The journal *Health Promotion Practice* routinely presents a section of "Book and Media Reviews." This section of the journal focuses on reviewing multiple types of media including books, guides, videotapes, CD-ROMs, software packages, and Web sites that are designed for health promotion and education practitioners. The following is a synopsis of a tool for a health promotion specialist to use in the development process of health communications planning: *CD Cynergy*. This CD-ROM can be used to assist the health promotion professional to systematically plan health communication interventions within a public health framework. As discussed by the editor, S. Gambescia: "This tool levels the playing field for process, language, techniques and strategies. The program starts with identifying the problem, not with the selected intervention . . . it provides tips and information about noncommunication interventions, acknowledging that health communication may not be the best or only intervention for a particular problem" (*Health Promotion Practice*, July 2002).

CD Cynergy presents a comprehensive introduction with a video, an overview of the program, and a how-to segment. The core of this tool is a six-phase step-by-step tutorial presenting substantial examples and additional resources that can be linked to each phase of the health communications process. A media library (with Version 1.2.1) contains 100 media samples such as radio spots, TV spots, and posters. The six phases of this tutorial are:

1. Problem definition and description
2. Problem analysis
3. Identifying and profiling audiences
4. Developing a communication strategy and tactics
5. Developing an evaluation plan
6. Launch/feedback

Version 1.2.1 will be revised and updated by the CDC.

An additional option is one of the workshops for health educators, health communicators, and other professionals held throughout the country by the Society for Public Health Education. Information is available on SOPHE's Web site or from SOPHE, 750 First Street NE, Suite 910, Washington, DC 20002, telephone 202-408-9804, e-mail *info@sophe.org*.

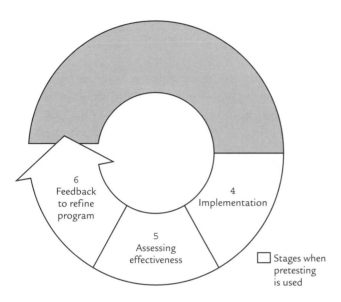

FIGURE 4.3   Stages in Health Communication

Media and messages   Pretesting systematically gathers target audience reaction to written, visual, or audio messages and media. In assessing the quality of media, program staff should document their having followed procedures that meet professional standards and follow well-established steps to create media (see Figure 4.3). Program planners who do not pretest media lose the opportunity to gain valuable insights into the quality of those methods of communication. A thorough review of formative evaluation methods for media is provided in "Making Health Communication Programs Work" (National Cancer Institute 2002).

The purposes of pretesting media in a formative evaluation are to improve communication before their diffusion and to document which alternatives will be most efficient and effective in the field. The concept of pretesting is simple; it involves measuring the reactions of a group of people to the object of interest, for example, a film, booklet, radio announcement, or poster. Pretesting should be done not only with members of the target audience but also in-house staff. The sophistication and budget that can be applied to conducting a pretest seem infinite—the resources expended by the advertising industry each year confirm this fact—but health organizations' budgets aren't.

In developing health information programs and revising existing messages and media, pretesting is an essential method for assessing ease of comprehension, personal relevance, audience acceptance, ease of recall, and other strengths and weaknesses of draft messages before they are produced in final form. A pretest should establish a target audience baseline and help determine if there are large cognitive, affective, perception, or behavioral differences within the target audience.

No absolute formula can be used to design a pretest or field trial. A range of simple or highly technical and costly methods and procedures are available. The acceptability and memorability of selected media and products may often be improved, however, without a major allocation of time or resources. A pretest should be tailored to your objective and should consider time, cost, resources, and availability of the target audience. Planners may have to decide which media will be formally pretested and which may undergo only internal staff review. This decision must be tempered by the risk of creating active opposition responses. CDC has recommended the following (CDC 1999):

Message Content
- Limit the number of messages.
- Tell readers what you want them to do.
- Tell readers what they'll gain from reading your material.
- Choose your words carefully.
- Be sensitive to cultural differences.

Text Appearance
- Use font sizes between 12 and 14 point.

Visuals
- Use visuals to help communicate your messages.
- Choose the best type of visual for your materials.
- Make visuals culturally relevant and sensitive.
- Make visuals easy for your readers to follow and understand.
- When illustrating internal body parts or small objects, use realistic images and place them in context.

Layout and Design
- Design an effective cover.
- Organize your messages so they are easy to act on and recall.
- Leave lots of white space.
- Make the text easy for the eye to follow.

Written materials   Written materials are almost always used in health promotion and education programs. The major concern is whether people can read and understand the material. Written materials should serve as aids to information transfer and should clarify and reinforce the principal messages specified in the program objectives. Using written materials as the principal behavior-change elements of your program is, however, archaic. Many professionally developed and field-tested written materials are available for most health problems and risk factors. Use a three-step process to assess program materials: (1) assessment of reading level, (2) analysis of content, and (3) review by content and health education specialists.

The program staff must first gather materials and review them thoroughly to determine which ones might serve program objectives best. Design written materials for efficient, low-cost distribution. Some can be modified for the target audience. They should be capable of capturing the interest of the audience and be presented in an imaginative, yet simple, fashion. It is important that terms, word choice, and other characteristics be chosen to promote reading. Ask the following major questions to assess the quality of materials: (1) What are the objectives? (2) Why use this medium to communicate this information? (3) For whom are the written materials intended? (4) Under what circumstances will people read it? (5) What languages or ethnic perspective do we need to consider? Use pretesting to gather words, phrases, and vernacular from target audiences, so that appropriate language can be used in materials, and to determine the most effective method for communicating information. These issues must be resolved during the development of written material before significant resources are spent.

The writer must select a succinct title, prepare a written text, and consider the number and type of illustrations to be used in constructing materials. The staff also must reach agreement on when, how, and how often the written materials will be introduced to participants. Programs should have a mechanism to document the distribution of written materials, for example, monthly, quarterly, and annually by type (American Association for Health Education 2002).

If a program uses written materials extensively, as aids to reinforce its educational efforts, staff may want to assess whether participants are using the information. In a study by the Rand Corporation for the Food and Drug Administration on informing patients about drugs, 236 men and women, who used 69 pharmacies in Los Angeles County, were asked seven questions to determine their behavioral responses to a written insert in a medication package (Winkler et al. 1981):

1. Do you remember a leaflet that came with your prescription?
2. Did you read it before you started taking erythromycin?
3. (If no): Did you get a chance to read it later?
4. After you read it, did you ever go back and read it again?

TABLE 4.12   Behavioral Responses to Leaflets

| Response | Experimental Condition | | | |
	Low Explanation, No Instructions	Explanation	Instructions	Explanation and Instructions
Read leaflet	77.6%	84.6%	70.3%	80.6%
Read before starting meds	67.2%	65.3%	64.1%	59.7%
Read more than once	36.2%	32.7%	31.3%	33.9%
Kept leaflet	53.4%	63.5%	51.6%	61.3%
Showed leaflet to someone else	22.8%	25.0%	29.7%	27.4%

Source: Winkler et al. (1981).

5. (If yes): Why did you read it again?

6. Did you keep the leaflet, did you throw it away, or what?

7. Did anyone else read the leaflet from your prescription?

Although many questions were examined in this study, e.g., variations in format, length, content, and style, the basic process was to determine what type of document worked best. The study used methods that have broad applicability to health programs. It conducted a qualitative assessment of participants' reactions to the package insert using a semantic differential scale. Individuals were asked to rate different pamphlets on the basis of their thoroughness and clarity of explanation, degree of stimulation, simplicity or complexity, level of reassurance, and factuality. Study results refuted the myth that "no one reads those things."

As Table 4.12 indicates, a very large proportion of subjects read the leaflet before starting to take their prescription, a significant percentage read it more than once, a majority kept the leaflet, and approximately 1 in 4 showed it to someone else. Many ongoing programs that use written information could use the questions, documentation, and formative evaluation design applied in this study. They determine, in a formative fashion, how effective written components of a program are in communicating information to program participants.

Visual materials, radio, and television   In pretesting visual aids, e.g., posters, a principal aim is to assess their ability to attract. In general, they should be attention getters, conveying one idea. The extent to which they are understandable, are educationally and ethnically acceptable, and promote audience involvement should be assessed. If a major fiscal expenditure is being made, multiple samples from the target audience at different locations may be needed. A small number of people may be sufficient—5 to 10 to pretest a poster. Although many questions can be asked, 10 are presented here that are often used by an interviewer or in a self-administered questionnaire to determine an individual's response to a visual aid:

1. What is the most important message presented?
2. Is this visual aid asking you to do something?
3. Is there anything offensive to you or other people who live in your community?
4. What do you like about it?
5. What do you dislike about it?
6. How would you rate it in comparison to others you have seen before?
7. Is the information new to you?
8. Are you likely to do what the visual aid asks?
9. Do you think the average person would understand it?
10. How would you improve it?

These questions and others that staff may consider appropriate should be asked as the visual is shown to each individual. The responses will provide insight into the attractiveness, comprehensibility, and acceptability of the visual aid (American Association for Health Education 2002).

The pretesting of radio and television announcements follows the general principles outlined for other categories of media. One difference, however, is the need to produce and pilot-test an announcement. Cost is a major factor to consider. A radio announcement can be easily taped on a recorder and a poster designed to rough form, but producing a TV announcement or program, even in preliminary form, can be expensive. Table 4.13 illustrates the questions that might be asked to pretest a radio announcement.

Health message testing service   For programs on a number of specific health problems, e.g., smoking cessation, breast self-examination, and physical fitness, the staff may choose to use a commercial health message testing service. This type of service provides a standardized system to assess audience response to radio and television messages about health to gauge the communication effectiveness of these messages. The system informs program planners of the audience's message recall, comprehension, and sense of the personal relevance and believability of the message, as well as identifying strong and weak communication points. In testing a message, the major concern is its appropriateness for its intended subgroup. To measure communication, a testing service examines the attention-getting

TABLE 4.13	Pretesting Characteristics
Characteristic	Questions
Attraction	Is the presentation interesting enough to attract and hold the attention of the target group? Do consumers like it?
	Which aspects of the presentation do people like most?
	What gained the greatest share of their attention?
Comprehension	How clear is the message? How well is it understood?
Acceptability	Does the message contain anything that is offensive or distasteful by local standards?
	Does it reflect community norms and beliefs?
	Does it contain irritating or abusive language?
Personal involvement	Is the program perceived to be directed to persons in the target audience?
	In other words, do the consumers feel that the program is for them personally, or do they perceive it as being for someone else?
Persuasion	Does the message convince the target audience to undertake the desired behavior?
	How favorably predisposed are individuals to try a certain product, use a specific service, originate a new personal health behavior?

ability of the message and audience recall of the main idea. Overall, a health message testing service can provide invaluable insights for refining draft message announcements, choosing between alternative messages, and planning future health promotion campaigns. It is, however, very expensive.

Television program evaluation and analysis by computer Current technology provides the most sophisticated evaluation and research of television productions through the application of microcomputer technology. Electronic analyses can be made of the effects of a media presentation, documenting an audience's reaction second by second. With this technology, it is possible to observe the effects of minute changes in presentation on the audience's attitudes, knowledge, and skill. This information gives program personnel the opportunity to manipulate covertly what audience members see and to analyze their responses instantaneously. It allows program personnel to collect instant feedback data on an infinite number of visual, graphic, verbal, and other configurations.

Although most service programs are not capable of applying this highly sophisticated method of assessing audience response, it is a powerful technique for pilot-testing media during the preproduction stage. Given the increased impetus to use multimedia in health promotion and education, this technology may be of particular relevance to national or statewide efforts for which detailed pilot testing of products is essential. But before investing in production costs that easily could run into six or seven figures, agencies need to perform careful preliminary assessments.

PRACTICE STANDARD

Health promotion programs should conduct pretests of their media and materials for the following effectiveness components: (1) attractiveness, (2) comprehension and readability, (3) acceptability, (4) audience involvement, and (5) persuasion.

Instrument development and pretesting   A well-documented deficiency in the literature is the failure of many program planners to establish the utility, reliability, and validity of their instrument data. Chapter 3, "Measurement in Evaluation," provided a detailed discussion of this issue. Examine all instruments to determine their relevance to the specified objectives of the program. In the development and pretesting of an instrument, program planners should demonstrate concern for the consumer. The instrument should be a manageable length—the shorter, the better. Collect only essential information from participants.

Instrument pretesting is a critical first step to ensure data quality and competencies. Rely heavily on instruments used by comparable programs; no program planner should develop a new instrument unless absolutely necessary. If, for example, the program is attempting to change the participants' personal health practices or beliefs, the staff should adapt forms identified in the literature or available from national agencies for surveying health risk factors, practices, knowledge, and beliefs, e.g., by the National Center for Health Statistics or Centers for Disease Control. Pretest instruments for such characteristics as time of administration, ease of comprehension, readability, sensitivity, reactivity of questions, organization of questions, and standardization of administration and scoring. First select a sample of individuals who are representative of the population for whom the instrument is prepared. Then test the instrument under conditions comparable to those in which it will be applied in the program setting.

Readability testing   Readability is another important aspect of pretesting written materials. Readability tests essentially determine the reading grade level required of the average person to understand the written materials. Readability estimates provide evidence only of the structural difficulties of a written document, that is, vocabulary and sentence structure. They indicate how well the information will be understood but do not guarantee the effectiveness of the piece. Pretests for readability are available and easy to apply. Many readability formulas exist (Dale and Chall 1948; Flesch 1948; Fry 1968; Klare 1974–1975), but the SMOG grading formula for testing the readability of educational material is one of the most commonly applied (McLaughlin 1969). Generally considered an excellent method of assessing the grade level that a person must have reached to understand the text, it requires 100% comprehension of the material read. To calculate the SMOG reading grade level, McLaughlin (1969) advises program personnel to use the entire written work that is being evaluated and to follow these six steps:

1. Count 10 consecutive sentences at the start, in the middle, and near the end of the text.
2. Circle all words with three or more syllables, including repetitions of the same word from this sample.
3. Total the number of words circled.
4. Estimate the square root of the total number of polysyllabic words counted.
5. Find the nearest perfect square and calculate the square root.
6. Add a constant of 3 to the square root to calculate grade (reading grade level) that a person must have completed to fully understand the text being evaluated.

Sentence length, word length, and difficulty affect the readability score. The SMOG formula ensures 90% comprehension; that is, a person with a tenth-grade reading level will comprehend 90% of the material rated at that level. This procedure can be applied to all texts prepared by a program for public consumption. "Making Health Communication Programs Work" (National Cancer Institute 2002) presents useful discussions of readability in general and in health-related literature. In addition, see "Clear and Simple: Developing Effective Print Material for Low Literate Readers" (NIH-NCI 1994).

CASE STUDY 4.4

Content Analysis

READABILITY TESTING AND CONTENT ANALYSIS

Readability testing examines the linguistic and structural qualities of written text, but it does not assess the content, difficulty of concepts, or appropriateness for a target audience. Content analysis is a systematic, quantitative description of the communication's content. The use of content analysis and readability assessment permits a more

---

Source: K. Glanz and J. Rudd (1990).

meaningful profile of the characteristics of currently available cholesterol education materials.

The following case study discussion represents an example by Glanz and Rudd of how to assess the readability and content of printed materials. The purpose of this case study, a condensed version of the article, was to review available print cholesterol education materials and to examine their readability and content.

METHODS: CRITERIA TO INCLUDE AND IDENTIFY MATERIALS

Inclusion Criteria

This analysis focused on print educational materials that met five criteria:

1. Focused on low-fat, low-cholesterol eating and/or was used by cholesterol education programs.
2. Available from government, voluntary agencies, professional associations, universities, or public education units of proprietary health organizations.
3. Could be distributed by health professionals or patient educators.
4. Patient "give-aways"; there might be some costs to providers, but materials should be free to patients.
5. Stand-alone educational materials that could be used in combination with other educational media or methods, e.g., slides, tapes, lectures, or counseling.

Identification of Materials

The first source of materials involved items received by the authors in their prior work in nutrition education. Materials and sources were identified through the Abstract Book of the National Cholesterol Conference of November 1988. Requests were also made directly to organizations involved in public and patient cholesterol education. These methods produced an incomplete list of materials: 38 items. (See source article for materials analyzed.)

ANALYSIS OF MATERIALS

Analysis of materials was completed in three steps: characterization of materials, assessment of readability level, and content analysis.

Characterization of Materials

Each item was cataloged by title, sources, date of publication, and primary intended audience: general public, public and screening participants, those identified with elevated cholesterol, and patients in treatment. Size was measured from unopened dimensions of the brochure or pamphlet. Length was assessed by word count and by number of pages, based on one page in an unopened state. Appearance was assessed by the presence of blank ("white") space between text, space of two or more lines between blocks of text, and use of visual images and print size.

Readability Analysis

Readability was assessed using two methods. The first, the SMOG grading formula, predicts the grade of a written passage correctly with a standard error of prediction of 1.5 grades. Because the SMOG is based on 100% comprehension of materials, we also use the FOG formula, which is based on 50% to 75% comprehension of the written

TABLE 4.14 Mean Readability Levels of Cholesterol Education Materials

	General	Audience Screening	High Chol.	Total
No. of Items	11	10	17	38
SMOG grade level	11.5	10.3	10.9	10.8
FOG grade level	11.4	11.0	10.9	10.9

Source: Reprinted from Glanz, K., and Rudd, J. 1990. Readability and content analysis of print cholesterol education materials. *Patient Education and Counseling* 16: 109–118. Copyright © 1990, with permission from Elsevier.

material. Both formulas give estimates of grade level of education required to understand the text.

Content Analysis

We assessed the presence or absence of nine content elements for each education brochure or pamphlet. Four elements were related to diagnosis of elevated cholesterol and related cardiovascular risk factors: discussion of HDL/LDL lipid fractions, the physiology of cholesterol elevation, other heart disease risks factors, and weight control or reduction. Five other elements were assessed:

1. Information about dietary behavior change and food choice, foods to emphasize or avoid
2. Use of brand names
3. Information on food preparation methods
4. Portion size
5. Distinction between saturated fat and polyunsaturated or other types of fats

ANALYSIS PROCEDURES

The analysis and coding procedure was pilot-tested on a sample of materials. An independent analysis of a subsample of materials was completed, followed by resolution of any discrepancies by agreement among raters.

RESULTS

Readability Assessment

The mean readability level of the materials was grade 10.8 (S.D. 1.50), SMOG grading formula, and 10.9 (S.D. 1.99), FOG grading formula. Approximately 70% of all items were written at a reading level of grade 10 or higher. As Table 4.14 shows, readability levels were uniform across audience categories. No significant correlation existed between reading level and length of the item, defined either in terms of word count or number of pages. There was a strong, significant, and positive correlation ($r = 0.78$) between SMOG and FOG readability levels. This adds confidence about the accuracy of the reading levels.

TABLE 4.15   Percentage of Items Containing Content Elements by Audience Category: Diagnosis and Risk-Related

Audience	Percentage with Content Element*			
	HDL/LDL	Physiol.	CHD Risk	Wt. Control
General (n = 11)	36.4[b]	54.5	45.5[b]	36.4
Screening (n = 10)	70.0[a]	90.0	90.0[a]	40.0
High chol. (n = 17)	47.1[b]	64.7	64.7[b]	58.8
Total (n = 38)	52.8	68.4	65.8	47.4

Source: Reprinted from Glanz, K., and Rudd, J. 1990. Readability and content analysis of print cholesterol education materials. *Patient Education and Counseling* 16: 109–118. Copyright © 1990, with permission from Elsevier.

* Explanation of content elements: Mention/discussion of HDL/LDL = HDL/LDL lipid fractions; Physiol. = physiology of cholesterol elevation; CHD Risk = other heart disease risk factors; Wt. Control = weight control/reduction. Within content elements, percentages with different superscripts indicate $P < 0.05$ by Mann-Whitney U-test (a's indicate significantly higher percentages than b's).

TABLE 4.16   Percentage of Items Containing Content Elements by Audience Category: Dietary Behavior Change, Food Information

Audience	Percentage with Content Element*				
	Food Types	Brands	Food Prep.	Portion	Sat. Fat
General (n = 11)	72.7[b]	0.0	72.7[b]	63.6	90.9
Screening (n = 10)	80.0[b]	20.0	70.0[b]	40.0	80.0
High chol. (n = 17)	100.0[a]	5.9	94.1[a]	70.6	88.2
Total (n = 38)	86.8	7.9	81.6	60.5	86.8

Source: Reprinted from Glanz, K., and Rudd, J. 1990. Readability and content analysis of print cholesterol education materials. *Patient Education and Counseling* 16: 109–118. Copyright © 1990, with permission from Elsevier.

* Explanation of content elements: Mention/discussion of Food Types = food groups/types; Brands = uses brand names; Food Prep. = preparation methods; Portion = portion size; Sat. Fat = types of fat (saturated/unsaturated). Within content elements, percentages with different superscripts indicate *P.*

Content Analysis

Table 4.15 presents the findings for diagnosis and risk-related content elements, audience category, and complete sets of materials. Statistically significant differences (Mann-Whitney U-test [23]) in the percentage of mentions within content elements across audience categories were determined. Approximately half the materials explained the meaning of HDL/LDL lipid fractions. Fewer than half addressed weight control and its role in cholesterol management. Mentions of HDL/LDL and other heart disease risk factors were slightly more frequent in materials for screening audiences. A similar but nonsignificant trend was evident for the elements of cholesterol physiology. Weight control was most often discussed for those identified with elevated levels (high chol.).

The results of the content analysis for dietary behavior appear in Table 4.16. Nearly all materials addressed types of foods, food preparation, and the distinction between saturated and other types of fat: 87%, 82%, and 87%, respectively. Less than two-thirds (60.5%) discussed portion size. Only 7.9% included brand names when recommending desirable food choices. The materials designed specifically for patients (high chol.) were significantly more likely to include types of foods and food preparation information. A similar but nonsignificant trend was evident for portion size and saturated-unsaturated fats. Within content elements, percentages with different superscripts indicate $P < 0.05$ by Mann-Whitney U-test (a's indicate significantly higher percentages than b's).

DISCUSSION

This assessment suggested that the majority of content was aimed at well-educated, middle-class, middle-aged, nonminority populations who are highly motivated to translate abstract concepts into food choices. There appeared to be a need to develop materials to reach important but underserved segments of the population, to tailor messages and materials to the needs of potential users, and to design materials with attention to the consumer's or patient's lifestyle. The implications of this study for practice are discussed in greater detail in the original article. *The Content Analysis Guidebook* by Nevendorf (2002) and *Process Evaluation for Public Health Interventions and Research* by Steckler and Linnan (2002) are comprehensive references on this topic.

SUMMARY

A PEM and different process evaluation methods are available to assess the quality of program implementation. Complementary quality control methods, standards, and guidelines are available to use in conducting a process evaluation of the feasibility of providing an ongoing health promotion and education program and its quality. Standards exist in the fields of health promotion education and health communications that apply to all elements discussed in this chapter. Program staff, evaluators, and administrators should know these established methods and be able to apply them in planning and evaluation.

5 | Qualitative Evaluation

Qualitative methods are anthropological techniques, particularly ethnography, applied to program evaluation (Fetterman 1989). In its purest form, ethnography—the study of culture and its meaning—requires that the anthropologist spend months or years participating in the life of a community. The ethnographer may observe how social groups interact under different circumstances, explore the significance artifacts hold in daily life or on special occasions, record field notes of striking ideas, and interpret the resulting data to convey insights into aspects of culture. In contrast to the ethnographer, the evaluator's primary objective is timely and practical feedback for program improvement. Hence, qualitative evaluations typically operate along shorter time frames than ethnographic studies. Moreover, in program evaluation, an in-depth field study is typically not as feasible as in an ethnographic study. Thus, the qualitative evaluator must be adaptive in applying ethnographic methods to assessing health promotion and education programs. One important adaptation is the primacy accorded the qualitative interview in most phases of program evaluation. This is in contrast to fieldwork as the mainstay of ethnographic study (Coffey and Atkinson 1996; Stake 1995).

This chapter provides an overview of qualitative evaluation methods. In general, qualitative approaches are useful because they focus on naturally occurring events in program settings. They are flexible and can be varied in the course of a study. They are effective at uncovering the significance that participants ascribe to program structures, processes, events, and outcomes (Miles and Huberman 1994). This type of practical significance is different from but complementary to statistical significance in experimental and quasi-experimental designs.

Illustrations of Qualitative Assessments by Evaluation Phases

Qualitative approaches are applicable to all four evaluation phases (i.e., evaluation Phases 1 and 2 are designed to determine program feasibility and impact under "ideal" circumstances, and in Phases 3 and 4 effectiveness evaluations occur under "day-to-day" conditions). Many of the same qualitative methods may be applied across all phases. Thus, the chapter's primary focus is on methodologies. Before we elaborate on methodology, the following examples illustrate several phases of qualitative applications.

Assessing the Underlying Assumptions of Health Promotion Interventions

Rugkasa and colleagues (2001) interviewed 85 children between the ages of 10 and 11 throughout Northern Ireland to explore how "childhood agency" may explain the beginning of smoking behavior among children. The study premise holds that peer pressure, often cited as a root cause, is an adult construction of childhood behavior. As such, it may misrepresent how children symbolize smoking. An understanding of social relationships among children as distinct from those of adults should be a factor in building program interventions. The interview data suggested that the children perceived smoking as an adult activity and as a taboo even by those who smoke. The authors rejected the notion that smoking is perceived as a "rite of passage" among preteens, because they recognize that smoking behavior resides among adults, and adults would object to their smoking. The authors hold that smoking can be better understood as a *status offense*, where the child is engaged in a breach of a taboo. Peer pressure assumes that children are passive in the face of pressure, but the authors' data indicated that children have robust means of refusing to take up smoking. Thus, programs based on building peer refusal skills may misinterpret how preadolescents symbolize children who smoke. *The study illustrated how qualitative assessments may build theory that informs health promotion program interventions.*

Assessing an Organization's Capacity to Implement Health Promotion Interventions

The National Cancer Institute (NCI) funded 21 state health departments and the District of Columbia to link with local organizations to stimulate the development of community interventions for cancer prevention and control. NCI intended the program to build capacity within state agencies to facilitate local programming. A qualitative evaluation was conducted to assess the capacity of the state health departments to facilitate local programming. Interviews and document reviews were the sources of study data. The evaluation indicated that state agencies had capacity in data gathering and interpretation, influence with an extensive network of providers, support for program mobilization, and oversight functions such as monitoring service contracts. State health agencies lacked capacity in providing programming expertise, hiring the appropriate personnel in a timely manner due to bureaucratic procedures, and fitting the state agencies' regulatory and programmatic responsibilities with NCI's emphasis on conducting research and publishing scientific manuscripts. The evaluators recommended that NCI assist state agencies in building capacity by providing technical expertise in identifying and implementing effective interventions, developing a better understanding of the time required for the interventions to produce the desired outcomes, and communicating more consistently with program representatives at the state health agencies (Goodman, Steckler, and Alciati 1997). *The study illustrates how qualitative evaluation methods can produce suggestions to refine program operations.*

Assessing the Reasons for the Lack of Programmatic Outcomes

In a randomized controlled study of AIDS prevention education in Uganda, Kinsman et al. (2001) administered a pre- and posttest questionnaire to students in their last year of primary school, the year in which the AIDS curriculum was taught. The authors then held focus group interviews with a sample of students who received the program. The questionnaire data indicated that the program produced few significant increases in knowledge about condoms and HIV transmission, attitudes about delaying sex and discrimination against people with AIDS, and behaviors such as the use of condoms. Focus group data indicated that the curriculum interventions were not implemented—an example of a Type III error (see Chapter 4). The primary reasons for the lack of implementation included lack of time in the curriculum and lack of teacher preparedness and comfort. The authors concluded that AIDS education needs to be incorporated into a nationally mandated curriculum on life-skills education, and future teachers should be required to participate in courses on teaching methods while in college. *The study illustrated how qualitative methods may complement quantitative evaluation in discovering why a program is not producing the desired outcomes and in suggesting remedies.*

Assessing the Unintended Outcomes Produced by a Health Promotion Program

Goodman and Steckler (1987–1988) evaluated a program to prevent smoking and use of alcohol among adolescents in a low-income housing development in North Carolina. The youth who participated in the program were between the ages of 11 and 15, were in middle school, and were referred by teachers who assessed a child to be at high risk. The program was operated by the county health department in coordination with several community agencies. The intervention consisted of a series of structured group activities for improving decision making, control of life's circumstances, and increased feelings of self-worth. The program proved generally effective in implementation and in producing the desired outcomes. For instance, the youth consistently reported that the program increased choices for problem solving and for sharing personal needs, and that they continued to use the techniques they learned even after the program ended. In addition to these results, the evaluation revealed that the program helped the local health department to overcome a negative image in the community, gain recognition from other health agencies, and develop an extensive library. Other community agencies reported greater trust with parents, more involvement with teachers, and greater community involvement in planning. Had the qualitative evaluation not been implemented, none of these findings would have been reported. *This type of evaluation can uncover unintended outcomes, both desirable and undesirable. They may be used to further develop a program.*

QUALITATIVE DATA METHODOLOGIES

Qualitative techniques can be broadly classified into those used for data collection and those applied to data analysis. For data collection, evaluators most frequently employ open-ended interviews, conduct on-site observations, take field notes, and review program documents. For data analysis, predominant methods include data coding to identify similar concepts (Coffey and Atkinson 1996); matrix displays for arraying data (Miles and Huberman 1994); and triangulation for bolstering internal validity (Denzin 1984). Numerous books and articles are devoted to each of these methods, with the work of Michael Q. Patton (e.g., 1997, 1990, 1982), a pioneer and a prolific writer on qualitative evaluation, being particularly noteworthy.

Cesario, Morin, and Santa-Donato (2002) described a methodology for scoring and rating the strength of qualitative evaluation research (QER) evidence. Multiple dimensions of QER can be assessed. The authors noted:

> The quality of evidence rating was based on the total scores for each of the five categories described below. A quality of evidence rating for each qualitative study was assigned using the legend below:
>
> Q I: Total score of 22.5–30 indicates that 75% to 100% of the total criteria were met.
>
> Q II: Total score of 15–22.4 indicates that 50% to 74% of the total criteria were met.
>
> Q III: Total score of less than 15 indicates that less than 50% of the total criteria were met.

Assessing Qualitative Studies

1. DV = Descriptive vividness
2. MC = Methodological congruence
   a. RD = Rigor in documentation
   b. PR = Procedural rigor

c. ER = Ethical rigor

d. C = Confirmability

3. AP = Analytic preciseness

4. TC = Theoretical connectedness

5. HR = Heuristic relevance

a. IR = Intuitive recognition

b. RBK = Relationship to existing body of knowledge

c. A = Applicability

Scoring Scale

3 = Good = 75%–100% criteria met

2 = Fair = 50%–74% criteria met

1 = Poor = 25%–49% criteria met

0 = No evidence that criteria met = <25% criteria met

DATA COLLECTION: THE QUALITATIVE INTERVIEW

The interview is considered the most important data-gathering device in qualitative evaluation (Coffey and Atkinson 1996; Fetterman 1989). The interview is distinct from other forms of data collection in its "open-endedness." Questions are generally broad in scope, such as, "How is the program successful?" or "Why was the program altered to meet its goals?" "How" and "why" questions predominate to elicit the details and nuances of program dynamics as perceived by the interviewee (Yin 1994).

Qualitative specialists emphasize that interviewees have "tacit knowledge," or a "taken for granted" quality about their thoughts and actions, a quality so integrated into their "mental maps" that they may not be aware of the underlying forces that drive perceptions and behavior (Spradley 1979; Agar 1986). For instance, an interviewee may suggest that parts of a program are so important that they cannot be candidates for alteration. The informant may not be aware of the deeper underlying reasons for such a restriction and, if asked directly, may give superficial or "surface" explanations, such as, "That program is at the very heart of our organization's mission." A "deeper-seated" reason may come out in conversation because deeper meanings are often encoded in linguistic form (Spradley 1979). For instance, in discussing the aforementioned program, the interview respondent may also say, "Our agency director developed that program and really believes in it." This statement goes deeper in explaining what "at the very heart of our organization" means, because the program's placement is most likely influenced by its support from the director. The interview subject may not make the connection between the program's central location and the director's support, but the connection is there as "tacit knowledge." It's the qualitative evaluator's job to realize the connection by inference. As we detail later in this chapter, "inference development" is a cornerstone methodology for qualitative analysis.

To elicit rich dialogue, the evaluator may ask the interviewee to describe a specific example of how the organization went about altering programs. Asking for illustrations, couching questions with how and why structures, and posing open-ended questions all are recommended devices for producing a rich array of data from the interview. Case Study 5.1 illustrates an evaluation study that used interviews to elicit a deeper structural interpretation for the limited degree of partnering that occurred among a project's stakeholders (Goodman et al. 2001).

CASE STUDY 5.1

Using Interviews in the Evaluation

A state department of health entered into a cooperative agreement with the Centers for Disease Control and Prevention (CDC) to implement a community-based, comprehensive diabetes prevention program. The cooperative agreement required that the state agency work in partnership with the county health department, community providers of diabetes treatment and care, and other community groups. The agreement mandated a community advisory board to "participate in program and policy decisions affecting the project and the community." In its application to CDC, the state health agency underscored the importance of "the partnership and coalition approach with . . . concerned, committed individuals and organizations to plan and implement a broad, comprehensive, community-based approach."

The program produced a great degree of conflict among project stakeholders, and lack of cooperation was hampering effective implementation. As part of the evaluation, interviews were conducted with CDC project representatives, university-based consultants, state health department administrators, local health department representatives, executive committee members, and work group leaders from the community. When those interviewed were asked why so much disharmony arose, the surface explanations pointed to personality conflicts. In analyzing interview data more closely, the evaluator reached a deeper understanding of factors that impeded a true partnership from forming. Although the cooperative agreement emphasized that the project would be a partnership, the interview data suggested that it operated more as a bureaucratic "chain of command." The partners had expectations that each would have a representative voice in decision making but felt overly controlled by those officially designated as responsible for program oversight. Although "personality differences" may have been a surface explanation, the following discussions with a project representative and an active community member reflect the underlying conditions that strained relationships:

It's the typical them and us syndrome which we see between the federal government and state government, and state government and local government. Issues of autonomy and control. We put a word out like "partnership" between CDC, the state, and the locals which is a nice word. But administratively we have a funding agreement with the state, and then the state has a contractual agreement with the county. When you juxtapose a nice word like partnership on top of fiscal accountability and accountability for deliverables, and when you have three entities that have unequal decision-making authority, and then negotiating all of that, I think that's part of the tension.

We have CDC funding for the project. The grant is to the state health agency, and then we have the state health agency contracting the grant to the county department of health. So you have all of these controlling factors.

The evaluation recommended that the concept of partnership be reconciled with the function of oversight, because community partnerships do not operate well as bureaucratic hierarchies. To enable partnership functioning, the project hired a group process consultant who was instrumental in helping the partnership function as a team.

Types of Open-Ended Interview Questions

Spradley (1979) lists five general classifications of open-ended questions:

1. *Grand tour questions* focus on what usually takes place: Could you describe a usual day on the project? Could you describe how a patient interaction typically occurs? Could you describe a typical interaction among project staff regarding program activities?

2. *Mini-tour questions* investigate smaller aspects of experience: Would you describe your typical day as a client counselor? Would you describe what you do when a client does not show up for a scheduled appointment? Would you draw a picture of the clinic facility, indicating in which parts of the facility you spend most of your day?

3. *Example questions* ask for illustrations of specific terms or actions: You mentioned that certain patient interactions are more difficult than others; can you describe an example of a difficult interaction with a patient? You have mentioned that community outreach was more effective than other aspects of the program; can you describe an example of how outreach was effective?

4. *Experience questions* ask interviewees about their own experience with aspects of the project: You have spent a considerable amount of time doing outreach; can you tell me about some of your experiences doing outreach? You mentioned that you find outreach rewarding; from your own experience, how has outreach been rewarding?

5. *Native language questions* encourage interviewees to translate terms and phrases most commonly used in a program setting: Could you describe the meaning of "nonadherence"? Why is nonadherence a concern? You

mentioned the term "code blue"; can you tell me all about code blue? Can you provide an example of a code blue situation?

The last example illustrates the necessity of mixing and matching different question types. Sometimes one type of question (e.g., the native language question, "What is code blue?") is combined with an experience question (e.g., "Can you describe your experiences in a code blue situation?"). This type of mixing and matching is important to elicit greater focus and deeper meaning behind surface explanations. The questions that follow the first in a sequence are termed "follow-ups" and "probes." They enrich data collection in the following ways (Rubin and Rubin 1995):

- They encourage the interview respondent to provide more detailed characterizations of program situations, interactions, activities, and sequences of events.
- They examine newly discovered ideas.
- They explore unusual premises.
- They test and modify emerging themes.

The how and why question construction is often used in follow-ups and probes.

Group Interviews

Group interviews and focus groups are different from the one-person interview. In a group, the interviewees interact with each other and with the evaluator. Through expanded conversation, each participant's perspective is enriched by that of the others. Usually, the conversations are layered with deep, contextual, and rich exchanges, thus producing valuable data. For maximum results, group participation must reach a critical mass. Krueger (1994) suggested that as few as 4 to as many as 12 group participants are an acceptable range, with 7 to 10 people being optimum. The range remains small enough for all members to have an opportunity to share insights, yet large enough to provide diversity of perspectives.

The focus group is a special type of group interview in its purpose and composition (Krueger 1994). Where the mixed-group interview often combines participants of different gender, age, title, position, or another such factor, the participants in the focus group are homogeneous in makeup, e.g., program staff who are in similar positions, program managers with other program managers, or a group of program clients. Homogeneous groupings allow for one set of program stakeholders to be heard "pure of voice," because the group articulates separately from other sets of stakeholders. Also, in mixed groups, program staff may be reticent to provide true answers in front of supervisors, or clients may be hesitant to speak out in front of staff (Gruber and Trickett 1987).

Methodological Considerations in Conducting Qualitative Interviews

Sampling   How to select a sample of interviewees is a central consideration for the qualitative evaluator. In the experimental design, *random sampling* is employed so that findings may be generalized to the population from which the sample was drawn. In the qualitative approach, the evaluator uses *purposive sampling* by selecting interview subjects that, taken together, provide a rich array of perspectives about the program under study. By comparing the perspectives across interview subjects, the findings may generalize as themes regarding the program being evaluated. Case Study 5.1 illustrates the deployment of a purposive sample (i.e., CDC project representatives, university-based consultants, state health department administrators and project staff, local health department representatives, executive committee members, and work group leaders) that was drawn to provide a rich array of perspectives about a community diabetes program.

Permission   An informed consent statement should be signed by each person before the interview begins. For individual interviews, the form should emphasize that the interview will remain confidential. For group interviews, the informed consent form should emphasize that confidentiality will be maintained by the evaluator, but cannot be assured for other group members. The interviewee should retain the right to refuse to answer any question. When the interview is tape-recorded, the respondent should be assured the right to shut the tape recorder off at any point during the interview without affecting his or her status in the program. When children are interviewed, permission should be obtained in writing from their parents.

Protocol development   As with all other methods, open-ended interviewing requires a protocol that serves as a guide for asking questions, probes, and follow-ups about important dimensions of the evaluation (Rubin and Rubin 1995). An illustration follows of an abbreviated interview protocol from an evaluation of the National Centers of Excellence in Women's Health that was funded by the U.S. Office on Women's Health (Goodman et al. 2002). The national designation as a Center of Excellence (CoE) and the funding that accompanied it were based on a competitive application process among academic medical centers. The qualitative evaluation focused on the opportunities and challenges that arose when integrating women's health centers into traditional academic medical settings. A section of the protocol that pertained to the CoE's status within the institution as a consequence of receiving national designation included the following questions, prompts, and follow-ups:

> *Question 1.* What aspects of the CoE are *most* valued by the institution?
> *Prompt.* For each aspect mentioned, prompt with *who values and why?*

Follow-up. For each aspect mentioned, follow up with *how has that value influenced CoE priorities?*

Question 2. What aspects of the CoE are *least* valued by the institution?

Prompt. For each aspect mentioned, prompt with *who does not value and why?*

Follow-up. For each aspect mentioned, follow up with *how has that influenced CoE priorities?*

Question 3. In what ways does the institution support the CoE?

Follow-up. How has support from the institution changed over time, if at all?

Question 4. How has the national designation affected the visibility of women's health in your institution?

Follow-up. Has the designation improved access to resources?

Prompt. If yes, how? Keep asking until all ways affected are described.

Other questions in the protocol concerned the history of women's health activities prior to the CoE designation, the characteristics of the CoE's five core components (clinical, research, educational, leadership, and community), a description of the CoE structure and location, and the perceived status of the CoE within the institution.

Interview flow   The qualitative interview requires more active listening than aggressive questioning (Yin 1994). Rubin and Rubin (1995) provided several suggestions to ensure that the interview flows smoothly. The evaluator starts with an informal chat to put the interview subjects at ease. To encourage rich conversation, the evaluator continues with core, nonthreatening questions, such as, "What about the program makes you feel particularly good?" or "How did the program achieve that good feeling?" Throughout the interview, the evaluator maintains a neutral posture in body language, facial expression, and tone of voice and should not pretend to be sympathetic or negative. The interviewer uses the interview protocol as a guide, and when an answer does not produce rich description or it provokes additional interest, the evaluator asks follow-up and probe questions. The interviewer should also keep the door open for questions from the interviewee and end with casual chatting that may result in additional data not captured in the interview. This additional data should be recorded in the field notes.

Time constraints are also an important consideration in the pacing of the interview. It is difficult to capture rich, descriptive data during short interview periods. Therefore, the interviewer must decide when the respondent is moving off track or providing a response that is too long. Even when pacing is going well, time limits may still reduce the dimensions of the interview. In such instances, the evaluator must decide what questions can be overlooked. To compensate, the evaluator may try to highlight the missed questions in other interviews, or through a follow-up interview by telephone. Recording devices are available so that telephone interviews may be taped directly into a recorder, but informed consent should always be obtained. In addition, the interviewees—whether by telephone or in person—should always have the option to go off the record, asking the interviewer to turn the tape recorder off.

Observation   Observing aspects of a program can be an integral part of a qualitative evaluation. For instance, observing a classroom when evaluating the effects of a tobacco prevention curriculum can provide important data about program implementation. Similarly, observations of clinics, community events, or any other type of program activity can provide insights that a recollection by interview simply cannot. Thus, from the ethnographer's point of view, participant observation is the preferred method, because it combines "participation in the lives of the people under study with maintenance of a professional distance that allows adequate observation and recording of data" (Fetterman 1989, 45). In qualitative evaluation, participant observation is sometimes feasible, particularly when the evaluator resides within the organization that runs the program. But professional distance is hard to maintain when the evaluator is on the inside. Given the subjectivity inherent in qualitative approaches, the opportunity to use an outside evaluator is advisable where feasible. For an expanded discussion of participant observation, see Jorgensen (1989).

When the evaluator is from the outside, opportunities to observe a program become quite limited. The evaluator loses most of the experiential aspects of participation, and the observations become more like snapshots than movies. To maximize the value of snapshot opportunities, a practical strategy termed "focused observation" can be used. It is a systematic way for the experienced eye to concentrate observations on predetermined aspects of a program. For instance, when visiting a clinic to interview the director, the evaluator may observe the waiting room, focusing on the comfort of the seating, the demeanor of the waiting room staff, the type of educational materials in the room, and even the smell of the waiting area. A protocol for such observations in a women's health clinic may be as simple as that in Figure 5.1.

How to observe   In general, observation consists of three primary elements: actors, actions, and settings. Collectively, they compose a social scene such as a classroom activity on drugs. The evaluator considers the teacher and students as the actors, the instructional process as the actions, and the classroom environment as the setting. Much can be gained by focusing observation on the interaction of the elements in a social scene. In the observation of the classroom the evaluator may focus on teacher style, expressiveness, and performance in

1. Chairs (if the chairs are all the same, they will not suit everyone)
   a. Comfortable for women of size (large seating area or chairs without arms)?
   b. Comfortable for older women (chairs that are not too low and have an arm to assist with standing)?
   c. Comfortable for shorter women (chairs that have a footrest or are lower to the ground)?
2. Reading material or other audiovisual/educational materials
   a. What health care materials are available regarding screening for cancer, heart disease, diabetes, osteoporosis?
   b. What magazines are available for pleasure reading while waiting?
3. Wall decorations
   a. Do they reflect women's art and issues (i.e., a Remington cowboy scene might not be the best decoration for a women's health clinic)?
4. Receptionist
   a. Is receptionist able to view waiting area to spot problems?
5. Climate
   a. What is quality of interaction between staff/clients, staff/staff, client/client?
   > None/busy/casual
   > Friendly/abrupt

FIGURE 5.1 Protocol for Observation of Clinic Waiting Area

delivering the lesson. Teacher style may be contrasted with student attentiveness; the quality of interaction among teacher and students; the use of visual aids; or the nature of the classroom as conducive to program delivery. Thus, actor, actions, and settings of the social scene are building blocks for understanding the program in action.

It is vital to remember that snapshots are moments frozen in time, and generalizations about such observations cannot be made on the basis of one picture alone. The more opportunities that the evaluation team has to observe, the more generalizations can be drawn. Deeper meanings may be encoded in repeated observations of actions within the context of the social setting including the rolling of eyes, the whispering among two participants, and other aspects of body language or verbal tone. These actions have symbolic meaning as "hidden transcripts"—interpretations, attitudes, perceptions, and behaviors that are not revealed to the evaluator because the informant is uncomfortable or distrustful of sharing the data with an outsider (Scott 1990).

Field notes Taking field notes is an important device for "rounding out" the data collection after an interview or observation session. The evaluator either writes down or describes on tape aspects of the contact that include:

- What people, events, or situations were involved
- Impressions of participants' demeanor
- Points of emphasis that emerged as most central to the session just concluded
- Possible hunches, speculations, or hypotheses that were stimulated by the session
- Additional questions to be asked of contacts as follow-up (Miles and Huberman 1994)

The choice of what to record depends on the detail needed and the degree to which interviewing or observation may have been intrusive, thus altering ordinary behaviors in natural settings. For interviews, the evaluator may record perceptions regarding the interviewee's degree of comfort, honesty, and openness during the interview, which can be taken into account when considering the validity of the interview. For observations, field notes are a main vehicle for recording data. The observer may use a written form for data collection, but such an approach can be obvious, obtrusive, and possibly disruptive of the scene being observed (Jorgensen 1989). Field notes should be jotted unobtrusively. Alternatively, the observer could record observations on tape once finished. Jotting down short notes (a few words) during the observation as cues for taping the details afterward is a useful combination of techniques. Where possible, field notes should be recorded on a tape recorder immediately after interviews and observations so that the impressions are fresh. Once compiled, field notes should become part of the written record and can be coded during data analysis in the same manner as transcribed interviews.

Logic models That programs have an underlying rationale or "conceptual model" is essential if the intervention activities are to be sound in construct (Kumpfer et al. 1993; Chen 1990; Scheirer 1996). During data collection, such models can be invaluable tools for understanding the program's operations and the results that they produce. The qualitative evaluation uses logic models for the following purposes:

- To provide evidence that the project is based on underlying conceptual precepts.
- To delineate the assumed causal linkages among these precepts.
- To allow for an evaluation as to how sound these precepts and linkages are.
- To enable an evaluation of how these precepts change over the course of the project.

- To facilitate further evaluation as to why the precepts may have changed.
- To allow for comparison between these precepts and the actual implementation of project activities to see if they are confluent.
- To allow the evaluator to pinpoint where the model for the project and its actual implementation deviate from each other.
- To facilitate exploration as to why such deviations may have occurred.
- To provide an evidence base for making causal attributions between implementation and outcomes.

Two types of models are important in qualitative evaluation. The first is a "model of problem," which outlines the risk factors that result in a health dysfunction. The second is a "model of action," which outlines the intervention activities that are directed at the risk factors and health dysfunction depicted in the model of the problem (Goodman and Wandersman 1994).

Figure 5.2 illustrates a model of the problem for breast and cervical cancer in South Carolina. The problem model is composed of three elements, each of which is in a column. The left column is the problem background, or the nature of the problem (which, in Figure 5.2, is expressed in terms of incidence and mortality). Other factors that can be represented in the problem background include demographic factors (who is affected by the problem), incidence and prevalence rates, morbidity rates (e.g., days lost from school or work), and mortality rates. The middle column contains the risk factors that contribute to the problem and suggest where interventions may be focused. In Figure 5.2 such factors include the lack of a breast and cervical cancer program that is sponsored by the state health department (possibly a factor in the lack of early screening and detection). South Carolina being a rural state, lack of access to such programs is a risk factor. In Figure 5.2, the third column reiterates the problem in terms of negative health results if the risk factors are not addressed effectively. Models of the problem are used to identify those factors that should be considered when building an intervention. If the intervention can address the risk factors in the middle column, then the results in the third column may be transformed into positive health outcomes.

Figure 5.3 is a model of action for a program that is directed to the risk factors in Figure 5.2. The model of action, like all such models, is composed of a series of "micro-steps" that are logically linked to illustrate how the program unfolds. Kumpfer et al. (1993, 7–8) define such models of action as a "logical series of statements that link the problems your program is attempting to address, how it will address them, and what the expected result is." Patton (1997) describes these steps as a means-ends hierarchy. The evaluator looks for the attainment of micro-steps in the order predicted by the model of action as a way of accounting qualitatively for internal validity (Yin 1994).

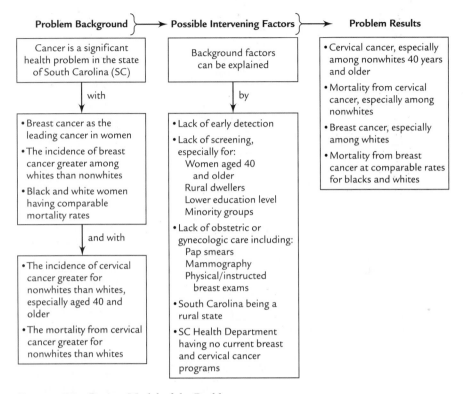

FIGURE 5.2   Project Model of the Problem

The model of action in Figure 5.3 begins in the upper left corner with the development of a statewide program that is operated by the state health department in conjunction with the American Cancer Society. Thus, one risk factor identified in the Figure 5.2 model of the problem is addressed, namely the lack of a statewide program spearheaded by the state health department. (Of course, whether the program operates effectively is another matter and would require a well-developed process evaluation.) The upper portion of Figure 5.3 further indicates that the state-supported program is well staffed and is directed at screening and addressing gaps in service for those who are screened positive and require a referral. Thus, other risk factors in Figure 5.2, such as accessibility of care, are accounted for in Figure 5.3. Once again, the quality of screening and follow-up care requires an effective process evaluation. Assuming that the program is well implemented, we can evaluate whether it helps in alleviating any of the conditions listed in Figure 5.2 under problem results, namely, the reduction of morbidity and mortality due to breast or cervical cancer. If the results are positive, then the model of action is in all likelihood an important intervention to study further and replicate.

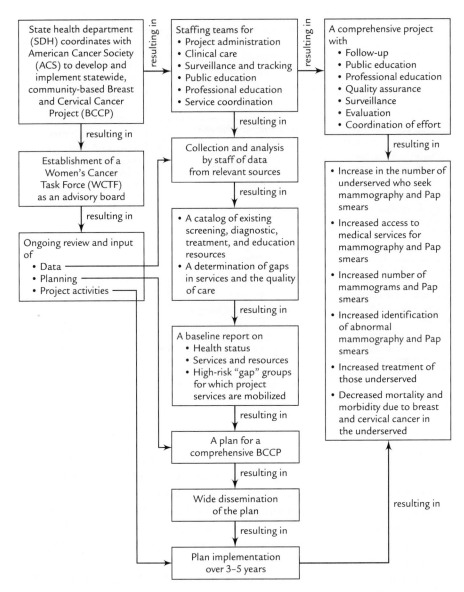

FIGURE 5.3   Project Model for the Breast and Cervical Cancer Project (BCCP)

Models like Figure 5.3 are termed "logic" models because they use the logic of "if . . . then" language construction. Figure 5.4 illustrates the "if . . . then" logic for constructing the model of action for the Breast and Cervical Cancer Project. Such logic models can be important vehicles for data collection and analysis. The evaluator may develop logic models by first collecting and reviewing original

If	Then
the state health department and American Cancer Society coordinate activities	a Women's Cancer Task Force an staff teams will result
the WCTF forms	it will advise the project on data needs, planning, and project activities
the WCTF provides input	it will influence the modification of data, planning, and activities
staff teams are formed	staff will collect and analyze data
data are collected and analyzed	a catalog of resources and the determination of gap groups will result
resources and gap groups are determined	a baseline report on health status, services, and gap groups will result
a baseline report is developed	a comprehensive plan will result
a comprehensive plan results	it will be disseminated
the plan is disseminated	it will be implemented over 3 to 5 years
the plan is implemented	comprehensive project activities will result
comprehensive project activities are implemented	outcomes including increased access to mammography and Pap smears, increased identification of abnormal results, and increased treatment will result

FIGURE 5.4   "If . . . Then" Constructions for Developing Logic Model of the Program's Action

grant submissions and requests for proposals. These documents often describe the funding and implementing organizations' rationale for the program (that is, the model of the problem) and the intervention approaches (or the model of the program's action) to be taken. By a systematic comparison of the models with quarterly and annual progress reports, the evaluator may identify gaps in activities, or activities that are inconsistent with the model. The evaluator builds questions about them into the interview protocol for discussion with stakeholders. Thus, the models become a valuable vehicle for collecting interview data. Moreover, during the interview, the evaluator may share the models with interviewees for an interpretation of their accuracy in depicting the program. The interviewees may respond by pointing out which aspects of the model occurred as indicated, which did not occur at all, or which were altered from the original plan. The evaluator may use follow-up and probe questions to prompt interviewees to further explain why and how the model was altered, thus giving insight into the dynamic processes underlying program implementation.

Several good resources are in print for developing logic models. Kumpfer et al. (1993) offer a step-by-step approach for logic model development, and Scheirer (1996) compiled a journal issue devoted to the development of such project templates. Goodman and Wandersman (1994) also provide a step-by-step approach for developing models to evaluate complex community programs, and the Kellogg Foundation (2002) has a guide for logic models.

Written records   Most programs have extensive written technical documents that provide a historical record. Yin (1994) distinguishes between documentation and archival records. The former includes letters, agendas, proposals, progress reports, newspaper clippings, and other written documents. Archival records include organizational charts, client records, and personal records such as telephone logs and calendars. Both forms of written evidence have the following attributes for qualitative evaluation:

- Stable—can be reviewed repeatedly.
- Unobtrusive—are noninteractive with the evaluation.
- Exacting—provide names, references, and details of events.
- Broad coverage—can span the life of a program.

Written records also have notable weaknesses as a source of evidence, the paramount limitation being that biases creep into the recording of written data, which are subtle and hard to glean. It is hard to know, for instance, what was left out or slanted from minutes of a meeting that were recorded months earlier. Also, another major hurdle is in securing access to program files and internal communications (Yin 1994). Access issues are best addressed in the process of contracting for the evaluation.

Program records can be analyzed in a manner similar to that for other forms of written data, like interviews and field notes (see the section below, "Data Analysis"). Records may also be used to develop logic models. The model in Figure 5.3 was developed by the following steps:

1. Compiling and chronologically ordering the Request for Application (RFA) from the funding agency, the original grant proposal, and subsequent reports (e.g., quarterly reports, renewal grants, and other project memoranda).
2. Reviewing the RFA and grant proposal to identify the project's original objectives, which were categorized as near-term, intermediate, and ultimate, and then linked by "if . . . then" logic, thus producing the model of the program's action.

3. Comparing the model to objectives and project status reported in subsequent reports to document how well program implementation matched the model of action.

4. Developing a list of interview questions to explore the instances where the model of action and program implementation diverged to better understand why deviation from the model occurred.

Equipment Used in Data Collection

The evaluator must be careful in preparing equipment in order to assure that data collection runs smoothly. Because interviews are the sine qua non of qualitative methods, tape recording devices are important. Verbatim transcripts increase accuracy, a prerequisite for producing reliable interpretations of informants' meaning. Use a high-quality tabletop recorder made for transcribing meetings. One with a multidirectional microphone can make all the difference in the world in producing audible data. Hand-held tape recorders and microcassettes are strongly discouraged because they produce ambient noise and do not have the sound quality of a multidimensional microphone. In one recent incident, a team of evaluators did not heed such advice and used hand-held devices with microcassettes. Several tapes were inaudible for transcription, thus wasting precious time and resources. Some cautious evaluators operate two tape recorders simultaneously during an interview. If one fails, the data are not lost. The best recorders are only as good as the quality of the audiotapes that are purchased. The added expense for high-quality tapes is negligible compared to the cost of losing data.

Video recordings and still pictures are other devices for documenting human interactions. Although videotaping and picture taking may be obtrusive, they become less so when the operator is at ease with each technology. Other means for reducing obtrusiveness include setting up the equipment and having supplies ready in advance of an encounter (be sure to have extra film, videotape, and audiotape), gaining permission for taping and picture taking, and using recording devices with sufficient frequency so that those being observed become accustomed to it.

Data Analysis

Qualitative data analysis consists of a series of steps that generally apply to all data analysis methods, including:

1. Affixing codes to written data
2. Placing inferences about the data in the margins of written records
3. Sorting data into similar and contrasting patterns

4. Incorporating the patterns into evaluation themes
5. Developing the themes into constructs for report writing (Miles and Huberman 1994)

The following sections elaborate on the steps in this process.

Step 1. Affixing codes to written data—types of coding   The code is the basic unit in qualitative analysis. When combined, codes are incorporated into larger analytical units that depict similar and different program patterns (Seidel and Kelle 1995). A variety of approaches can be used for coding qualitative data, including the methods described in the following paragraphs.

Simplification and reduction   This is used to help define and classify elements of a program or other social situation. For instance, Spradley (1979) interviewed "people in the bucket," the term jailed transients used to refer to themselves. Spradley further coded his interview data to classify the "types" of "people in the bucket," including "bulls"—those hired to oversee prison life; "inmates"—those who have been arrested; and "civilians"—those who cook or provide nursing services. Within categories, subcategories are possible. For instance, one type of inmate is a "trustee" who may perform different roles such as hospital orderly, barber, garbage collector, and patrol constable. Coffey and Atkinson (1996) consider simplification and reduction coding to be advantageous for rendering broad analytical categories of codes into manageable proportions. Using Spradley's example, simplification and reduction coding is produced by filling in the X in the following statement: X is a type of "person in the bucket." Every time an illustration is found in the text of an interview, the evaluator codes it by the "type of person" identified in a quote from the text. In the end, the list can be reduced to a number of types, as Spradley illustrates.

Enumeration coding   This is a special category of reduction and simplification coding used to quantify qualitative data. Table 5.1 illustrates reduction and simplification used to categorize the benefits derived from a cancer prevention and control program operating in four state health departments (Goodman, Steckler, and Alciati 1997). The benefits are broken down into main categories ("Capacity development," "Increased commitment to cancer interventions"), which are further broken down into subcategories (e.g., "Program infrastructure," "Data applications," etc.). Additionally, the table uses enumeration coding by inserting the number of times a type of benefit was mentioned in the interviews. The right-hand column, labeled "State," has four subcolumns: A, B, C, and D, each representing one of the four state health departments. The numbers within each subcolumn represent how many times a category was mentioned by respondents

TABLE 5.1   Benefits Received from Implementing DBIR: Number of Mentions

Category	Subcategory	Elements	State A	B	C	D
Capacity development (138)	Program infrastructure (63)	Networking (23)	5	10	3	5
		Cancer prevention programming (19)	3	2	10	4
		Credibility (10)	1	5	3	1
		Legislative influence (9)		1	8	
		Funding (2)	1		1	
	Data applications (40)	Formatted data (17)	16	1		
		Establish applications to cancer control (15)	11	3	1	
		Interpreted data (5)	1	1		3
		Grant development (3)	2	1		
	Staff capability (35)	Expertise (30)	1	22	4	3
		Personnel (5)	3	1	1	
Increased commitment to cancer interventions (18)	Administrative commitment (11)	Programming (6)	2	3		1
		Administrative investment (5)			1	4
	Networking (7)	Local level (4)		3	1	
		State level (3)				3

from each of the four state health departments. For example, the main category of "Capacity development" has 5, 10, 3, and 5 citations, respectively, for the health departments. When the citations are added across the rows (A through D), the sum equals 23, the number in parentheses under the element for "Networking." "Networking" is one of several elements that comprise the "Program infrastructure" subcategory. If all the elements under this subcategory are added, they produce 63 citations. Similarly, if all of the citations in the subcategories for "Capacity development" are summed, they add up to 138.

The advantage of enumeration coding is that it produces a general sense of the strength of each category. Enumeration coding produces two types of information related to strength: code intensiveness and code extensiveness. The number of times a code appears within a document is an example of code intensiveness, or the relative frequency of the code in comparison with other codes. Code intensiveness is illustrated in Table 5.1 because the codes are organized by those that were mentioned most frequently. That is, the category "Capacity development," with 138 citations, is placed above the category "Increased commitment to cancer interventions," with only 18. Similarly, the subcategory "Program infrastructure," with 63 citations, is placed above the ones with lower numbers of citations. The same pattern holds true for the elements. It should be clear that, with 138 code citations, "Capacity development" is perceived as a more pervasive benefit than "Increased commitment," with 18. By enumerating codes in this manner, the evaluator has a way of discerning which categories are most intensive, thus most thematic of benefits.

In contrast to code intensiveness, the extensiveness of a code is indicated by the number of cases in which the same code surfaces. In Table 5.1, code extensiveness is reflected across the rows by counting the number of state health departments that cited the same benefit. For example, "Networking" appears as the first element under the category "Capacity development" because it is most intensive, with 23 citations. It is also most extensive in that it is cited several times across all four state health departments, with 5, 10, 3, and 5 citations, respectively. In contrast, the element labeled "Formatted data" under the subcategory "Data applications" is less extensive; it is cited by only two state health departments. Although less extensively cited than "Networking," "Formatted data" is quite intensive for state health department A, because it was coded 16 times. Thus, it is a major benefit for this one state health department, but not for any of the others.

The preceding illustration suggests that enumeration coding for both intensiveness and extensiveness should be made with caution. Should more weight be given to "Networking" as an element since it is extensive than to "Formatted data," which is less extensive but quite intensive at one site? Moreover, one strong statement may be as powerful as several perfunctory quotes. Counting for intensiveness does not take into consideration the sentiment or conviction conveyed within the body of a quote. It is up to the evaluator to decide the proper balance to be struck among enumerated codes. In making such determinations, the evaluator can check field notes to see if the respondent was noted as presenting instances of strong sentiment, or the evaluator may go back to the interview respondents afterwards to gauge whether they agree with the relative order of importance given to each code category. Most qualitative computer software packages include enumeration coding as a basic feature and can help the evaluator save time by aggregating and counting similar codes (Coffey and Atkinson 1996; Weitzman and Miles 1995).

Cross-category coding   This is a method for answering core evaluation questions by associating different coded sets of information. The community-based diabetes project discussed earlier in the chapter provides an example of cross-category coding. A central evaluation question concerned how groups of project stakeholders perceived each other, because perceptions can influence the degree of cooperation among project partners, a trait necessary for effective implementation. Table 5.2 is an array of the stakeholders involved in the diabetes project. During data analysis, stakeholder interviews were coded by three categories: the stakeholder group holding the view (the perceiver—top row of Table 5.2); the stakeholder group being viewed (the perceived—left column of Table 5.2); and the view that is held (the perception—cells of Table 5.2).

By coding across these categories of stakeholders, an array of viewpoints was produced for in-depth analysis. For instance, by looking across the first row of Table 5.2, the evaluator can see how CDC was perceived in relationship to the project. Notice that the state and county health departments viewed CDC as needing to improve communication; the community executive committee experienced CDC as controlling and inflexible; and CDC perceived itself as being parental and having high expectations, but also as consultative. It is important that such differing views surface in the evaluation, because CDC's perception as consultant was not shared by other stakeholders who were important to the project's success. What CDC perceived as high expectations and parental attitude may have contributed to the other groups experiencing CDC as controlling. These differences, when brought to the surface by an evaluation, can pave the way for shared recognition and enhanced cooperation, whereas conflicting perceptions that do not surface may be cause for disruption.

A similar procedure can be used to depict how one group of stakeholders perceives all others. In Table 5.2, for instance, the attributions in the column "Community Work Groups" indicate that they perceived all other groups with some shade of criticism: CDC is perceived as an overseer; the state health department is bureaucratic; the county health department does not get along with others; and the executive committee is not accessible for input. The work groups perceived themselves as desiring to work well with others and being frustrated because of a dearth of volunteers. When the data in the table are scanned in this manner, the evaluator observes a potentially negative pattern. The work groups, having direct contact with community members and service providers and being negatively disposed to others, could compromise program implementation. Yet, other groups, like CDC and the executive committee, were positively disposed to the work groups (see the row labeled "Community Work Groups"). When one group is negatively disposed to most others, and that perception is not shared, the project can be compromised. Cross-category coding can help to highlight such tensions.

A third way that cross-category coding may be used is in combination with enumeration coding. To illustrate, the cells in Table 5.2 have comments that can be categorized generally as positive, negative, or neutral. For instance, CDC is

TABLE 5.2 Types and Perceptions of Stakeholders

Perceived	CDC	State Health Department Administration	County Health Department Project Staff	Community Executive Committee	Community Work Groups	University Consultants
CDC	Parental High expectations Consultative	Pressured to show results Need improved communication	No direct communication	Controlling Inflexible	Shares information Overseer	Supportive Visionary
State Health Department Administration	Micromanaging	Provide administrative oversight Too "hands on"	Inflexible	Insensitive to community participants Micromanaging	Bureaucratic	High expectations High demands Low support
County Health Department Project Staff	Machinery that makes project operate	[No perceptions provided]	Highly community involved High expertise	Concerned Committed	Does not get along well with others	Staff unfairly treated

Perceiver

Community Executive Committee	Controlling	Sounding board for policy Interface	Facilitative Frustrated with bureaucratic requirements	Clearinghouse for ideas Made sacrifices, frustrated with bureaucratic requirements	Formal No input into their deliberations	Not knowledgeable about how they function
Community Work Groups	Catalysts for activities	Variable effort Lack of clarity of purpose	Some involved at high level Involvement varies	Diligent Well defined and focused	Desire to work well with others Frustrated due to lack of volunteerism	Enthusiastic Not all equally involved
University Consultants	Strong expertise Supportive Differing levels of involvement	Strong expertise Differing levels of involvement	Strong expertise Helpful resources	Strong expertise Differing levels of involvement	Strong expertise Supportive	Limited amount of time

perceived positively by the university consultants as supportive and visionary; the state health department is perceived negatively by the county health department as inflexible; the community executive committee is perceived by the state health department as a sounding board for policy, which is more a statement of fact rather than a positive or negative attribution. By counting how many positive, negative, and neutral attributions are made, the evaluator can enumeration the general dispositions of each stakeholder group. Where negative attributions outweigh those that are positive or neutral, this may have implications for the type of feedback that the evaluator may want to share for optimizing project functioning. As with enumeration coding in general, the evaluator should be careful in relying too heavily on numbers per se, because one negative attribution may be felt so strongly that it can far outweigh several positive attributions.

Semantic construct coding   This is an elaboration of simplification and reduction coding. Recall that Spradley used a semantic construct—X is a type of inmate—to define categories of inmates. Table 5.1 uses a similar semantic device—X is a type of program benefit—to produce categories of benefits for state health department cancer prevention and control interventions. Table 5.1 best illustrates semantic construct coding because the coding delineates a taxonomy of benefits consisting of categories, subcategories, and elements, which is more than just a simplified and reduced list. When codes are so arranged into taxonomies, semantic construct coding is used to full effect.

    To produce such a taxonomy, the evaluator starts with a question from the interview protocol, for instance, "How is the program beneficial?" If the interview produced rich data, the interview respondent should have talked about program benefits. In the analysis phase, the interview data are transcribed, so the discussion of program benefits is in written form. The evaluator reads the transcript text on benefits and considers the following semantic construct: X is an example of a benefit. Where such examples are found, the evaluator codes the text, noting the type of benefit produced, thus "filling in" the X in the semantic construct. When the relevant sections of the interview are completely coded for benefits, a list of benefits results.

    At this stage, the evaluator has produced simplification and reduction codes. By then discerning how benefits are similar and different, the evaluator begins to develop taxonomies by using a semantic construct termed a *dyadic contrast*. Comparing one benefit from the list to another, the evaluator asks, "How is X benefit different from (or similar to) Y benefit?" When all the benefits are so defined, the evaluator decides on category terms that characterize all the benefits that are grouped together as similar. For instance, the main benefit categories in Table 5.1, "Capacity development" and "Increased commitment to cancer interventions," were derived from the elements in the table. This was accomplished by first asking how the elements were similar or different, resulting in the subcategories of "Program infrastructure," "Data applications," and "Staff capability." These three subcategories, taken together, are indicative of "Capacity development" as an overall category of benefit produced by the DBIR project in state health departments. In short, by using semantic constructs to distinguish between characteristics of benefits, a taxonomy of benefits results.

Evaluators may differ on which elements belong under various subcategories and categories. Thus, it is useful to have more than one person working independently to produce a taxonomy. Then the individual evaluators share their taxonomies and work towards consensus in developing a unified taxonomy. Working as a team is preferable, if not always feasible, to working alone. When working solo, the evaluator should try to come up with several different ways for classifying the elements within categories. Whether working as a team or alone, list the reasons that support or undermine the placement of each element in a taxonomy. The reasons should be supported or disputed based on the data coded from the interviews.

The possible applications of semantic construct coding are limited only by the quality of the data and the evaluator's ability to think creatively about constructs. For example, semantic constructs might be: X is a challenge experienced by a program; X is a source of program support; X is a source of program turbulence; X is a perception of project functioning; X is an outcome produced by the project. Semantic constructs should be developed and contoured in partnership with the program to be evaluated.

Relational coding   In this extension of semantic construct coding, a construct is embedded within a cause-and-effect relationship. Examples of cause and effect include: X benefit (or challenge) was caused by Y conditions (or circumstances), or X benefit (or challenge) resulted in Y conditions (or circumstances). Say that an interview subject states, "The program was most helpful to me because it gave me the opportunity to demonstrate the skills that I learned in my evaluation course at the university. As a result, I was given a positive annual job performance rating and received a nice raise in pay." In applying relational coding to such a statement, the evaluator could code as follows: "demonstrating skills" is a benefit that was caused by "learning from my evaluation course," resulting in "a positive job rating." By placing the benefits in a taxonomy, the evaluator could then see if any of the causes and results that were associated with particular benefits formed patterns. If, for instance, high levels of demonstrated skills typically resulted in pay raises, then such incentives might influence the working climate of the implementing organization. Conversely, if skills are not recognized and rewarded, the evaluator may want to explore the consequences to staff motivation and morale. When using relational coding, the data must contain descriptions that include cause-and-effect statements. Therefore, when developing interview protocols, the evaluator should include probes and follow-ups to stimulate cause-effect discourse.

Step 2. Placing inferences about the data in the margins of written records
From the ethnographer's standpoint, "people everywhere learn their culture by observing other people, listening to them, and then making inferences" (Spradley 1979, 8). In qualitative evaluation, drawing inferences begins during the data collection process and is a main objective of data analysis (Stake 1995). Take, for example, the data in Table 5.3, from an evaluation of a program for young teens who were in danger of abusing drugs (Goodman and Steckler 1987–1988). The demographic data in the table clearly indicate that the residents of the community being studied are predominantly African American, are under the age of 18, and have a large percentage (40%) of households headed by females who, with monthly payments being low, mainly rent. The average household has less than four individuals. These data can be gleaned directly from the table, but what other assumptions or inferences might be drawn that are not as obvious? For instance, given the low home ownership rate and low cost of rent, might one infer that the community lives in subsidized housing? Additionally, with less than four individuals per household, 40% being headed by females, and the average age under 18, might one infer that many of the households headed by poor, young women reflect a social condition that has been termed "the feminization of poverty"? Considering that the community is African American, might one also infer that poverty is a basis for health inequality, because minority groups tend to be affected disproportionately (Krieger 2000)?

Of course, all inferences that are drawn from the data should be verified. For the inferences drawn from Table 5.3 to take on a more dynamic flavor, the evaluator could collect observational data (composed of actors, actions, and settings—see page 185, "How to Observe") regarding the nature of the community. Even during the interview, the evaluator could test inferences that arise on the spur of the moment by probing or asking follow-up questions. During the interviews with teens in the drug prevention program, the evaluator became interested in understanding how the program activities buffered the children from abusing drugs. The evaluator followed up with an experience question (see page 181), asking, "Can you describe an example of how the program helped students avoid drugs?" When a teacher responded by describing how well children enrolled in the program performed in school, the evaluator wondered whether the students recruited into the program already were among the higher achievers in the class, thus producing a "halo effect." Therefore, the evaluator probed further with an example question (see page 181), inquiring, "You mentioned how successful the children were who were referred to the program. Can you describe

TABLE 5.3   Demographic Characteristics of the Neighborhood

Characteristic	Number	Percent
Total residents	6,142	100
African Americans	5,534	90.1
Age < 18 years	2,645	43.1
Age 10–15 years	1,015	16.5
Total no. housing units in census tract	1,865	100
No. occupant-owned	529	28.4
Average monthly rent	$110	
Average no. persons per household	3.52	
No. female-headed households	714	
No. two-parent households	496	
Median family income	$5,331	

examples of the types of children you referred to the program?" In response to this probe, the teacher indicated that those referred typically were not performing at an average level in school, were often quiet and did not participate in class, and wouldn't volunteer for extracurricular activities. Consequently, the initial inference about a halo effect was disconfirmed.

Inferences are most often drawn when the evaluator is coding an interview. During the coding process, the evaluator reads the text to fill in a semantic construct such as "X is a type of program achievement." In the process of coding, the evaluator infers from the text that part of the children's achievements resulted from having committed staff who worked overtime. The evaluator writes the inference directly into the margin next to the interview text. During the entire coding process, the evaluator adds such inferences into the margins, looking, at the same time, for data that confirm or disconfirm previous inferences that were drawn. All inferences, and data that are confirming and disconfirming, are noted in the margins. When the coding is completed, the evaluator assembles all the inferences and confirming or disconfirming data, grouping them by themes. For instance, if many examples surface of staff commitment as contributing to program success, then a theme may emerge as an important evaluation finding regarding the positive influence of staff on the intervention effect. Most qualitative software packages allow for inferences to be placed in the margins of an interview text file along with corresponding codes. Some packages can aggregate inferences for the evaluator so that they can be readily tested for confirming and disconfirming data.

Step 3. Sorting data into similar patterns and contrasting patterns   Matrix displays are used for arraying qualitative data that result from coding and categorizing. Table 5.2 is an example of a matrix display. Miles and Huberman (1994) present a thorough discourse on matrix arrays and provide an assortment of matrix applications for qualitative data. Possibilities for matrix displays include arrays of time, importance, concept, critical incident, and project role (the latter illustrated in Table 5.2). As previously noted, arraying the data in a matrix display facilitates the development of inferences, patterns, and themes.

Step 4. Incorporating the patterns into evaluation themes   The inferences that are drawn can be used to discover patterns. Where inferences are consistent, they become thematic features to be highlighted in reporting the evaluation findings. Where inferences are inconsistent or in conflict with one another, then a method like "breakdown and resolution" may be used to resolve discrepancies (Denzin 1984). During the breakdown phase, the evaluator first identifies in what ways the inferences are at odds. Then, during resolution, the evaluator explores ideas for linking inferences until they can be reconciled under a unified theme. For example, in a study of the mechanisms for sustaining a health promotion program, turnover of staff and participants appeared to have a positive effect on the program's viability. Because turnover often signifies program turbulence and instability, for it to have a positive effect on the program was perplexing. To reconcile this putative inconsistency, the evaluator explored in what way turnover could be functional for the program. A pattern emerged suggesting that those who left the program often disagreed with its core goals and functions. Thus, those who remained helped solidify program identity and those who left defined through turnover what they did not support (Steckler and Goodman 1989).

Step 5. Developing the themes into constructs for report writing   The themes that emerge may be synthesized into constructs that are the raw materials for generating an evaluation report. In developing constructs, the evaluator must take pains to assure their validity prior to reporting because subjectivity may lead to shortcomings and misinterpretations. Stake (1995) suggests that the main method is triangulation, or the combining of multiple sources of evidence. Triangulation can take several forms, including informant, methods, data, evaluator, time, and theory (Denzin 1984; Yin 1994). The simple combining of methods to reduce or unify constructs is what Coffey and Atkinson (1996) call "vulgar triangulation," because different methods explore different facets of the data. Thus, the use of different methods should be geared towards an appreciation for complexity and variety. To avoid the pitfalls of vulgar triangulation, the technique can best be applied by aggregating the themes according to the study questions that they inform. Then the themes under each study question are triangulated in order to develop the construct to be reported. In qualitative evaluation, such constructs should coincide with the evaluation questions that inform the study. With this tack, triangulation is not methods focused, but themes focused. The following steps are suggested for triangulating themes into constructs:

- Provide each theme with a title.
- Place each theme title under the study question.
- Next to each theme title, indicate what aspect of the question it informs.
- Rank each aspect in the order of importance to the question it informs.
- Next to each aspect, list the ways in which it is complementary to the others.
- Next to each aspect, list the ways in which it differs from the others.
- Organize report writing according to the rankings and ways that the themes are complementary and different for each evaluation question to be answered.

The Case Study as an Evaluation Methodology

The primary purposes of the case study are to discover how a program functions as a dynamic system and to examine how the environment in which it operates affects program functioning (Stake 1995). Yin (1994) writes that the qualitative case study is "the preferred strategy when 'how' or 'why' questions are being posed, when the investigator has little control over events, and when the focus is on a contemporary phenomenon within some real-life context" (p.1). Program evaluation often fits these criteria. As previously noted, how and why questions are used in qualitative evaluation to produce rich and thick description of interviewees and can also be used as the main questions for the evaluation. The evaluator has little control over program events; the evaluation is the study of real life and contemporary events. Another hallmark of the case study evaluation is the use of multiple data collection and analysis methods to produce an in-depth, storylike quality in describing the program dynamics and the results that they produce. The evaluator often uses vignettes and quotes to dramatize the description, thus bringing the reader in direct contact with the views and sentiments of program participants (Stake 1995).

CASE STUDY 5.2

Combining Methods of Evaluating Data

The case is a study of a breast and cervical cancer program funded by the Centers for Disease Control. The case not only illustrates how methods are combined to produce a rich depiction of the program but also elucidates a story about survival and creativity in the wake of events that could have undermined the program's ability to operate. The evaluation was retrospective and assessed the program from its inception in 1990 through 1997.

PROGRAM BACKGROUND

The Breast and Cervical Cancer Project (BCCP) was a multiyear, statewide effort devoted to diagnosing and treating breast and cervical cancer. BCCP originated from the Breast and Cervical Cancer Mortality Prevention Act, Title XV, which was passed by Congress in 1990. The act provided for funds to the Centers for Disease Control and Prevention (CDC), which awarded breast and cervical cancer prevention projects to eight states, including the one depicted in this case. The award was made to the state health department to focus on six major service areas, which included:

- Providing breast and cervical cancer screening to low-income women by private physicians and clinics under contract to the state health department.
- Making referrals for medical treatment for women who needed it.
- Developing and distributing public information and education to increase the use of screening services.
- Providing education to health professionals to improve the screening process.
- Establishing ways to monitor the quality of screening.
- Establishing appropriate surveillance programs.

The logic models for the program appear in Figures 5.2 and 5.3.

THE CASE EVALUATION

The evaluation questions, along with the data that inform each question, are included in Table 5.4. Data collection used both quantitative (screening and billing forms, patient records) and qualitative (reports, documents, and interviews) sources of data.

CLIENT DEMOGRAPHIC CHARACTERISTICS

The data from patient records indicate that African Americans represented 59% of the project's clientele, whites 38%, and others 3% of the total (0.02% had no specification for race). Across groups, approximately 35% were under 40 years of age, 58% had no data recorded for health insurance, and 27% had no health insurance.

PROJECT IMPLEMENTATION

The quarterly reports for Years 1–5 were reviewed to document objectives reported as accomplished, partially accomplished, not accomplished, and having insufficient information to judge level of accomplishment. The results are summarized in Table 5.5. The left-hand column lists the objectives that were reported in quarterly reports over 5 years. The reports categorized the objectives by (1) administration/management, (2) project planning, (3) data systems, (4) implementation of project activities, and (5) project outcomes. Two members of the evaluation team independently reviewed all annual and quarterly reports to judge the level of accomplishments of each objective. Since the reports were organized by objective with a narrative for each indicating its status, the evaluators could readily judge the level of accomplishment. The evaluator ratings are

TABLE 5.4   Evaluation Questions and Data Collection Sources

Questions	Data Source
What were the sociodemographic characteristics of BCN patients who were screened?	Screening and billing forms
What was the likelihood of breast cancer and cervical cancer by age, race, and insurance type?	Screening and billing forms, patient records
What was the presumed "model of action" proposed for BCN?	Project annual and quarterly reports
How did the presumed "model of action" compare with actual project implementation?	Project annual and quarterly reports
What were the perceived benefits produced by BCN?	Interviews and program documents
What were the areas of perceived improvements needed by BCN?	Interviews and program documents
How were community approaches effective?	Interviews and program documents
How could community educational approaches be improved?	Interviews and program documents
How were the relationships between BCN and service providers perceived?	Interviews and program documents
What adjustments in practice did providers make due to BCN?	Interviews and program documents
What were the perceived barriers to screening?	Interviews and program documents
What were the perceived barriers to follow-up?	Interviews and program documents

indicated at the top of Table 5.5: "+" indicates that the evaluators rated the objective as met; "0" indicates that the objective was partially met; "−" indicates that the objective was not met; and "?" indicates that there was insufficient information in the quarterly and annual reports to ascertain the level of accomplishment of the objective.

The numbers 1–5 across the top row of the table stand for each of the 5 years for which the objectives were rated, with a total rating across the 5 years appearing in boldface. Notice that the 5 years are repeated for each type of rating. The cells contain the number of objectives for each category in the left column by the rating they were assigned. For example, there was one staffing objective in Year 1 and one in Year 2, both being rated as met. At the bottom of each row, the overall percentages are listed for the ratings of each objective by fiscal year, with the total percentages appearing in boldface.

Overall, 102 objectives (51%) were met, 46 objectives (23%) were partially met, 37 objectives (18%) were not met, and 17 objectives (8%) could not be fully analyzed.

TABLE 5.5   Status of Objectives by Project Year (FY91/92–FY95/96)

Fiscal Years

Objective	+ 1	+ 2	+ 3	+ 4	+ 5	+ T	0 1	0 2	0 3	0 4	0 5	0 T	− 1	− 2	− 3	− 4	− 5	− T	? 1	? 2	? 3	? 4	? 5	? T
Administration/ Management	·																							
Staffing	1	1				2						0						0						0
Contract oversight	3	6	3	4	3	19						0	1					1	1			1		2
Fiscal development	·				1	1						0			1	1	1	3						0
Project Planning	·																							
Plan development		2		1		3						0	1	1				2						0
Program planning	·							1				1						0						0
Data Systems	·																							
Community health need profiles	1	2	2	1	1	7	1			1		2			1			1				1	1	2
Surveillance and tumor registry	1	1	1			3	1	1				2	1	1	1			3				2	2	4
Client tracking		2		1	1	4	2	1	1			4	2	1	2	1		6						0
Community health services profiles	1				1	2					1	1						0						0
Client record/Billing	1				1	2			1	1	1	3		2				0						0
Project evaluation	·					0		1	2			3			2		2	4				3		3

Implementation of Project Activities																								
Task force/coalition	2	3		2	7					1		1	1		1		1	1					1	1
Professional education	2	2	1	1	6					1		1	1		2	1	1	4	1				1	1
Information dissemination	2	6		4	12	1	2					3	1	1	1	2		3					1	1
Community initiatives (other than information dissemination)		1	2		3		1	2		1		3	1	1	2	1		4						0
Quality assurance audits		1	3	3	7		2			1		3	1					1						0
Interorganizational service arrangements with ACS					3			1	1			2						0						0
Project Outcomes																								
Service-related	1	4	2	2	11		4	1	3			8		1	1			0						0
Client-related		3			3		1	2	2	3		8	1		1	1	1	3			2		1	3
Community education	2	2			2	1						1						0						0
Professional education	1	1	2	1	5							0			1			1						0
Total	16	37	16	17	16	102	7	12	11	9	7	46	4	7	15	7	4	37	1	0	2	7	7	17
Percent by Fiscal Year	57	66	36	435	47	51	25	21	25	23	21	23	14	13	34	18	12	18	4	0	5	18	21	8

Thus, more than half of the objectives were fully met and almost three-quarters of the objectives were met to a considerable degree. The table also indicates the percentage of objectives met by category. For instance, objectives for administration and management were largely met, but the development of data systems had a mixed record, with the surveillance and tumor registry system slower to develop along with the rescreening and follow-up of clients.

The clinical records indicate that the project's level of effort was sufficient to screen 32,301 women, with 84% reporting no recent breast symptoms, and 15% reporting symptoms. Of the 31,703 patients who were given a clinical breast examination (CBE), 87% did not require a follow-up examination, and 13% required follow-up because of any abnormalities found. In total, 2,459 patients were identified with abnormal mammograms and 828 patients with abnormal Pap smears.

BENEFITS AS OUTCOME DATA

The benefits produced were derived using semantic construct coding to develop a taxonomy and enumeration coding to produce levels of code intensiveness. The interview data produced five major categories of project benefits that were cited by stakeholder groups, including benefits to women served (83 citations), benefits to the community at large (72 citations), organizational benefits (42 citations), benefits to professional services (24 citations), and benefits to the external environment (12 citations). The numbers in parentheses are enumerations of the number of codes per category. Each of the categories has several subcategories. For instance, stakeholders cited four subcategories of benefits to women served: medical (53 citations), behavioral (20 citations), educational (7 citations), and social (2 citations). To support the elements in the resulting taxonomy and to provide a "richness" in reporting the data, quotations were added to the final report to illustrate the respondents' perceptions of program benefits. Several of these quotations follow.

> *Provider:* I feel like [the volunteer workers] are reaching women that probably would not come in and have a mammogram. We do screenings with our mobile program. We have volunteers recruiting the women, so we actually go to their community and do the mammograms. We actually bring it to their door and they have someone on our mobile or a different mobile to do the clinical breast or the Pap smear. We really are reaching those women that wouldn't have it, and have found some cancers. Of course, those women that come into the hospital too have the mammogram done. They wouldn't have. They couldn't afford it. I get a lot of calls during the course of the day of people asking "How can I get a mammogram? I don't have any insurance; I'm not able to afford this and I have a lump." It's nice to be able to give them the referring physician's name for BCCP. It's nice to be able to answer them with something positive. Not saying, "I'm sorry, we can't help you."

> *Volunteer:* I've seen personal cases where women have found a lump or something suspicious and it scared them because they knew they didn't have the money to do anything with it. But they knew the danger of not having something done. BCCP enabled them to check it out. I've seen many grateful women because they were told everything's okay.

> *Outreach worker:* Most of these women who went through BCCP would not have gone without a doubt because they did not have money. They did not have insurance. They don't have jobs that provide insurance. No one told them the impor-

tance of having a mammogram. A lot of women are afraid to have mammograms. Through BCCP, we were able to share with them all the information and that made them a lot more comfortable. A lot of women weren't that uncomfortable with it but didn't have the money. Now they could go someplace through the BCCP and didn't have to pay and that really played a big part.

DHEC staff: BCCP reached women that have never been reached before and gave them screening services that they would not have otherwise gotten.

CDC representative: I think one of the main successes is that they have been able to reach quite a few women. Their numbers have been quite good. They have gotten good penetration into minority populations, particularly African Americans.

Note how the quotes are consistent across respondents. This is a form of triangulation by informant through a comparison of responses that are confirming, thus supportive of the theme that women screened through BCCP would not otherwise have been screened. The interviews were also triangulated with data from client records, which indicate that of the 32,301 women screened, 2,459 had abnormal mammograms and 828 had abnormal Pap smears, with the mean ages for the women being 45.4 and 37.1 years, respectively. This form of triangulation by method is an example of how data sources are enriching, for not only were women in a gap group being served, but the data demonstrate that the program also was effective in screening and surfacing case morbidity.

The evaluation of BCCP also pointed out needed improvements, including those involving the sufficiency of project management (57 citations), directions from CDC (37 citations), resources (37 citations), and project approach (34 citations). Just as with project benefits, project needs were placed in a taxonomy, counted for intensiveness within and extensiveness across interviews, and dramatized with quotations. Again, both semantic construct and enumeration coding were used in developing the taxonomy.

A CASE EXAMPLE OF PROGRAM TRANSFORMATION FOR SURVIVAL

Case study evaluations provide opportunities to convey important vignettes that emerge from the themes regarding a program and its operations. For BCCP, an interesting story unfolded regarding the overnight transition of the program from the state health department to the American Cancer Society. The evaluation was able to document the transition visually through a series of logic models, one for each year of BCCP's operations. By putting the models in chronological order, the evolution of changes in operations was depicted. To illustrate, Figures 5.3 and 5.5 are the same, but the latter indicates how parts of the model evolved over time. The evolution tells an important story about the BCCP project that is illustrated by the changes in the model.

From 1990 to 1993, BCCP was the sole domain of the state health department, as indicated by the dotted line in the upper left box that omits the American Cancer Society (ACS) until 1993. Also, in the first year, the project did not have components or outcomes, indicated by the dotted "Xs" across the two boxes on the right. As a result of its work in the first year, project staff recognized the need to implement a comprehensive program and become outcome focused. Hence, the two right boxes were added after Year 1. This indicates an evolution to a more comprehensive approach.

In Year 3, a community health planning model called PATCH (Planned Approach to Community Health) was incorporated as a structure for coordinating the project

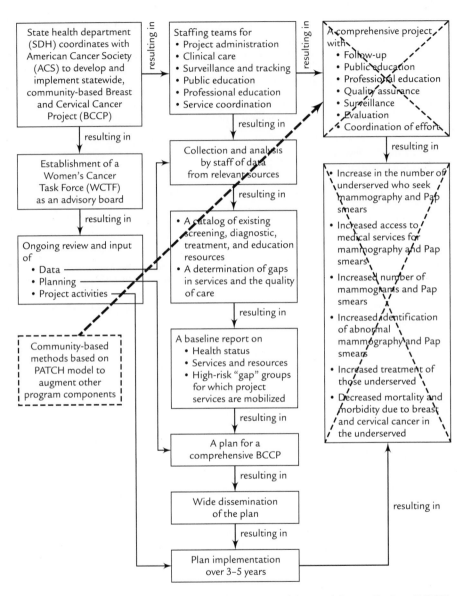

FIGURE 5.5 Evolving Project Model for the Breast and Cervical Cancer Project (BCCP)

components. PATCH, a model developed by the Centers for Disease Control and Prevention, enhanced project implementation by providing a structure for community-based activities. In Year 5, staff were incorporated into teams, as indicated by the dotted line in the upper middle box. Teaming was the result of a process evaluation that led to restructuring for more coordination.

Perhaps the most dramatic change in the model of action occurred in Year 3, when CDC entered into an agreement with the national American Cancer Society to establish a framework for joint activities in cancer prevention and control. Following the national accord, the state health department and the regional ACS developed a memorandum of agreement to combine resources to recruit women at risk for breast and cervical cancer into screening services. The state health department began to utilize ACS, its staff, educational materials, and volunteer networks to promote awareness, education, and the recruitment of women into services. These changes are reflected in the model of action beginning in 1993 (box in the upper left corner).

In the actual evaluation, six different logic models were drawn (1990–1995). By developing the models prior to conducting interviews, the evaluator realized the importance of the program shift to ACS and included questions about its effect on the program. The introduction of such questions produced a deeply nuanced theme, which is indicated by the story that surfaced regarding why ACS was incorporated into the program's model of action. The evaluation goes on to illustrate the unforeseen benefits of a governmental health agency partnering with ACS, a private, nonprofit organization. The story picks up in 1995, two years after the partnership was established. With the election of a new governor who was committed to reducing the size of state government, the staff hired and trained to conduct the BCCP program were in jeopardy of losing their jobs. Consequently, the leadership of the state health department and ACS arranged for the transition of the project staff from governmental to ACS employ. This feat is a remarkable accomplishment, made more so since the transition literally happened overnight—on a Friday, the staff worked for the state, and on the next Monday, they worked for ACS. Respondents elaborated on the reasons for the shift:

> This is my story. It was dramatic and it came about because we had a new governor who began to downsize state government. That was a statement he was going to make for his political party. And he was going to carve off this, that, and the other from the health department—they were faced with downsizing.

> The state health department had an opportunity to move out twenty-five positions or so [to ACS] and save the program. Had they kept all those positions, through an attrition process, people with superior length of duty [at the state health department] would have moved into those positions because most BCCP staff had been state employees for only three years. They would've all been history, and people who knew nothing would have taken positions in BCCP. And so, moving BCCP to ACS was a good marriage.

> We were going through an organizational upheaval here at the state health department. There was pressure to reduce the head count in the central office of the agency by 100 positions. That put people who had been recently hired or who were on temporary grant positions at much risk. We believed that BCCP was at much risk of losing its people, not losing the project. We would have been given "gifts" of other people who got bumped from somewhere else. We didn't know what would happen, so we were looking for alternative ways to do the project and not have it dismantled by the monster reduction in force that was happening. But the other thing was, it seemed like it made sense. In our state, ACS is a community organization, with links in the community doing cancer control, eager to develop better connections into parts of the population that they didn't historically reach. This was a

chance to build the capacity of that organization to do some things that we historically haven't been terribly successful at.

In short, the case evaluation produced important lessons about the fragility of climate in which even effective projects like BCCP operate, and about the strategic importance of partnerships with organizations in different sectors. Most likely, the BCCP project was saved by the ability of state government to transition its project staff to the private sector with great haste. Such lessons gleaned from case evaluations have a resonance that can be generalized beyond the one project being assessed.

SUMMARY

This chapter provides an overview of the place for qualitative methods in program evaluation. Methods can be used for several purposes and across all four phases of evaluation. Regardless of the purpose, a qualitative evaluation tends to use the same sets of methods for data collection and analysis. For data collection, we have emphasized the primacy of the interview supplemented by observations, field notes, document reviews, and logic models. For data analysis, coding becomes the basic unit in a process of inference building towards pattern and the themes of the evaluation. The case study triangulates methods to produce a rich and nuanced depiction of program functioning. When qualitative methods are so triangulated, and when they are used in combination with quantitative evaluation approaches, the resulting evaluation is all the richer in its blending of nuances.

6 | Formative and Impact Evaluations

Federal and state public health agencies, nongovernmental organizations, not-for-profit or for-profit companies, and foundations that fund large-scale health promotion programs typically require an evaluation of behavioral impact. Valid evaluations of impact, however, often are not conducted because of the poor technical expertise of staff, lack of time, and/or lack of resources. Evaluations also fail when qualitative, process, and formative evaluations are not conducted to identify program strengths and weaknesses. Before an allocation of significant fiscal resources to a new or ongoing program is made, a carefully designed evaluation plan and monitoring system need to be field-tested. HP programs need to pilot-test the extent to which a program can be successfully implemented and the extent to which it has produced desirable behavioral changes among participants.

As discussed in Chapter 1, an evaluability assessment should be conducted to determine if a behavioral impact evaluation is feasible. This requires a budget and a written program plan and objectives; specification of the type, frequency, and intensity of intervention methods; and well-defined measurement and data-collection procedures. A formative evaluation, including a description of methods to pilot-test and to document routine program implementation, should be planned. The authors are often asked to consult on the evaluation of programs for which one or several of the core intervention or assessment components are lacking or for which evaluation plans are not well defined. So, before an evaluation design is selected, a program may have to go back to step 1 or 2 to specify program procedures and methods, address related issues, and revise a draft plan.

Evaluation planners need to gain competence and confidence in selecting program evaluation designs and applying them to and modifying them for a population at risk and the unique characteristics of each setting. Evaluation staff need to be able to choose from alternative evaluation designs, basing decisions on factors such as:

- Characteristics of the target health and behavior problems
- Objectives of a program

- Purposes/types of the evaluation
- Availability of program and evaluation resources
- Phase of intervention development

When preparing an evaluation plan, program staff need to identify and to attempt to control for the numerous possible sources of bias that will affect, if not compromise, interpretation of data and results. Realistically, however, each individual program component cannot and should not be evaluated to determine its specific impact. Multiple methodological issues raised in previous chapters must be addressed before concluding that a program has had a significant impact on behavior. A thorough appreciation of evaluation and measurement principles and intervention methods, described in the literature related to a program, is needed to answer one enduring, primary question: Can the observed change in a behavioral impact rate, if statistically significant, be attributed to the health promotion program?

EVALUATION DESIGNS

A design specifies when, from whom, how, and what program procedures, interventions, and measurements will be applied during program implementation. It is a schematic diagram of a well-organized evaluation. If successfully implemented, a rigorous experimental design should allow conclusions to be drawn with confidence. It enables a program to estimate, with varying degrees of certainty, what level of change would be produced if participants had not been exposed to the HP intervention. As presented in Table 6.1, three categories of evaluation design are important for this discussion: experimental, quasi-experimental, and non-experimental. Biases that each evaluation has to address are presented in the next section.

FACTORS AFFECTING INTERNAL VALIDITY OF RESULTS

Although in principle an evaluation should be concerned with internal and external validity, health promotion programs should be primarily concerned with internal validity. This enables staff to make optimal use of resources, time, and personnel to maximize the opportunity to produce desired changes. External validity is almost always beyond the scope or capacity of an individual program. Attempts to create a program that is generalizable, e.g., statewide or systemwide dissemination, may attenuate the efficacy of the unique characteristics and synergy of program personnel and participants, so that few or no changes are produced.

Internal validity is defined as the extent to which an observed impact, a significant improvement in cognitive, skill, behavioral, health status, or economic

TABLE 6.1   Categories of Evaluation Design

Design	Description
Nonexperimental design	Includes one E group but no C or $\underline{C}$ group. Typically asserts little or no control over the major bias to internal validity.
Quasi-experimental design	Includes an experimental (E) group and a comparison ($\underline{C}$) group created by methods other than random assignment and includes observations of both groups, both prior to and after application of intervention (X) procedures. It may yield interpretable and supportive evidence of behavioral impact, asserting varying degrees of control over several biases, but usually not all that bias internal validity.
Experimental design	Includes random assignment of an experimental (E) and a control (C) group, and observations of both groups, prior to and after application of the intervention (X) procedures. It yields the most interpretable and defensible evidence of behavioral impact, asserting the greatest degree of control over the major factors that bias or compromise the internal validity of results.

indicator rate, can be attributed to a planned intervention. Did a planned, replicable intervention (X) produce the significant increase in the impact rate (O)? Is X the only or the most plausible explanation for the significant changes in O, or can all or part of the observed change be attributed to other factors? Are the results unequivocal and defensible?

External validity is defined as the extent to which an observed, significant change in a behavioral or health impact rate, attributed to a feasible, replicable intervention and documented by multiple evaluations with high internal validity, can be generalized to other program settings and to comparable populations at risk, e.g., workers in a similar industry, patients using comparable clinical services, or students in other demographically comparable school systems. External validity is primarily addressed by multiple Phase 3 and 4 program evaluations. It is supported by a meta-analysis of the evidence. If numerous Phase 3 and 4 evaluation results are consistently positive and have high internal validity, a health promotion intervention may have external validity.

A CONTEMPORARY SYNTHESIS OF BIASES TO INTERNAL VALIDITY

The evaluation literature (e.g., Campbell and Stanley 1966) has traditionally identified eight common factors as threats (biases) to internal validity of observed results. Each factor presented in Table 6.2 may confound or bias interpretation

TABLE 6.2 Traditional Threats to Internal Validity

Threat	Definition
1. History	Bias from significant, unplanned national, state, local, or internal administrative organizational events or exposures occurring at the program site during the evaluation study period that may produce behavior change by participants. *Example:* A legislature imposes a new statewide tax of $0.50 on tobacco.
2. Maturation	Bias from natural, biological, social, or behavioral changes occurring among the participants or staff members during the study period, such as growing older, staff becoming more skilled, or becoming more effective and efficient in program delivery. *Example:* A 10-year-old child matures socially and psychologically as a 13-year-old adolescent in an urban setting where peers encourage sexual activity.
3. Testing	Bias from taking a test, being interviewed, or being observed. *Example:* An adult in a cholesterol reduction program is interviewed by a nutritionist about amount of fiber or fat intake, prompting a socially desirable response or changes in fat/fiber intake behavior over a short period of time.
4. Instrumentation	Bias from changes in the characteristics of measuring instruments, observation methods, or data-collection processes, affecting the reliability and validity of instruments. *Example:* Evaluators use a carbon monoxide method of ascertaining smoking levels at baseline and a behavioral report at follow-up.
5. Statistical regression	Bias from the selection of an experimental, control, or comparison group on the basis of an unusually high or low level or characteristic yielding changes in subsequent measurements. *Example:* A program is used to select and study a group of employees at least 30% overweight at the beginning of a weight-reduction program.
6. Selection	The identification of a control (C) or comparison ($\underline{C}$) group not equivalent to the E group, because of demographic, psychosocial, or behavioral characteristics. *Example:* A group of 100 adult smoking community residents is chosen as a comparison group to 100 adult smoking university employees.
7. Participant attrition	Bias introduced in impact data by nonrandom, systematic, or excessive attrition (10% or more) of experimental (E), control (C), or comparison ($\underline{C}$) group participants. *Example:* In a stress-management course, 40 of 100 participants from the C group and 20 of 100 from the E group drop out of the program. Those experiencing high stress levels drop out in greater numbers, because they cannot devote time to the program due to other commitments.
8. Interactive effects	Any combination of the above seven threats.

TABLE 6.3   Biases to Attribution of Impact and Internal Validity

Type of Bias	Dimensions	Issues
Measurement	Validity (V) Reliability (R)	Methods and procedures to produce accurate and reproducible data
Selection	Participation rate (P) Attrition rate (A)	Representativeness of the study sample of a defined population at risk
Historical	External events (H) Internal events (I) Intervention (X)	Type, frequency, intensity, and duration of exposure to planned and unplanned events

of behavioral impact by independently or collectively producing all or part of an observed change in a rate.

Contemporary evaluation planning methods and 25 years of evaluation research studies in health promotion demand a revision and synthesis of the traditional eight threats to validity by Campbell and Stanley (1966). As noted in Table 6.3, these eight sources of bias (threats) to the internal validity of evaluation results should be grouped into the three primary sources of bias:

1. Measurement bias

2. Selection bias

3. Historical bias

The literature and the experience of the authors confirm that these three and their interactions are the most frequent and serious biases that compromise evaluation results. An evaluation team needs to know the major factors that confound evaluation results and to learn how best to control for each. It needs to know how each design enables an evaluation to rule out plausible, alternative explanations of impact.

Measurement Bias

As discussed in Chapter 3, the first and most critical bias to attribution of behavioral impact is *measurement*. It has two core sources of potential bias or error: poor validity (V) and poor reliability (R). Each evaluation must present empirical evidence of the accuracy and stability of its data, collected prior to and during an evaluation, to confirm measurement quality. A primary concern is the extent to which an evaluation has used standardized and replicable measurement methods, representing the "gold standard" of the measurement science base for all dependent and independent variables. Elimination of these two sources of bias must occur before an evaluator can accurately assess if, and how much, change in an impact rate has occurred. Randomization, however, does not "control" for poor measurement; it merely distributes poor baseline and follow-up data equally. This bias category combines threats 3 and 4 of Campbell and Stanley.

Selection Bias

The second bias to attribution of impact is *selection*. It has two sources of bias: participation (P) rate and attrition (A) rate of the target population. A program must describe the eligibility criteria for the defined population at risk (population denominator) for its evaluation and enumerate the total number/percent of eligible participants: Do the eligibility criteria (inclusion/exclusion) produce bias? A primary question *not* addressed by many evaluation reports is: What percent of all eligible subjects participated and what percent refused to (participation rate, P)? How representative of the population at risk is the evaluation study sample? Among participants eligible for a follow-up, who were lost to follow-up, who initially agreed to participate but decided to withdraw or drop out of the evaluation (attrition rate, A)? All subjects who were randomized should typically be used to compute an impact rate: intent to treat policy. The primary selection question is: How representative are the results? Can the results of an evaluation be applied to the defined population in this setting?

Each rate $(P$ and $A)$ defines how small or large a selection bias was in an evaluation and can be used to determine the internal validity of results. The ability to generalize evaluation results to a defined population may be severely limited or impossible if each of these selection biases is not addressed in planning and implementing an evaluation. A formative evaluation of measurement and intervention procedures is needed to ensure they can be routinely implemented. It should produce insights that will significantly reduce refusals at the onset of an evaluation and attrition of participants during the evaluation. An evaluation needs to present a comparison of the baseline characteristics of the eligible participants who agreed and the participants who were eligible but refused or dropped out. This bias combines threats 2, 5, 6, and 7 of Campbell and Stanley.

Historical Bias

The third bias to attribution of impact is *history*. It has three primary sources of bias. First—what transient or enduring external historical events (H) may be a plausible cause(s) of significant changes in a behavioral impact or health outcome rate? For example, a powerful, nationwide event that had a substantial external impact on all evaluation studies in progress was the terrorist attacks in New York and Washington, D.C., on September 11, 2001. Second—what internal (I) programmatic, historical events may have occurred during the evaluation, e.g., changes in organizational or program administration and/or policy, structure, staffing, or resources? Third—what specific intervention procedures (X_n) were delivered or not delivered to what percentage of eligible evaluation participants? The issue is the extent to which planned exposure to the program (X)—intensity, duration, and frequency of delivery of specific intervention procedures—was documented (process evaluation) and the degree of standardization, replicability, and stability (fidelity) of intervention procedures by staff. This bias represents threats 1 and 2 of Campbell and Stanley.

An evaluation will not be able to attribute observed changes to an intervention unless measurement, selection, and historical biases are ruled out. It is important to stress: An evaluation design does not always "control" for each of the three biases. The purpose of a design is to create E versus C group equivalence at baseline and follow-up. An experimental design, if successfully implemented, equally distributes, by randomization, known and multiple unknown variances for biases that are independent predictors of change. A randomized design attempts to equally distribute the combination of independent external history (H), internal history (I), or treatment (X) exposures among E and C group participants. A good plan and successful formative evaluation will significantly improve control over each of these biases.

EVALUATION DESIGN NOTATION

Learning the basic notation of evaluation design is necessary for efficient communication. A small set of letters, representing different elements of a design, are used in discussions in other sections of this chapter:

Notation	Definition
R	Random assignment of an evaluation study participant (or unit) to a group.
E	Experimental (intervention or treatment) group: $E_1, E_2, E_3,$ $\ldots, E_n$ indicates planned exposure of the group to different intervention procedures.
C	Control (equivalent) group established only by random assignment; indicates no exposure to an intervention or exposure to a minimum or standard intervention procedures.
$\underline{C}$	Comparison group established through any method other than randomization.
X	Intervention procedures applied to an E group: $X_1, X_2, X_3, \ldots,$ X_n indicates an intervention consisting of multiple, different procedures.
n	Number of participants in the E, C, or $\underline{C}$ group.

O	An observation or measurement to collect data, including tests, interviews, visual or audio ratings, or record reviews: O_1, O_2, O_3, . . . , O_n indicates multiple measurements at different times.
T	Time when an observation, assignment to a group, or application of intervention procedures has occurred: T_1, T_2, T_3, . . . , T_n indicates repeated observations.

EVALUATION DESIGNS

There are very few evaluation designs that are sufficiently methodologically rigorous to produce valid, interpretable results. Five designs (discussed below) are the most likely choices used to evaluate a health promotion program. More complex designs, e.g., multifactorial designs, are possible but are typically beyond the resources of an ongoing program. Multifactorial designs are conducted to determine multiple questions about the independent (X_1) and interactive $(X_1 + X_2)$ effects of intervention procedures. These types of designs are usually applied in a Phase 1 or Phase 2 evaluation research study, which has extensive scientific expertise, resources, staff, and time to meet its multiple/complex implementation, training, and analytical demands. A multisite community group evaluation design presents many complex issues. Comprehensive discussions of evaluations that plan to use a site as the unit of randomization, intervention, and analysis (not individual participants), such as a school, county, city, hospital, or factory, are presented by McKinley et al. (1996) and Murray (1998).When a group design is applied, stratification and matching of units, prior to randomization, is strongly recommended (see Case Study 6.4).

The program setting or target population may make it more difficult to conduct an evaluation of high methodological quality. A common constraint is the challenge of applying the experimental model: a randomized design with baseline and follow-up measurement of the E group and C group. Unfortunately, because of a lack of training, confidence, or resources program staff often do not select more rigorous and methodologically stronger evaluation designs. Always start with the most rigorous design possible and then, if necessary, modify it to the setting. If you start off planning an evaluation by compromising on methodological rigor, you have lost an opportunity to examine the total program or program elements before all design possibilities have been thoroughly explored. Although compromise on the use of the experimental model when planning and conducting an evaluation should be rare, it may not be feasible for some programs, agencies, and settings. The evaluation literature confirms that one type of quasi-experimental design—time series—can be applied in special circumstances. However, if a funding agency requires certainty about efficacy or effectiveness, an experimental design should be the first choice.

TABLE 6.4   Biases to Internal Validity of Selected Designs

Design	(M) Measurement		(S) Selection		(H) History			Σ Bias
	(1) V	(2) R	(3) P	(4) A	(5) H	(6) I	(7) X	(8) Σ
1. One group pretest and posttest: E_1 or $\underline{C}$ O X O								
2. Nonequivalent comparison group: E_1 O X_1 O $\underline{C}$ O O								
3. Time series: E OOOO X OOOO								
4. Multiple time series: E OOOO X OOOO $\underline{C}$ OOOO OOOO								
5. Randomized pretest and posttest with a control group: R E O X O R C O O								

V = validity; R = reliability; P = participation rate; A = attrition rate; H = external events;
I = internal events; X = program; O = observation; Σ = sum of M + S + H

The five options, Design 1 to Design 5, presented in Table 6.4 in an ascending hierarchy, represent an increasing ability to produce defensible evidence of impact. Table 6.4 presents information on the potential independent sources of bias to the internal validity of the five common evaluation designs. Each design needs to be examined to assess the degree to which a program will be able to attribute an observed impact to the application of your program.

Although there may be rare exceptions, all quasi-experimental and non-experimental designs have significant independent and synergistic threats to internal validity. Even when a randomized design—Design 5—is used, however, evaluation results may be equivocal or compromised, unless plausible alternative explanations of impact are ruled out. The methodological issues in selecting these five designs are described in the following section. As noted in Table 6.4, there are seven potential sources of biases or plausible explanations to internal validity, and an eighth source (Σ), interactive effects.

Note   No notation is placed in the body of Table 6.4 to signify that each design and source of bias needs to be examined in the context of each individual evaluation.

Design 1: One-Group Pretest and Posttest

Design 1 is the most basic design (nonexperimental) for a program assessment. This design has many problems of inference and typically controls for few or none of the three primary sources of bias. It should not be used to assess program impact. Although it is tempting to attribute an observed change that occurred between O_1 and O_2 to the intervention (X), a number of alternative explanations are plausible. For example, other historical events, unplanned exposures, or unexpected activities involving program participants between O_1 and O_2 may partially or fully explain an observed significant change. The longer the time period between O_1 and O_2, the more probable it will be that historical (H) or (I) events or other exposures will influence results. In addition, measurement error or atypical participant-selection characteristics may also explain observed changes.

Design 1, although not ideal, may be used to conduct a pilot test of a program, however, if the interval between O_1 and O_2 is short and if significant selection and measurement biases can be ruled out. A program may need to assess the immediate or short-term impact of a health education intervention for patients or the impact of training on staff knowledge, skills, or behavior. Maximum control over measurement reliability and validity and data-collection methods and completeness should be asserted to control for this bias, regardless of the size or purpose of the evaluation. If baseline and follow-up measurements (O) are valid and occur prior to and soon after the intervention (X), e.g., 1 month before and 1 month after, measurement and history may not be plausible threats to the interpretation of short-term impact.

The primary weakness of Design 1 is the extent to which participants selected for the program are comparable to typical users of other clinics, schools, and work sites in an HP program. By determining the comparability of those who do and do not participate, an evaluation may be able to estimate selection biases. The staff-training program to improve assessment of knowledge and skills of Type 2 diabetic patients presented in Chapter 3, Table 3.5, is an example of the application of this design.

Example A program conducts an assessment of patient smoking status at three of six clinic sites that provide prenatal care services to Medicaid patients. On the first visit to the three maternity clinics during a 2-month period, 60 smokers, 20 at clinic 1, 20 at clinic 2, and 20 at clinic 3, complete a brief smoking knowledge, health beliefs, and current smoking status form (O_1). An expired breath–carbon monoxide (CO) test value is recorded as part of the program to inform each patient about her level of tobacco exposure. All 60 patients received the normal patient education program (X_1): a 3-minute, one-to-one counseling session plus a one-page brochure on risk. A follow-up interview of 50 of the 60 patients at a second or third visit is performed as part of a patient's normal visit.

A self-report of smoking status and a CO assessment are performed (O_2) again. This group can be referred to as the usual care program group. If this group of 60 patients is used to compare (see Design 2) an existing program (X_1) to a new program ($X_1 + X_2$), it should be called a comparison (C) group.

The following hypothetical impact might be documented between the onset of pregnancy (O_1) and the second or third prenatal visit (O_2): (1) an increase in maternal and infant smoking health belief–perceived risk score, 60% to 95%, and (2) a decrease in smoking rate from 60 smokers to 57 smokers based on self-report and CO value. This level of impact, a 5% quit rate (3/60), with possible selection and measurement biases to internal validity acknowledged, provides a program with an empirical estimate of the behavioral impact of the existing patient education program.

The major methodological questions are: How comparable are the 60 patients to the typical patient population from the three sites and for all six sites (selection bias)? How accurate is the self-report and CO value (measurement bias)? How plausible are internal (I) or (X) or external (H) exposure explanations of the 5% quit rate (historical bias)?

Design 2: Nonequivalent Comparison Group

Design 2 builds on Design 1 by adding a second group: an experimental group (E_1). The dashed line in Table 6.4 between the intervention (E_1) group and the comparison (C) group (Design 1) confirms creation of the groups by a method other than randomization. An example of the application of this design would be the introduction of a new program with three new patient education procedures at the prenatal care sites ($X_2 + X_3 + X_4$): X_2 is a 10-minute video for patient and family; X_3 is a brief telephone reinforcement call; X_4 is a 1-minute reinforcement counseling session at the next clinic visit. A comparison of the strengths and weaknesses of Designs 1 and 2 suggests that the addition of a second group *may* improve a program's ability to rule out some alternative explanations of impact.

Example   Biases may be partially dealt with by ensuring that neither the C nor the E_x group, from the same or different sites, is selected because of an extreme trait. A same-site C group is the best choice. Design 1 observation methods are repeated in Design 2. As noted in Design 2, the same baseline (O_1) and follow-up (O_2) observations are necessary for both groups at all sites. The observations must use the same instruments and methods and have standardized measures of high quality. After staff are trained to routinely provide the new program procedures ($X_2 + X_3 + X_4$ to E_1), a CO plus self-reported quit rate of 11.7% (7/60) is confirmed at a second or third follow-up visit. A comparison of the old HP program (X_1) impact rates of (C) 5% vs. (E) 12% for the new HP program provides encouraging results. The extent to which this design improves controls for selection bias remains an issue: How comparable at baseline was each cohort of E and $\underline{C}$, 60 patients? An excellent example of the application of this design is presented in Gebauer et al. (1998).

Design 3: Time Series

Design 3 can be applied if a program can:

- Establish the periodicity and pattern of the impact rate being examined for a well-defined population at risk.
- Observe at multiple monthly/quarterly data points, typically 1 to 2 years before and 1 to 2 years after the new intervention (X_n) was introduced.
- Establish the validity, reliability, and completeness of measurement.
- Collect data unobtrusively as part of an existing monitoring system.
- Document introduction of an intervention (X_n) at a specific time and, if planned, withdrawal of the intervention abruptly at a specific time.

The application of a time-series design (TSD) requires an adequate number of observations to document impact rate trends. A minimum of 50 data points for assessing an impact has been recommended (Glass et al. 1975; Ostrom 1978). Although an evaluation team should be aware of the complexity of analytical issues in applying a TSD, it may consider using it with fewer data points. Observation and analysis of behavior change trend rates over time, even with fewer than 50 data points (for example, two to four baseline and two to four follow-up assessments), represent a significant improvement over Design 1. In using a TSD, more data points *may* increase the validity of results, so that an evaluation makes stronger causal inferences. The observation points should occur at equal intervals and cover a sufficient time period to confirm preintervention and postintervention variations for an impact rate.

If applying a TSD, as in all designs, an evaluation team needs to examine the extent to which this quasi-experimental design can control for measurement, selection, and historical biases. Did external or internal historical, nonprogram events or activities confound interpretation of the observed results? Because the principal issue in applying a TSD is to document the significance of a trend in an observed rate, the treatment must be powerful enough to produce shifts in an impact rate considerably beyond the normally observed variations in the rate. The plausibility of the impact of factors such as weather, seasonality, decreases in personnel, and changes in resources must be carefully examined. The threat of external historical (H) and internal historical (I) bias increases significantly with the extended duration of a TSD evaluation.

Time-series designs (TSD) and time-series analysis (TSA) continue to have limited application in health promotion evaluation literature. Cook and Campbell observed in 1979 that large untapped sources of data can be accessed:

> A surprising amount of time-series data is already available, and more will be as the pressure for indicators increases. On the assumption that recent and future data are of better technical quality than was sometimes the case in the past, we can expect to see an increasing use of time-series analyses based on federal, state and local sources.

Biglan et al. (2000) more recently noted:

> Greater use of interrupted times-series experiments is advocated for community intervention research. Time-series designs enable the development of knowledge about the effects of community interventions and policies in circumstances in which randomized controlled trials are too expensive, premature, or simply impractical.

A Phase 4 program evaluation may be the most likely type to use a TSD.

This design is especially appropriate when a new tax, policy, or law is passed that prohibits, reduces, or mandates changes in population behavior, e.g., cigarette tax, seat belt and helmet laws, age of alcohol purchase, and higher or lower speed limits. Only through replication of an HP evaluation with the same intervention using a TSD and the production of reports of consistently significant evidence of impact over time can valid conclusions about impact be made. An application of this design is included in Case Study 6.2. Another excellent example of the TSD design was presented by Ma, Shive, and Tracy (2001).

Design 4: Multiple Time Series

A multiple time-series (MTS) design is a quasi-experimental design in which impact rates are studied at different times over several years for an experimental (E) group and a comparison (C) group. This design includes all methods and issues of Design 3, plus the addition of a comparison (C) group time series from similar sites or units of comparison, e.g., states, schools, counties, or work sites. The addition of the comparison group *may* strengthen the program's control over the primary three biases. The MTS design can only be applied in situations where retrospective and prospective databases exist and are accessible or where an organization can periodically observe rates for program participants, e.g., monthly, quarterly, and annually for both defined populations and areas: E and C groups. The primary methodological issue in MTS is the comparability of E vs. C at baseline and at each follow-up measurement: selection bias. Because the comparison sites are typically other states, facilities, or geographic area, it is always difficult to match sites on all of the major predictor variables to reduce a selection bias.

A barrier to the use of this design is the need for the same multiple observations of the comparison ($\underline{C}$) group before, during, and after the intervention program begins. Unless the data are valid, current, complete, accessible, and routinely reported in a timely manner, the observations, typically representing 3 to 5 years of data, may not be comparable or may be too time- and resource-intensive to collect. The major issue is to be able to say with reasonable assurance that, before the program, a stable, comparable pattern of impact measurements was confirmed for both the $\underline{C}$ and the E groups/sites. New health policy legislation and taxation legislation are typical health promotion interventions for specific populations and locations for which a single or multiple time series may be the strongest design to use to evaluate impact over time.

Design 5: Randomized Pretest and Posttest with an E and C Group

An experimental design enables the evaluator to establish by randomization two groups, E and C, not significantly different at baseline for any independent or dependent variables that are predictors of impact. Eligible participants are randomized within each/all study sites. There are several methods of conducting an experimental study. A common approach is to evaluate an existing program (X_1) for a C group by comparing it to an E group that receives a hypothetically more effective program ($X_1 + X_2 + X_3$). Standardized assessments at baseline and follow-up are conducted of all E and C group participants. If you have a large number of participants (200+) interested in an HP program, they can be assigned by random selection (R) within sites to the E and C groups. Random assignment may be done all at once, if participants enter the program together, or you may assign participants randomly as they sign up and enter the program over time. This design should produce excellent control over the three major biases to internal validity, assuming no major implementation problems. Confirmation that the randomization process has been to an established equivalent group, however, is essential. Case Study 6.4 and all case studies in Chapter 7 are examples of Design 5.

QUASI-EXPERIMENTAL DESIGNS AND BIAS

A quasi-experimental design (Designs 2, 3, 4), by definition, does not control for all measurement-selection-historical biases. Selection bias is always the principal issue when a quasi-experimental design is used. LaLonde and Maynard (1987) and Grossman and Tierney (1993), in "The Fallibility of Comparison Groups," provided sound methodological and analytical discussions about the use of $\underline{C}$ groups and quasi-experimental designs. They noted,

Despite using a comparison group explicitly designed to overcome many of the self-selection issues that are endemic to quasi-experimental methods and using a variety of statistical methods to control for selection bias, quasi-experimental designs are still subject to the threat that the comparison group did not adequately represent the appropriate non-treatment state.

There is a lack of consensus in the literature about what analytical methods are the most appropriate for nonequivalent comparison group design (Rubin 1974; Kenny 1979; Cook and Campbell 1979; Grossman and Tierney 1993). The four common methods of statistical analysis of quasi-experiments are (1) analysis of covariance (ANCOVA), (2) ANCOVA with a reliability correction, (3) raw score change analysis, and (4) standardized change score analysis. Each method typically produces different results, and frequently the validity of the results of each analysis is questioned. These analytical problems have been examined and discussed in the literature for 25 years; for example, see Kenny (1979, Chap. 11).

Although statistical methods continue to improve, statistical adjustment methods cannot fully adjust for known—and *especially multiple unknown*—self-selection characteristics of participants or matched groups/sites. After matching on one or two baseline (pretest) variables, in almost all cases, it becomes impossible to match on other salient, predictor characteristics. The initial pretreatment differences from known—and especially the significant unknown—selection characteristics make all E and C group posttest comparisons problematic. Ask: What percent of the variance is predicted by the variables used to match? Caution is always strongly advised in applying and interpreting results from a quasi-experimental study.

Shadish (2000) and other contributing authors in a special volume on research design, *Donald Campbell's Legacy*, provided a synopsis of the history and enduring issues inherent to quasi-experimentation. Six empirically supported recommendations were made:

1. Select internal—same site—rather than external comparison subjects.
2. Avoid participants' self-selection into E or C conditions.
3. Consider selecting comparison groups matched on stable pretest measures.
4. Include pretests on the dependent variable (or proxy pretests if true pretests are not possible) and use to adjust the posttest.
5. Use sensitivity analyses to explore possible effects of hidden bias and different selection assumptions.
6. Significantly reduce or prevent attrition by pilot-testing.

ESTABLISHING A COMPARISON ($\underline{C}$) GROUP

Although randomization is the best choice, an experimental design may not be feasible in some situations. A nonequivalent $\underline{C}$ group may represent the only feasible alternative, especially for Phase 4 program impact–dissemination evaluations. This may occur in a setting where a program's philosophy and policy require delivery of a new "best practice" program to all participants at all sites. It may then be necessary for an evaluator to create a comparison group. In using a nonequivalent $\underline{C}$ group, an evaluator is attempting to replicate an experimental study in every way with the exception of randomization. In identifying a $\underline{C}$ group, give considerable attention to selecting individuals or groups who are as similar to the E group as possible. The rationale and methods for identifying individuals, units, or groups to serve as a $\underline{C}$ group must be well defined. When a comparison group ($\underline{C}$) and not a control group (C) is established, the potential effect size of a program, however, is likely to be reduced (Boruch 1976). Evaluation study results and the internal validity of conclusions are almost *always* attenuated when a quasi-experimental design is applied.

An evaluation plan needs to create a comparison ($\underline{C}$) group that is highly comparable to the E group. In establishing a $\underline{C}$ group, baseline similarities and differences between the $\underline{C}$ and the E groups must be documented. The following methods are suggested for selection of the $\underline{C}$ group to improve your chances of assessing impact. Selection and historical biases are the most significant biases to address in this design. Measurement bias may be addressed, if the validity and reliability of baseline and follow-up data are empirically documented prior to and during the evaluation.

Matching with External Units

An opportunity may exist to match program data at program sites (E group) to program data in a comparable area ($\underline{C}$ group) where the new intervention to be provided will not be introduced. This method is not feasible, however, unless a uniform database exists or can be introduced at all alternative locations. Examples include public health clinics, hospitals, schools, or work sites. In identifying subjects to serve in a $\underline{C}$ group, select approximately the same number of individuals per site as in the E group. If the $\underline{C}$ site has a monitoring system, you may be able to identify a number of units whose participants may have demographic traits comparable to the E group. The difficulty in using this method is gaining the cooperation of intact groups or sites in other settings. An example of the method of matching by unit is presented in Windsor and Gutter (1982).

Matching with Internal Units-Participants

Another option is to apply Design 1 twice at the same sites. All assessment methods and procedures are standardized. The eligibility criteria and sample size

TABLE 6.5   Baseline Data for _E_ and _C_ Groups

Variable	_E_ (n = 280)	(_C_) (n = 170)	Significance Level (P)
Age (years)	45.7	44.1	NS
Annual income	$9,077	$8,776	NS
Years in school	11.3	11.5	NS
Black female	25%	28%	NS
White female	75%	72%	NS
Has a family doctor	79%	84%	NS
Has had uterus removed	24%	23%	NS
MD visit: ≤6 months	74%	77%	NS
Mean cognitive score	71.8	70.9	NS
Mean belief score	1.45	1.47	NS
Breast self-examination: ≤3 months			SIG, 0.01
None	33%	23%	
One	20%	23%	
Two	19%	14%	
Three or more	27%	40%	
Pap smear			NS
None	22%	14%	
Fewer than 12	55%	56%	
More than 12	23%	30%	

Source: Windsor et al. (1980, 203–218).
NS = not significant; SIG = significant

are kept standard for both cohorts. The example described in Design 2, if successfully implemented, will provide an optimal nonequivalent comparison group evaluation. For example, using the same site for the _C_ group from January to June and for the _E_ group from July to December may assert very good control over selection bias.

Participant- or Peer-Generated _C_ Groups

One alternative method to create a _C_ group is to have participants match themselves with a nonparticipant friend. In the participant-generated method, participants identify one or two friends who are very much like them, e.g., in age, sex, race, and socioeconomic status (SES). Participants are asked to provide the names and phone numbers of these nonparticipant friends, who would be contacted by program staff. This method, used to establish the _C_ group reported in Table 6.5, may be an efficient way to create a nonrandomized comparison (_C_) group (Windsor et al. 1980). One problem with participant generation, however, as observed in Table 6.5, may be the failure of a significant proportion of treatment group participants to identify a comparison friend. Using this method may also result in interaction between E and $\underline{C}$ subjects, increasing the potential for contamination of $\underline{C}$ subjects. This possibility should be monitored by a process evaluation.

ESTABLISHING A CONTROL GROUP

The key question in establishing a C group is: Does it adequately control for the predictors of behavioral impact, such as risk status, age, gender, or education? Each baseline variable may have an independent or interactive effect, producing or explaining part of an observed rate. Ideally, E and C randomization produces identical groups for all dependent-impact variables and independent variables significantly associated with the dependent variables. An equivalent control group will typically assert control over the independent variables, so that small biases from M-S-H are minimized by equal distribution. It asserts this control by distributing evaluation study participants with specific baseline characteristics equally between E and C groups. An assumption in making a comparison between E and C groups is that the groups were equivalent before introduction of the intervention (X). An E group is used to determine whether program participants have improved as a result of exposure to the intervention by comparing them to a C group that was not exposed or to those exposed to a minimal intervention. Equivalence must be documented: Random assignment does not always produce equivalent groups at baseline.

An issue that frequently has limited C group establishment is that program staff may not want to withhold the intervention (X) from E group participants. This may seem an insurmountable barrier at first glance, but in practice it need not be. Remember: An evaluation is planned to determine if significant changes have occurred from exposure to the new intervention. Valid impact data on the internal validity of an existing program or the new program may not be available. Although the standard or minimum program should not be withheld, the intensity, duration, and types of methods and materials or the frequency of application of program elements can be varied. A comparison of the C group, the standard health promotion program (X_1), is made to the E group—"best practice" program ($X_1 + X_2 + X_3$). Ask practical questions: How effective is the existing program? What new methods could be feasibly applied in the program settings that might significantly increase the current level of impact? If the existing intervention time/intensity/frequency/resources are increased by 20% or 50%, is it likely to be significantly more effective?

Random Assignment

Randomization of participants into E and C groups is the best method of establishing groups for evaluation purposes and of asserting control over biases to in-

TABLE 6.6   Establishing a Control Group for a Delayed-Treatment Program

Baseline Observations	Program 1 Starts	Program 2 Starts	Follow-Up
$O_1 \, R \, E \, (n = 120)$	$X_1 \, O_2$	O_3	O_4
$O_1 \, R \, C \, (n = 120)$	O_2	$O_3 \, X_1$	O_4

ternal validity. Multiple computer programs are readily available to generate a random assignment list for each site. If participants are randomly assigned as they are recruited, assignment may take a number of forms. If the number of participants is large, e.g., more than 200, then simple random assignment may be adequate to establish equivalent groups at each evaluation site. A program planner, however, may choose a stratification, matching, or blocking within the site system prior to randomization at each evaluation site to achieve greater precision. Participants are grouped at baseline by demographic characteristic predictive of an impact rate, e.g., age/gender/race, with other participants with similar characteristics matched or clustered. They are then randomly assigned within cluster within a site to the E or C group.

Delayed Treatment

A common misinterpretation of an experimental design is that the administration of an intervention (X_N) is an all-or-nothing choice. In the simplest of delayed approaches, about half of the participants from an applicant pool are randomly selected to serve as E or C group participants. Because program resources are almost always finite, e.g., a work site health promotion program, cohorts of workers may be phased into a program over time. One-half of the eligible applicants (E group) are exposed to the new program initially, and one-half later (C group), e.g., in 1 to 3 months. In this way, eligible participants are randomly assigned to immediate (E) or delayed (C) treatment, with each having an equal opportunity to participate. Randomization is the fairest and most equitable method of selecting initial program participants in a case where a large number of eligible participants are interested but all cannot be served at the same time. This design is especially useful for a Phase 1 formative evaluation.

Table 6.6 shows a diagram of the delayed-treatment method. At T_1 a group of participants sign up for a program. Using the parameters $\propto = 0.05$, power = 0.80, $P_1 = 0.10$, and $P_2 = 0.30$, a sample of 120 per group is chosen. Of the 240+ who agree to participate, 120 are randomly assigned to group E and 120 to group C. Sample size formulas and calculations per group are presented in a later section of this chapter. P_1 is an estimate of the probability of the behavior that an evaluation expects to document among a C group, e.g., $P_1 = 10\%$ or the current rate of weekly activity among a group of white-collar employees in a large, urban commercial company. P_2 is the expected estimate of the probability of the behavior an evaluation expects to document among an E group, e.g., $P_2 = 30\%$, or the expected increased rate due to the new intervention methods.

A baseline observation (O_1) is performed during the recruitment period, but prior to the start of the program. At T_2 participants assigned to group E are exposed to the program (X_1); those assigned to group C are not exposed. Follow-up observations (O_2) are made of both groups. At a predetermined time in the future (T_3), e.g., in 3 months, group C participants are exposed to the program over a 30/60/90-day period. In this example, it would be prudent to assign 120 to each group, using an estimate of $\leq 20\%$ lost to follow-up, to ensure at least ≥ 100/group at follow-up. This approach is particularly useful in confirming immediate and short-term (1–3 months) estimates of program impact. A formative evaluation of a program in the early stages of development, using this design, may be the most feasible method of assessing immediate or short-term impact.

A Multiple-Component Program

An evaluation may be designed to apply combinations of different interventions to some participants and withhold components from others. If a large number of participants want to participate in a program and there is a need to assess the impact of different components, investigators may decide to conduct a randomized, factorial study. In this evaluation the objective is to determine the differential impact of the multiple components of a program by exposing subsamples of participants to different components. Important structural dimensions characteristics of the program such as duration, frequency of reinforcement, and intensity may be examined to determine which individual or combined elements are the most efficacious.

As indicated in Table 6.7, the initial pool of 360+ recruited applicants can be randomly assigned to three "equivalent" groups ($n = 120$). Participants in each group may be exposed to single parts of a program or combinations. The C group might receive nothing or a minimum core intervention.

A New Program

If your agency decided to develop or present a totally new program or a new version of an ongoing program, it could randomly assign half the participants to be exposed (E_1) to the standard program (X_1) and half (E_2) to the new, enriched (best practices) program ($X_2 + X_n$), for purposes of comparison of impact. As indicated in Table 6.8, having recruited and established baselines for a pool of 240 participants, you randomly assign each to participate in program X_1 or program X_2. Follow-up observations are conducted as in other group designs. An evaluation of which program was the most effective can then be made.

TABLE 6.7   Establishing a Control Group for a Multiple-Component Program

Baseline Observations, T_1	Program Starts, T_2	Program Ends, T_3	Follow-Up, T_4
$O_1 \, R \, E_1 \, (n = 120)$	$X_1 \, X_2 \, X_3 \, O_2$	O_3	O_4
$O_1 \, R \, E_2 \, (n = 120)$	$X_1 \, X_2 \quad O_2$	O_3	O_4
$O_1 \, R \, C_1 \, (n = 120)$	$X_1 \quad O_2$	O_3	O_4

TABLE 6.8   Establishing a Control Group for a New Program

Baseline Observations, T_1	Program Starts, T_2	Program Ends, T_3	Follow-Up, T_4
$O_1 \, R \, E_1 \, (n = 120)$	$X_1 \, O_2$	O_3	O_4
$O_1 \, R \, E_2 \, (n = 120)$	$X_2 \, O_2$	O_3	O_4

COMPARABILITY OF EVALUATION STUDY GROUPS

Establishing the baseline comparability of E and C or $\underline{C}$ groups in a quasi-experimental or experimental evaluation is essential. The objective of comparing baseline data on the E and C or $\underline{C}$ groups is to confirm that no major differences existed for predictors of an impact rate between these groups prior to the evaluation and program exposure. Data in Tables 6.5 and 6.9 portray the comparability of E, C, and $\underline{C}$ groups participating in two published studies.

Table 6.5 presents baseline statistics for 450 female participants in a formative evaluation of a rural cancer control program (Windsor et al. 1980). Randomization was not possible in this program. The $\underline{C}$ group was identified using a peer-generation method—female participants each were asked to identify a nonparticipant friend of the same age and gender. The data indicate that the two groups were very similar at baseline for several sociodemographic factors, physician utilization, cognitive and health belief scores, and behavioral reports. The noted exception was the higher baseline level of breast self-examination reported by the $\underline{C}$ group. It should be noted that the two groups were likely different for multiple characteristics we could not measure. Each of these independent characteristics may have been associated with the impact rate, representing unknown selection bias. Another problem was the difference in sample size between the E and $\underline{C}$ groups. Baseline data in Table 6.9 from the multiple risk factor intervention trial (MRFIT), involving 12,000+ participants and three comprehensive screens, which confirmed equivalence, can be contrasted with Table 6.5.

Data from these two studies, a small demonstration project in a rural southern county with limited resources and a large NIH-funded randomized clinical

TABLE 6.9   Mean Values of Selected Variables Among MRFIT Participants Assigned to Special Intervention (*E*) and Usual Care (*C*)

Variables	Units	*E*	*C*
Values at first screen			
Serum cholesterol	mg/dL	253.8	253.5
Diastolic blood pressure	mm Hg	99.2	99.2
Cigarette smokers	%	63.8	63.5
Cigarettes/day smoked	No.	33.7	34.2
Framingham 6-year risk of CHD death	%	3.12	3.15
Values at second screen			
Age	years	46.3	46.3
Diastolic blood pressure	mm Hg	91.2	91.2
Systolic blood pressure	mm Hg	136.0	135.8
Percentage on blood pressure medication	%	19.6	19.1
Weight	lb.	189.3	189.1
Drinks/week	No.	12.5	12.7
Serum			
Fasting glucose	mg/dL	99.5	99.3
Thiocyanate plasma	μmol/L	131.0	131.1
Total cholesterol	mg/dL	240.3	240.6
HDL cholesterol	mg/dL	42.0	42.1
LDL cholesterol	mg/dL	159.8	160.3
Triglycerides	mg/dL	194.7	193.9
Values at third screen			
Diastolic blood pressure	mm Hg	90.7	90.7
Cigarette smokers	%	59.3	59.0
Cigarettes/day smoked	No.	32.4	32.8
		(*n* = 6,428)	(*n* = 6,438)

Source: Sherwin et al. (1981, 402–425).

trial, confirmed that program resources and capacity are predictors of the ability of investigators to establish study group comparability. The amount and type of data collected will vary dramatically according to a program's purpose and resources, but all programs must establish the baseline characteristics of *E*, *C*, or *C* group participants and comparability.

Determining Sample Size

One of the most frequently asked questions in planning an evaluation is: How large should the C or $\underline{C}$ and E groups be? The minimum number of participants to be recruited in each group must be estimated as part of the planning process and prior to implementation. Knowledge of what the sample size should be for each study group is necessary to ensure sufficient statistical power in data analysis and interpretation. It also will be used to determine

- Estimated duration of the evaluation
- Estimated staffing needs
- Estimated evaluation costs

It is essential information for drafting an annual program evaluation budget and for preparing a time/task-line for implementation. A meta-evaluation or meta-analysis and/or a pilot test should be conducted at all sites to provide the necessary information to determine sample size needs.

Two types of error need to be considered in planning an evaluation: Type I and Type II. A null hypothesis is a hypothesis of no significant differences between the E and C groups. A Type I error is the probability of rejecting a null hypothesis (H_0) when it is true. Because the objective of a program is to have a significant impact (reject H_0), E and C groups must be large enough to have the opportunity to reject the null. Regardless of the total number in each group, the E and C groups should be approximately the same size.

Four statistics are used to determine the most efficient E and C group sample size. The first step is to select a level of statistical significance. An accepted convention to be used for an evaluation is $\propto = 0.05$. *Note:* In a formative evaluation (Phase 1), $\propto = 0.10$ may be used as an adequate level to test statistical significance and to empirically derive estimates of sample size. The use of $\propto = 0.10$ versus $\propto = 0.05$ can be justified, because the program is trying to get a valid, preliminary estimate of promising new intervention methods. One of the primary purposes of a Phase 1 evaluation is to produce initial estimates of effect size or level of behavioral impact. If a meta-evaluation or meta-analysis and Phase 1 and Phase 2 evaluation results confirm a consistent effect size, and there is no concern about harm, a one-tailed test should be applied to estimate sample size and to evaluate behavioral impact in Phase 3 and Phase 4 evaluations.

Having specified the $\propto$ level, step 2 requires selection of a "power" level for the evaluation. Consider the $1 - \beta$ level, the probability of accepting a null hypothesis when it is not true: committing a Type II error. It is concluded that a program did not produce a significant effect when it could. The literature recommends the following parameter for an evaluation of a health promotion program:

typically, a health promotion evaluation will select power $(1 - \beta) = 0.80$ when $\alpha = 0.05$ (Cohen and Cohen 1975).

In step 3, the expected impact levels are estimated from either an ME or an MA or, better, from program data: a natural history study or formative evaluation. An estimate of the current level of impact, the effect size (ES), produced by X, is needed. The process of estimating ES is described in the following example. An MA and a pilot test indicate that the self-initiated weight loss rate (P_1) annually for a 12-month period for HMO members is approximately 10%: $P_1 = 0.10$. Weight loss can be defined as having at least 5% reduction of initial weight. The MA confirms that a reasonable expectation of behavioral impact for a weight loss program in an HMO population at a 6-month follow-up is 20%: $P_2 = 0.20$. With these four parameters, $\alpha = 0.05$, power $= 0.80$, $P_1 = 0.10$, and $P_2 = 0.20$, a standard sample size table can be used to estimate how many participants in both the E and C groups an evaluation must have at O_1 and O_2 to test the significance of a rate difference. The formula in Fleiss (1981) to estimate sample sizes for comparison of rates is:

$$\bar{P} = \frac{P_1 + P_2}{2}$$

$$n' = \frac{\left(c_{\alpha/2}\sqrt{2\bar{P}\bar{Q}} - c_{1-\beta}\sqrt{P_1 Q_1 + P_2 Q_2}\right)^2}{(P_2 - P_1)^2}$$

$$n = n' + \frac{2}{|P_2 - P_1|} = \text{(continuity correction)}$$

Data presented in Table 6.10 for a two-tailed test on proportion specify the sample sizes needed for E and C groups for different α, power, P_1, and P_2 statistics. Using the statistics from the example, data in the table indicate that the program would need $\boxed{219}$ participants *per group at follow-up* to confirm as statistically different the hypothesized difference between P_1 (C group) and P_2 (E group). These data refute the common misconception that 100+ participants are needed per group. The use of (113) and $\triangle 71 \triangle$ subjects per group, respectively, would require a program to produce a behavioral impact of at least a 25% or 30% rate to statistically confirm that the E minus C group difference was significant. The likelihood, then, of finding a statistically significant difference between the E and C groups with sample sizes of $n = 100+$ each, where $P_1 = 0.10$ and $P_2 = 0.20$, is a little higher than chance (50/50).

The underlying theory in deciding on sample sizes is based on hypothesizing an expected level of impact. If the literature and empirical evidence suggest that a program will have an effect size of $P_1 = 0.10$ vs. $P_2 = 0.20$, and this level of impact is programmatically or organizationally important, then using the Fleiss data in Table 6.10 and the same α, power, and P values, each study group (E and

TABLE 6.10   Sample Sizes per Group for a Two-Tailed Test on Proportions: $P_1 = 0.10$

P_1	α	Power			
		0.95	0.90	0.80	0.50
0.20	0.01	471	397	316	189
	0.05	348	286	219	117
0.25	0.01	238	202	162	98
	0.05	117	146	113	62
0.30	0.01	149	126	102	63
	0.05	111	92	71	40

Source: Adapted from Fleiss (1981, 262).

C) will need approximately 219 people at follow-up. If the evidence suggests that the impact of a program will be large, e.g., $P_1 = 0.10$ and $P_2 = 0.25$, then a sample size of 113 per group is needed at follow-up. It is prudent to randomize an extra 10% or 20% of participants per group to ensure an adequate number of end-point observations. A pilot test will help determine what percent to over-sample. Accordingly, an evaluation using the parameters presented may need to recruit and to randomize approximately 500 participants.

This method also identifies how long the evaluation will take. It defines how many participants need to be recruited each week/month at each evaluation site. It can be used to estimate staffing needs per site. This critical methodological issue must be addressed in all impact evaluation plans to improve the quality of future interventions and to improve the HP science and practice base. Because of the complexity of determining sample size and selecting appropriate impact analysis methods, biostatistical consultation should be sought.

CASE STUDIES: SCIENCE INTO PRACTICE

We present five case studies to illustrate the strengths and weaknesses of the quasi-experimental and experimental designs discussed in this chapter. They have been selected because they are part of the published literature and represent programs with different purposes and samples of participants: adults and youth, clinic and community, school and work site settings. The first case is a detailed discussion of a Phase 1 formative evaluation study. It provides a review of the methodological issues common to the developing, pilot-testing, and evaluation of a new health promotion program.

CASE STUDY 6.1

A Formative Evaluation in Maternal and Child Health Practice: The Partners for Life Nutrition Education Program for Pregnant Women

INTRODUCTION

Public health interventions often fail to have an impact for many reasons, including failure to deliver program components as planned, failure to standardize and pilot-test intervention methods, and/or failure to monitor the delivery of the intervention or assessments. These problems may be avoided if formative and process evaluations are conducted as part of program development. In a formative evaluation, all health education intervention and measurement procedures should be applied under normal conditions. Information derived from a Phase 1 formative evaluation, if successfully implemented, should be used to revise program methods prior to planning a large-scale Phase 2 efficacy evaluation.

BACKGROUND

The Mississippi State Department of Health identified patients' lack of knowledge and skill and poor overall nutritional status at conception and during pregnancy as primary contributing factors of a high rate of low birth weight and infant mortality. More than 95% of pregnant women in the Delta region, a six-county area, received maternal health services at the county health department. These women were eligible for the Special Supplemental Program for Women, Infants, and Children (WIC) services. WIC clients received two 15-minute educational sessions for every 6 months of participation. Although nutrition education is a standard component of the WIC program, little data existed on how local programs provided nutrition education or behavioral impact. Additionally, two 15-minute patient education sessions represent an intervention with limited potential to alter dietary behavior. A meta-evaluation confirmed that the behavioral impact of nutrition education during pregnancy had not been documented (Boyd and Windsor 1993).

The Freedom from Hunger Foundation of California (FHF) joined with the Mississippi Cooperative Extension Service and the state Department of Health to establish the Partners for Life Program (PFLP) to address nutrition problems in the Delta region. The primary aims of the PFLP project were to build a partnership between the WIC and the Expanded Food and Nutrition Education Program (EFNEP) and to plan, implement, and evaluate the impact of nutrition education on the dietary-related behaviors associated with infant and maternal health. Because of the encouraging results of evaluations of EFNEP, which involved a more personalized instruction, the PFLP decided that changes could be made in EFNEP to meet local program needs. Prior to integrating EFNEP and WIC methods, however, it was necessary to change the focus of the EFNEP model from general nutrition education to a more tailored program.

Source: N. Boyd and R. Windsor, "A Formative Evaluation in Maternal and Child Health Practice: The Partners for Life Nutrition Education Program for Pregnant Women," *Maternal and Child Health Journal* 7, no. 2 (June 2003): 137–143.

STUDY LOCATION

Leflore County, a county representative of the six-county Delta region, was selected as the site for a 2-year formative evaluation. The formative evaluation was designed to assess intervention strengths and weaknesses of the PFLP prior to its implementation in the multicounty region: a Phase 2 efficacy evaluation. The objectives of the PFLP were:

- To develop a new EFNEP curriculum tailored to pregnancy.
- To recruit and train peer EFNEP educators.
- To develop and validate patient assessment instruments.
- To conduct a review of intervention forms and procedures.
- To convene focus groups among participants to determine the utility and acceptability of the new curriculum.
- To pilot-test the new curriculum under normal conditions.
- To determine behavioral impact.

METHODS

Program Development

An advisory committee of physicians, nurses, nutritionists, health educators, and other health professionals with MCH expertise provided guidance about program content validity, structure, and process. The committee defined eight essential content areas: (1) maternal and infant nutrition; (2) health problems and solutions; (3) eating healthy and healthy baby; (4) how to make decisions; (5) saving for mother and baby; (6) food, friends, and fun; (7) caring for the baby; and (8) preparation for delivery. The EFNEP content was altered to meet the nutritional needs of pregnant women and was designed to be delivered in eight consecutive weekly sessions of 60 minutes each. The content and methods focused on improving patient knowledge and skill. Discussion and demonstration in the clients' homes and an interactive education/teaching style was the delivery format. A draft of the PFLP was reviewed and revised, based on the comments of two external nutrition education experts.

Peer Educator Recruitment and Training

The PFLP staff recruited five local female peer educators whose qualifications included being African American, a mother, and a high school graduate. These women received an intensive 3-month training program from the PFLP staff. The PFLP director used this group's advice to revise the program. The five peer educators completed their training by delivering the new intervention to a sample of 25 WIC-eligible pregnant women in their homes. The PFLP director was present to provide feedback and to critique the peer educators' presentations.

Focus group discussions with patients were convened periodically to provide information about clients' use and acceptance of, satisfaction with, and recommendations for change in the new curriculum. Qualitative evaluation data, combined with process evaluation measures, provided the planning/evaluation team with the information to determine what adjustments to the project procedures and intervention content should be made.

Instrumentation

Lesson objectives and content were used to develop a 28-item nutrition in pregnancy knowledge test. Two experts in nutrition education and instrument development reviewed the test for content validity. This instrument was administered to a sample of 63 pregnant women in Leflore County who met eligibility criteria. The test internal consistency analysis confirmed an $r = 0.71$ (Kuder-Richardson 21). Item analyses were performed to determine item-to-total correlation coefficients and item difficulty. Three items were too easy and one test item was found to be too difficult. A 24-hour dietary behaviors recall instrument was also administered to the pilot sample of 63 patients. A random subsample of ten 24-hour dietary recalls was independently rated by two nutritionists to determine interrater reliability by Kappa (K) statistic. The interrater reliabilities were poor to excellent: meat: $K = 0.50$; fruits and vegetables: $K = 0.60$; milk and dairy products: $K = 0.65$; and breads and cereals: $K = 0.90$.

Formative Evaluation Design

A randomized, experimental E vs. C group design was used. A computer-generated random assignment procedure was used to assign each patient at the Leflore County Health Department to the C or E group, after informed consent. The C group received the standard WIC program and the E group received standard WIC services plus the new PFLP program.

Estimation of Sample Size

Achievement of two objectives was assessed: (1) nutrition knowledge and (2) 24-hour dietary recall score. A moderate effect size was used to estimate sample size, based on a 24-hour dietary recall score. An $\alpha = 0.10$ was used instead of the traditional 0.05, because this was a formative evaluation and there were no safety or harm issues: power was 0.80. Based on these statistics, 120 subjects per group were needed to evaluate and to derive initial estimates of E vs. C group behavioral differences.

Measurement and Analysis Methods

All women completed the following: (1) a baseline questionnaire, which included demographic information, (2) a nutrition knowledge test, and (3) a 24-hour dietary recall. At the completion of the eighth nutrition education lesson for E group women, all were scheduled for the posttest assessments: (1) nutrition knowledge and (2) 24-hour dietary recall. Behavioral impact was assessed by comparing the posttest scores of the E and C groups on (1) the nutrition knowledge test, (2) the total score on the 24-hour dietary recall, and (3) each of the four components measured by the 24-hour dietary recall.

An analysis of covariance (ANCOVA), with the pretest scores as covariates, assessed between-group differences in the posttest scores. Guthrie and Scheer's method of scoring the 24-hour dietary recall was applied. A total score was derived by summing the four food group scores; the maximum score was 16. Within-group changes in the four food groups were evaluated by comparing the pretest servings with posttest servings. The dependent t-test was used for these analyses.

Process Evaluation

A process evaluation model developed by Windsor et al. (1994) was used to monitor the implementation of the patient assessment and nutrition education procedures of the PFLP. As shown in Table 6.11, the number of clients exposed to each procedure (B)

TABLE 6.11   Process Evaluation of the PFLP

Procedures	(A)	(B)	(C)	(D)	(E)
1. Pretest knowledge	240	236	98	100%	.98
2. Pretest 24-hr. recall	240	238	99	100%	.99
3. Lesson 1	120	85	71	95%	.75
4. Lesson 2	120	81	68	95%	.71
5. Lesson 3	120	76	63	95%	.67
6. Lesson 4	120	69	57	95%	.61
7. Lesson 5	120	59	49	95%	.52
8. Lesson 6	120	59	49	95%	.52
9. Lesson 7	120	50	42	95%	.44
10. Lesson 8	120	46	38	95%	.40
11. Posttest knowledge	240	115	48	90%	.53
12. Posttest 24-hr. recall	240	101	42	90%	.47

Program Implementation Index:

$$PII = \frac{.98 + .99 + .75 + .71 + .67 + .61 + .52 + .52 + .44 + .40 + .53 + .47}{12} = .63$$

(A) = eligible patients; (B) = patients exposed; (C) = exposure rate—B/A;
(D) = performance standard; (E) = index—C/D

was divided by those eligible to participate (A) to compute an exposure rate (C). The implementation index for each of the 12 procedures was calculated by dividing the exposure rate (C) by the performance standard (D) established prior to program implementation. A performance standard of 100% was set for assessment procedures 1 and 2. Given the reality of program delivery and follow-up in public health settings, where some participant attrition is typically observed, a performance standard of 95% exposure was set for procedures 3 to 10. A performance standard of 90% was applied to assessment procedures 11 and 12.

RESULTS

Process Evaluation

Process evaluation data are presented in Table 6.11. As shown in column A of Table 6.11, 240 patients were randomly assigned to either the E (120) or C (120) group. For assessment procedures 1, 2, 11, and 12, all 240 patients were eligible. Only the 120 women assigned to the E group were eligible for exposure to procedures 3 to 10. A decrease in exposure was documented between procedures 3 and 4: PII = 0.75 and PII = 0.71. Decreases in exposure were observed throughout the eight-lesson intervention delivery: from PII = 0.75 for procedure 3 to a low for procedure 10, PII = 0.40. The index increased slightly for procedures 11 (0.53) and 12 (0.47). The PII was 0.63— a much lower rate than the recommended PII $\geq$ 0.90.

TABLE 6.12   Baseline Comparability of E and C Groups

Variable	E Group	C Group
Age	22 yrs.	23 yrs.
Education	11 yrs.	11 yrs.
Race (black)	92%	92%
Persons in household	4.2	4.1
	(n = 48)	(n = 65)

TABLE 6.13   Program Efficacy: Knowledge and 24-Hour Dietary Recall

			Knowledge			
Experimental	Mean	S.D.	Control	Mean	S.D.
Pretest	21.18	3.78	Pretest	20.75	3.52
Posttest	28.50	3.71	Posttest	19.68	3.91
Difference	7.32		Difference	1.07	
	n = 48			n = 65	

ANCOVA $F = 32.35$ (df = 1,110), $p = 0.0001$

			Total 24-Hour Dietary Recall Score			
Experimental	Mean	S.D.	Control	Mean	S.D.
Pretest	10.38	2.38	Pretest	10.58	2.25
Posttest	11.86	2.66	Posttest	11.13	2.05
Difference	1.48		Difference	0.55	

ANCOVA $F = 2.76$ (df = 1,110), $p = 0.09$

Formative Evaluation

Baseline data for study participants in Table 6.12 indicated no significant E vs. C differences. The random assignment process established equivalent groups. As shown in Table 6.13, at the posttest the E group scored significantly higher in nutrition knowledge ($p = 0.0001$) and in the total score on the 24-hour dietary recall ($p = 0.09$) than did the C group.

Comparisons on dietary intake for each food group are shown in Table 6.14. At the posttest, the E group consumed significantly more servings of meat (E group = 5.03 vs. C group = 3.95, $p = 0.03$), fruits and vegetables (E group = 3.89 vs. C group = 2.83, $p = 0.09$), and bread and cereals (E group = 8.91 vs. C group = 6.95, $p = 0.002$) than did the C group. No difference at the posttest was observed for consumption of milk and dairy products (E group = 0.93 vs. C group = 0.83, $p = 0.23$).

TABLE 6.14   24-Hour Dietary Recall of Meats, Vegetables, Breads/Cereals, and Milk

Experimental	Mean	S.D.	Control	Mean	S.D.
Pretest	5.09	3.06	Pretest	4.78	2.58
Posttest	5.03	2.92	Posttest	3.95	3.01
Difference	−0.06*		Difference	−0.83†	

ANCOVA $F = 4.84$ (df = 1,110), $p = 0.03$
* dependent $t = -0.12$, $p = 0.55$ (df = 47)
† dependent $t = -2.59$, $p = 0.01$ (df = 64)

Within-group comparisons of pretest and posttest servings revealed that the E group increased their daily intake of vegetables and fruits by nearly 1⅔ servings ($p = 0.009$), increased daily intake of breads and cereals by more than 1¾ servings ($p = 0.007$), and increased daily intake of milk and dairy products by almost ½ serving ($p = 0.01$). E group intake of meat was unchanged from pretest to posttest.

Within-group changes in dietary consumption among C group women showed an inconsistent eating pattern at the posttest compared with the pretest. C group decreased their daily consumption of servings of meat by almost 1 serving ($p = 0.01$) and breads and cereals by nearly ½ serving per day ($p = 0.04$). The C group women showed a daily increase in fruits and vegetables at the posttest assessment by almost 1 serving ($p = 0.04$). No change in milk and dairy products intake was observed among C group women.

Note   Because of the substantial selection bias introduced by the 55% attrition rate, none of these results can be plausibly attributed to the intervention.

IMPLICATIONS FOR PRACTICE

Public health interventions based on a thorough needs assessment of the target population and a well-trained cohort of providers have the most potential for success. Unfortunately, many interventions are implemented without a formative evaluation of assessment or intervention procedures. This evaluation of the PFLP demonstrated limited behavioral impact and identified serious problems with the intervention delivery, participant attrition, and measurement. The intervention produced several increases in nutrition knowledge and reported dietary intake. However, there were two major issues of concern. Although the E group nearly doubled its mean daily intake of milk to approximately 1 serving per day, this level of consumption was considerably below the recommendation of 4 servings daily for pregnant women. The second major issue was whether the changes in the observed dietary intake were sustained after birth. Sustainability was not assessed in this formative evaluation.

The program implementation index (PII = 0.63) confirmed that it was substantially below the recommended PII = 0.90. A record review of program delivery by the peer educators revealed that the average time taken to deliver the intervention was

134.6 days, or approximately 19 weeks. This dramatically exceeded the time planned, 8 to 10 weeks, by the program developers. The peer educators were trained to deliver the program in 8 consecutive weeks prior to the onset of the third trimester, because this is the period of the greatest fetal growth. Unfortunately, the PFLP peer educators altered the delivery policy and plan. They decided to spread out the eight lessons to maintain client contact during the entire prenatal period.

The failure to complete program delivery during the predetermined time frame prevented additional nutritional behavior changes from occurring among the E group. A Type III error was committed in this formative evaluation, i.e., failure to implement the health education program as planned (Basch et al. 1985). Part of the problem can also be attributed to the FHF philosophy and policy that the evaluation be conducted "independent" of the program. Simply put: After the evaluators (Windsor and Boyd) had collaboratively developed the evaluation plan, they had no responsibility or authority to monitor implementation. All data were derived after completion of the PFLP.

In addition to documenting that the eight nutrition lessons had not been delivered as planned, the evaluators documented the level of acceptability of participants. Focus groups indicated that the increased length of time between lessons caused a loss of patient interest and made their time commitment too great.

A retrospective record review revealed that only 15 E group clients completed five lessons or more but could not be located for the posttest. In addition, 55 C group clients could not be located for the posttest assessment. Lack of follow-up measurement introduced a significant selection bias to this evaluation. Although the attrition rate in the E and C groups was much higher than that generally observed in regular EFNEP programs, with more than 20% of the women having moved during pregnancy, the attrition rate was similar to recent studies conducted in WIC settings. The total number of nutrition education lessons also contributed to patient attrition. Also, some content may not be critical to dietary behavior change. The last two lessons, for example, focus on the preparation for childbirth and baby care and appear to be unrelated to the primary objective of the intervention, i.e., improved maternal nutrition during pregnancy. A reduction in the number of intervention sessions from eight to six should make it more attractive to clients.

The nutrition knowledge test and the 24-hour dietary recall were adequate tools to measure the intervention impact. However, a review of the 24-hour dietary recall revealed minor problems. A single 24-hour dietary recall, for example, may not be a reliable estimate of dietary behavior, particularly if the recall was obtained for a day that differed radically from the typical eating pattern. Rush and Kristal (1982) assessed the reliability of the instrument among 520 low-income pregnant women and found it to be $r = 0.70$ when four dietary recalls were obtained.

Although obtaining multiple 24-hour recalls may be time-consuming and expensive, gathering multiple 24-hour dietary recalls from a representative subsample of study participants (e.g., 20%) is essential to enhance the validity and reliability of this measure. The validity of the 24-hour dietary recall depended on the interviewer obtaining accurate estimates of the proportion of food eaten and the manner in which the food was prepared. Because client diets were self-reports, external verification of dietary behavior of a 20% stratified subsample would have been a stronger measure. Biochemical assessment, significant other reports, and clients' submissions of weekly grocery receipts are three alternative methods. Although biochemical analysis is the most reliable and valid, it is also the most expensive.

CONCLUSION

Despite thorough planning, this formative evaluation documented no impact and significant implementation problems. Because the authors (the evaluation team) were asked not to be a part of the ongoing program by the foundation, the opportunity to monitor and correct this problem was not possible. It is important for program planners and evaluators to use these methods, results, and insight to make significant program changes in problem areas prior to implementation of a Phase 2 evaluation. Only when all major implementation problems have been addressed will the intervention be sufficiently strong to have the potential to be routinely delivered and to produce the desired behavioral effect.

CASE STUDY 6.2

Communication Methods and Evaluation Designs for a Rural Cancer Screening Program

BACKGROUND AND OBJECTIVES

The Alabama Department of Public Health, like many state health departments, established a cancer-screening program (CSP) in the 1970s, initially with National Cancer Institute support. Its purpose was to remove barriers such as availability, accessibility, acceptability, and cost to service use in local rural communities. The CSP had 50 clinics in operation at the end of 1981 and had screened approximately 11,000 women over a 10-year period, 90% of whom were members of families below the poverty level. Of those newly screened, 57% reported that they either never had a Pap smear, had not had one within the last 2 years, or did not remember ever having had one.

A collaborative effort with representatives from the University of Alabama–Birmingham (UAB) faculty, the Alabama State Health Department, and the Cooperative Extension Service was initiated in 1978 to develop, implement, and evaluate a community-based Cancer Communications Program. The objective of the program was to increase the number of high-risk women using the CSP in Alabama during the second quarters of 1979 and 1980. The Hale County screening program was selected as a demonstration site because it had a large pool of high-risk women over 35 years of age (approximately 3,500); it was similar to a number of counties in south-central Alabama; and it had been operational for several years. Residents in this county were predominantly black, poor, and rural, with limited access to primary health care services and personnel.

INTERVENTION

As shown in Table 6.15, five elements were identified as the principal components of the CSP community intervention in this Phase 1 formative evaluation. A multiple-component intervention was used because the literature and the experience of the

---

Source: Windsor, Cutter, and Kronenfeld (1981).

TABLE 6.15   Elements, Channels, and Purposes
of the Hale County Intervention

Element	Channels of Communication	Purposes
1. Community organization (X_1)	Local lay and professional leaders	Increase acceptance and support Demonstrate and increase program credibility
2. Mass media (X_2)	Electronic and print media: radio, local newspaper, church and club newsletters, posters, and bulletin boards	Increase awareness of and interest in program message Reinforce program message
3. Lay leadership (X_3)	Leadership training: standardized package	Increase assumption of responsibility by locals in community or group Decrease misinformation Increase program acceptance by groups through peer participation and pressure
4. Interpersonal group sessions (X_4)	Group process: 1- to 2-hour standardized cancer education program session	Increase efficiency of networking Increase adaptability to personal evaluation and responsibility Increase motivation and social support Increase personalization of messages Increase legitimacy of at-risk role
5. Interpersonal individual sessions (X_5)	Individual word-of-mouth diffusion	Increase persuasion Increase efficiency of diffusion Increase salience of messages Increase trial and adoption

Source: Windsor, Cutter, and Kronenfeld (1981, 37–45).

investigators strongly confirmed that no single source of exposure could be expected to have a significant impact on the behavior of the target group. Combinations of messages from multiple salient channels, particularly interpersonal sources at repeated intervals, were designed and applied.

Two community health education programs were implemented separately in Hale County during April, May, and June of 1979 and 1980. The principal messages communicated by the programs during the 3-month interventions were: (1) Women over age 35 who had never had a Pap smear were at higher risk for cervical cancer and should contact the CSP; and (2) cervical cancer was highly curable if detected in its early stages. The first intervention program, in Table 6.15, was applied in 1979. A local planning group was established consisting of representatives of the health department, extension service, county medical society, and UAB (X_1). A local mass media campaign was planned and implemented (X_2). The community health organization effort recruited and trained 39 female lay leaders, 21 white and 18 black, from existing women's groups (X_3). The leaders received a three-hour standardized training session to conduct programs for women's groups throughout the county. They held 45 cancer communications meetings with about 15 to 20 participants each. They were provided standardized methods and materials for the 1- to 2-hour sessions. Approximately 750 women were documented as having directly participated in this Cervical Cancer Communications Program (X_4). Word-of-mouth diffusion by participants to friends (X_5) was strongly reinforced at the sessions.

EVALUATION DESIGN

A time-series design (TSD) with one repeated treatment was chosen to evaluate the behavioral impact of the Cancer Communications Program. The computerized data system of the CSP of the Alabama Department of Health was used to unobtrusively confirm the number of new users by monthly and quarterly report. These data were examined to determine the extent to which the two interventions increased CSP use by new users beyond what was normally observed. In applying a TSD, this project

- Established the periodicity of the pattern of behavior being examined.
- Collected behavioral data unobtrusively.
- Confirmed multiple data points 1 year before and 1 year after the intervention.
- Applied and abruptly withdrew the intervention during a specific time period.

This design was used because it was the most rigorous quasi-experimental design feasible for conducting a formative evaluation of a public health program of this type in a field setting.

FORMATIVE EVALUATION IMPACT

Figure 6.1 illustrates the frequency (number) of new users by quarter and by year for Hale County. A new user was defined as an individual who had not previously used the Alabama CSP. An examination of the pattern of Figure 6.1 for the 3-year period suggested a significant difference in CSP use during the two intervention periods. The frequency of CSP new users for the five baseline quarters prior to the first intervention period (X) was relatively stable, although the increase in the frequency of new users in the second quarter of 1978 suggested a seasonal variation. An increase of 345% in new users, from 20 to 89, was observed for the second quarter of 1979, the intervention quarter. In other words, 89 new clients used the service during this period, compared with an average of 15 in 1978 and a maximum of 20 for the second-quarter baseline in 1978.

As noted in Figure 6.1, another increase in client use, from 20 to 50 (approximately 150%), was observed during the second intervention period (Y). In the aggregate, an estimated 100 more new users were motivated to use the CSP than would be expected from the pattern observed during the nonintervention periods in 1978 and 1979. Throughout the 3-year period, the demographic characteristics of the new users

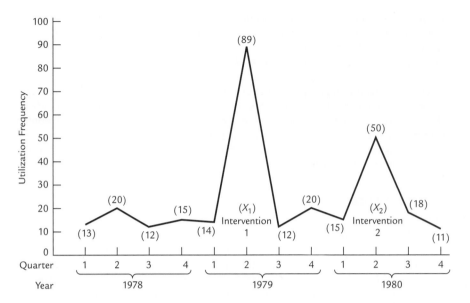

FIGURE 6.1   Frequency of New CSP Users by Quarter and Year *Source:* Windsor and Cutter (1981).

remained relatively stable, suggesting that the two interventions had an effect on similar women.

An analysis of the new-user increase using a linear regression model found that the observed frequencies for the intervention quarters were significantly higher ($P > 0.01$) than the observed frequencies for the nonintervention quarters. An examination of utilization data from a contiguous matched county revealed no changes in CSP use by new users of the magnitude noted in Hale County. It was concluded from the available evidence that the increases in new CSP users in Hale County were *primarily* due to the two interventions.

INTERNAL VALIDITY

Program evaluators should consider whether a number of factors other than the intervention produced an observed impact. Using the Hale County project data, each of the major factors noted was examined to see if it produced the increases observed. The main question asked for each source of bias was: Could this factor have produced part or all of the observed change?

Measurement Bias

Because the data observed were unobtrusive measures of behavioral impact (CSP use), this factor could not be a plausible explanation for the observed change during the intervention periods. No direct contact occurred between study personnel and clinic users. The TSD controlled for the effects of multiple observations by using unobtrusive measurement. An examination of the instruments and data-collection procedures used by the CSP confirmed a high degree of standardization. No documentation errors were apparent to the investigators during the 3-year observation period. CSP instruments and personnel remained constant, and the increased service utilization by new users was easy to confirm. All CSP users were confirmed as Hale County residents. It was concluded that measurement bias did not represent a plausible explanation for the observed increases in behavior.

Selection Bias

No $\underline{C}$ group was used in this study. In addition, the demographic characteristics of those motivated to use this service were comparable to those of new and previous users. The information available suggested that selection did not play a significant role in producing the observed change. The evaluators assessed the extent to which the observed change was a statistical artifact. The demographic characteristics, age distribution, and racial makeup of the users for the 3-year period were stable. Although it was confirmed that more women used the service, those new users were not significantly different from previous new users. The level and type of new CSP users were relatively stable during the nonintervention period.

Hale County was selected because it was generally comparable to a number of rural counties in south-central Alabama and not because of any extreme characteristic or screening problem. The evidence suggested that the observed increases were not due to a regression effect. Because the impact variable of this study was CSP use by new users, attrition by study participants was not an issue. Although this factor frequently represents a problem in an evaluation and might have represented a problem in this study if a concern had been repeat-user attrition (missed appointments), it could not have compromised the internal validity of the observed results.

New CSP users throughout the rural county were all women with similar socioeconomic characteristics. An examination of the age and racial characteristics of the county population and CSP users confirmed a high degree of demographic stability and homogeneity. No significant social, biological, or psychological changes among female residents of this county were apparent. A maturation effect, therefore, was not a plausible explanation for the impact.

Historical Bias

Because a TSD was applied, historical effects represented a potential threat to the internal validity of the results. In examining the possibility that historical events caused the observed increase, the evaluators found that no local, countywide, area, state, or national cancer communication program or cancer event had occurred during the 3-year demonstration project period. The Hale County CSP was selected because it had been operating for 2 years and was considered a stable and mature program: no apparent historical effects. Local or county organizations that might have had an independent effect on CSP use were collaborators with or supporters of the project. No changes in CSP use of the magnitude noted in Hale County were evident in several adjacent counties. Although a seasonal variation was observed in the spring, even considering this fluctuation, the magnitude of program impact was 3.5 times more than the baseline use in 1978: 89 new users vs. 20 new users. The fluctuation in the spring (baseline) quarter of 1978 was most likely due to American Cancer Society fundraising and screening-promotion efforts introduced each spring throughout Alabama. No significant administrative or staffing changes (*I*) occurred during the study period.

From this evidence and statistical analyses, it was concluded that history represented an implausible explanation for the increases observed.

SUMMARY

The assessment of the three principal threats to internal validity confirmed that the most likely reason for the observed significant behavior changes in CSP use was the Cancer Communications Program applied in the spring of 1979 and 1980. This conclusion was strengthened by the replication of this evaluation in Year 2. The observed increases were statistically and programmatically important. The formative evaluation methods and issues examined were useful for planning future and ongoing community health education–cancer control efforts.

CASE STUDY 6.3

Community-Wide Smoking Prevention: Long-Term Outcomes of the Minnesota Heart Health Program and the Class of 1989 Study

BACKGROUND AND OBJECTIVES

The Class of 1989 Study was designed to test the efficacy of a smoking-prevention program as part of a larger effort to reduce heart disease in entire communities. It was a substudy of the Minnesota Heart Health Program (MHHP), a population-based, community-wide cardiovascular disease prevention program. It was hypothesized that the impact of the school-based smoking prevention program for adolescents would be maintained if the program were part of a 5-year effort implemented within the schools and within the communities. This was a Phase 2 efficacy evaluation.

EVALUATION METHODS

The design of the Class of 1989 Study was determined by the parent project, the MHHP. Two of six MHHP communities were selected: Minnesota (*E*) and North Dakota (*C*). A quasi-experimental design was used to assess the impact of the school health education program provided as part of the community-wide cardiovascular disease prevention program in Moorhead, Minnesota. All sixth-graders enrolled in public schools in both *E* and *C* communities participated in a baseline survey in 1983. This cohort was surveyed annually each April until graduation in 1989. The annual survey was a cross-sectional sample of all students. Cohort data were also analyzed due to the availability of identifying information from the cross-sectional samples.

The behavior impact data for this project were derived from the annual cross-sectional and cohort surveys. A test-retest correction for smoking intensity for this population was $r = 0.99$. Saliva thiocyanate samples were obtained to validate self-reports

---

Source: Perry, Kelder, Murray, and Klepp (1992).

from a random sample of 50% of the classrooms. A cutoff of ≤79 micrograms per milliliter was used. A nonequivalent comparison group design (Design 2) was implemented to evaluate the impact of the intervention in the 13 grade schools and 7 high schools in the Moorhead community.

INTERVENTION

The smoking intervention, the Minnesota Smoking Prevention Program, was implemented in 1984 at the beginning of the seventh grade. The primary focus of the intervention was to prevent tobacco use by attempting to influence the social and psychological factors that encourage smoking initiation. The purpose of this MHHP was to restructure the adult social and physical environment related to cardiovascular disease prevention. Detailed discussions of the intervention are presented in the full report of this case study and other sources referenced in the case study. The MHHP intervention was applied in 1983, 1984, and 1985, in addition to the school-based adolescent smoking-prevention program. Thus, all students were indirectly exposed to the larger, community-wide MHHP behavioral intervention over the 5-year period. The adolescent cohorts in the intervention community were also exposed to the seven strategies of the MHHP:

1. Population-based screening
2. Food-labeling education
3. Community organization citizen task force
4. Continuing education of health professionals
5. Mass media
6. Adult education at work sites, churches, and the like
7. Youth education

PROGRAM IMPACT

The cross-sectional and cohort smoking impact data were analyzed to assess differences between the two communities for each year from 1983 to 1989. No significant baseline differences were documented between the two study communities. Data are presented in Figure 6.2 on the smoking prevalence cohort sample by grade, reflecting significant differences for the experimental and comparison cohort for each observation year. At the end of high school 14.6% of the cohorts sampled from the experimental (E) community were smoking, compared with 24.1% from the comparison ($\underline{C}$) community. The saliva sample confirmed the self-reported data, indicating a false-negative report in the E group community of 9.8% and in the $\underline{C}$ group community of 6.5%.

INTERNAL VALIDITY

Measurement Bias

The baseline equivalence of the two communities for the larger MHHP study and the adolescent smoking-prevention studies was well documented. The smoking prevalence rates for the sixth grade for both communities were comparable. In addition,

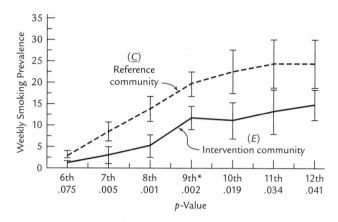

Figure 6.2 Smoking Prevalence of the Cohort Sample, by Grade. *Source:* Perry et al. (1992).
*Smoking prevalence adjusted for false-negatives in ninth grade.

the self-report data on smoking status were confirmed by saliva thiocyanate tests. A thorough discussion of the methods used to analyze the cohort and cross-sectional data is presented in the study. The discussion of the analyses presented convincing evidence of the comparability of groups and assessments of changes over time. This study used both self-reports and saliva thiocyanate levels to confirm smoking behavior. The data document a very high quality of instrumentation and measurement. Measurement error or misclassification was likely to have been small. Measurement of smoking behavior was accurate and stable.

Selection Bias

The selection of the communities and the schools was based on the larger cardiovascular disease prevention study. They reported a demonstrated *E* versus *C* group "equivalence." Presentation of data on the two communities would, however, have been preferable. Although it is likely that some differences existed between the two communities, the use of both cohort and cross-sectional samples and the capacity to define community and parent characteristics supported the conclusion that selection biases were probably small. The sophistication of the sampling frame, statistical analyses, thoroughness of measurement, and follow-up procedures also provided evidence that selection bias was probably a modest threat to the validity of the reported results. The small number of sites, however, always makes it difficult to completely rule out selection bias.

The issue of attrition and attrition analysis is dealt with directly by this report. The magnitude of intervention differences associated with attrition was examined by the investigators and found to be small. Thus, although some attrition occurred, it was well documented. The characteristics of students lost to follow-up were considered in the assessment of the efficacy of the smoking-cessation program. This issue was addressed in the discussion.

Historical Bias

When a nonequivalent comparison group design is applied, particularly where the unit of analysis is an entire community, and when the evaluation study is conducted over an extended period of time (5 years), examining the role that historical events may have played in producing behavior change is especially important. Information presented in the case study through documentation of events over the study period in both communities provided good evidence that the impact of historical events was probably minimal. Independent surveys in the general area confirmed that the rates of smoking in a comparison adolescent cohort were comparable to those observed in independent surveys. It would appear that the ongoing activities at the national, state, and local levels relating to adolescent smoking cessation probably affected both the E and C communities equally. The observed gradual rise in smoking initiation rates the E and C community is consistent with the expected annual increases in the incidence and prevalence rates among adolescents observed in the literature.

The psychosocial changes occurring among the two adolescent cohorts on the basis of information provided and noted in the literature reflect anticipated rates of experimentation and adoption of new behaviors. The maturation of the class of 1989 from sixth grade to twelfth grade appeared comparable in both adolescent cohorts. The design asserted good control for this threat to validity.

SUMMARY

This evaluation study is an excellent example of the application of evaluation principles and intervention methods for school- and community-based studies. The study was well designed, reflecting a high level of quality and methodological rigor for a quasi-experimental study. The conclusions reported by the investigators reflect a high level of internal validity. The results are likely to be generalizable to other midwestern communities with comparable community/adolescent demographics. The observed differences between the E and C communities were large, significant, and enduring. In contrast, other evaluation studies of the impact of adolescent smoking-prevention programs have found no impact or have documented substantially diminished impact over time. This evaluation study documented a large impact (50%) for a cohort representative of the population at risk in these communities. The optimism reflected in the Class of 1989 Study discussion on efficacy was well grounded.

These results indicated that a smoking-prevention program integrated into an existing school health education curriculum, and strongly maintained and reinforced over time by a community-wide multiple–risk factor cardiovascular prevention trial, can produce a large, sustained, lower rate of smoking initiation among adolescents. This case study represents an excellent follow-up of an earlier Phase I formative evaluation of school-based smoking-cessation interventions by Perry and colleagues (1980). A major lesson to be learned is that it takes the most sophisticated expertise, substantial resources, and excellent cooperation from study partners to successfully conduct a quasi-experimental evaluation.

CASE STUDY 6.4

Gimme 5 Fruit, Juice, and Vegetables for Fun and Health: Outcome Evaluation

BACKGROUND AND OBJECTIVES

This study was designed to test the effectiveness of a fourth-grade and fifth-grade curriculum, consisting of 12 sessions each year, lasting approximately 45 to 55 minutes per session. The multicomponent intervention, based on social-cognitive theory, included newsletters, videotapes, and so on in addition to the curriculum. The evaluation included 7-day food records, psychosocial measures from students, telephone interviews with parents, and observational assessments. Its primary objective was to increase the consumption of fruits, juices, and vegetables (FJV) among fourth- and fifth-grade students. This was a Phase 3 effectiveness evaluation.

METHODS

This study included 16 volunteer elementary schools matched within school districts on variables that could modify treatment effects, such as enrollment size, percentage of students on free or reduced-price lunches, and student turnover. Following matching, 8 schools were randomly assigned to the E group and 8 were randomly assigned to the C group. Schools were the unit of random assignment and analysis. Sample size estimates were based on a priori effect sizes, with 80% power. Teachers and students of the E group schools received the 6-week, 12-session grade-appropriate intervention from January through February 1995–1996. The evaluation design of the study is diagrammed in Table 6.16.

Comprehensive baseline assessments were conducted for students and E and C schools prior to randomization. Students' 7-day food consumption records were collected at three points in time, as noted in Table 6.16. This included consumption of breakfast, lunch, dinner, and snack. Psychosocial measures are included through fruit and vegetable knowledge, snack preferences, outcome expectation, and self-efficacy. Parents were also interviewed with regard to the availability and accessibility of FJV.

Extensive psychometric analyses were performed for all measures collected by this evaluation. A thorough process evaluation was conducted including documentation of curriculum implementation for both fourth- and fifth-grade teachers. Documentation of school lunch menus, performance of parent telephone interviews to document availability and accessibility of FJV, and point-of-purchase education delivery were also performed.

INTERVENTION

The 24-session curriculum, consisting of 12 sessions of 45–55 minutes each, delivered within a 6-week period during grades 4 and 5, was based on social-cognitive theory. It was designed to elicit participatory activities among the elementary school children.

Source: T. Baranowski, M. Davis, K. Resnicow, et al., "Gimme 5 Fruit, Juice, and Vegetables for Fun and Health: Outcome Evaluation," *Health Education and Behavior* 27, no. 1 (February 2000): 96–111.

TABLE 6.16   Evaluation Research Design: Gimme 5

Baseline Data Collection	Random Assignment	Fourth-Grade Intervention	Mid-date Collection	Fifth-Grade Intervention	Postdata Collection
O_1	E	X	O_2	X	O_3
O_1	C		O_2		O_3

Source: Baranowski, et al. Copyright © 2000 by Society for Public Health Education. Reprinted by permission of Sage Publications, Inc.

The five primary objectives were:

1. To increase FJV availability and accessibility at home through role plays and student activities.
2. To enhance student preferences by encouraging students to taste fast, simple, and easy recipes prepared in class.
3. To train students in their FJV snack and meal preparation skills.
4. To train students in goal-setting to increase FJV intake.
5. To train students in problem-solving skills.

Teachers from each of the participating schools attended a 1-day, 6-hour workshop during a regularly scheduled in-service training day each year. More than 95% of the teachers completed the training both years. *Gimme 5* daily newsletters were given to students to take home to share with their parents. In-class assignments were designed to help students make better decisions about the selection, preparation, and consumption of FJV. Three MTV-format videotapes for each grade level were sent to parents at 2-week intervals to reinforce the *Gimme 5* curriculum.

PROGRAM IMPACT

A total of 1,732 children completed a 7-day food record in Year 1; 1,864 children completed it in Year 2; 1,946 completed the record in Year 3; and 1,253 completed a food record for all three years. As noted in Table 6.17, the E and C groups were equivalent at baseline for all dietary factors.

As indicated in Figure 6.3, a significant impact was observed among the experimental group for FJV combined. This evaluation demonstrated that a school nutrition education program based on social-cognitive theory could positively enhance student FJV consumption. The documented effect size of 0.2 servings was comparable to replications of the *Gimme 5* program in Minnesota, California, and New Orleans.

INTERNAL VALIDITY

This study is an excellent example of a Phase 3 effectiveness evaluation of health education methods for young children in a school setting. The analytical and psychometric methods, discussed in detail in this report, represented a strong systematic application of impact evaluation methods used in planning, implementation, and analysis.

TABLE 6.17   Baseline Values for Dietary and Psychosocial Variables

7-Day Food Record	n	Year 1 E	Year 1 C
Fruits and vegetables (F & V)	3,347	2.3 (0.1)	2.4 (0.1)
All vegetables	3,347	1.1 (0.1)	1.2 (0.1)
Fruit and juices	3,347	1.2 (0.1)	1.2 (0.1)
Self-efficacy: eating F & V	3,138	42.3 (1.0)	44.2 (1.0)
Social norms	3,171	11.7 (0.3)	12.5 (0.3)
Knowledge	3,171	9.4 (0.3)	9.4 (0.3)

Source: Year 1 excerpted from Baranowski, et al. Copyright © 2000 by Society for Public Health Education. Reprinted by permission of Sage Publications, Inc.

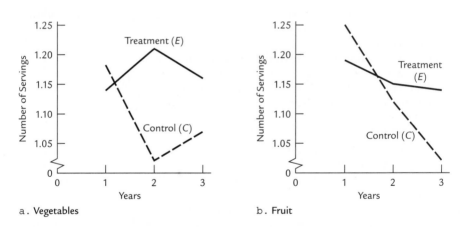

a. Vegetables   b. Fruit

FIGURE 6.3   Least Squares Means for Fruit and Vegetable Consumption for Treatment and Control Groups Among the Cohort Sample at Three Time Points
Source: Baranowski, et al. Copyright © 2000 by Society for Public Health Education. Reprinted by permission of Sage Publications, Inc.

As noted, the 7-day self-reported food record, although validated in previous research, was an impact rate based on self-report. Some error, acknowledged in the report, was likely to have occurred: measurement bias. An examination of the extent to which this study controlled for the principal sources of bias to internal validity reveals excellent control for history and selection.

SUMMARY

In summary, this evaluation represented an example of how to apply rigorous evaluation methods and procedures to document the feasibility and effectiveness of health education and health promotion interventions in the schools. It is also an exemplary example of a theory-based evaluation.

CASE STUDY 6.5

Breast-Feeding Initiation in New York City, 1979 to 1996

BACKGROUND AND OBJECTIVES

The New York City Health Department's Bureau of Maternity Services designed a program to increase breast-feeding prior to infant discharge from all New York City hospitals as a primary program objective. The purpose of this Phase 4 program evaluation was to determine whether or not the new policy and subsequent programmatic activities of the bureau significantly increased changes in breast-feeding among infants born in all New York City hospitals and municipal hospitals from 1979 to 1996. All New York City hospitals were surveyed daily over a 2-month period every 2 years from 1979 to 1996. This evaluation is a very good example of a time-series design to assess the impact of an ongoing system-wide public health program: a Phase 4 evaluation.

PROGRAM EVALUATION DESIGN

The survey period consisted of 3 months in 1979, 1 month in 1980, and the months of April and May for each succeeding year. Every day for the 2-month period, from 1984 to 1996, a member of the hospital staff identified as the lactation coordinator filled out forms at the time of discharge. She documented the number of infants discharged each day, how they were being fed at the time of discharge, and whether they were private or public health patients. A standardized form was used throughout the evaluation. The behavioral impact data of the breast-feeding initiative was derived from the annual estimates. It was reported as a time series, reflecting the total number of patients discharged, percent breast-feeding, and percent feeding formula only.

INTERVENTION

The intervention, named the Breast-Feeding Initiative (BFI), consisted of multiple components. Initially, from 1979 to 1984, the BFI consisted of department teams visiting hospital maternity services to encourage staff to promote breast-feeding. A citywide consensus development group, both governmental and academic, was created to further influence professional commitment and routine recommendations. In 1984 the New York State Department of Health established a code (policy) requiring that each hospital with maternity services have a lactation coordinator (LC) as part of regular staff. Each LC had the primary responsibility for routine provision of breast-feeding

Source: K. Rosenberg, C. McMurtrie, B. Kerker, et al., "Breast-Feeding Initiation in New York City, 1979 to 1996," *American Journal of Public Health* 88, no. 12 (1998): 1850–1852.

TABLE 6.18   Private Patients in New York City Voluntary Hospitals: Method of Infant Feeding at Time of Hospital Discharge, 1979–1996

Year	Total No. Discharged	Any Breast-Feeding No. (%)	Formula Only No. (%)
1979	11,127	4,357 (39)	6,770 (61)
1980	3,731	1,649 (44)	2,082 (56)
1982	7,883	3,769 (48)	4,114 (52)
1984	8,167	4,441 (54)	3,726 (46)
1986	8,822	4,441 (50)	4,381 (50)
1988	9,302	4,942 (53)	4,360 (47)
1990	9,457	5,162 (55)	4,295 (45)
1992	9,039	5,064 (56)	3,975 (44)
1994	7,894	4,958 (63)	2,936 (37)
1996	7,869	5,189 (66)	2,680 (34)
Total	83,291	43,972 (53)	39,319 (47)

Note: Any breast-feeding = "breast only" plus "breast and formula."

education for all women delivering at her hospital. There was considerable local emphasis during the entire intervention period on breast-feeding education for physicians and nursing maternity providers and tracking the introduction of the new code/policy.

RESULTS

Data presented in Tables 6.18 and 6.19 document the method of infant feeding at time of hospital discharge from 1979 to 1996. Table 6.18 reflects all hospitals and Table 6.19 represents hospitals that served Medicaid patients. As indicated, there was a significant increase—from 29% to 58%—in any breast-feeding at the time of discharge for all hospitals. In addition, a very substantial and consistent increase—15% in 1979 to 55% in 1996—was documented among the municipal hospital patients. A concurrent decrease in formula-only feeding was confirmed. The 15% to 55% increase in all New York City hospitals and in all New York City municipal hospitals was statistically significant. The proportions increased every year in every survey throughout the evaluation.

INTERNAL VALIDITY

Measurement Bias

Each hospital designated a specific individual (lactation coordinator) who was responsible for recording and reporting all data. Because the data were only reported every other year by the same person, for a 2-month period, the measurement error was probably small. Using a comparison of discharges with citywide live births during each study period, it was confirmed that approximately 80% of all live births were docu-

TABLE 6.19   Medicaid Service Patients in New York City Voluntary Hospitals: Method of Infant Feeding at Time of Hospital Discharge, 1979–1996

Year	Total No. Discharged	Any Breast-Feeding No. (%)	Formula Only No. (%)
1979	5,431	1,165 (21)	4,266 (79)
1980	1,953	438 (22)	1,515 (78)
1982	3,703	972 (26)	2,731 (74)
1984	3,600	987 (27)	2,613 (73)
1986	3,878	1,104 (28)	2,774 (72)
1988	4,391	1,398 (32)	2,993 (68)
1990	5,252	1,711 (33)	3,541 (67)
1992	5,771	2,095 (36)	3,676 (64)
1994	5,952	2,532 (43)	3,420 (57)
1996	5,368	2,613 (49)	2,755 (51)
Total	45,299	15,015 (33)	30,284 (67)

Note: Any breast-feeding = "breast only" plus "breast and formula."

mented as consistent with the data reported in this evaluation. An important strength of this survey is that the data on method of infant feeding were collected by a professional and not by patients. Data related to breast-feeding, use of alcohol, tobacco, and drugs, and other types of sensitive information would be likely to have high social desirability.

It is notable that although the increase was observed each year throughout the evaluation period in New York City, this increase was in contrast to the decrease in national breast-feeding rates for both public and private maternity patients in the United States. This trend provides increased support for the internal validity of the estimates. The report noted that the method of infant feeding may be overestimated, especially in the last 5 years, because the average days in the hospital for a vaginal delivery in New York and throughout the United States decreased from 4 days to less than 3 days. It would appear that measurement bias is an unlikely explanation for the increases observed at both city hospitals and municipal hospitals.

Selection Bias

These data represent the total population for all New York City hospitals, including all city hospitals and municipal hospitals. It does not seem possible that the bias was introduced by the exclusion of any particular type of hospital or numbers of hospitals. A weakness, however, in the report is that it does not identify the total number of hospitals or the total number of New York City municipal hospitals. This information was available in the New York City Department of Health and does not represent a serious deficiency. The report would have been strengthened by a description of the characteristics of program users over time. Although it would appear that selection bias is an unlikely plausible explanation for the observed improvement in breast-feeding initiation rates at hospital discharge, more data are needed to examine this issue.

Historical Bias

A strength of this evaluation is the use of *all* eligible units and patients to document the behavioral impact rate of the breast-feeding intervention. The information provided would indicate that, relatively speaking, within each of the hospitals staff had an ongoing responsibility to provide lactation education services and equipment for all patients. Although it is likely that lactation coordinators changed over time, given the specific responsibilities and the completeness of the data provided by the facilities to the New York Public Health Department, it would not appear that internal (*I*) historical events were plausible explanations for the increase in breast-feeding rate at discharge. The combined application of the ongoing breast-feeding initiation–patient education program by regular designated staff and the external policy (*H*) were well documented. The consistent increases over time provided additional evidence that external history was unlikely to be a source of significant change.

SUMMARY

This evaluation is a very good example of how a well-defined, ongoing public health program for a specific population at multiple individual sites or for a large municipal area can assess behavioral impact over time. It is reasonable to conclude that the BFI in New York was successful; its evaluation had very good internal validity. Other comparable health promotion programs might use a single time-series design in the future, especially in the early stages of evaluation. If it were perceived as a 3- or 5-year program, quarterly rates per year could be used. A multiple time-series design could also be applied; this would include matching 10 (*E*) and 10 (*C*) hospitals, clinics, or sites.

SUMMARY

In evaluating the efficacy or effectiveness of a health promotion program, there are multiple critical methodological issues to address. The time frame, resources, and capacity of a program must be considered prior to making a final decision about the specific design or methods to propose and implement. In making a decision about an evaluation design, the potential factors affecting internal validity, factors that compromise or bias estimates of program impact, must be considered. A number of evaluation designs exist, but very few are useful for program evaluators. The five designs identified in this chapter—one-group pretest and posttest, nonequivalent comparison group, time series, multiple time series, and randomized pretest and posttest with control group—are adequate to excellent choices. In deciding what design to implement, the evaluator needs to fully appreciate the strengths and weaknesses of each.

Because designs play a prominent role in increasing the probability of a demonstrable significant effect, an effect size must be estimated and a decision made about the needed sample size during the planning of an evaluation. There are a few good ways to establish a *C* or *C̲* group. An evaluator needs to consider what problems will arise in implementing an evaluation that includes two or three study groups. Although, at first glance, using a randomized design may seem impossible, more careful thought about the key questions to be answered, combined with a consultation and literature review, may provide insight into the use of a control group instead of a comparison group in evaluating a program. Regardless of the type of design or group used, the baseline comparability of study groups must be established.

In summary, the theory and applications discussed in this chapter represent an essential body of information an evaluation team must know and be able to apply to successfully plan, manage, and evaluate a health promotion program.

7 | Cost Evaluation

Cost-effectiveness analyses began to be conducted for a variety of federal and state programs in the mid-1960s. The Report of the President's Committee on Health Education (USDHEW 1971) recommended: "Cost analysis studies should be made to determine the long-term effectiveness of health education programs in reducing personal health care costs for persons with specific types of health problems." This report was the first national consensus statement about the need for cost analyses of health education–promotion programs. Very few applications of the principles and methods of cost analyses, however, were published in the health promotion and education literature in the 1970s (Thompson and Fortress 1980). Rogers et al. (1981) reported one of the first reviews of the cost-effectiveness of health promotion programs.

Multiple peer review journals in the 1980s and 1990s, such as the *American Journal of Public Health*, *American Journal of Health Promotion*, and *Health Education Research*, and specialty health-related journals reported cost analyses of health promotion and education interventions for diverse problems, settings, and populations (Barry and DeFriese 1990). Documentation of the salience of successful program implementation, quality, behavioral impact, and associated costs was recognized by program managers and policy makers as important information for decision making, as illustrated in *Health Promotion in the Workplace* (O'Donnell and Ainsworth 1984). A report from the Brookings Institute, *Evaluating Preventive Care* by Russell (1987), was one of the first discussions of the efficacy and cost analyses of health promotion programs to improve the health of older people. It included a review of the related literature for health effects, types of interventions, and cost-effective analysis in six health promotion program areas: (1) drug therapy for hypertension control, (2) smoking, (3) exercise, (4) dietary calcium uses, (5) obesity counseling, and (6) alcohol use. "Guidelines for Cost Effectiveness Evaluations" were also presented. The importance of conducting cost analyses for health promotion programs is well established (Tengs et al. 1995).

OBJECTIVES

The objectives of this chapter are to provide a basic discussion of principles, methods, and applications of cost analyses to plan, implement, and evaluate health promotion programs. It is beyond the scope of this chapter to present a comprehensive review of all types of cost analyses. Thorough discussions are readily available in the health economics literature. A very readable primer was presented by Barry and DeFriese, "Cost-Benefit and Cost-Effectiveness Analysis for Health Promotion Programs," in *American Journal of Health Promotion* (1990). An excellent first choice for a comprehensive discussion of the multiple dimensions and complexity of cost-analysis methods for health promotion and disease prevention programs is *Prevention Effectiveness: A Guide to Decision Analysis and Economic Evaluation* (Haddix et al. 1996).

Six types of cost-analysis evaluations are frequently cited in texts (Warner and Luce 1982; Luce and Elixhauser 1990):

1. Cost-effective analysis (CEA)
2. Cost-benefit analysis (CBA)
3. Cost-utility analysis (CUA)
4. Cost-minimization analysis (CMA)
5. Cost of illness (COI)
6. Quality-of-life (QALY)

This chapter focuses only on CEA and CBA, because they are the methods most frequently applied by health education–promotion programs. Selected characteristics of four types of economic evaluations are presented in Table 7.1.

COST-EFFECTIVE ANALYSIS

The objective of a health promotion program evaluation is to determine which intervention methods produced a significant change (positive or negative) in an impact rate from a baseline rate: e.g., increased participant knowledge, increased self-care skill, increased medication adherence, increased or decreased utilization of health services, or decreased workdays lost. Typically, a health promotion program evaluates the impact of different educational, behavioral, or communications interventions for an experimental (E) group or a control (or minimal intervention—C) group. *Cost-effective analysis* (CEA) is an evaluation method designed to assess program-intervention alternatives according to costs and effectiveness in the production of a measurable behavioral impact or health outcome. In performing a CEA, two intervention alternatives—E vs. C—are compared,

TABLE 7.1 Measurement of Costs and Consequences in Economic Evaluations

Type of Study/Analysis	Measurement/ Valuation of Costs in Both Alternatives	Identification of Consequences	Measurement/ Valuation of Consequences
Cost-effectiveness	Dollars	Single effect of interest, common to both alternatives, but achieved to different degrees	Natural units (e.g., life-years gained, disability-days saved, points of blood pressure reduced, etc.)
Cost-benefit	Dollars	Single or multiple effects, not necessarily common to both alternatives, and common effects may be achieved in different degrees by the alternatives	Dollars
Cost-utility	Dollars	Single or multiple effects, not necessarily common to both alternatives, and common effects may be achieved to different degrees by the alternatives	Healthy days or (more often) quality-adjusted life-years
Cost-minimization	Dollars	Identical in all relevant respects	None

Source: Drummond et al. (1997). Reprinted by permission of Oxford University Press.

using common measurement methods, to confirm the level of achievement of program educational and behavioral objectives. Impact data are examined in the context of personnel and nonpersonnel resources—costs (input)—expended to accomplish the observed degree of impact (output). This computation enables the evaluator and policy maker to identify which method provided optimal effectiveness in relation to its cost.

COST-BENEFIT ANALYSIS

Cost-benefit analysis (CBA) is an evaluation method in which two or more intervention alternatives, and associated E group vs. C group impact rates, are compared according to monetary costs (input) and monetary benefits—savings (output). Program costs and program benefits are measured in dollars. Benefits are often called consequences. Because CBA compares each alternative in monetary terms, the evaluator documents whether a specific method has a benefit that exceeds its associated costs and determines which method has the lowest cost-to-benefit ratio. One of the major issues raised about CBA is that it is often difficult, because of methodological and/or philosophical reasons, to place a dollar value on *all* program benefits (Rice and Hodgson 1982; Barry and DeFriese 1990).

PURPOSE OF CEA AND CBA

The general purpose of CEA and CBA is to serve as an analytic evaluation tool to provide insight about program efficiency. It should foster better decision making about resource allocation. A cost analysis requires accurate documentation of expended fiscal resources to implement a health promotion program. Data confirming measurement validity and reliability, successful program implementation (process evaluation), and internal validity of results (impact evaluation) must be available. Thus, before initiating a cost analysis, the evaluator must address the multiple critical issues identified in Chapters 1 to 6. The principles and basic steps of applying the principles of CEA and CBA are well described in the literature. The application of these methods and the assignment of monetary values to human experience or a social program may, however, be problematic. When applying CEA and CBA, it is important to appreciate the technical sophistication of these two evaluation methods and when appropriate to seek special expertise to perform cost analyses.

Another important issue to consider in planning a program and defining its costs is: What do specialists (experts) define as the most appropriate minimum HP program, e.g., clinical practice guidelines, that licensed, credentialed, and trained specialists should be providing to all eligible individuals who should participate? Program quality should be the primary issue in deciding what health promotion program should be delivered to a specific population at risk and specific setting. Costs are only one dimension of a program used in decision making.

COST ANALYSIS METHODS

There are six sequential steps in performing a CEA or CBA: (1) Define the population and extent of the problem; (2) define the behavioral or health objectives; (3) define program costs—input; (4) define the cost—perspective; (5) document impact or outcome—output; and (6) perform sensitivity analyses.

Step 1: Define the Population and Problem

The first step in a cost analysis is to document the extent of the problem (numerator) among a defined population at risk (denominator). The incidence or prevalence rate of the problem is specified in epidemiological, behavioral, or clinical terms, for example, "Among a cohort of 1,000 adults over age 50 who are members of XYZ HMO and who work for the ABC Company, 300, or 30%, have a diagnosed case of high blood pressure." If the problem is, for example, high blood pressure or injuries among a defined cohort of ABC employees, "What are the rates of blood pressure control or personal injury, associated morbidity, and utilization of employee health services and care attributable to these two problems?" Each rate and individual HMO member with a risk factor has associated financial expenditures for his or her condition. If the incidence rate, e.g., increased percentage with HBP controlled, is decreased, it should represent an opportunity to evaluate associated economic benefit or savings.

In defining the baseline incidence or prevalence rate of a problem, be it a state or city low-birth-weight prevention program for pregnant Medicaid patients who smoke, or workers at XYZ Company, the next step is to identify the population-attributable risk (PAR), or the primary, major cause(s) of the health problem. In smoking and pregnancy, for example, the PAR for low birth weight is 20%. In this chapter, the primary risk factor(s) are assumed to be behavioral and amenable to change. This step defines, in theory, how much—what percent of the health status indicator—is caused by risk factors that can be changed. Elimination of the risk factors, in theory, eliminates the PAR and dramatically reduces or may eliminate the incidence rate. If the population risk is dramatically reduced or eliminated, associated excess costs should be substantially reduced and benefits/savings observed.

Step 2: Define Health or Behavioral Objectives

Description and quantification of program objectives in measurable terms and documentation of a baseline rate for the population at risk are critical steps for an evaluation and cost analysis. Following the definition of the extent of the health and associated behavioral problems among the target population, the next step is to define measurable objectives derived from valid baseline measures against which different intervention methods are to be compared. A meta-analysis will document the range of impact rates (effect sizes) for specific populations at risk. It is assumed, during this process, that technical and program capabilities exist to measure highly valid and reliable output: behavioral impact or health outcome rates. In some cases, the measurement of an objective may be complicated, e.g., measurement of the quality-of-life years added due to an intervention. But most health promotion program health status outcomes (e.g., uncontrolled hypertension, or high blood cholesterol levels) or a behavioral outcome (changes in smoking status, or weight loss) can be measured in valid and reliable ways. Defining multiple objectives for each program should be possible.

Excellent examples of measurable health-status and risk-reduction objectives are presented in *Healthy People 2010* (USDHEW 2000).

Almost all major health promotion program objectives are measurable, and instruments and methods exist to confirm status at different times for a defined population at risk. In some cases, however, objectives are not easily measurable, such as reduction of suffering or stress. Thus, it is more difficult to establish these types of objectives as endpoints of a health promotion program. As noted in Chapter 6, programs must define how much of a rate they expect to change (effect size) and specify how many participants they must have to perform analyses of the significance of an effect.

Step 3: Define the Program Costs—Input

In Chapters 2 and 4 considerable emphasis was placed on the need to define intervention procedures and the need to empirically confirm that the core set of program-intervention procedures was delivered to the target population as planned: Was a process evaluation planned and conducted? To conduct a cost analysis, a program must describe the number, frequency of contact, and duration of the program procedures used to intervene. It is presumed that the meta-evaluation and formative evaluation that the intervention used had an opportunity to modify the behavioral objectives prepared in step 2. There will always be one or possibly two intervention alternatives in a health promotion program. One alternative is the usual education or information intervention (C group). One or two special interventions (E group) are always provided.

Feasibility and costs are a critical dimension in the selection of alternative methods of intervention at the onset. In most cases, in the development of and decision to deliver a health promotion program, interventions are created or selected because they are appropriate to a setting or specific health or behavioral problem and the population at risk.

This step requires documentation of the costs associated with program delivery: staff time per group or individual contact, number of contacts, and amount/cost of materials distributed. A comprehensive process evaluation provides this information. In the specification of costs, program staff document all budgetary resources expended to provide the program to participants. In general, these costs can be divided into direct costs (personnel and nonpersonnel) and indirect costs (facilities rent, maintenance, etc.). Whether to use indirect costs in a computation is an individual program judgment that depends on the extent to which the organization requires these costs to be used: Who is paying for it?

Personnel costs   The major cost associated with the delivery of health promotion and education programs is personnel time: typically 80% to 90% of a budget. A detailed description of the intervention specifies how much individual staff time is expended to provide the different components of the intervention. As noted in Chapter 4, a program flow analysis of 10 or more clients at each site should provide good estimates of the cost per participant.

In an employee fitness program, for example, a master's-trained exercise physiologist might use 20 hours twice per week to deliver a 10-week aerobics class for each group of 20 employees. Employees do not participate during company time. The instructor may have to spend an additional 10 hours in preparation: 1 hour per session. If you assume a $40,000 per year salary for this person, with a 20% fringe benefit rate (.20 × $40,000 = $8,000), then the total salary costs would be $48,000 per year. The hourly rate for this staff member would be $23.07 (48,000 ÷ 2,080 hours). Thus, the total personnel costs to deliver this type of program to 20 employees would be $692.10 ($23.07 × 30 hours): $34.06/employee.

If equipment is minimal and available, it may not be included as part of direct costs. A company could estimate the cost of space used (rent/sq. ft) for classes, because this space could be used for profit-making activity. Additional costs to the company could be considered, depending on whether the program was delivered on company time or employee time. It might be zero if on employee time, or the average hourly wage of the 20 employees if conducted on company time. Costs of staff communication with employees, of scheduling, and/or facilities setup would also be incurred and could be counted. Another dimension of a cost analysis may be participant co-payment to defray costs, e.g., $10 or $20 per employee. The cost per employee would then be $14.06 or $24.06.

Equipment and material costs   In marketing and delivering HP programs, materials such as books, paper, handouts, leaflets, and posters may be used. In addition, specialized equipment may be needed, such as for an exercise class. Equipment costs used for multiple programs and purposes can be estimated, with the estimation of dollars equivalent to that proportion of the time in which the equipment is used solely for your intervention. Materials and equipment costs should be easily documented.

Facilities costs   Facilities costs reflect the monetary value of use of the physical space in which a program is provided. All property space can be valued. An estimate of the cost per square foot for classroom or meeting space can be computed. The cost per square foot times the hours of use divided by the total number of possible hours of use produces a crude estimate of facilities costs. When facilities are rented, a lease contract would specify the facilities costs. Unless space has to be rented, on-site facilities costs may not be used in cost analyses.

A simple worksheet (see Chapter 2) can be constructed to estimate the total personnel or nonpersonnel input costs allocated to deliver the health promotion program.

Step 4: Define the Cost-Analysis Perspective

Each evaluation needs to clarify what perspective it will apply in its analysis. There are two basic perspectives used in cost analyses: societal or agency. In a large percent of cost evaluations for health promotion programs designed to change population-based behavior, an agency-provider perspective is taken.

Societal perspective   All health-related costs for health care, hospitalization, and related treatment-management services would be included in this perspective. In the societal perspective other indirect costs may be included, e.g., gains or losses directly associated with the morbidity or mortality of the target audience. All costs borne by the client within the at-risk group, such as out-of-pocket payment for drugs or medications, transportation costs, loss of work due to the condition or participation in the health promotion program, or child-care expenses would be counted or estimated. It is more difficult to measure client costs such as pain or anxiety, which may also be included and a monetary value placed on them.

Third-party or agency perspective   The principal focus of this perspective is the cost associated with health/medical care expenses associated with a condition or disease and the expenses avoided as a result of the intervention. Other costs, such as patient loss of productivity, travel, and so forth are not part of the third-party perspective. Health maintenance organizations, managed-care organizations, and the federal/state governments pay for and/or reimburse for related costs for specific problems among the target group of a health promotion program. The perspective of the health promotion–disease prevention program includes those direct costs associated with the costs of providing the program. The perspective here is essentially: How much does it cost the funding agency to treat the health problem for each member of a health plan, or to provide the health promotion program?

Step 5: Document Behavioral Impact or Health Outcome Rates—Output

The next step in the performance of a cost analysis is to confirm the educational, behavioral impact, and/or health outcome. What was the effect size for each rate? Were the program objectives achieved? What benefits (consequences) occurred from program exposure? In examining these output data, the methodological issues related to internal validity, defined in Chapters 2 to 6, must be addressed. Empirical evidence must be presented to confirm that the changes in impact or outcomes observed are attributable to the intervention methods. Cost analysis should not be performed unless a methodologically rigorous evaluation has been conducted to provide valid evidence of results.

A health promotion program, e.g., fitness and weight control, may document that method 1 produced an effectiveness level of "5% less weight than at baseline observation" at a 6-month follow-up. Method 2 produced an effectiveness level of "5% more weight than at baseline observation." When comparing method 1 against method 2, the relative cost is considered for delivery of method 1 and method 2, and output data are compared in the context of effectiveness (weight loss). This computation produces a cost-effective ratio (CER). Looking at this example from a CBA perspective, you might be able to examine the costs of method 1 and method 2 and document the benefits (if any can be expected) of the method in monetary terms, e.g., Were a reduction in workdays lost and cost savings observed? Absenteeism rates, if attributable to the method, that produce a decrease in workdays lost may translate into monetary savings. In the CBA evaluation of method 1 versus method 2, a cost-to-benefit ratio (CBR) may be computed and total economic savings-benefit reported.

Step 6: Perform Sensitivity Analysis

The purpose of sensitivity analysis (SA) is to estimate costs using different assumptions to determine how much the cost savings and the CER or CBR would change. Before an organization establishes a new policy or new program and commits a large amount of money to its development and routine delivery, a clear picture of program efficiency is needed. Sensitivity analysis may produce four important results for a program:

1. Dependence on a specific assumption of a conclusion of impact
2. Assumption that does not significantly affect a conclusion
3. Confirmation of the assumption of the minimum or maximum value that a cost factor must have for a program to appear worthwhile
4. Issues and uncertainties deserving future cost-analysis evaluation

If a statistically significant impact is documented, these results should be examined in the context of variations of costs for input and output at different sites or with different groups of program participants. For example, personnel and material costs vary from state to state, and the level of behavioral impact will vary from site to site. An organization might decide in a sensitivity analysis to increase personnel or total intervention costs by 10% or 20% and/or to decrease the observed effect size by 10% to 20%. These assumptions may be varied as part of the SA program, using low-medium-high estimates of effect size. An HP program documents what changes would occur in the conclusions with these variations. It is important to emphasize that when performing a sensitivity analysis, the magnitude of the variations and assumptions should be reasonable. Case Studies 7.1 and 7.3 provide an application of SA.

VALUATION

A discussion of costs should also include consideration of the value of monetary resources for purposes other than allocation to a health promotion and education program. Simply put, if a school system, company, managed-care organization, or public health agency budgets and spends (invests) $100,000 annually in a health promotion program, those funds are not available for other income-producing opportunities. It is also important to recognize that all program costs and expenditures are not incurred at the present time. Costs are incurred over a period of years and the benefits, real or estimated savings, typically occur over a longer period of time. The issue is estimating the costs and benefits of a program throughout its effective lifetime. The term used to consider the value of current and future dollars in a cost analysis is *discounting*.

As reflected in Table 7.2, future dollar costs and benefits are reduced, or "discounted," to reflect the fact that dollars spent or saved in the future should not weigh as much as dollars spent or saved today. The basic premise of discounting is that an organization has the option to invest an amount of money in units, e.g., $10,000, in an activity. If $10,000 is invested, it may yield $500 at a CD rate of 5%, for a total of $10,500 each year. Concurrently, during this year the consumer price index reports an inflation rate. If the inflation rate during the year is 3%, then the sum of $10,000 will have the investment buying power of only $9,700 in the next year.

The choice of the most appropriate discount rate, typically 3% or 5%, depends to a large extent on how inflation rates are addressed. If all items in the costs of the program are expected to increase at the same rate as inflation, there are two choices in discounting. First: Inflate future costs and use a larger discount rate to allow for inflation. This is called the "inflation-adjusted discount rate." Second: Do not inflate future costs and use a smaller discount rate to not allow for inflation. Financial calculators have discount functions, and financial software packages for personal computers can easily perform these calculations.

In the applications of CEA and CBA, there are a number of health problem areas for which cost analyses may be complex and very imprecise. The literature must be reviewed and specific expertise sought for a program area to ascertain

Table 7.2 Discount Table				

Present value of $1 discounted to the 5th year:

n	1%	2%	3%	4%	5%
1	0.9901	0.9804	0.9709	0.9615	0.9524
2	0.9803	0.9612	0.9426	0.9246	0.9070
3	0.9706	0.9423	0.9151	0.8890	0.8638
4	0.9610	0.9238	0.8885	0.8548	0.8227
5	0.9515	0.9057	0.8626	0.8219	0.7835

Source: Excerpted from Haddix et al. (1996).

how each issue—costs discounting, inflation, and sensitivity analysis—needs to be addressed. Consultation with a health services researcher/health economist is recommended.

Case Studies

The following three case studies provide examples of the application of cost analysis methods. Case Study 7.1 describes methods used to conduct a CEA of two different health education methods for public health patients in prenatal care. Case Study 7.2 describes the application of CEA to health education methods for adults with asthma in a pulmonary medicine clinic. Case Study 7.3 presents an application of CBA to an evaluation of the behavioral impact and estimated savings from health education methods for pregnant smokers in public health maternity clinics for a state Medicaid system.

Case Study 7.1

CEA: Public Health Patients in Prenatal Care

INTRODUCTION

The 1985 Institute of Medicine's report "Preventing Low Birth Weight" identified smoking during pregnancy as a contributing factor in 20 to 40 percent of low birth weights among infants of women receiving public assistance in the United States. A major recommendation of the report was to consider the issues of relative costs and benefits of

Source: Windsor, Warner, and Cutter (1988).

formulating public health policy about health education methods designed to increase birth weight. Lack of adequate data prevented the committee from estimating the additional public expenditure required to finance the recommended public health education program. The Institute of Medicine's report and recent reviews of the intervention research literature concluded that estimates of the cost-effectiveness and cost benefits of health promotion and education methods to increase birth weight were not available. This paper presented the results of a cost-effectiveness evaluation derived from a randomized trial designed to evaluate the effectiveness of self-help smoking-cessation methods for pregnant women in public health maternity clinics. The research methods, self-help interventions, and results have been discussed in detail elsewhere.

Cost-effectiveness analysis refers to the comparative evaluation of the costs (input) and behavioral impact (output) of three cessation methods for pregnant smokers used in the randomized trial. These analyses were performed to provide decision makers, such as directors of maternal and child health and public health education programs, with information to evaluate cessation methods.

METHODS

A randomized pretest-posttest design was used in the evaluation. At the time of their first clinic visit, pregnant smokers—a total of 309 women from three prenatal clinics—were assigned to one of the three groups. Baseline comparability of the three groups was confirmed. Group 1, the standard information control group, received information in nonfocused interaction on smoking and pregnancy, requiring about 5 minutes during the first prenatal visit. Group 2 received the standard clinic information on smoking plus a copy of "Freedom from Smoking in 20 Days," a manual published by the American Lung Association (ALA) (1980). Group 3 received the standard clinic information plus the pregnancy-specific self-help manual "A Pregnant Woman's Self-Help Guide to Quit Smoking."

The "Pregnant Woman's Guide" went through extensive internal and external review before it was given to Group 3. All skills were pilot-tested with pregnant smokers at each of the clinics. A prototype of the guide was produced representing a standardized smoking-cessation method that professionals in prenatal care could use to educate their patients. Three pregnant women who participated in the pilot study of 50 pregnant smokers and who had used the guide to become ex-smokers served as editorial consultants.

Groups 2 and 3 also received an informational packet entitled "Because You Love Your Baby," on the risks of smoking and the benefits of quitting, disseminated by the ALA. The patient education methods used to teach the use of the self-help manual for Groups 2 and 3 were standardized and presented in approximately 10 minutes at the first prenatal visit by the same woman, a baccalaureate-trained health education specialist. No smoking-cessation intervention methods were provided to the 309 women after their first visits.

Smoking status was confirmed at mid-pregnancy and end of pregnancy, using patient self-reports and saliva thiocyanate tests with a cutoff value of 100 micrograms per milliliter or less. Women lost to follow-up were counted as smokers.

Cost Analysis

Intervention costs were estimated by identifying associated resources, determining their unit values (prices), multiplying the number of units of each by its price, and summing across all resource categories. The principal resources used were personnel and the self-help educational materials. No costs for the use of facilities were estimated. The cessation methods were applied during normal clinic hours in the three public health facilities and thus did not produce incremental or differential facilities costs. Because almost no supplies were used beyond those used during the normal visits to the clinics, supply costs were treated as zero. The one exception was the supplies needed for the saliva thiocyanate tests. These tests are unlikely to be used in any everyday clinic setting and hence were not considered to be a resource cost associated with self-help methods. From a social perspective, the client's time also was a resource, although it would not be relevant to any agency director dealing with program budgets. We adopted the perspective of the agency for this analysis.

Estimating Personnel Costs

A health education specialist with a BS degree counseled Groups 2 and 3. A nurse with a BSN, however, is the most likely person to provide smoking-cessation methods as part of prenatal care. Personnel costs vary from state to state, by type of personnel and by level of training. Based on interviews with personnel unit officials of health departments of same-size major cities, we estimated the average wage (in 1986) for clinic health department nurses at $20,000, with fringe benefits totaling an additional 20%, for a total personnel cost of $24,000 per nurse per year. Thus, the hourly labor cost per nurse was estimated at $12 (assuming 40 hours per week and 50 workweeks per year).

As noted previously, the average time spent at first visit in Groups 2 and 3 to educate each woman about how to use the self-help guides was about 10 minutes. Two brief follow-up nonintervention contacts were conducted to collect saliva samples and self-reports of smoking status. Each follow-up took an additional two minutes. Although the follow-up contacts were not designed to be part of the patient education intervention, patients may have perceived them to be part of it. Additionally, in practice, prenatal staff is likely to make inquiries about patient smoking status at subsequent clinic encounters. A verbal statement of encouragement such as "Keep up the good work" was made for women in Groups 2 and 3 who had quit.

Actual personnel time per client should be counted, for a total of approximately 15 minutes for Groups 2 and 3. Group 1 required 5 minutes of staff time per client at first visit, with an additional combined 5 minutes for the midpoint and end-of-pregnancy follow-ups. Total personnel time per client in Group 1 was about 10 minutes. In all cases, personnel time was valued at the appropriate fraction of the hourly rate defined previously. The cost of each ALA cessation manual to the project in 1983 was $4, and the cost of each "Pregnant Woman's Guide" was also $4. Thus, the total costs and personnel time were the same for Groups 2 and 3.

RESULTS

The end-of-pregnancy quit rates were 2% in Group 1, 6% in Group 2, and 14% in Group 3. Quitters were confirmed by combining patients' self-reports of smoking status at follow-up with their saliva thiocyanate values.

Table 7.3 represents the cost per patient and cost-effectiveness ratios by study group. The ratios suggested that the pregnancy-specified, tailored self-help methods provided to Group 3 patients were more cost-effective in encouraging smoking cessation than either the standard smoking cessation information provided to Group 1 or the self-help methods for Group 2. These estimates suggest that the Group 3 methods

TABLE 7.3   Cost-Effectiveness of Three Smoking-Cessation Methods

Group	Cost per Patient	% Quit	Cost-Effectiveness
1. Information	$2.08	2%	$104.00
2. ALA manual	$7.13	6%	$118.83
3. Guide	$7.13	14%	$50.93

Cost-effectiveness = cost per patient divided by number who quit (effectiveness).

Group 1 = information in a nonfocused interaction on smoking and pregnancy.

Group 2 = information plus the "Freedom from Smoking" manual of the ALA.

Group 3 = information plus a self-help guide for pregnant women.

can achieve smoking cessation at less than half the cost of either of the two alternatives tested. Group 1 methods were the least costly on a per patient basis, but the increase in effectiveness associated with the Group 3 methods is sufficiently greater than the increase in the per patient cost of delivery to make this intervention more cost-effective. Compared with that of Group 1, Group 2's effectiveness is not sufficiently greater to compensate for its greater cost.

DISCUSSION

Sensitivity Analysis

The reported findings are based on several assumptions about costs and effectiveness. We performed several sensitivity analyses to assess whether the basic conclusions depended on the precise estimates employed in the analysis. Specifically, we addressed the following questions:

1. Is the finding of the greater efficiency of the Group 3 ("Pregnant Woman's Guide") approach dependent on the precision of its effectiveness? The guide is more cost-effective because it shares the highest cost with the ALA manual but is more effective (14% versus 6%). There is, however, a substantial margin for the guide to be less effective than observed without losing its cost-effectiveness. The observed quit rate could be halved, and the guide would remain the most cost-effective of the three methods. We conclude, therefore, that the superiority of the pregnancy-specific method is not likely to be dependent on the precision of the estimate of its effectiveness. The guide will remain preferred to the ALA manual as long as its effectiveness is greater, a function of the identical cost. The guide must be 3.4 times more effective to maintain superiority over the standard information approach. The 1988 cost of the guide of $4 versus the cost of $7 for the "new" ALA manual for pregnant smokers makes the guide even more cost-effective because of its significantly lower cost.

2. Is the cost effectiveness of the group methods dependent on the precise estimate of the cost of staff time, the dominant cost of intervention? Allowing the hourly rate for labor costs to vary by 20% above our estimate, equivalent

to base annual salaries of $24,000, we find that the pregnancy-specific self-help cessation method substantially dominates the two alternatives even when the high hourly rate is used for the guide and the low hourly rate is used for the two alternatives.

3. Do the cost estimates of the materials significantly affect the findings? No. The cost of the Group 3 methods could be nearly twice that observed. The third alternative would remain the most cost-effective.

Social Cost Versus Accounting Cost

From a social perspective, the value of the patient's time could be included as a resource cost. From an agency perspective, the perspective adopted in this analysis, client's time was not a resource on which departmental funds must be expended. Hence, it is not a program budget component. It may be useful, however, to consider briefly how inclusion of the value of the patient's time might affect our analysis. As in the case of personnel, only the incremental time required by the interventions represents an intervention cost. Time expended by patients traveling to clinics and waiting to be seen by the health professionals is not a relevant cost. Patients incur these costs for regular, periodic clinic exams. In this context, incremental clinic time spent by patients is identical to staff time.

For patients in Groups 2 and 3, however, there is an additional incremental cost, namely, the time to read and use the self-help packages. If this extra time totals about 1 hour (7 days × 8–10 minutes), patients in Groups 2 and 3 will spend 75 minutes on the intervention. Patients in Group 1, by contrast, will devote only the additional 10 minutes also experienced by staff. If we value patient's time at $3.35 per hour (minimum hourly wage in 1986), the value of each patient's time required for Group 1 methods is about $56 (0.166 per hour × $3.35), while that required for Group 2 and 3 interventions is $419 (1.25 per hour × $3.35). This adds 27% ($0.56 divided by $2.08) to the per patient cost for Group 1 and 59% ($4.19 divided by $7.13) to the cost for Group 2 and 3 methods; cost-effectiveness ratios increase similarly. Under these circumstances, the Group 3 methods remain the most cost-effective and Group 2's the least cost-effective.

Program and Policy Implications

A clear responsibility exists to provide efficient and effective methods to pregnant women to help them quit smoking. Increased attention is also needed to assist maternal and child health programs in the planning, management, and evaluation of smoking-cessation programs for pregnant smokers. This evaluation and analysis indicated that simple verbal statements about risk were ineffective and inefficient. These data, and data from other evaluation studies, suggested that the typical informational content and methods of prenatal care education related to smoking needed to be significantly revised. Counseling should include specific smoking-cessation and maintenance methods to help the pregnant woman become and remain a nonsmoker. If a public health department expects to achieve a quit rate greater than 2–3%, increases in resources and time will have to be allocated.

Personnel costs associated with the provision of effective cessation methods can be absorbed by most ongoing prenatal education programs with small allocations of personnel time. Training requirements for nurses to use self-help methods are also modest. Initial in-service training and periodic training for new prenatal care nurses on how to teach the use of self-help methods as part of a prenatal education would take approximately 2 hours, resulting in a training cost of $24 per nurse (at $12 per hour). This cost, however, would be spread out over a year for counseling all pregnant smokers. An additional cost of approximately $0.24 per patient would be incurred if 100 pregnant smokers were counseled. Training time and costs, therefore, could double from 2 to 4 hours ($24 to $48) and only increase the cost for 100 patients counseled to about $0.50 each. Although not tested in this study, it is also likely that the $0.24 to $0.48 cost per patient would be reduced, because almost all prenatal care education programs would provide this type of patient education as part of a small group. Additionally, in cases where there was little staff turnover, the cost would be further reduced in proportion to the number of pregnant smokers counseled. Total training costs would be very low.

Because the 2% control group quit rate observed in this study (3) was comparable to other reported quit rates (2–4%) for pregnant smokers after initiating prenatal care, perhaps only 20,000–40,000 of the annual cohort of approximately 1 million pregnant smokers are being motivated to quit by information approaches after initiating prenatal care. If the pregnancy-specific self-help methods and corresponding 14% quit-smoking rate observed in this trial could be applied to this cohort, there might be 140,000 quitters. This estimate is likely to be conservative, however, because more affluent and educated pregnant smokers who are provided cessation methods exhibit quit rates of approximately 25%.

The estimated cost of prenatal care, including delivery and postpartum care for a normal delivery, was (in 1985) approximately $2,000–$3,000. The cost of neonatal delivery in Level II or Level III hospitals using low-to-medium estimates was approximately $14,000–$20,000. Although estimating clinical outcomes and cost-benefit ratios was not a purpose of this evaluation, we noted that if this type of self-help method were used, additional direct costs might be avoided due to reduced hospitalization and morbidity related to increased birth weight.

Applying the cost estimates from Table 7.3 to the 1 million pregnant smokers who delivered each year (in the 1980s and 1990s), the total cost for universal application of self-help methods would be approximately $7 million. The total investment across the 50 states, therefore, would be small, an insignificant proportion of the total private or public sector costs associated with low birth weight. The potential savings would appear to be substantial.

CASE STUDY 7.2

CEA: Adults with Asthma in a Pulmonary Medicine Clinic

INTRODUCTION

The prevalence of asthma among adults in the United States is 3–6%. There are more than 500,000 hospitalizations and 3,500 deaths from asthma per year. Multiple studies of adults with asthma confirmed adherence levels of only 30–40%. Educational

Source: Windsor, Bailey, et al. (1990).

intervention studies have reported methodological problems, used small sample sizes, lacked cost analyses, and presented inconclusive results. This evaluation study was designed to document *efficacy*—the level of behavioral impact produced by a health education program with optimal resources—and *costs*—personnel and materials needed to routinely deliver the program.

METHODS

The study was conducted at a university-based Comprehensive Pulmonary Medicine Clinic. Patients who had a primary diagnosis of asthma, used medications daily, and met the following diagnostic criteria were eligible: recurrent episodes of wheezing or dyspnea; objective evidence of significantly increased airway resistance during episodes; and improvement in the airway when symptom-free. Of the 280 adults older than age 17 meeting the criteria screened between April 1986 and March 1987, 267 (95%) participated.

Following informed consent and baseline assessment, 135 patients were randomized to a control group and 132 patients to an experimental group. Patients were stratified by level of asthma severity within each of 11 physician practices prior to randomization. Using pilot study data, an estimated possible improvement in adherence of 20% or more for 12 months, and an anticipated 10% attrition rate, the need for at least 120 patients in each study group was defined.

HEALTH EDUCATION INTERVENTION

The experimental (*E*) group received a peak flow meter and a standardized program from a health education specialist:

- A 30-minute one-to-one session with instruction on peak flow meter use, inhaler use skills, and use of *A Self-Help Guide to Asthma Control*
- A 60-minute asthma support group session of four to six patients and asthma control partners
- Two brief telephone reinforcement calls within one month of the group session

One-to-one discussions and a review of all methods and materials were conducted with clinic nurses and all 11 participating pulmonary physicians. Four focus group sessions with patients were held to develop the intervention. All educational components and evaluation methods were pilot-tested.

MEASUREMENT

All patients received a baseline and 12-month follow-up medical and behavioral assessment, including four behavioral outcomes: (1) correct inhaler use, (2) inhaler adherence, (3) medication adherence, and (4) total adherence rating. A 10-item observational checklist documented inhaler use and skill (IU). Medication adherence (MA) and inhaler adherence (IA) were assessed using instruments adapted from the literature. Psychometric analyses (Cronbach's alpha) confirmed marginal to adequate reliability: $r(MA) = 0.69$, $r(IA) = 0.64$, and $r(IU) = 0.78$. Item analyses confirmed minimum item-discrimination coefficients: $r \geq 0.20$. A total adherence score was derived by combining patient scores on the medication and inhaler adherence scales.

More than 85% of the patients used an inhaled bronchodilator and continuous theophylline. Theophylline levels were analyzed on the two follow-up assessment days

TABLE 7.4   Baseline Patient Characteristics by Study Group

Characteristics	Control Group (*n* = 135)	Experimental Group (*n* = 132)
Sex: female	71%	61%
Race: black	28%	32%
Median age	49	50
Median years of education	13	13
Current smoker	13%	10%
Asthma severity		
Mild	39%	37%
Moderate	45%	48%
Severe	17%	16%

Source: Windsor et al. (1990). Used by permission of The American Public Health Association.

to indirectly corroborate patient adherence reports. Patients were informed that their theophylline level would be analyzed to assess adherence. Although theophylline level is an imperfect measure of adherence and does not reflect adherence to nontheophylline medications, behavioral studies of adults who know a method is available to validate self-reports document a significant reduction in deception rates (bogus pipeline or pipeline effect).

BEHAVIOR INTERVENTION RESULTS

Data in Table 7.4 confirmed group equivalence at baseline. A comparison of the 13 patients who refused (5% refusal rate) versus the 267 who participated confirmed no baseline differences by gender, race, age, education, and asthma severity. Thirty-four of the control group patients (25%) and 8 of the experimental group patients (6%) were lost to follow-up. Analyses of baseline data confirmed that the 42 dropouts were not significantly different from the 238 participants. Within the intervention group, use of the asthma guide was reported by 124 patients (94%); 110 (89%) participated in the group session; and 124 patients (94%) received both reinforcement calls.

The behavioral impact of the intervention is presented in Figure 7.1. Using a 95% confidence interval (CI) to evaluate differences between rates of group improvement, a consistent pattern of adherence was confirmed for a 12-month period. Significant improvements for the intervention group in inhaler skills use (CI = 0.29, 0.61), inhaler adherence (CI = 0.24, 0.50), medication adherence (CI = 0.31, 0.57), and total adherence score (100% adherence) (CI = 0.28, 0.59) were observed. Little behavior change was observed in the control group.

COST ESTIMATION AND ANALYSIS

Patient time and intervention development costs were not used to compute program costs. An MPH-health education specialist provided the intervention, but a nurse would be the typical provider. A salary of $25,000 plus a fringe benefit rate of 20% was used to estimate nursing cost: $30,000 per year/2,080 hr. = $14.42/hr. Total personnel time costs for the experimental group were $24.03: component 1 = $7.21,

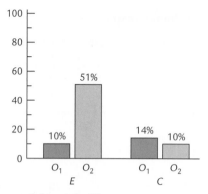

a. Inhaler use checklist
All ten items—Correct

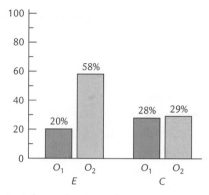

b. Inhaler adherence scale
All six items—Yes

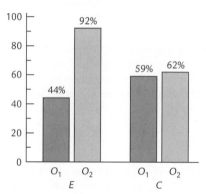

c. Medication adherence scale
All six items—Yes

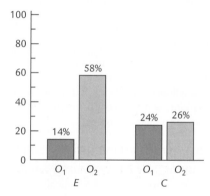

d. Total adherence scale
All twelve items—Yes

FIGURE 7.1 Behavioral Impact by Type and Study Group

component 2 = $14.42, and component 3 = $2.40. The asthma guide cost $8.00, for a total intervention cost of $32.03/patient. The total control group costs for a 10-minute general discussion about the importance of adherence and two brief follow-up contacts for a total of 15 minutes were $3.61/patient. Cost analyses presented in Table 7.5 confirmed the need to allocate resources to significantly increase patient adherence.

DISCUSSION

The significant increase in adherence documented in the *E* intervention group exceeded those of previous reports. Although some proportion of patient self-reports of adherence may represent a "social desirability" response, psychometric analyses indicated good measurement of behavioral impact. The very high recruitment rate confirmed that adults with asthma were interested in taking an active role in their self-management

TABLE 7.5   Cost-Effectiveness of the Health Education Program

Group	Cost per Patient	Adherence Score Improvement	Total Cost-Effectiveness*
Control group ($n = 135$)	$3.61	+2%	$243.68
Experimental group ($n = 132$)	$32.03	+44%	$96.09

*Cost-effectiveness = total cost per group divided by adherence score increase.

and would participate in a health education program integrated into routine asthma care. Near unanimous positive anecdotal comments about the intervention by nurses, physicians, and patients were observed. Feasibility and patient and provider acceptance were very high. From an administrative and programmatic perspective, these results indicated that this type of intervention may have potential for adaptation by other asthma programs. However, in an attempt to maximize efficacy, an intervention was provided that may have been too resource-intensive and costly for other asthma-care sites. Although the methods and results reported here and elsewhere were encouraging, future health education research needs to evaluate the impact of a streamlined health education program on health services utilization, for example, ambulatory care, emergency care, and hospitalization and clinical outcomes.

CASE STUDY 7.3

CBA: Pregnant Smokers in Public Health Maternity Clinics

INTRODUCTION

Maternal smoking causes infant morbidity and mortality. The elimination or reduction of active and passive maternal and fetal exposure to cigarette smoke is a high priority. The need for effective smoking-cessation methods among pregnant women, particularly high-risk public health populations, is well defined.

Multiple randomized clinical trials and evaluation studies have reported estimates of the behavioral impact of cessation methods for pregnant smokers and have assessed medical cost outcomes. Only one clinical trial has evaluated the behavioral impact and the cost-effectiveness of cessation methods among pregnant smokers in a public health maternity setting. Cost-benefit analyses of health education methods for that setting are not available. This report presents the results of the Birmingham Trial II, an evaluation of the behavioral impact and cost benefits of a health education program for pregnant smokers in public health maternity clinics.

Source: Windsor, Lowe, et al. (1993).

METHODS

This study was conducted from 1986 to 1991 at the four highest-census maternity clinics, representing 85% of the annual cohort, of the Jefferson County Health Department (JCHD) in Birmingham, Alabama. A fifth JCHD clinic with a small census did not participate. Evaluation and data collection methods were adapted from Trial I, conducted at the JCHD from 1982 to 1985 (see Case Study 7.1).

A formative evaluation was planned from July 1986 to August 1987 to conduct a prospective natural history study prior to pre–Trial II to document smoking prevalence and quit rates attributable to routine prenatal care and risk information; to train the health counselors; and to pilot-test the intervention, measurement, and data collection methods.

Screening interviews at the first prenatal visit from September 1, 1987, to November 30, 1989, identified 4,352 patients: 1,381 (31.7%) reported smoking at conception. Of the 1,381, 1,171 were current smokers (26.9%) and 210 patients were self-initiated quitters (4.8%) before their first visit. A current smoker was defined as "a patient who self-reported during the first prenatal visit at least one puff of one cigarette in the last seven days." An assessment study using self-reports and salivary cotinine analyses confirmed that 74 (35%) of the 210 self-initiated quitters relapsed before delivery.

Of the 1,171 smokers screened, 110 (9.4%) were ineligible for one or more of the following reasons: (1) were not pregnant, (2) were ineligible for care, (3) were very late entry into care ($\geq$32 weeks), (4) did not stay for the first visit, (5) did not return for care, (6) were Trial I participants, (7) were prisoners, and/or (8) had difficulty reading the baseline questionnaire. Of the 1,061 women eligible, only 67 patients (5.7%) refused to participate. Thus, 994 smokers were enrolled in Trial II.

Evaluation Design

A prospective randomized pretest, posttest control group evaluation design with mid-pregnancy and end-of-pregnancy assessments of smoking status from self-reports and saliva cotinine tests was implemented. Random assignment of 994 patients was performed at the first prenatal visit after informed consent using a computer-generated system: experimental (*E*) group = 493 patients and control (*C*) group = 501 patients. After randomization, 93 *E* group and 87 *C* group patients became ineligible because of withdrawal from the public health maternity system, a miscarriage, or an abortion. A total of 814 pregnant smokers were eligible for a follow-up: *E* group = 400 and *C* group = 414.

Formative and Process Evaluation

The formative evaluation, conducted at the four clinics, included a pretrial with a sample of 269 patients (100 smokers and 169 nonsmokers) recruited from 300 consecutive intakes. A 35% smoking prevalence rate (105/300) and a 10% refusal rate (31/300) was observed. The sample of 100 smokers served as a prospective historical comparison group (*C* group) to document pretrial baseline prevalence rates and "normal" quit rates from the first visit to the third trimester and childbirth. Data and saliva collection methods were reviewed by clinic nurses and administrators and field-tested with the 269 patients.

Intervention time, barriers to routine use, and patient participation rates were documented for each clinic. Focus group discussions were held with five to eight patients at each clinic to field-test the *E* group intervention. As a part of the formative evaluation, the intervention was pilot-tested, reestablishing the feasibility of routinely providing cessation methods and confirming patient and provider acceptance.

A process evaluation system was pilot-tested with the sample of 269 patients. Monthly, quarterly, and annual clinic reports were prepared to document the level of implementation of the three intervention components and each measurement procedure.

Health Education Methods

The health education intervention had three components.

> *Component 1:* During the first visit, a standardized health education cessation skills and risk-counseling session of approximately 15 minutes was provided from a trained female health counselor to *E* group patients. Patients were taught how to use a seven-day self-directed cessation guide (R. Windsor, K. Amburgy, and L. Artz, unpublished cessation guide, 1987) with a sixth-grade reading level. The guide and counseling session were modified methods from Trial I. Following completion of Trial II, the self-help guide was revised for dissemination purposes.

During follow-up visits patients received components 2 and 3:

> *Component 2:* Clinic patient reinforcement methods were provided. A chart reminder form was put in the medical record, and a medical provider letter was sent to patients within seven days.

> *Component 3:* Social support methods were provided in the form of a buddy letter, a buddy contract, and a buddy tip sheet. Each patient was also sent a one-page quarterly "newsletter" with testimonial information on successful quitters, additional risk information, and cessation tips.

All 814 *E* and *C* group patients were strongly urged to quit and were given two pamphlets: "Smoking and the Two of You" (an American Lung Association pamphlet), which provided risk and benefit information, and "Where to Find Help If You Want to Stop Smoking," with a contact name, phone number, and cost of local programs.

During a 30-minute group prenatal education class at the first visit as part of standard prenatal care, a nurse presented the risks of smoking and the importance of quitting to all patients in about 2 minutes. No staff participated in continuing education on smoking cessation and no changes were observed in the staff counseling behavior during the study.

Measurement

Patients completed a one-page screening form, informed consent, and a self-administered questionnaire to document baseline smoking status, health beliefs, and commitment to quit. Saliva samples were tested using a standardized radioimmunoassay (RIA) protocol by the Clinical Biochemistry Laboratory of the American Health Foundation (AHF). Patients were informed that their saliva would be analyzed. Smoking status was reassessed by self-reports and cotinine tests at approximately four to eight weeks after the first visit (midpoint observation) and as soon as possible after the thirty-second week of gestation (endpoint observation). Only one follow-up was performed for patients who started care during the sixth and seventh month of pregnancy. A cotinine value of ≤30 ng/mL was used as the cutoff to validate self-reports of cessation.

Because a dose-response relationship exists between maternal smoking and intrauterine growth retardation, in addition to documenting quit rates, significant reduction rates were also documented for *E* and *C* group patients. A patient was defined as a "significant reducer" if her follow-up cotinine value was 50% or less than her baseline value, e.g., 200 ng/mL to ≤100 ng/mL.

Compliance Assessment

Compliance needs to be documented to establish the feasibility of implementation and patient use of all health education methods or programs. *E* group patients completed a self-administered questionnaire at the midpoint follow-up to document the number of days the guide and cessation methods were used. They had to report use of the guide four or more days and use of five or more cessation methods to be counted as "compliant."

Cost Estimation

The cost to deliver the intervention was personnel time and education materials. Because an agency perspective was used in our cost analyses, patient time, facilities costs, and intervention development costs were not used in our estimates. Although a health counselor provided the intervention, a nurse would be the usual provider. A salary of $30,000 plus a fringe benefit rate of 20 percent was used to estimate staff cost ($36,000 per year/2,080 hours = $17.31 per hour). Personnel costs for routine use of the 15-minute intervention including brief reinforcement would be about $4.33/patient ($17.31 × 0.25). The guide costs were approximately $5.00/patient, but large-volume printing—5,000 copies—reduces the cost to about $1.25/patient. The costs of educational materials, reproduction, and labor are about $0.40. The total intervention cost is about $6.00/patient.

Two minutes were spent at the first visit to provide the *C* group one-to-one risk information and materials. That, plus brief contacts at follow-up visits, which may have served as reinforcement, produced a total of 5 minutes, so total cost amounted to about $1.50/patient ($17.31 × 0.083).

Cost-Benefit Analyses of Statewide Dissemination

Smoking population attributable risk (SPAR) for low birth weight (LBW) has been documented at 20% to 30%. A low estimate of this risk was used to estimate the potential impact of statewide dissemination of the intervention of the LBW incidence in Alabama in 1990.

The benefit of dissemination, defined as the estimated number of LBW infants preventable by cessation, was based on the estimated net incremental health care costs of a low-birth-weight birth provided by the Office of Technology Assessment (OTA): $9,000 (low estimate) and $23,000 (high estimate). These estimates include three components: (1) hospitalization and physician costs at birth; (2) hospitalization costs in the first year of life (hospital costs only); and (3) long-term health care costs of treating an LBW infant. These estimates, including discounting by the OTA, were adjusted to 1990 dollars by the inflation rates of the consumer price index/medical care component of the Bureau of Labor statistics: 5.8% (1987), 6.9% (1988), 8.5% (1989), and 9.6% (1990). The discounted, inflation-adjusted, OTA low estimate of $12,104 and the OTA high estimate of $30,935 were used in our cost-benefit calculations.

TABLE 7.6   Comparability of Study Groups by Baseline Variables

Baseline Variable	C Group (n = 100)	E Group (n = 400)	C Group (n = 414)	Total (n = 814)	Refused (n = 67)
Mean age, years	23.8	24.1	24.7	24.6	27.5
Mean education, years	12.1	12.4	12.4	12.4	13.7
Mean EGA[a]	3.8	3.9	4.1	4.0	4.1
Race: % black	52	50	54	52	49
Cotinine (ng/ml)					
Mean	121	117	109	114	N/A
SD	103	100	91	96	N/A

[a] EGA = Estimated gestational age at entry into care (units = months)

RESULTS

Data in Table 7.6 confirm the baseline equivalence of the E and C groups. The C group (historical comparison group) of 100 pregnant smokers was comparable to the E and C groups. The refusals were similar to the study participants. At baseline about 45% of the patients exhibited low (≤99 ng/mL) and 40% moderate (100 to 199 ng/mL) levels of cotinine exposure. No E versus C group or black versus white differences in mean baseline cotinine values were observed.

Process Evaluation

Process evaluation data from monthly, quarterly, and annual clinic reports confirmed the following E group exposure rates by health education component: component 1 = 100%, component 2 = 88%, and component 3 = 100%. The intervention was successfully provided by nine different counselors to 400 patients at the four JCHD clinics over a 27-month period.

Patient Compliance Rates

Data confirmed that 63% of the E group reported use of the guide at least four days or more and the use of five or more cessation methods. This rate was comparable to the E group compliance rate of Trial I—65%. Eighty-two percent of the E group and 60% of the C group reported a quit attempt.

Behavioral Impact

The behavioral impact of the health education methods is reported in Table 7.7. Only patients who self-reported quitting at their first and second follow-up visits(s) and who had a cotinine value <30 ng/mL were counted as "quitters." Approximately 15% of the 814 patients were lost to follow-up; all were counted as failures. A comparison of the baseline characteristics of patients lost to follow-up and participants confirmed no significant differences.

As noted in Table 7.7, the E group had significantly higher quit rates than the C and C groups. Among the E group black patients the intervention increased quit rates by

TABLE 7.7   Quit Rates by Race and Study Group

Race	E Group Quit Rate %	n	C Group Quit Rate %	n	C̲ Group Quit Rate %	n	95% CI (E − C)	p = Value
Black	18.1[a]	210	10.7[b]	242	N/A		(0.8, 13.9)	0.03
White	10.0[a]	190	5.2[b]	172	N/A		(−0.6, 10.2)	0.08
Total	14.3	400	8.5	414	3.0	100	(1.4, 10.1)	0.01

[a]$p = 0.03$
[b]$p = 0.07$

7.4% and among E group white patients the intervention increased quit rates by 4.9% ($p = 0.03$ for blacks, $p = 0.08$ for whites). Black patients in the E and C groups had substantially higher quit rates than white E and C group patients.

Relapse was assessed from mid-pregnancy to delivery. The E group had a significantly higher relapse rate (14%) than the C group (8%) ($p = 0.001$). Analyses of baseline variables—age, education, EGA, race, and cotinine value—to document cessation predictors revealed that E group participation, baseline cotinine, and race were significant.

As noted in Table 7.8, although E and C group white patients had lower quit rates than black patients, E group white patients had a significantly higher reduction rate than black patients in the E group ($p = 0.05$) or white patients in the C group ($p = 0.05$). Although not statistically significant ($p = 0.07$), overall, the E group had a 27% higher reduction rate than the C group. Including the quitters as significant reducers, the "behavior change rate" was 31.0% in the E group versus 20.8% in the C group ($p = 0.001$).

Sensitivity, specificity, and the positive predictive value of the cotinine test to validate end-of-pregnancy self-reports of smoking status were 86%, 74%, and 93%, respectively. A comparison of self-reports to cotinine values of ≥31 ng/mL confirmed a total deception rate of 28%: E group = 32% and C group = 17%. No differences in deception rates, however, were observed between black and white patients in either the E or C groups.

Estimated Behavioral Impact of Statewide Dissemination

The E group, C group, and $C̲$ group differences in quit rates were 6% ($E − C$) and 11% ($E − C̲$). However, the E group and $C̲$ group quit rates in Trial II ($E = 14\%$ versus $C̲ = 3\%$) were comparable to those in Trial I ($E = 14\%$ versus $C = 2\%$). Both trials were conducted at the same JCHD sites among patient cohorts equivalent at baseline by SES, age, education, EGA, cotinine values, and percent black. However, only component 1 was provided to the patients in Trial I. *The addition of five minutes of intervention time and components 2 and 3 in Trial II did not produce a higher quit rate in the E group.* Thus, a 10-minute time period, only intervention component 1, and the average $E − C$ quit rate difference of 12% (Trial I, $E − C̲ = 12\%$, and Trial I, $E − C̲ = 11\%$) were used to estimate the potential behavioral impact and cost benefit.

TABLE 7.8   Significant Reduction Rates by Race and Study Group[a]

Race	E Group %	E Group n	C Group %	C Group n	95% CI	p = Value
Black	12.9	210	11.6	242	(−4.8, 7.3)	0.68
White	21.1	190	13.4	172	(0.0, 15.4)	0.05
Total	16.8	400	12.3	414	(−0.4, 9.3)	0.07

[a] Patients who quit were not counted as significant reducers.

Although a 12% quit rate difference may be possible at many prenatal clinics, it may represent an estimate of the efficacy (best estimate) of the behavioral impact of the intervention. Accordingly, the 12% quit rate difference was attenuated to 8% to reflect the effectiveness (typical estimate) of the intervention in routine use by prenatal nurses. If the intervention had been provided to the estimated 4,800 smokers ($0.30 \times 16,000$ prenatal patients) in the 1990 Alabama public health cohort, an additional 384 quitters ($0.08 \times 4,800$) might have been produced.

Estimated Impact of Statewide Dissemination on LBW Rate

A low-birth-weight (LBW) rate of about 12% to 13% has been observed among the Alabama public health cohort for several years, resulting in about 2,000 LBW infants each year ($0.125 \times 16,000$). Using a LBW-SPAR = 0.20 (low estimate), about 400 smoking-attributable LBW infants ($0.20 \times 2,000$) were born in the 1990 cohort. If the 8% difference to estimate the intervention's potential to reduce the incidence of smoking-attributable low birth weight had been used, an estimated 32 fewer LBW infants (0.08×400) might have been prevented by statewide dissemination and routine use of the intervention.

Estimated Cost Benefit of Statewide Dissemination

Based on the Office of Technology Assessment's discounted, inflation-adjusted estimates of excess health care costs (low estimate = $12,104 and high estimate = $30,935), 32 smoking-attributable LBW infants cost an excess of between $387,328 and $989,920.

Because data from Trial I and Trial II confirmed that component 1 delivered during a 10-minute session produced the behavioral impact, the total cost per patient can be reduced from $6.00 to $4.50 (staff time—15 to 10 minutes). Our cost-benefit analysis was based on the prevention of LBW infants among the estimated Alabama public health maternity cohort of 4,800 smokers. Because the cost benefit of dissemination was expressed as a net cost difference (economic benefit minus cost) among all 4,800 women who might have received the intervention, not just quitters, our costs to disseminate the intervention to the estimated 4,800 pregnant smokers would be approximately $21,600/year ($4,800 \times 4.50).

The cost-benefit ratio for the low estimate is $1 : $17.9 and for the high estimate is $1 : $45.8. The net difference between benefit and cost is $365,728 (low estimate) to $968,320 (high estimate) in favor of the intervention.

Sensitivity Analysis

We examined the sensitivity of these estimates in relation to changes in two parameters: intervention cost and estimated economic benefit. We varied the intervention cost from $4.50 (low estimate) to $9.00 (high estimate). We varied the health benefit by reducing the smoking population attributable risk from 0.20 to 0.15, thereby further reducing the estimated number of preventable low birth weights from 32 (low estimate) to 24 (very low estimate).

Data from evaluation studies confirmed that a quit rate difference (*E* minus *C* group) of 6% to 12% is achievable. Because we used an impact rate difference of 8% (low estimate), this parameter is likely to reflect the rate achievable in public health practice and is unlikely to vary substantially. However, costs for personnel and materials to routinely provide the intervention will vary. If we increase the total intervention costs 50%—moderate increase—from $4.50 to $6.75 ($6.75 × 4,800 = $32,400), the cost-to-benefit ratio (CBR) is: low estimate = $1 : $12.0, high estimate = $1 : $30.6. If costs were increased by 100%—high increase—($9.00 × 4,800 = $43,200), the CBR low estimate = $ 1 : $9.0 and high estimate = $ 1 : $22.9. The net difference between benefit and cost favors the intervention: $344,128 (low estimate) and $946,720 (high estimate).

If we increase the intervention cost by 100% (high increase) and decrease the estimated benefit (LBW-SPAR 0.20 to 0.15) by 25% (very low estimate), the CBR low estimate = $1 : $6.7 (24 × $12,104/$43,200) and high estimate = $1 : $17.2 (24 × $30,935/$43,200). Thus, for each $1 spent on smoking cessation, $7 to $17 in medical care costs might be saved. The net difference between the economic benefit and excess cost favors the intervention: The low estimate is $247,296 and the high estimate is $699,240.

Thus, variations in estimates of behavioral impact, smoking-attributable risk, excess health care cost, or discount rates did not affect the conclusions about the cost benefit and potential net savings of the intervention. The estimated cost-benefit ratios from this study and thus the net economic benefits were substantially higher than the cost-to-benefit ratio of $1 : $3.4 for prenatal care reported by the Institute of Medicine.

DISCUSSION

This behavioral impact and cost-benefit evaluation recruited 94% of a cohort of pregnant smokers from multiple clinics over a 27-month period. When considered along with evidence from Trial I and results of other intervention studies, this study confirms that an additional 6% to 12% quit rate difference is achievable in public health clinics.

An evaluation study of WIC patients in Michigan, which adapted Trial I self-help methods and the ALA self-help cessation methods, reported quit rates of 11% (*E*₁ group, self-help methods), 7% (*E*₂ group, risk information methods), and 3% (*C* group, no intervention). Another evaluation study in Washington, D.C., undertaken among a predominately black cohort of pregnant smokers who received the guide plus one-to-one counseling and other intervention materials, reported a quit rate based on self-reports of "about one-third." If the 33% self-reported quit rate is adjusted by applying our 32% *E* group deception rate, a 22% quit rate is derived. This quit rate is similar to the 18% quit rate of the *E* group black patients in Trial II.

The 8% *C* group quit rate in Trial II was much higher than the *C* group quit rate in Trial I—2%, the observed quit rate among our Trial II C̲ group (historical comparison group)—3%, and the *C* group in the Mayer et al. (1990) WIC study—3%. The Trial II *C* group received brief, one-to-one verbal and written risk information and strong encouragement to quit. These data suggested that, as implemented, the Trial II *C* group may have become a "minimum intervention group." Strong, one-to-one advice to quit, reinforced with readable risk information and RN/MD reinforcement, may have increased the "normal" quit rate observed in this public health setting from 2–4% to 6–8%.

These results and other efficacy and cost-effectiveness analyses have also documented that dissemination of these methods may reduce the incidence of LBW and reduce associated excess health care costs. Estimates of the impact of dissemination of "tested" health education methods to the 1990 U.S. Public Health cohort of approximately 1 million pregnant women, 350,000 pregnant smokers, and 120,000 LBW infants indicate that approximately 1,920 fewer LBW infants (120,000 × PAR 0.20 × 0.08) might have been prevented. Assuming a cost per public health patient of $6.75, the total cost to deliver the intervention to the total 1990 U.S. Medicaid cohort would have been approximately $2.4 million ($6.75 × 350,000 pregnant smokers). Thus, a net economic benefit of approximately $20 to $56 million might have been produced by dissemination. Annual dissemination to the U.S. maternity cohort of more than 1 million pregnant smokers (4.0+ million × 0.25 smokers) may also help achieve approximately 31% to 78% of the *Healthy People 2000* objectives for pregnant smokers.

These estimates of impact, however, reflect only a small part of the economic, health, and emotional benefits to women, infants, and their families. A national effort is needed in the 1990s to change prenatal care policy and the health education process and content for pregnant smokers. Continuing education programs must be expanded to improve the cessation counseling methods and skills of health care practitioners. As dissemination plans are prepared, Phase 4 evaluations will also be needed to document the degree to which health education methods are adopted in public and private maternity health care settings and to measure their behavioral and clinical impact.

SUMMARY

At the onset of planning, all evaluators should consider the estimated cost implications—input and output—of their health promotion intervention methods. The efficiency of intervention methods in producing either impact or outcome rates described in nonmonetary terms, or impact or outcome rates described in dollars and cents, should be routinely documented. The OTA of the U.S. Congress concluded in 1981 that health care decision making could be improved by the process of identifying and considering all the relevant costs and benefits of a decision. From a philosophical perspective, however, it is also important to emphasize that a singular preoccupation with cost analyses and judging a program's worth or value solely on the basis of cost is not justifiable.

Cost-effectiveness analysis or cost-benefit analysis should not serve as the sole or primary determinant of health care–program decision making. Program efficiency is only one part of the rationale to decide, for example, to provide drug education to children in elementary schools; or exercise, fitness, and diet classes to workers; or a mass-media program to influence use of prenatal care earlier in a pregnancy; or to increase use of high blood pressure medications. A broader range of issues reflecting concern for the welfare of a target population by an agency or organization and ethical and legal responsibilities should be the primary guide to decisions to allocate resources and provide programs.

The Evaluation Report

As discussed in Chapter 2, an effective health education program most often is created by the application of logical thinking to a public health problem. The evaluation report is the document that ties together a problem, program, and analysis of program impact. This synthesis is done by presentation of data to illustrate, if observed, cause-and-effect relationships. When a program fails to yield an expected impact, the report is a vehicle to explore explanations. The evaluation report is also a medium of communication. Therefore, while you are preparing it, you must keep in mind the people to whom it is directed. If the audience is varied, prepare different forms of a report emphasizing in each the issues and ideas of greatest interest to a particular group of readers.

The evaluation report is not a massive historical document describing events and results for future generations, although such a document may be worth preparing. Rather, it is an immediate, dynamic, succinct communication to those with specific interest in the program. The report discusses program process and outcomes and serves to guide others in making future related health promotion and education decisions. It is not the length but the quality of the report that makes it acceptable. It may be used to decide if and how to revise the existing program, to expand the program to other sites or settings, or to increase, reduce, or rearrange staff or budget. The major evaluation concern covered in a report is the program's efficacy: Did it yield what was expected? If not, why not? In the following pages, we delineate the sections of a comprehensive report. The extent of each section depends on the specific audience to whom the report is directed.

THE AUDIENCE

To what audience must you communicate? The first question to ask yourself is, Whom do I want to reach with this document? Then you ask, Which elements and aspects of the evaluation of the program are of greatest importance to that reader? In day-to-day practice, the unit administrator in the sponsoring organization will likely be the first person to see a draft of the report. Next the directors of the agency or organization may see it. If the program has been funded by outside grants, a report must communicate results of interest to the source of grant support. If the program results add to or clarify dimensions of health education practice, your colleagues will be interested. When a program complements medical or nursing practice, other providers may have an interest. If the program has produced changes with strong implications for community health and health services, local residents and news media may be interested.

Reports that communicate to each of these audiences differ in range, length, complexity, and language. Each, however, draws from the same data set. Much of the material generated in developing the original program plan will be useful in writing each version. It is generally a mistake to try to write one report to address the interests of all the potential audiences. Although there may be some standard sections in all reports (the same material repeated in each), some sections must be specifically tailored toward target audiences and provide more complete material about their interests.

The process of communicating to several audiences is made more efficient by preparing a document with interchangeable parts. The statistical analysis, for example, may be presented in great detail for some audiences and only briefly summarized for others. The administrative pattern for operating the program may be described elaborately for some readers and barely mentioned for others.

FORMAT

If you have followed the evaluation methods discussed in this book and have collected data both at predetermined points in a program and at the end of the program period, then you will have much data in hand when report-writing time arrives. You will also have a logically conceived program plan or blueprint to enumerate the expected behavioral impact and health outcomes of the program. Preparing evaluation reports therefore should start with a review of the original plan, data, and analysis and interpretation of the data. Organize this information into a clear, well-documented presentation. Table A.1 provides a suggested outline for the sections of this communication.

Executive Summary (Abstract)

The first section is the executive summary. Because most evaluators have been influenced by their academic training, some tend to prepare reports that assume the readers have a widespread academic interest and are willing to plod through voluminous material to find the important points. Few people have either the time or the patience to search through many pages to find the pearls. A good evaluation report presents its findings at the beginning. The readers know the re-

TABLE A.1   Evaluation Report Outline

1. Title page
2. Executive summary (abstract)
3. Table of contents
4. Program purpose
   a. Aims and objectives
   b. Participant description
5. Program description
   a. Educational—behavioral methods
   b. Contents—process—time
   c. Staffing
6. Evaluation methods
   a. Process evaluation
   b. Impact—outcome evaluation
7. Results
   a. Quantitative analysis
   b. Qualitative analysis
   c. Cost analysis
8. Conclusions—recommendations

sults at the outset. One way to accomplish this is to prepare an executive summary and to make this the first page of the evaluation report. The summary should concisely describe the program's objectives, methods, processes, and results. Write the summary, like the report, without jargon and in the active voice. If you need to use scientific or technical words, define them for readers.

The summary should present essential evaluation material in language the intended readers will understand. The quality of the summary often dictates whether the full report will be read. It should be followed by a clearly numbered and accurately referenced table of contents. Some people refuse to read reports without a well-labeled table of contents. They may be justified because its absence demonstrates a significant deficiency in the report writers.

Program Purpose and Key Evaluation Questions

Readers of the report need to be told what the program intended to achieve. Readers also need to know why achieving the goal was important—the benefits. If the program expected, for example, to help overweight employees lose weight, why is this valuable? The reasons may be different for the reader who is the employee's spouse and for the reader who is the chief executive officer of the company.

It is important not to assume that the reader has background information about the program and its potential worth. Assume the reader does not. Prepare a clear, direct description of the program purpose and potential benefit—do not exaggerate. Describe the characteristics that make the program unique. Include a profile of the participants. Obviously, a program is valuable because of the particular people it aimed to assist. Why was it important to reach them?

The major evaluation questions should be spelled out in this section. They are the measuring sticks of whether the program achieved its purpose. This list of the questions that guided your evaluation, whether it is long or short, should be self-explanatory once the reader has gone through your description of purpose.

Program Description

Once readers have grasped the purpose of the program and reviewed the questions that guided evaluation of it, they will want to understand what the program "looked like." To say that the program was "self-management training" is not enough. What was the training? Where? When? How did it occur? You need to include five elements in this program description, more or less extensively depending on the audience for your report:

1. *The basic nature of the education.* What theoretical principles of education were used? For example, was the program based on social cognitive and social support theory? Was it a combination of organized peer group support and rehearsal of specific health skills? Was it counseling from professionals? Was it provision of information through various media? Was it based on group problem solving?

2. *The content of the program.* What material was presented? How was it presented at each learning session?

3. *The logistics and process of the program.* What was the location of the educational sessions, their frequency, and their duration? What number of hours, days, or weeks was assessed?

4. *The number and deployment of staff.* What kind of training did they receive before inception of the program? What was the average number of participants in the sessions?

5. *The administrative support provided.* What number and deployment of program managers, coordinators, secretaries, and other administrative personnel were used?

This description should enable readers to envision a learning session with the educators and participants doing what they would typically do. A complete narrative would include examples of the behavioral objectives set, how learners were enabled to reach the objectives, and how achieving the objectives was related to the overall purpose of the program.

Evaluation Methods

Describe for readers the methods of program assessment. The methods and design selected from the possibilities presented in Chapters 2–6 should be presented. Discuss two dimensions: the design (Chapter 6) that enabled you to ascertain the impact and outcomes of the program (e.g., whether employees changed their eating patterns and lost weight) and the process evaluation (Chapter 4) that enabled you to make judgments about the quality of the program (e.g., whether the staff performed as expected or the anticipated average level of participation in group discussions was reached). These two dimensions are best described separately. The quality assessment measures what actually occurred in the program. The evaluation design measures the results. In health education programs, both are exceedingly important and should be reported. Readers will have more or less interest in quality assessment, however. Your audience will be more interested in the design to determine the impact of the program. Once persuaded that this dimension was adequately addressed, many readers will want to know more about process. In this section, like the others, you must determine how much material is appropriate for the reader. When in doubt, mention the material in the body of the report. Include a narrative description in an appendix.

The description of your evaluation design should include use of control groups, sampling procedures, sample size, and the reliability and validity of the data. In describing these points, discuss not only what judgments each element allows you to make about the program but also what judgments cannot be made. Describe limitations of the study. As we discussed in previous chapters, using highly controlled evaluation techniques in natural settings is often difficult. Almost all quasi-experimental designs and all process assessment methods are flawed. It is your responsibility to recount the ways in which the evaluation procedures are deficient. This demonstrates to the readers that you have thought about and tried to account for evaluation weaknesses.

Next, present a description of the ways in which you collected data to answer each evaluation question. If you used several techniques, the limitations of each should be discussed. For example, if some data were collected in face-to-face interviews, how candid and forthcoming were respondents? How did you guard against interviewer bias? If you used hospital records as a source of data, how accurate and consistent were the records completed by health personnel? It is important for you to show that you anticipated, and wherever possible addressed, problems in data collection. Some readers like to see samples of questionnaires or other instruments for collecting data, but do not put questionnaires in the body of a report; put them in the appendix.

Results

Describe how you analyzed the data. If a large data set was collected and you used a computer, mention how the data were managed and what computer program you used. Few practitioners have the resources to write special statistical programs; most use standard packages. It is sufficient, in most cases, to name the program and mention why it was selected. Within each program, several statistical options are generally available. Report which statistical procedures were used for each kind of evaluation question. Describe any adjustments or corrections in the tests that were made. If your audience comprises measurement specialists and statisticians, however, you will have to give much more detail on why you selected these tests. You may also need to discuss more fully the limitations of the procedures in analyzing the given variables and the evaluation questions considered important.

If you collected primarily qualitative data or for some other reason did not use a computer and analyzed the data by hand, describe the methods used and the statistical tests applied. Some reports have only percentages computed by hand. Simple statistical procedures are easy to compute, especially with a pocket calculator. When you have made the effort to design an evaluation and collect quantitative data in the ways suggested in this text, you need to employ these simple tests. In reporting them, make clear the standards for accepting statistical significance. If statistically significant, was it important?

Some of your data will have been analyzed "qualitatively" (e.g., content analysis, rating by experts, tabulation of observations over time, or in other ways). Describe the methods used in enough detail so readers can judge how careful, comprehensive, and consistent the procedures were. If several raters have been used to review data, report interrater reliability. Similarly, discuss your view of the stability of the data. If there were major problems in analyzing the data, describe and clarify these problems in this part of the report.

The data analysis section should help readers see how the data were handled and in what ways they were interpreted by the evaluators. This section should illustrate that the results in the pages to follow are based on reliable data and a careful, generally conservative, analysis.

Program Costs

With increasing frequency, health promotion and education programs are being asked to comment in fiscal terms on the cost effectiveness and cost benefits of programs. Some administrators want a detailed cost analysis. As discussed in

Chapters 2 and 7, there are several ways to ascertain the effectiveness and benefits of a program, given its costs. These formulas are rarely definitive, but where they can be applied they provide some indication of whether the goals attained were beneficial and whether the program was the most effective vehicle for reaching the goal. Often it is not possible to illustrate cost effectiveness or benefit because data needed from other sources are not available. Then, as discussed in Chapter 7, approximations are used and educated guesses made. Even when data are not available for a sophisticated analysis, you should be able to demonstrate what the program cost the sponsoring organization and estimate or give examples of the kinds of savings the education might yield. These figures, as described previously, are easy to compute.

Conclusions and Recommendations

Although this section is positioned fairly late in the report, it is frequently the one to which readers flip immediately after the executive summary. The focal point of the document, it answers the evaluation questions. There are at least two common errors report writers make here: (1) claiming more than the evidence suggests and (2) claiming things not suggested in the evidence at all. Both are lethal errors to be avoided at all costs.

In an evaluation report, you want to present not only positive findings (significantly more men in the program lost more weight than did men in the control group) but also negative ones (fewer men attended the second half of the program than the first half). The objective of this part of the report is both to present and interpret findings and to explore explanations for results. If fewer men attended as the program continued, what were some possible reasons? Did they tire of the program? Were the later sessions less relevant to their needs? Were there changes in their work schedules? Did every person reach his weight-loss goal early? The world rarely operates just as you expect, and an evaluation report that reads as if all went perfectly is at best inaccurate and at worst dishonest. The report gives you the opportunity to make guesses or present additional data to show why the intended results were not achieved or why your expectations were reached or exceeded.

It is important to present data for every evaluation question posed and to interpret the meaning of each finding in relation to the overall aims of the program. In other words, you need to say why a particular finding is more or less important, given the impact and outcomes expected. This lends a perspective of the programmatic significance of your results. The statistical significance of a finding is an indication that the changes observed from before to after the program did not occur randomly. Programmatic significance means that the changes had value to the participants and program planners, given all that the program tried to accomplish.

Tables and graphs are often useful to depict findings, but you should not overwhelm readers with them in the body of the report; append them. Only a few very pertinent and revealing tables or graphs should be included in the findings section. Similarly, the narrative should not repeat what is shown in the tables. It should interpret, enhance, or expand on the data presented. You should describe all significant findings in the text in narrative form. Refer readers to tables in the appendix for further detail when data are extensive.

The section should end with a brief summary of the findings and some general conclusions about the program and its accomplishments. The more analytic the review of findings and conclusions, the better. This means thoughtful consideration of each result within the context of your program. It means not drawing conclusions about the program for which there are no empirical data (error 2 mentioned earlier) or making more of a finding than is really there (error 1). It seems only fair that you should explicitly caution readers about conclusions. The soundness of the program can be undermined by sloppy or grandiose "analysis" and presentation of its results. The findings and conclusion section is the most important part of the evaluation report and reflects your genuine understanding of the problem, what the program intended to accomplish, and the extent to which aims were met.

Many readers will expect you to make recommendations based on program outcomes. However, you must determine what kinds of recommendations are suitable based on the characteristics of the audience for the report. It is most appropriate for you to make programmatic rather than policy recommendations unless you were specifically asked to do the latter. A recommendation that a successful program be expanded to a larger audience is well within the prerogative of an evaluator. A recommendation that a hospital change its reimbursement pattern to accomplish this end is not. Recommendations, like conclusions, must be derived from the findings of the evaluation. Adding extraneous recommendations not supported by the data simply weakens the general effectiveness of the report. Some writers even refer to specific evidence in the body of the report when putting forward their suggestions.

Keep in mind—the most successful program can generally use fine-tuning. The recommendations section is an opportunity to call attention to ways a program may be made even stronger. Quality assessment data and findings that describe the processes of program implementation can be particularly useful in recommending change or adjustments in content and process. The questions usually addressed in a recommendations section are similar to those below:

1. Should the learning-approach process or content of the program be revised? If so, in what way?
2. Should the program staffing patterns be changed in any way?

3. Should there be changes in the types of personnel implementing the program?
4. Should there be adjustments in the budget allocations to various elements of the program?
5. Is the program generalizable to other groups of learners? If so, in what way might it best be expanded? How might it best be replicated?

DISSEMINATION TO DECISION MAKERS

One of the biggest complaints of evaluators is the underutilization of data. Findings are rarely used as much as they could be. Getting the report read by the right people does not occur by magic. If you want your evaluation report to influence decisions, you must think through how best to reach the decision makers. One way to do this, as we have discussed, is to ensure that the material in your report is targeted to the interests of a specific audience. But there are other things you can do to generate interest.

According to Zweig and Marvin (1981), the education of any group (in this case, decision makers) by any other group (in this case, evaluators) cannot happen without a process that respects the institutions, culture, and practices of each. In other words, you must carefully consider the individuals or groups you hope will use your report. How can you present your case for using the report so that it respects their point of view? Zweig and Marvin also suggest that evaluators need a conception of evaluation that takes into account the secondary place of evaluative information in day-to-day decision making. The decision maker will use your data as only one input into the decision. Your report is primarily only to you. You must determine how your findings directly and indirectly relate to the priorities of the decision maker you want to reach. Spell out the uses of the data to that person's interests.

Sichel (1982) believes that it is critical to give key individuals previews of the report. We strongly agree. Relevant drafts of information should be shared with decision makers in advance of open discussion or submission of the report. By having them review the material, you accomplish two things. First, you increase the chances that your material will be accepted by the decision maker. When you speak with him or her on an individual basis, you can better address that person's individual concerns. You eliminate the element of surprise and can verify that you have been sensitive to the decision maker's position and perspective. Second, you can emphasize the policy implications and usefulness of the report to that particular decision maker. You also take the opportunity to sell the decision maker on using your findings.

A report that sits on the shelf is of little use. Develop a strategy for reaching key people and assisting them to make data-based decisions.

FINAL THOUGHTS

Anonymity

During the data-collection period, it is likely that you assured program participants that the actions and opinions they allowed you to document would be anonymous in all evaluation documents. It is crucial to honor this commitment. No section of the report should be written so that the identity of individuals is revealed or can be deduced. The institutions, organizations, and services that were part of your program may also wish to remain anonymous. Before writing the report, determine how specific you can be in your description of people, places, and events while not violating participants' anonymity.

Sensitivity

Few things can unnerve even people with the strongest egos more than the idea of being evaluated. Successful evaluators approach both their subjects and their task in a way that reassures people that they are not being judged or labeled in negative ways. The evaluation report must be written with sensitivity. Even in the rare case when only a few people will see the document, a large measure of sensitive wording and phrasing of ideas is the most professional approach. You also want to ensure that the report is not offensive to those who have participated. To accomplish this end, you might ask someone familiar with the program but outside the evaluation team to read a draft of the report before it is completed and distributed. The reviewer should be asked to judge its sensitivity to people, places, and events. This reader must, of course, be a trusted person who is pledged to keep confidential all that the document contains.

Confidentiality

Because evaluation reports—even glowingly positive ones—can be sensitive documents, you must accord them a certain confidentiality. Determine at the outset the readership of the report. With members of the program hierarchy, compile lists of those who are to receive the various forms of the document. Discuss with the administrators how the report is to be treated after its initial distribution. Will it be made freely available to all who express an interest in the program? Will it be given out only with the permission of someone within the sponsoring organization? Will it be marked "confidential"? Will it be piled at the doorway so that every visitor can pick it up? You need to know the ground rules for handling and distribution of the report.

Objectivity

The chapters of this text have stressed that the primary task of evaluators is to look objectively at a problem and the program designed to address it. Next, they must organize program descriptions and assessment data into clear communications for specific groups of readers. Objectivity must be reflected in every page of every evaluation report. In many ways, developing a health education program is the art of professional health education practice; evaluation is the science. To develop future programs to assist people to prevent and manage illness more fully, health educators must learn from the evaluations of current programs. In this sense, every health education program has the opportunity to contribute to the knowledge base of practice in addition to assisting individual learners. It is only by conducting careful, objective program evaluations and communicating the results to others in the most objective way that the art and science of health promotion and education can be enhanced.

Specification of the Role of the Entry-Level Health Educator

AREA OF RESPONSIBILITY V

The entry-level health educator, working with individuals, groups and organizations, is responsible for:

Evaluating Health Education (12%)

The entry-level health educator, working with individuals, groups and organizations, is responsible for:

Function:	A. Participating in developing an evaluation design. (24%)
Skill:	1. The health educator must be able to assist in specifying indicators of program success.
Knowledge:	The health educator must be able to:
	a. differentiate between what can and cannot be measured (e.g., knowledge gained, changes in morbidity rates due to health education).
	b. translate objectives into specific indicators (e.g., knowledge gained, values stated, behaviors mastered).
	c. describe range of methods and techniques used for educational measurement (e.g., inventories, scales, competency tests).
	d. list steps involved in evaluative activities (e.g., setting standards, specifying objectives, developing criteria for achievement of objectives).
Skill:	2. The health educator must be able to help to establish the scope for program evaluation.

Source: U.S. Department of Health and Human Services, Public Health Service, *Initial Role Delineation for Health Education. Final Report,* prepared for the National Center for Health Education, DHHS Publication no. (HRA) 80-44 (Washington, D.C.: Government Printing Office, 1980), pp. 78–82.

Knowledge: The health educator must be able to:

    a. define scope of evaluation efforts (e.g., match standards with goals, explain relationship between activities and outcomes).

    b. describe feasibility of evaluative activities (e.g., time availability, resources, setting, nature of the program).

    c. explain the beliefs and purposes behind health education activities (e.g., value to consumers, increased control over health matters, informed public).

Skill: 3. The health educator must be able to help develop methods for evaluating programs.

Knowledge: The health educator must be able to:

    a. identify various measures for determining knowledge, attitudes and behavior (e.g., questionnaires, self-assessment inventories, knowledge tests).

    b. describe data available for evaluation (e.g., program attendance, reports of behaviors, survey data, letters from consumers and others, test scores).

    c. list strengths and weaknesses of various data collection methods (e.g., value of self-report, expense of observing behavior).

Skill: 4. The health educator must be able to participate in the specification of instruments for data collection.

Knowledge: The health educator must be able to:

    a. describe advantages and disadvantages of "home-made" and commercial instruments (e.g., utility, cost, timeliness).

    b. identify sources of instruments (e.g., professional organizations, research organizations, consultants, textbook publishers).

Skill: 5. The health educator must be able to assist in the determination of samples needed for evaluation.

Knowledge: The health educator must be able to:

    a. define sample concepts (e.g., stratified, random, convenience, universe).

    b. identify strengths and weaknesses of sampling techniques (e.g., sampling error, skewed results, normal distributions, precision of estimates).

Skill: 6. The health educator must be able to assist in the selection of data useful for accountability analysis.

Knowledge: The health educator must be able to:

      a. describe the uses of cost-benefit analysis (e.g., modify programs, select alternative(s) from competing choices).

    The entry-level health educator, working with individuals, groups and organizations, is responsible for:

Function: B. Assembling resources required to carry out evaluation. (22%)

Skill: 1. The health educator must be able to acquire facilities, materials, personnel and equipment.

Knowledge: The health educator must be able to:

      a. describe facilities, materials and equipment needed (e.g., telephones, typewriters, computers).

      b. identify required expertise and sources for expertise (e.g., survey methodology from universities, physician for clinical study, experts in evaluation).

      c. identify ways of obtaining necessary facilities, materials, expertise and equipment (e.g., personal visitations, formal requests, budgetary requisitions).

Skill: 2. The health educator must be able to train personnel for evaluation as needed.

Knowledge: The health educator must be able to:

      a. describe the process for assessing training needs (e.g., listing skills needed, reviewing skills of available personnel, comparing skills with program requirements).

      b. describe steps for implementing training programs (e.g., specifying learning objectives, selecting instructional methods, carrying out methods, evaluating).

Skill: 3. The health educator must be able to secure the cooperation of those affecting and affected by the program.

Knowledge: The health educator must be able to:

      a. describe how to involve relevant parties in the evaluation process (e.g., explaining importance, answering questions, asking for cooperation).

      b. identify importance of safeguarding rights of individuals involved (e.g., explanation of purposes and procedures, confidential record-keeping).

      c. explain methods to maintain interest in program evaluation (e.g., importance of the work, reinforcement of effort, communication techniques, presentation of evaluation results).

The entry-level health educator, working with individuals, groups and organizations, is responsible for:

Function: C. Helping to implement the evaluation design. (30%)
Skill: 1. The entry-level health educator must be able to collect data through appropriate techniques.
Knowledge: The health educator must be able to:
   a. identify the applicability of various techniques to a given situation (e.g., observations, interviews, questionnaires, written tests).
   b. describe how to acquire data from existing sources (e.g., scan newspapers, review journal articles, scan morbidity and mortality data, health records).
   c. distinguish between quantitative and qualitative data (e.g., counts vs. expressions of satisfaction, changes in physical indices vs. loss of interest).
Skill: 2. The health educator must be able to analyze collected data.
Knowledge: The health educator must be able to:
   a. identify basic statistical measures (e.g., counts, means, medians).
   b. describe processes of statistical analysis (e.g., selected analysis based on stated concern, collecting data, use of statistical techniques).
   c. explain the results of statistical analysis (e.g., report data, make inferences, draw conclusions).
   d. identify steps in analyzing qualitative data (e.g., developing categories, ascribing meaning to data, making inferences).
   e. explain how data may be kept and used as needed (e.g., record-keeping system, computer storage, filing systems, progress reports).
Skill: 3. The health educator must be able to interpret results of program evaluation.
Knowledge: The health educator must be able to:
   a. identify relationships between analyzed data and program objectives (e.g., objectives met, reasons for lack of achievement, changes in program reflected in data).
   b. recognize importance of looking for unanticipated results (e.g., appearance of seemingly unrelated results, significant deviations from what was expected).

    c. identify variables necessary for interpretation of data (e.g., SES, sex, age, medical diagnosis).

    d. recognize risks of drawing conclusions not fully justified by the data (e.g., program's value to other fields, program successes, program failures).

The entry-level health educator, working with individuals, groups and organizations, is responsible for:

Function:	D. Communicating results of evaluation. (25%)
Skill:	1. The health educator must be able to report the processes and results of evaluation to those interested.
Knowledge:	The health educator must be able to:

    a. describe how to organize, write and report findings (e.g., objectives, activities, results, interpretation, conclusions).

    b. translate evaluation findings into terms understandable by others (e.g., professionals, consumers, administrators).

    c. explain various ways to depict findings (e.g., graphs, slides, flipcharts).

Skill:	2. The health educator must be able to recommend strategies for implementing results.
Knowledge:	The health educator must be able to:

    a. list strategies that can be used for implementation (e.g., involve those affected, explain results to given audiences, propose new or modified programs).

    b. identify implications from findings for future programs or other actions (e.g., alert others beyond programs, publish reports on programs and their evaluation).

Skill:	3. The health educator must be able to incorporate results into planning and implementation processes.
Knowledge:	The health educator must be able to:

    a. describe how program operations can be modified based on evaluation results (e.g., discussions with personnel, proposed changes in objectives/methods/content).

    b. explain how evaluation results are part of the planning process (e.g., formative vs. summative evaluation, self-renewal of programs).

References

Abramson, J. H. 1985. Prevention of cardiovascular disease in the elderly. *Public Health Review* 13: 65–223.

Aday, L. A. 1991. *Designing and conducting health surveys.* San Francisco: Jossey-Bass.

Agar, M. H. 1986. *Speaking of ethnography.* Qualitative Research Methods Series, vol. 2. Beverly Hills, Calif.: Sage.

Alkin, M. C. 1980. *A user-focused approach in conducting evaluations: Three perspectives.* New York: Foundation Center.

Alvares, A. P., Kappas, A., Eiseman, J. L., Anderson, K. E., Pantuck, C. B., Pantuck, E. J., Hsiao, K. C., Garland, W. A., and Coriney, A. H. 1979. Intraindividual variation in drug disposition. *Clinical Pharmacology and Therapeutics* 26(4): 407–419.

American Association for Health Education. 2002. *CD Cynergy: A tool for health communication planning and evaluation.*

American College of Sports Medicine. 1980. The recommended quantity and quality of exercise for developing and maintaining fitness in healthy adults. *Journal of Physical Education and Recreation* 1: 17–18.

American Lung Association (ALA). 1980. *Freedom from smoking in 20 days.* New York: Author.

American Public Health Association, Committee on Professional Education. 1957. Educational qualifications and functions of public health education. *American Journal of Public Health* 47: 1.

Axelrod, M. 1975. Ten essentials for good qualitative research. *Marketing News* 10 (Mar. 14): 10–11.

Baker, F., and McPhee, C. 1979. Approaches to evaluating quality of health care. In *Program Evaluation in the Health Fields*, vol. 2, ed. H. C. Schuberg and F. Baker, 187–204. New York: Human/Sciences Press.

Bales, R. 1951. *Interaction process analysis.* Reading, Mass.: Addison-Wesley.

Bandura, A. 1977. *Social learning theory.* Englewood Cliffs, N.J.: Prentice Hall.

Bandura, A. 1982. Self-efficacy mechanism in human agency. *American Psychologist* 37: 122–147.

Bandura, A. 1986. *Social foundations of thought and action: A social cognitive theory.* Englewood Cliffs, N.J.: Prentice Hall.

Baranowski, T. 1989–1990. Reciprocal determinism at the stages of behavior change: An integration of community, personal, and behavioral perspectives. *International Quarterly of Community Health Education* 10(4): 297–327.

Baranowski, T. 1992–1993. Beliefs as motivational influences at stages in behavior change. *International Quarterly of Community Health Education* 13(1): 3–29.

Baranowski, T., Bee, D., Rassin, D., Richardson, J., and Palmer, J. 1989–1990. Expectancies toward infant-feeding methods among mothers in three ethnic groups. *Psychology and Health* 5: 59–75.

Baranowski, T., Domel, S., Gould, R., Baranowski, J., Leonard, S., Treiber, F., and Mullis, R. 1993. Increasing fruit and vegetable consumption among 4th and 5th grade students: Results from focus groups using reciprocal determinism. *Journal of Nutrition Education* 25(3): 114–120.

Baranowski, T., Evans, M., Chapin, J., Wagner, G., and Warren, S. 1980. Utilization and medication compliance for high blood pressure: An experiment with family involvement and self–blood pressure monitoring in a rural population. *American Journal of Rural Health* 6(1–6): 51–67.

Baranowski, T., Henske, J., Dworkin, R., Clearman, D., Dunn, J. K., Nader, P. R., and Hooks, P. 1986. The accuracy of children's self-report of diet: The Family Health Project. *Journal of the American Dietetic Association* 86(10): 1381–1385.

Baranowski, T., Henske, J., Simons-Morton, B., Palmer, J., Hooks, P., Tiernan, K., and Dunn, J. K. 1990. Dietary change for DVD prevention among Black-American families. *Health Education Research* 5(4): 433–443.

Baranowski, T., and Simons-Morton, B. 1991. Children's physical activity and dietary assessment: Measurement issues. *Journal of School Health* 61(5): 195–197.

Baranowski, T., Sprague, D., Henske, J., Seale, D., and Harrison, J. 1991. Accuracy of maternal dietary recall for preschool children: Socioeconomic status and day care factor. *Journal of the American Dietetic Association* 91(6): 669–674.

Baranowski, T., and Stables, G. 2000. Process evaluations of the 5-a-day projects. *Health Education and Behavior* 27(2): 157–166.

Baranowski, T., Tsong, Y., and Brodwick, M. 1990. Scaling of response scale adverbs among Black-American adults. *Perceptual and Motor Skills* 71: 547–559.

Barry, P., and DeFriese, G. 1990. Cost-benefit and cost-effectiveness analysis for health promotion programs. *American Journal of Health Promotion* 4(6): 448–452.

Bartholomew, K., Parcel, G., Kok, G., and Gottlieb, N. 1999. *Intervention mapping.* Mountain View, Calif.: Mayfield.

Basch, C. E. 1987. Focus group interview: An underutilized research technique for improving theory and practice in health education. *Health Education Quarterly* 14(4): 411–448.

Basch, C., Sliepcevich, E., Gold, R., et al. 1985. Avoiding type III errors in health education program evaluation: A case study. *Health Education Quarterly* 12(3): 315–331.

Becker, M. H. 1976. Sociobehavioral determinants of compliance. In *Compliance with therapeutic regimes,* ed. D. C. Sackett and R. B. Haynes, 40–50. Baltimore: Johns Hopkins University Press.

Bernstein, I. N., ed. 1976. *Validity issues in evaluative research.* Sage Contemporary Social Science Issues, vol. 23. Beverly Hills, Calif.: Sage.

Biglan, A., Ary, D., and Wagenaar, A. C. 2000. The value of interrupted time-series experiments for community intervention research. *Prev. Sci.* 1 (Mar. 1): 31–49.

Biron, P. 1975. Dosage, compliance and bioavailability in perspective. *Canadian Medical Association Journal* 115: 102–113.

Boatman, R., Levin, L., Roberts, B., and Rugen, M., ed. 1966. Professional preparation in health education in schools of public health: A report prepared for the 1965 annual meeting, Association of Schools of Public Health, Ad Hoc Committee on Health Education. *Health Education Monographs* 21: 1–35.

Boruch, R. 1976. Coupling randomized experiments and approximations to experiments in social program evaluation. In *Validity issues in evaluative research*, ed. I. N. Bernstein, 35–57. Sage Contemporary Social Science Issues, vol. 23. Beverly Hills, Calif.: Sage.

Boyd, N. F., Pater, J. L., Ginsburg, A. D., and Myers, R. E. 1979. Observer variation in the classification of information from medical records. *Journal of Chronic Diseases* 32: 327–332.

Boyd, N. R., and Orleans, C. T. 1999. Intervening with older smokers. In *Helping the hard-core smoker: A clinician's guide*, ed. D. F. Seidman and L. Covey. Mahwah, N.J.: Lawrence Erlbaum Associates.

Boyd, N. R., and Orleans, C. T. 2002. Smoking cessation for older adults. In *Treating alcohol and drug use in the elderly*, ed. A. M. Gurnack, R. Atkinson, and N. Osgood. New York: Springer.

Boyd, R., and Windsor, R. 1993. A meta-evaluation of nutrition education research among pregnant women. *Health Education Quarterly* 20(3): 327–345.

Bradburn, N. M., and Sudman, S. 1979. *Improving interview method and questionnaire design*. San Francisco: Jossey-Bass.

Bradburn, N., and Sudman, S. 1982. *Asking questions: A practical guide to questionnaire construction*. San Francisco: Jossey-Bass.

Bravo, G., and Potivin, L. 1991. Estimating the reliability of continuous measures with Cronbach's alpha or the intraclass correlation coefficient: Toward the integration of two traditions. *Journal of Clinical Epidemiology* 44: 381–390.

Bruner, J. S. 1973. *Beyond the information given*. New York: Norton.

Bruvold, W. 1993. A meta-analysis of adolescent smoking prevention programs. *American Journal of Public Health* 83(6): 872–880.

Cambre, M. 1981. Historical overview of formative evaluations of instructional media products. *Educational Communication and Technology Journal* 29(1): 3–25.

Campbell, D. 1969. Reforms as experiments. *American Psychology* 24(4): 409–429.

Campbell, D. 1975. Assessing the impact of planned social change. In *Social research and public policies*, ed. G. M. Lyons. Hanover, N.H.: Dartmouth College Public Affairs Center.

Campbell, D. T., and Fiske, D. W. 1959. Convergent and discriminant validation by the multitrait-multimethod matrix. *Psychological Bulletin* 56(2): 81–105.

Campbell, D., and Stanley, J. 1966. *Experimental and quasi-experimental designs for research*. Chicago: Rand McNally.

Carlton, R. A., Lasater, T. M., et al. Pawtucket Heart Health Program Writing Group. 1995. The Pawtucket Heart Health Program: Community changes in cardiovascular risk factors and projected disease risk. *Am. J. Public Health* 85: 777–785.

CDC, HIV/AIDS Prevention Research Synthesis Project. November 1999. Compendium of HIV prevention interventions with evidence of effectiveness. Atlanta, Ga.: CDC.

CDC Office of Communication. April 1999. *Scientific and technical information simply put*, 2nd ed.

Cesario, S., Morin, K., and Santa-Donato, A. 2002. Evaluating the level of evidence of qualitative research. *JOGNN* 31(6): 708–714.

Chen, H. T. 1990. *Theory-driven evaluations*. Newbury Park, Calif.: Sage.

Clark, N. 1999. Community/practice/academia partnerships in public health. *American Journal of Preventive Medicine* 16 (3S).

Clark, N. M. 1978. Spanning the boundary between agency and community. *American Journal of Health Planning* 3(4): 40–46.

Clark, N. M., Feldman, C. H., Evans, D., Millman, E. J., Wasilewski, Y., and Valle, I. 1981. The effectiveness of education for family management of pediatric asthma: A preliminary report. *Health Education Quarterly* 8(2): 166–174.

Clark, N., and Gakuru, O. N. 1982. The effects on health and self-confidence of collaborative learning projects. *International Journal of Health Education* 1(2): 47–56.

Clark, N. M., and Pinkett-Heller, M. 1977. Developing HSA leadership: An innovation in board education. *American Journal of Health Planning* 2(1): 9–13.

Coffey, A., and Atkinson, P. 1996. *Making sense of qualitative data: Complementary research strategies*. Thousand Oaks, Calif.: Sage.

Cohen, J. 1960. A coefficient of agreement for nominal scales. *Educational and Psychological Measurement* 20: 37–46.

Cohen, J., and Cohen, P. 1975. *Applied multiple regression/correlation for the behavioral sciences*. Hillsdale, N.J.: Erlbaum.

Committee for the Study of the Future of Public Health, Division of Health Care Services, Institute of Medicine. 1988. The future of public health. National Academy Press.

Cook, T. D., and Campbell, D. T. 1979. *Quasi-experimentation: Design and analysis for field settings*. Boston: Houghton Mifflin.

Cook, T. D., and Campbell, D. T. 1983. The design and conduct of quasi-experiments and true experiments in field settings. In *Handbook of industrial and organizational psychology*, ed. M. D. Dunnette. New York: Wiley.

Cook, T. D., and Reichardt, C. S., eds. 1979. *Qualitative and quantitative methods in evaluation research*. Beverly Hills, Calif.: Sage.

Coyle, S., Boruch, R., and Turner, C., eds. 1991. Evaluating AIDS prevention programs, expanded ed. Prepared by the Panel on the Evaluation of AIDS Interventions, National Research Council. Washington, D.C.: National Academy Press.

Cronbach, L. J. 1951. Coefficient alpha and the internal structure of a test. *Psychometrika* 16: 297–334.

Cummings, A. R. 1992. Quality control principles: Applications in dietetics practice. *Journal of the American Dietetic Association* 92: 427–428.

Dale, E., and Chall, J. 1948. A formula for predicting readability. *Educational Research Bulletin* 27(Jan. 2): 11–20, (Feb. 17): 37–54.

Daltroy, L., and Goeppinger, J., eds. 1993. Arthritis health education [Special issue]. *Health Education Quarterly* 20(1).

Delbecq, A. L. 1974. Contextual variables affecting decision making in program planning. *Decision Sciences* 5(4): 726–742.

Delbecq, A. L., Van de Ven, A. H., and Gustafson, D. 1975. Group techniques for program planning: A guide to nominal group and Delphi processes. Glenview, Ill.: Scott, Foresman.

Deniston, O., and Rosenstock, I. 1968a. Evaluation of program effectiveness. *Public Health Reports* 83(4): 323–335.

Deniston, O., and Rosenstock, I. 1968b. Evaluation of program efficiency. *Public Health Reports* 83(7): 603–610.

Deniston, O., and Rosenstock, I. 1973. The validity of non-experimental designs for evaluating health services. *Health Service Reports* 88(2): 153–164.

Denzin, N. K. 1984. *The Research Act.* Englewood Cliffs, N.J.: Prentice Hall.

Dial, C., and Windsor, R. A. 1985. A formative evaluation of health education—water exercise program for class II and class III adult rheumatoid arthritics. *Patient Education Counseling* 7(1): 33–42.

Domel, S., Baranowski, T., Davis, H. C., et al. 1993. Measuring fruit and vegetable preferences among 4th and 5th grade students. *Preventive Medicine* 22: 866–879.

Donabedian, A. 1966. Evaluating the quality of medical care, Part 2. *Milbank Memorial Fund Quarterly* 44: 166–206.

Drummond, M. F., O'Brien, B. J., Stoddart, G. L., and Torrance, G. W. 1997. *Methods for the economic evaluation of health care programmes.* Oxford University Press.

DuRant, R. H., Baranowski, T., Davis, H., Thomson, W. O., Puhl, J., Greaves, K., and Rhodes, T. 1992. Reliability of heart monitoring in three-, four-, and five-year-old Anglo-, Black-, and Mexican-American children. *Medicine and Science in Sports and Exercise* 24: 265–271.

Dwyer, F., and Hammel, R. 1978. An experimental study: Patient package inserts and their effects on hypertensive patients. *Urban Health* 7(June): 46.

Easton, E., Easton, M., and Levy, M. 1977. Medical and educational malpractice issues in patient education. *Journal of Family Practice* 4(2): 276.

Edmundson, E. W., Luton, S. C., McGraw, S. A., Kelder, S. H., Layman, A. K., Smyth, M. H., Bachman, K. J., Pedersen, S. A., and Stone, E. J. 1994. CATCH: Classroom process evaluation in a multicenter trial. *Health Educ. Q.* (Suppl 2): S27–S50.

Evans, D., Clark, N. M., Feldman, C. H., Rips, J., Kaplan, D., Levison, M. J., Wasilewski, Y., Levin, B., and Mellins, R. B. 1987. A school health education program for children with asthma aged 8–11 years. *Health Education Quarterly* 14(3): 267–279.

Farquhar, J. W., Fortmann, S. P., Flora, J. A., et al. 1990. Effects of communitywide education on cardiovascular disease risk factors: The Stanford Five-City Project. *JAMA* 264: 359–365.

Farquhar, J., Maccoby, N., et al. 1977. Community education for cardiovascular health. *Lancet* 1(June 4): 1192–1195.

Feinstein, A. R. 1977. Clinical biostatistics XLI: Hard science, soft data, and the challenges of choosing clinical variables in research. *Clinical Pharmacology and Therapeutics* 22(4): 485–498.

Fetterman, D. M. 1989. *Ethnography: Step by step.* Applied Social Research Methods Series, vol. 17. Newbury Park, Calif.: Sage.

Flanders, N. 1960. Interaction analysis: A technique for quantifying teacher influence. Paper distributed by Far West Laboratory for Educational Research and Development, San Francisco.

Flay, B. R. 1986. Efficacy and effectiveness trials (and other phases of research) in the development of health promotion programmes. *Preventive Medicine* 15: 451–474.

Fleiss, J. 1981. *Statistical methods for rates and proportions.* New York: Wiley.

Fleiss, J. L., and Gross, A. J. 1991. Meta-analysis in epidemiology with special reference to studies of the association between exposure to environmental tobacco smoke and lung cancer: A critique. *Journal of Clinical Epidemiology* 44: 127–139.

Flesch, R. 1948. A new readability yardstick. *Journal of Applied Psychology* 32: 221–233.

Freudenberg, N. 1989. *Preventing AIDS: A guide to effective education for the prevention of HIV infection.* Washington, D.C.: American Public Health Association.

Freudenberg, N., Feldman, C. H., Clark, N. M., Millman, E. J., Valle, I., and Wailewski, Y. 1980. The impact of bronchial asthma on school attendance and performance. *Journal of School Health* 50(9): 522–526.

Friere, P. 1970. *Pedagogy of the oppressed.* New York: Seabury.

Fries, J. F., Green, L. W., and Levine, S. 1989. Health promotion and the compression of morbidity. *Lancet*, 481–483.

Fry, E. 1968. A readability formula that saves time. *Journal of Reading* 11: 513–516, 575–578.

Gebauer, K., et al. 1998. A nurse-managed smoking-cessation intervention during pregnancy. *J. Obstet. & Gynecol. in Nursing* 21: 47–53.

Glanz, K., and Rimer, B. K. 1997. *Theory at a glance: A guide for health promotion practice.* NIH Publication no. 97-3896, National Cancer Institute, Bethesda, Md.

Glanz, K., and Rudd, J. 1990. Readability and content analysis of print cholesterol education materials. *Patient Education and Counseling* 16: 109–118.

Glaser, B. G., and Strauss, A. L. 1967. *The discovery of grounded theory: Strategies for qualitative research.* New York: Aldine.

Glass, G. V. 1976. Primary, secondary, and meta-analysis of research. *Educ. Res.* 5: 3–8.

Glass, G. V., McGaw, B., and Smith, M. L. 1981. *Meta-analysis in social research.* Beverly Hills, Calif.: Sage.

Glass, G., Wilson, V., and Gottman, J. 1975. *Design and analysis of time series experiments.* Boulder: University of Colorado, Laboratory of Educational Research.

Goodman, R. M., LiBurd, L. C., and Green-Phillips, A. 2001. The formation of a complex community program for diabetes control: Lessons learned from a case study of Project DIRECT. *Journal of Public Health Management and Practice* 7(3): 19–29.

Goodman, R. M., Seaver, M. R., Yoo, S. Y., Dibble, S., Shada, R., Sherman, B., Urmston, F., Milliken, N., and Freund, K. 2002. A qualitative evaluation of the National Centers of Excellence in Women's Health program. *Women's Health Issues* 12(6): 291–308.

Goodman, R. M., and Steckler, A. 1987–1988. The life and death of a health promotion program: An institutionalization case study. *International Quarterly of Community Health Education* 8(1): 5–21.

Goodman, R. M., Steckler, A., and Alciati, M. H. 1997. A process evaluation of the National Cancer Institute's Data-Based Intervention Research program: A study of organizational capacity building. *Health Education Research* 12(2): 181–197.

Goodman, R. M., and Wandersman, A. 1994. FORECAST: A formative approach to evaluating the CSAP Community Partnerships. *Journal of Community Psychology* CSAP special issue: 6–25.

Green, L. 1974. Toward cost-benefit evaluations of health education: Some concepts, methods, and examples. *Health Education Monographs* 2(1): 34–64.

Green, L. 1977. Evaluation and measurement: Some dilemmas for health education. *American Journal of Public Health* 67(2): 155–161.

Green, L., and Brooks-Bertram, P. 1978. Peer review and quality control in health education. *Health Values: Achieving High-Level Wellness* 2(4): 191–197.

Green, L., and Figa-Talamanca, I. 1974. Suggested designs for evaluation of patient education programs. *Health Education Monographs* 2(1): 54–71.

Green, L., and Kreuter, M. 1991. *Health promotion planning: A diagnostic approach.* Mountain View, Calif.: Mayfield.

Green, L. W., and Kreuter, M. W. 1991. *Health promotion planning: An educational and ecological approach,* 2nd ed. Mountain View, Calif.: Mayfield.

Green, L., and Kreuter, M. 1999. *Health promotion planning: An educational and ecological approach.* 3d ed. Mountain View, Calif.: Mayfield.

Green, L., Kreuter, M., Deeds, S., and Partridge, K. 1980. *Health education planning: A diagnostic approach.* Palo Alto, Calif.: Mayfield.

Green, L., Levine, D., and Deeds, S. 1975. Clinical trials of health education for hypertensive outpatients: Design and baseline data. *Preventive Medicine* 4: 417–425.

Green, L. W., and Lewis, F. M. 1986. *Evaluation and measurement in health education.* Mountain View, Calif.: Mayfield.

Greene, J. C., and Caracelli, V. J. 1997. Advances in mixed-method evaluation: The challenges and benefits of integrated diverse paradynes. *New directions for evaluation,* no. 74. San Francisco, Calif.: Jossey-Bass.

Greene, R. 1976. *Assuring quality in medical care.* Cambridge, Mass.: Ballinger.

Grossman, J., and Tierney, J. P. 1993. The fallibility of comparison groups. *Evaluation Review* 17(5): 556–571.

Gruber, J., and Trickett, E. J. 1987. Can we empower others? The paradox of empowerment in the governing of an alternative public school. *American Journal of Community Psychology* 15(3): 353–371.

Guba, E., and Lincoln, Y. 1989. *Fourth-generation evaluation.* Newbury Park, Calif.: Sage.

Haddix, A. C., Teutsh, S., Shaffer, P., and Donet, D., eds. 1996. *Prevention effectiveness: A guide to decision analysis and economic evaluation.* New York: Oxford University Press.

Handbook for certification of health education specialists. 1990. New York: National Commission of Health Education Credentialing.

Haug, M., and Ory, M. 1987. Issues in elderly patient–provider interactions. *Research on Aging* 9: 3–44.

Health Education Monographs editors. 1977. Guidelines for health education preparation and practice. *Health Education Monographs* 5(1): 1–18.

Heaney, C., and Goldenhar, J., eds. 1996. Worksite health programs. *Health Education Quarterly* 23(2): 133–136.

Hermanson, B., Omenn, G. S., Kronmal, R. A., Gersh, B. J., and participants in the Artery Coronary Surgery Study. 1988. Beneficial six-year outcome of smoking cessation in older men and women with coronary artery disease. *New England Journal of Medicine* 319: 1365–1369.

Hochbaum, G. 1962. Evaluation: A diagnostic procedure. *Studies and Research in Health Education,* vol. 5. Geneva: World Health Organization, International Conference on Health and Health Education.

Hochbaum, G. 1965. Research to improve health education. *International Journal of Health Education* 8(1): 141–148.

Hunter, J. E., and Schmidt, F. L. 1990. *Methods of meta-analysis.* Newbury Park, Calif.: Sage.

Institute of Medicine. 1997. *Linking research to public health practice: A review of the CDC's program of centers for research and demonstration of health promotion and disease prevention.* Washington, D.C.: National Academy Press.

Inui, T. 1978. A common bond: Exploring the interface between health education and quality assurance. *Journal of Quality Assurance* 10(Oct.): 6–7.

Israel, B. A., and Rounds, K. A. 1987. Social networks and social support: A synthesis for health educators. In *Advances in health education and promotion: A research annual,* ed. W. B. Ward, S. K. Simonds, P. D. Mullen, and M. Becker. Greenwich, Conn.: Jai Press.

Iverson, D., and Kolbe, L. 1983. Evaluation of the national disease prevention and health promotion strategy: Establishing a role for schools. *Journal of School Health* 53: 294–302.

Janis, I. L. 1983. *Counseling on personal decisions: Theory and research on short-term helping relationships.* Westover, Mass.: Murray.

Janis, I., and Mann, L. 1977. *Decision making.* New York: Free Press.

Johnson, S. M., and Bolstad, O. D. 1973. Methodological issues in naturalistic observation: Some problems and solutions for field research. In *Behavior change: Methodology, concepts, and practice,* ed. L. A. Hamerlynck, L. C. Handy, and E. J. Mash. Champaign, Ill.: Research Press.

Joint Committee on Standards for Education Evaluation. 1981. *Standards for evaluations of educational programs, projects, and materials.* New York: McGraw-Hill.

Jorgensen, D. L. 1989. *Participant observation: A methodology for human studies.* Applied Social Research Methods Series, vol. 15. Newbury Park, Calif.: Sage.

W. K. Kellogg Foundation Evaluation Handbook. 2002. W. K. Kellogg Foundation, Battle Creek, Mich.

Kenny, D. 1975. A quasi-experimental approach to assessing treatment effects in the nonequivalent control group design. *Psychology Bulletin* 82: 345–362.

Kenny, D. A. 1979. *Correlation and causation.* New York: John Wiley.

Kinsman, J., Nakiyingi, J., Kamali, A., Carpenter, L., Quigley, M., Pool, R., and Whitworth, J. 2001. Evaluation of a comprehensive school-based AIDS education programme in rural Masaka, Uganda. *Health Education Research* 16(1): 85–100. Cary, N.C.: Oxford University Press.

Kish, L. 1965. *Survey design.* New York: Wiley.

Kish, L. 1987. *Statistical design for research.* New York: Wiley.

Klare, G. 1974–1975. Assessing readability. *Reading Research Quarterly* 1: 62–102.

Kreuter, M. 1985. Results of the school health education evaluation. *Journal of School Health* 8.

Krieger, N. 2000. Discrimination and health. In L. F. Berkman and I. Kawachi, *Social Epidemiology.* Oxford, U.K.: Oxford University Press, 36–75.

Krueger, R. A. 1994. *Focus groups: A practical guide for applied research,* 2nd ed. Thousand Oaks, Calif.: Sage.

Kumpfer, K. L., et al. 1993. *Measurements in prevention: A manual on selecting and using instruments to evaluate prevention programs.* U.S. Department of Health and Human Services, Center for Substance Abuse Prevention, Technical Report 8. Rockville, Md.: Government Printing Office.

Laboratory Standardization Panel of the National Cholesterol Education Program. 1990. Recommendation for improving cholesterol measurement. NIH Publication no. 90-2964. Bethesda, Md.: National Heart, Lung and Blood Institute.

LaLonde, R., and Maynard, R. 1987. How precise are evaluations of employment and training programs? Evidence from a field experiment. *Evaluation Review* 11(4): 428–451.

Larry, R., chair. 1973. Report of the president's committee on health education. New York: Publication Affairs Institute.

Leupker, R. V., Murray, D. M., Jacobs, D. R., Mittelmark, M. B., Bracht, N., Carlaw, R., Crow, R., Elmer, P., Finnegan, J., Folson, A. R., Grimm, R., Hannan, P. J., Jeffrey, R., Lando, H., McGovern, P., Mullis, R., Perry, C. L., Pechacek, T., Pirie, P., Sprafka, M., Weisbrod, R., and Blackburn, H. 1994. Community education for cardiovascular disease prevention: Risk factor changes in the Minnesota Heart Health Program. *American Journal of Public Health* 84(9): 1383–1393.

LeVee, W., ed. 1989. New perspectives on HIV-related illnesses: Progress in health services research. National Center for Health Services Research, Public Health Service, U.S. Department of Health and Human Services. Washington, D.C.: Government Printing Office.

Little, A. 1976. A survey of consumer health education programs. Final report submitted to the office of the Assistant Secretary for planning and evaluation/health on contract no. HEW 100-75-0082. Washington, D.C.: Department of Health, Education and Welfare.

Liu, K., Cooper, R., Mackeever, J., Byington, R., Soltero, I., Stamler, R., Gosch, F., Stevens, E., and Stamler, J. 1979. Assessment of the association between habitual salt intake and high blood pressure: Methodological problems. *American Journal of Epidemiology* 110(2): 219–226.

Lofland, J. 1971. *Analyzing social settings.* Belmont, Calif.: Wadsworth.

Lorig, K., and Holman, H. 1993. Arthritis self-management studies: A twelve-year review. *Health Education Quarterly* 20(1): 17–28.

Luce, B., and Elixhauser, A. 1990. Standards for the socioeconomic evaluation of health care services. (A. Culyer, ed.) New York: Springer Verlag.

Ma, G., Shive, S., and Tracy, M. 2001. The effects of licensing and inspection enforcement to reduce tobacco sales to minors in Greater Philadelphia, 1994–1998. *Addict. Behav.* 26(5): 677–687.

Manzella, B. A., Brodes, C. M., Richards, J. M., Jr., Windsor, R. A., Soong, S-j., and Bailey, W. C. 1989. Assessing the use of metered dose inhalers by adults with asthma. *Journal of Asthma* 26: 223–230.

Matchar, D., and Samsa, G. 1999. The role of evidence reports in evidence-based medicine: A mechanism for linking scientific evidence and practice improvement. *The Journal of Healthcare Quality: The Joint Commission Journal:* 522.

Mayer, J. P., Hawkins, B., and Todd, R. 1990. A randomized evaluation of smoking cessation interventions for pregnant women at a WIC clinic. *Am. J. Public Health* 80: 76–78.

McCormick, K., and Moore, S. Nov. 1994. Clinical practice guideline development: Methodology perspectives. UDHHS.

McGraw, S., McKinley, S., McClements, L., Lasseter, T., Assaf, A., and Carleton, A. 1989. Methods in program evaluation: The process evaluation system of Pawtucket Heart Health Program. *Evaluation Review* 13(5): 459–483.

McGraw, S. A., Sellers, D. E., and Stone, E. J. 1996. Using process data to explain outcomes: An illustration from the child and adolescent trial for cardiovascular health (CATCH). *Evaluation Review* 20(3): 291–312.

McKinley, J., et al. 1996. Evaluation review. *Journal of Applied Social Research* 20(3): 237–352.

McKnight, J. L. 1978. Community health in a Chicago slum. *Development Dialogue* 1: 62–68.

McLaughlin, G. 1969. SMOG grading—a new readability formula. *Journal of Reading* 12(May): 639–646.

McLeroy, K. R., et al. 1990. Tobacco prevention in North Carolina public schools. *J. Drug Educ.* 20(3): 257–268.

McLeroy, K. R., Clark, N. M., Simons-Morton, B. G., Forster, J., Connell, C. M., Altman, D., and Zimmerman, M. A. 1995. Creating capacity: Establishing a health education research agenda for special populations. *Health Educ. Q.* 3 (Aug. 22): 390–405.

McNabb, W. L., et al. 1985. Self-management education of children with asthma: Air wise. *American Journal of Public Health* 75(10): 1219–1220.

McShane, L. M., Clark, L. C., Combs, G. F., Jr., and Turnbull, B. W. 1991. Reporting the accuracy of biochemical measurement for epidemiologic and nutrition studies. *American Journal of Clinical Nutrition* 53: 1354–1360.

Miles, M. B., and Huberman, A. M. 1994. *Qualitative data analysis: An expanded sourcebook.* Thousand Oaks, Calif.: Sage.

Miller, J., and Lewis, F. 1982. Closing the gap in quality assurance: A tool for evaluating group leaders. *Health Education Quarterly* 9(1): 55–66.

Moore, S. R. 1986. Smoking and drug effects in geriatric patients. *Pharmacy International* 7: 1–3.

Morgan, G. D., Noll, E. L., Orleans, C. T., et al. 1996. Reaching midlife and older smokers: Tailored intervention for routine medical care. *Preventive Medicine* 25: 346–364.

Mullen, P. D., Simons-Morton, D. G., Rameriz, G., Frankowski, R. F., and Green, L. W. 1997. A meta-analysis of trials evaluating patient education and counseling for three groups of preventive health behaviors. *Patient Education and Counseling* 32: 155–173.

Multiple Risk Factor Intervention Trial (MRFIT). 1981. V: Intervention on smoking. *Preventive Medicine* 10(4): 476–500.

Mumford, E., Schlesinger, H. J., and Glass, G. V. 1982. The effects of psychological intervention on recovery from surgery and heart attacks: An analysis of the literature. *American Journal of Public Health* 72(2): 141–151.

Murray, D. 1998. *Design and analysis of group randomized trials.* New York: Oxford University Press.

National Cancer Institute. 2002. *Making health communications programs work.* Washington, D.C.: National Institutes of Health.

Neaton, J., Broste, S., Cohen, L., Fishman, E., Kjelsberg, M., and Schoenberger, M. 1981. The Multiple Risk Factor Intervention Trial (MRFIT), VII: A comparison of risk factor changes between the two study groups. *Preventive Medicine* 10(4): 519–543.

Neiger, B. L., Barnes, M. D., Lindsay, G. B., Schwartz, R. H., Lancaster, R. B., and Chalkley, C. M. 2000. Unifying research and practice in public health education: Analysis and comparison of two consensus conferences. *Health Promotion Practice* 1(2): 168–177.

NIH Consensus Development Program. Consensus Statement February 11–13, 1997. Vol. 15, no. 2.

Norman, S., Greenberg, R., Marconi, K., Novelli, W., Felix, M., Schechter, C., Stolley, P., and Stunkard, A. 1990. A process evaluation of a two-year community cardiovascular risk reduction program: What was done and who knew about it? *Health Education Research* 5(1): 87–97.

Nunnally, J. C. 1978. *Psychometric theory*, 2nd ed. New York: McGraw-Hill.

O'Donnell, M. P., and Ainsworth, T. 1984. *Health promotion in the workplace*. New York: Wiley & Sons.

Ogden, H. 1978. Recent developments in health education policy. *Health Education Monographs* 6 (suppl. 1): 67–73.

Ogden, H. 1980. Health education as an element of U.S. policy. *International Journal of Health Education* 23(3): 150–155.

Orleans, C. T., Rimer, B., Fleisher, L., Keintz, M. K., Telepchak, J., et al. 1989. *Clear Horizons: A quit smoking guide especially for those 50 and over*. Philadelphia: Fox Chase Cancer Center.

Ostrom, D. 1978. *Time series analysis: Regression techniques*. Quantitative Applications in the Social Sciences series. Beverly Hills, Calif.: Sage.

Paganini-Hill, A., and Hsu, G. 1994. Smoking and mortality among residents of a California retirement community. *American Journal of Public Health* 84: 992–995.

Patton, M. 1980. *Quantitative evaluation methods*. Beverly Hills, Calif.: Sage.

Patton, M. Q. 1982. *Practical evaluation*. Beverly Hills, Calif.: Sage.

Patton, M. Q. 1990. *Qualitative research and evaluation methods*, 2nd ed. Newbury Park, Calif.: Sage.

Patton, M. Q. 1997. *Utilization-focused evaluation: The new century text*, 3rd ed. Thousand Oaks, Calif.: Sage.

Perry, C., Kelder, S., Murray, D., and Klepp, K. 1992. Community-wide smoking prevention: Long-term outcomes of the Minnesota Heart Health Program and the Class of 1989 Study. *American Journal of Public Health* 82(9): 1210–1216.

Perry, C., Killen, J., Telch, M., Slinkard, L.A., and Danaher, B. G. 1980. Modifying smoking behavior of teenagers: A school-based intervention. *American Journal of Public Health* 70(7): 722–725.

Prochaska, J. O., and DiClemente, C. C. 1983. Stages and processes of self-change of smoking: Toward an integrative model of change. *Journal of Consulting and Clinical Psychology* 51: 390–395.

Puska, P., Koskela, K., and McAlister, A. 1979. A comprehensive television smoking cessation program in Finland. *International Journal of Health Education* 22(4, suppl.): 1–28.

Reichardt, C. S., and Rallis, S. F., eds. 1994. The qualitative-quantitative debate: New perspectives. *New directions for program evaluation*, no. 61. San Francisco, Calif.: Jossey-Bass.

Rice, D. P., and Hodgson, T. A. 1982. The value of human life revisited. *American Journal of Public Health* 72(6): 536–537.

Rimer, B., et al. 1986. Research and evaluation programs related to health education for older persons. *Health Education Quarterly* 13(4).

Rimer, B. K., Glanz, D. K., and Rasband, G. 2001. Searching for evidence about health education and health behavior interventions. *Health Educ. Behav.* 2(Apr. 28): 231–248.

Rimer, B. K., Orleans, C. T., Fleisher, L., Cristinzio, S., Resch, N., Telepchak, J., and Keintz, M. K. 1994. Does tailoring matter? The impact of a tailored guide on ratings and short-term smoking-related outcomes for older smokers. *Health Education Research* 9: 69–84.

Rogers, P., Eaton, E., and Brown, J. 1981. Is health promotion cost-effective? *Preventive Medicine* 10: 324–339.

Rosenstock, I. 1960. Gaps and potentials in health education research. *Health Education Monographs* 8: 21–27.

Rosenstock, I. 1975. General criteria for evaluating health education programs. In Proceedings of the NHLI working conference on health behavior, May 12–15, ed. S. M. Weiss. DHEW Publication no. (NIH) 76-868. Washington, D.C.: Government Printing Office.

Rossi, P. H., ed. 1982. Standards for evaluation practice. *New Directions for Program Evaluation* 15(September). San Francisco: Jossey-Bass.

Rossi, P. H., and Freeman, H. E. 1993. *Evaluation: A systematic approach*, 5th ed. Newbury Park, Calif.: Sage.

Rossi, P., Freeman, H., and Wright, S. 1979. *Evaluation: A systematic approach*. Beverly Hills, Calif.: Sage.

Rossi, P., and Williams, W., eds. 1972. *Evaluating social programs: Theory, practice and politics*. New York: Seminar Press.

Roter, D. 1977. Patient participation in the patient-provider interaction: The effects of patient question asking on the quality of interaction, satisfaction, and compliance. *Health Education Monographs* 5(4): 281–315.

Rubin, D. 1974. Estimating causal effects of treatments in randomized and nonrandomized studies. *Journal of Educational Psychology* 56(5): 688–701.

Rubin, H. J., and Rubin, I. S. 1995. *Qualitative interviewing: The art of hearing data*. Thousand Oaks, Calif.: Sage.

Rugkasa, J., Kennedy, M. B., Abaunza, P. S., Treacy, M. P., and Knox, B. 2001. Smoking and symbolism: Children, communication and cigarettes. *Health Education Research* 16(2): 131–142.

Rush, D., and Kristal, A. R. 1982. Methodologic studies during pregnancy: The reliability of the 24-hour dietary recall. *Am. J. Clin. Nutr.* 35(5 Suppl): 1259–1268.

Russell, L. B. 1987. *Evaluating preventive care: Report on a workshop*. Washington, D.C.: Brookings Institute.

Sallis, J. F., Howell, M. F., Hofstetter, C. R., Elder, J., Caspersen, C. J., Hackley, M., et al. 1990. Distance between homes and exercise facilities related to the frequency of exercise among San Diego residents. *Public Health Reports* 105: 179–185.

Salzer, M. S., Nixon, C. T., Schut, L. J., Karver, M. S., and Bickman, L. 1997. Validating quality indicators. Quality as relationship between structure, process, and outcome. *Eval. Rev.* 3(June 21): 292–309.

Sanders, J. Joint Committee on Standards for Educational Evaluation. 1994. *The program evaluation standards*, 2nd ed. Thousand Oaks, Calif.: Sage.

Sanstad, K. H., Stall, R., Goldstein, E., Everett, W., and Brousseau, R. 1999. Collaborative community research consortium: A model for HIV prevention. *Health Educ. Behav.* 2(Apr. 26): 171–184.

Schafer, R. B. 1978. Factors affecting food behavior and the quality of husbands' and wives' diets. *Journal of the American Dietetic Association* 72: 138–143.

Scheirer, M. A. 1996. A user's guide to program templates: A new tool for evaluating program content. *New directions for evaluation*, no. 72. San Francisco: Jossey-Bass.

Scheirer, M. A., Shediac, M. C., and Cassady, C. E. 1995. Measuring the implementation of health promotion programs: The case of the Breast and Cervical Cancer Program in Maryland. *Health Education Research* 10(1): 11–25.

Schlundt, D. G. 1988. Accuracy and reliability of nutrient intake estimates. *Journal of Nutrition* 118: 1432–1435.

Scott, J. C. 1990. *Domination and the arts of resistance: Hidden transcripts.* New Haven, Conn.: Yale University Press.

Scriven, M. 1972. Pros and cons about goal-free evaluation. *Evaluation Comment* 3(4): 1–4.

Sechrest, L., Perrin, E., and Bunker, J., eds. 1990. *Research methodology: Strengthening causal interpretations of non-experimental data.* Rockville, Md.: AHCPR.

Seidel, J., and Kelle, U. 1995. Different functions of coding in the analysis of textual data. In U. Kelle, ed., *Computer-aided qualitative data-analysis: Theory, methods, and practice,* 52–61. London: Sage.

Sepulveda, J., Fineberg, H., and Mann, J., eds. 1982. *AIDS prevention through education: A world view.* New York: Oxford University Press.

Shadish, W., Cook, T., and Leviton, L. 1991. *Foundations of program evaluations.* Newbury Park, Calif.: Sage.

Shadish, Leonard, and Bickman, eds. 2000. *Validity and social experimentation: Donald Campbell's legacy.* Newbury Park, Calif.: Sage.

Shea, S., Basch, C. E., Wechsler, H., and Lantigua, R. A. 1996. The Washington Height-Inwood Healthy Heart Program: A 6-year report from a disadvantaged urban setting. *Amer. J. of Pub. Health* 86: 166–177.

Sherwin, R., Kaelber, D., Kezdi, R., Kjelsberg, M., and Thomas, H., Jr. 1981. The multiple risk factor intervention trial (MRFIT), II: The development of the protocol. *Preventive Medicine* 10(4): 402–425.

Shinn, M., Lehmann, S., and Wong, N. W. 1984. Social interaction social support. *Journal of Social Issues* 40(4): 55–76.

Shortell, S., and Richardson, W. 1978. *Health program evaluation.* St. Louis: Mosby.

Sichel, J. 1982. *Program evaluation guidelines.* New York: Human Sciences Press.

Siemiatycki, J. 1979. A comparison of mail, telephone and home interview strategies for household health surveys. *American Journal of Public Health* 69: 238–244.

Simmons, J. J., Salisbury, Z. T., Kane-Williams, E., Kauffman, C. K., and Quaintance, B. 1989. Interorganizational collaboration and dissemination of health promotion for older Americans. *Health Education Quarterly* 16(4): 529–550.

Simons-Morton, B., and Baranowski, T. 1991. Observation methods in the assessment of children's dietary practices. *Journal of School Health* 61(5): 204–207.

Snyder, L. B., and Hamilton, M. A. 2002. A meta-analysis of the U.S. health campaign effects on behavior: Emphasize enforcement, exposure, and new information, and beware secular trends. In R. C. Hornik, ed., *Public health communication: Evidence for behavior change.* Mahwah, N.J.: Lawrence Erlbaum.

Society for Public Health Education, Ad Hoc Committee. 1968. Statement of functions of community health educators and minimum requirements for their professional preparation with recommendations for implementation. Professional preparation of community health educators, National Commission on Accrediting. Washington, D.C.: Department of Health, Education and Welfare, Public Health Service, Centers for Disease Control.

Society for Public Health Education, Ad Hoc Task Force on Professional Preparation and Practice of Health Education. 1977a. Guidelines for the preparation and practice of professional health educators. *Health Education Monographs* 5(1): 75–89.

Society for Public Health Education, Committee on Professional Preparation and Practice of Community Health Educators at the Baccalaureate Level. 1977b. Criteria and guidelines for baccalaureate programs in community health education. *Health Education Monographs* 5(1): 90–98.

Somers, A., ed. 1976. *Promoting health: Consumer education and national policy.* Germantown, Md.: Aspen Systems.

Special Committee on Aging, United States Senate. 1986. *Developments in aging,* vol. 3. Washington, D.C.: U.S. Government Printing Office.

Spector, P. 1981. *Research designs.* Quantitative Applications in the Social Sciences Series, no. 23, ed. J. L. Sullivan. Beverly Hills, Calif.: Sage.

Spradley, J. P. 1979. *The ethnographic interview.* Fort Worth, Tex.: Harcourt Brace Jovanovich.

Stake, R. E. 1995. *The art of case study research.* Thousand Oaks, Calif.: Sage.

Starfield, B. 1974. Measurement of outcome: A proposed scheme. *Milbank Memorial Fund Quarterly* 5(1): 39–50.

Steckler, A., and Goodman, R. M. 1989. How to institutionalize health promotion programs. *American Journal of Health Promotion* 3(4): 34–44.

Steckler, A., and Linnan, L. 2002. *Process evaluation in public health interventions.* San Francisco: Jossey-Bass.

Steckler, A., McLeroy, K. R., Goodman, R. M., Bird, S. T., and McCormick, L. 1992. Toward integrating qualitative and quantitative methods: An introduction. *Health Education Quarterly* 19(1): 1–135.

Stevens, R., Feucht, T., and Roman, S. 1991. Effects of an intervention program on AIDS-related drug and needle behavior among intravenous drug users. *American Journal of Public Health* 81(5): 727–729.

Stone, A., Shiffman, S., Schwartz, J., et al. 2002. Patient non-compliance with paper diaries. *British Medical Journal* 324: 1193–1194.

Stone, E. 1994. Process evaluation in the multicenter child and adolescent trial for cardiovascular health (CATCH). *Health Education Quarterly* (suppl. 2) S1–S143.

Stone, E. J., Pearson, T. A., Fortmann, S. P., and McKinlay, J. B. 1997. Community-based prevention trials: Challenges and directions for public health practice, policy, and research. *Annual Epidemiology* S7: S113–S120.

Stone, E., Perry, C., and Luepker, R. 1989. Synthesis of cardiovascular behavioral research for youth health promotion. *Health Education Quarterly* 16(1): 155–169.

Suchman, E. 1967. *Evaluative research: Principles and practice in public service and social action programs.* New York: Russell Sage Foundation.

Sudman, S. 1976. *Applied sampling.* New York: Academic Press.

Tengs, T. O., Adams, M. E., Pliskin, J. S., Safran, D. G., Siegel, J. E., Weinstein, M. C., and Graham, J. D. 1995. Five hundred life-saving interventions and their cost effectiveness. *Risk Analysis* 15: 369–390.

Thompson, M., and Fortess, E. 1980. Cost-effectiveness analysis in health program evaluation. *Evaluation Review* 4(4): 549–568.

U.S. Congress, House. 1975. National Health Planning and Resources Act of 1974, Public Law 93-641, 93rd Congress.

U.S. Congress, House. 1976. National Consumer Health Information and Health Promotion Act of 1976, Public Law 94-317, 94th Congress.

U.S. Congress. 1988. *How effective is AIDS education?* Office of Technology Assessment. Washington, D.C.: Government Printing Office.

U.S. Department of Health, Education and Welfare. 1971. Findings and recommendations: National activities in support of health education. Report of the President's Committee on Health Education. Washington, D.C.: Government Printing Office.

U.S. Department of Health, Education and Welfare. 1977. *Handbook for improving high blood pressure control in the community.* National Institutes of Health, National Heart, Lung, and Blood Institute. Washington, D.C.: Government Printing Office.

U.S. Department of Health, Education and Welfare. 1978a. *Preparation and practice of community, patient, and school health educators.* DHEW Publication no. (HRA) 78-71. Washington, D.C.: Government Printing Office.

U.S. Department of Health, Education and Welfare. 1978b. *Pretesting in cancer communications.* National Institutes of Health. DHEW Publication no. (NIH) 78-1493. Washington, D.C.: Government Printing Office.

U.S. Department of Health and Human Services. 1980a. *Initial role delineation for health education: Final report, prepared for the National Center for Health Education.* Public Health Service. DHHS Publication no. (HRA) 80-44. Washington, D.C.: Government Printing Office.

U.S. Department of Health and Human Services. 1980b. *Promoting health/preventing disease: Objectives for the nation.* Public Health Service. Washington, D.C.: Government Printing Office.

U.S. Department of Health and Human Services. 1989a. *Guide to clinical preventive services.* Preventive Services Task Force. Washington, D.C.: Government Printing Office.

U.S. Department of Health and Human Services. 1989b. *Making health communication programs work: A planner's guide.* National Institutes of Health. NIH Publication no. 89-1493. Washington, D.C.: Government Printing Office.

U.S. Department of Health and Human Services. 1989c. *Reducing the health consequences of smoking: 25 years of progress. A report of the surgeon general.* U.S. Public Health Service, Centers for Disease Control, Center for Health Promotion and Education, Office on Smoking and Health. DHHS Publication no. (CDC) 89-8411.

U.S. Department of Health and Human Services. 1990a. *Development and evaluation of comprehensive federal physical fitness programs.* Washington, D.C.: Government Printing Office.

U.S. Department of Health and Human Services. 1990b. *Healthy people 2000: National health promotion and disease prevention objectives.* Washington, D.C.: Government Printing Office.

U.S. Department of Health and Human Services. 1990c. Long-term psychological and behavioral consequences and correlates of smoking cessation. In *The health benefits of smoking cessation: A report of the surgeon general.* U.S. Public Health Service, Centers for Disease Control, Center for Health Promotion and Education, Office on Smoking and Health. DHHS Publication no. (CDC) 90-8416, 532–555; 561–578.

U.S. Department of Health and Human Services. 1991. *Clearing the air.* Rockville, Md.: Public Health Service, National Institutes of Health, National Cancer Institute, PHS Publication no. 91-1647.

U.S. Department of Health and Human Services. 1992a. *Cultural competence for evaluators*, ed. M. Orlandi, R. Weston, and L. Epstein. OSAP Cultural Competence Series. DHHS Publication (SAMHA) no. 92-1884. Washington, D.C.: Government Printing Office.

U.S. Department of Health and Human Services. 1992b. *Health behavior research in minority populations*, ed. D. Becker, R. Hill, J. Jackson, et al. NIH Publication (NHLBI) no. 92-2965. Washington, D.C.: Government Printing Office.

U.S. Department of Health and Human Services. November 2000. *Healthy People 2010.* Washington, D.C.: Government Printing Office.

U.S. Department of Health and Human Services. November 2001. Closing the health gap: Reducing health disparities affecting African Americans. HHS Factsheet.

Verbrugge, L. M. 1980. Health diaries. *Medical Care* 18(1): 73–95.

Vladeck, B. C. 1984. The limits of cost-effectiveness. *American Journal of Public Health* 74(7): 652–653.

Wallerstein, N. 1992. Powerlessness, empowerment, and health: Implications for health promotion. *American Journal of Health Promotion* 6: 197–205.

Warner, K. E., and Luce, B. R. 1982. *Cost benefit and cost effectiveness analysis in health care.* Ann Arbor, Mich.: Health Administration Press.

Webb, E. J., Campbell, D. T., Schwartz, R. D., and Sechrest, L. 1966. *Unobtrusive measures: Noncreative research in the social sciences.* Chicago: Rand McNally.

Weingarten, V., Goodfriend, S., and Harris, C. 1976. *Health education demonstration at Roosevelt Hospital.* New York: Institute of Public Affairs.

Weiss, C. 1972. *Evaluation research: Methods for assessing program effectiveness.* Englewood Cliffs, N.J.: Prentice Hall.

Weiss, C. 1973a. Between the cup and the lip. *Evaluation* 1(2): 49–55.

Weiss, C. 1973b. Where politics and evaluation research meet. *Evaluation* 1(3): 37–45.

Weiss, C. H. 1995. Nothing as practical as good theory: Exploring theory-based evaluation for comprehensive community initiatives for children and families. In J. P. Connel, et al., *New approaches to evaluating community initiatives: Concepts, methods, and context.* Washington, D.C.: The Aspen Institute.

Weiss, C. H. 1998. *Evaluation,* 2nd ed. Englewood Cliffs, N.J.: Prentice Hall.

Weitzman, E. A., and Miles, M. B. 1995. *Computer programs for qualitative data analysis: A software sourcebook.* Thousand Oaks, Calif.: Sage.

Williams, J. H., Belle, G. A., Houston, C., et al. 2001. Process evaluation methods of a peer-delivered health promotion program for African American women. *Health Promotion Practice* 2(2): 135–142.

Windsor, R. A. 1981. Improving patient education assessment skills of hospital staff. A case study in diabetes. *Patient Counseling and Health Education* 3(1): 26–29.

Windsor, R. A. 1986. The utility of time series analysis in evaluation health promotion and education programs. *Advances in Health Education and Promotion* 1: 435–465.

Windsor, R. A., Bailey, W., Richards, J., Manzella, B., Soong, S-j., and Brooks, M. 1990. Evaluation of the efficacy and cost effectiveness of health education methods to increase medication adherence among adults with asthma. *American Journal of Public Health* 80(12): 1519–1521.

Windsor, R. A., Baranowski, T., Clark, N., and Cutter, G. 1984. *Evaluation of health promotion and education programs.* Mountain View, Calif.: Mayfield.

Windsor, R. A., Boyd, N. R., and Orleans, C. T. 1998. A meta-evaluation of smoking cessation intervention research among pregnant women: Improving the science and art. *Health Education Research* 13: 419–438.

Windsor, R. A., and Cutter, G. 1981. Methodological issues in using time series designs and analysis: Evaluating the behavioral impact of health communication programs. In *Progress in clinical and biological research*, vol. 83: *Issues in screening and communications*, ed. C. Mettlin and G. Murphy, 517–535. New York: Liss.

Windsor, R. A., and Cutter, G. 1982. Quasi-experimental designs for evaluating cancer control programs in rural settings. In *Advances in cancer control research and development. Proceedings of the third conference on cancer control*, ed. C. Mettlin and G. Murphy, 517–555. New York: Liss.

Windsor, R. A., Cutter, G., and Kronenfeld, J. 1981. Communication methods and evaluation design for a rural cancer screening program. *American Journal of Rural Health* 7(3): 37–45.

Windsor, R. A., Cutter, G., Morris, J., et al. 1985. Effectiveness of self-help smoking cessation intervention research among pregnant women: A randomized trial. *American Journal of Public Health* 76(12): 1389–1392.

Windsor, R. A., Kronenfeld, J., Ory, M., and Kilgo, J. 1980. Method and design issues in evaluation of community health education programs: A case study in breast and cervical cancer. *Health Education Quarterly* 7(3): 203–218.

Windsor, R. A., Lowe, J. B., Perkins, L. L., Smith-Yoder, D., Artz, L., Crawford, M., Amburgy, K., and Boyd, N. B., Jr. 1993. Health education for pregnant smokers: Behavioral impact and cost benefit. *American Journal of Public Health* 83(2): 201–206.

Windsor, R. A., and Orleans, C. T. 1986. Guidelines and methodological standards for smoking cessation intervention research among pregnant women: Improving the science and art. *Health Education Quarterly* 13(2): 131–161.

Windsor, R. A., Roseman, J., Gartseff, G., and Kirk, K. A. 1981. Qualitative issues in developing educational diagnostic instruments and assessment procedures for diabetic patients. *Diabetes Care* 4(4): 468–475.

Windsor, R. A., Warner, K., and Cutter, G. 1988. A cost-effectiveness analysis of self-health smoking cessation methods for pregnant women. *Public Health Reports* 103(1): 83–87.

Windsor, R., Whiteside Jr., H., Solomon, L., Prows, S., Donatelle, R., Cinciripini, P., and McIlvain, H. 2000. A process evaluation model for patient education programs for pregnant smokers. *Tobacco Control 2000* 9 (suppl. 3): iii29–iii35.

Windsor, R. A., Woodby, L. L., Miller, T. M., Hardin, J. M., Crawford, M. A., and DiClemente, C. C. 2000. Effectiveness of agency for health care policy and research clinical practice guidelines and patient education methods for pregnant smokers in Medicaid maternity care. *American Journal of Obstetrics and Gynecology* 182: 68–75.

World Health Organization, Expert Committee on Health Education of the Public. 1954. First report. WHO Technical Report Series, no. 89. Geneva: World Health Organization.

World Health Organization, Expert Committee. 1969. *Planning and evaluation of health education services*. WHO Technical Report Series, no. 409. Geneva: World Health Organization.

World Health Organization. 1980. *Health program evaluation: Guiding principles for application of the managerial process for national health development*. Geneva: World Health Organization.

World Health Organization. 1981. *Development of indicators for monitoring progress toward health for all by the year 2000*. Geneva: World Health Organization.